Present Laughter

'Present mirth hath present laughter
What's to come is yet unsure . . .'
                                    Twelfth Night

Present Laughter

A Personal Anthology of Modern Humour

Selected by *Alan Coren*

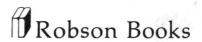 Robson Books

FIRST PUBLISHED IN GREAT BRITAIN IN 1982 BY
ROBSON BOOKS LTD., BOLSOVER HOUSE, 5-6
CLIPSTONE STREET, LONDON W1P 7EB. COPY-
RIGHT IN THIS ANTHOLOGY © 1982 ALAN COREN

Present laughter.
  1. English wit and humor
  I. Coren, Alan
  827'.914'08   PN6175

ISBN 0-86051-191-X

Printed in Hungary

Contents

Introduction by **ALAN COREN**   9

WOODY ALLEN   15
The Kugelmass Episode

V. S. NAIPAUL   28
The Quarrel with Ramlogan

CLIVE JAMES   39
Princess Daisy

CYRA McFADDEN   49
Leonard as a Lover

P. G. WODEHOUSE   53
Jeeves in the Springtime

S. J. PERELMAN   70
Strictly from Hunger

KEITH WATERHOUSE   81
Flag of Inconvenience

RING LARDNER   86
The Love Nest

MALCOLM BRADBURY   100
Conference Purposes

JAMES JOYCE   114
Appetites

DAMON RUNYON 118
Sense of Humour

MICHAEL FRAYN 129
Identity Crisis

ARTHUR MARSHALL 136
Here We Go Again

PHILIP ROTH 141
Suicide

ROBERT GRAVES 150
Earth to Earth

PAUL JENNINGS 156
Red-blooded ¾rose

JOSEPH HELLER 159
The Soldier in White

BERNARD LEVIN 173
The Luck of the Irish

BEACHCOMBER 180
Hotel Superbe v The Filthistan Trio

TOM STOPPARD 189
The Funeral of the Year

JOHN UPDIKE 197
Bech Enters Heaven

TOM SHARPE 211
The Fall of the House of Hazelstone

ALEX ATKINSON 225
The Eyes of Texas are Upon You

PAUL DEHN 232
A Woman of a Certain Class

ALEXANDER FRATER 237
Scoop

GEOFFREY WILLANS 242
How To Be Topp

THOMAS BERGER   245
Blacked Up

BASIL BOOTHROYD   262
Nobody Knows The Trouble

J. P. DONLEAVY   266
My Painful Jaw

CARYL BRAHMS & S. J. SIMON   269
An Historic Night at the Old Vic

KINGSLEY AMIS   285
Focusing Session

BRUCE JAY FRIEDMAN   296
Gun Law

EVELYN WAUGH   303
The Agony of Captain Grimes

MYLES NA GOPALEEN   313
The Archaeology Institute

GWYN THOMAS   318
The Treatment

N. F. SIMPSON   322
A Matter for the Courts

RICHARD CONDON   337
Walter Slurrie Goes to Washington

MILES KINGTON   347
London's Villages

LEONARD Q. ROSS   353
Mr K*a*p*l*a*n

ROBERT MORLEY   359
France and the French

RANDALL JARRELL   369
Mrs Robbins

SELLAR & YEATMAN   373
The Three Henries

JEFFREY BERNARD   377
  Sweet Sixteen

NIGEL DENNIS   380
  The Pukey

PATRICK RYAN   386
  The Tattooed Lady

STANLEY REYNOLDS   394
  Ill Met By Moonlight

ANGUS WILSON   400
  A Visit in Bad Taste

A. P. HERBERT   408
  Cricket in the Caucasus

RUSSELL DAVIES   418
  A Year in Miniature

DOROTHY PARKER   424
  Here We Are

RICHARD GORDON   435
  The Wild Life of Suburbia

ROBERT BENCHLEY   440
  The Tooth

E. S. TURNER   448
  Grand Tour 2000

ANTHONY BURGESS   453
  Don Carlo

H. L. MENCKEN   467
  Chiropractic

JOHN WELLS   475
  I'm Getting Mallied in the Morning

JAMES THURBER   479
  The Night the Bed Fell

Acknowledgements   484

Introduction

Nobody who met my old man ever forgot him.

The first thing you saw was the sabre scar across his head. The wound had been stitched up by a big mulatto *chanteuse* who had gone in with the first ENSA wave at Salerno, and the only way she could work the needle without passing out was to stay drunk; the scar went from right over his left eye to the nape of his neck. It looked like a zip. It looked like you could take hold of one end and pull and all my old man's brains would be lying there on the half-shell, like some big delicacy at Les Pyramides or that place on the Arno where Black Jack Horowitz strangled the peacock the night the rain never stopped and we all tried to put together *The Oxford Book of Secretarial Verse.*

My old man's left arm was the size of anyone else's thigh, and it was tattooed in the shape of a cabriole leg. One of his favourite party pieces was where he went out of the room and came back a couple of minutes later as a Regency card table. People still talk about that. His right arm stopped at the elbow: the rest had been left inside the turret of a Tiger tank after the lid came down, somewhere in the Ardennes Forest. I always meant to go there some day and look for this big white ulna with a lot of rust and spent Spandau cartridge-cases around it, but I never did, and I suppose I never shall now.

When he came back from the War, he just laughed about
it, at first. But then, one night in the winter of 1945, he
suddenly said:
'You're going to have to help me at the brewery, son.'
I said: 'I'm only seven, dad.'
It was the first and only time my old man hit me. If he had
hit me with the left, I should not be here now; but it was the
right he threw, and being short it had neither the range nor
the trajectory, but it hurt just the same when the elbow
connected.
Later on, he quietened down and asked me what I
intended to do with my life if I didn't want to hump barrels.
'I want to do anthologies, dad,' I said.
He looked at me hard, with his good eye; the other one is
still rolling around near El Alamein, for all I know.
'What kind of a job is that for a man?' he said.
'I don't think I'm cut out for humping barrels, dad,' I said.
He spread his arms wide; or, more accurately, one wide,
one narrow.
'It doesn't have to be barrels. There'll be other wars, you
could go and leave limbs about.'
I nodded.
'I thought about that, dad. I could be a war anthologizer. A
war provides wonderful opportunities, collected verses,
collected letters, collected journalism, things called *A
Soldier's Garland* with little bits of Shakespeare in. Did you
know that Rupert Brooke's *The Soldier* has appeared in no
less than one hundred and thirty-eight anthologies, dad,
nearly as often as James Thurber's *The Secret Life of Walter
Mitty*?'
He thought about this for a while.
'Is there money in it?' he said at last.
'Dear old dad!' I said. 'An anthologizer doesn't think
about money. He is pursued by a dream. He dreams of
making a major contribution to gumming things
together. He dreams of becoming a great literary figure
like Palgrave or Quiller-Couch.'
'And how do you go about learning to anthologize, son?'

I smiled, but tolerantly

'You can't learn it, dad. It comes from the heart and the soul. Fifty pounds would help.'

People have asked me, three decades on, in colour supplements, on chat shows, what the major influence on my work has been. I tell them that it wasn't Frank Muir, it wasn't Philip Larkin, it wasn't even Nigel Rees or Gyles Brandreth, important though these have undeniably been: it was the day my old man took his last fifty pounds out of his wooden leg, and set me on my path.

I left school soon after that. There was nothing they could teach me that would not be better learned in the real world: the experience of felt life is what lies at the still centre of all the great anthologies. I shipped aboard a coaler on the Maracaibo run, and I discovered what a Laskar likes to read in the still watches of the stifling equatorial night. My first anthology, a slim volume and privately circulated, consisted of buttocks snipped from *Health and Efficiency* interlarded with Gujarati limericks and reliable Portsmouth telephone numbers. Juvenilia, perhaps, and afflicted with the sort of critical introduction that I have long since learned always goes unread, but no worse than, say, the annual *Bedside Guardian*.

Two years later, I jumped ship at Dakar, and took up with a Senegalese novelty dancer who had a tin-roofed shack down by the harbour and a brother who worked three days a week as a roach exterminator in the British Council library. It was perhaps the most idyllic and fruitful period of my life: it was mornings of grilled breadfruit and novelty dancing on the roof overlooking the incredible azure of the Indian Ocean, and afternoons of studying the anthologies her brother would steal from the library, the absence of which, when noticed, he would attribute to the kao-kao beetle which subsisted, he said, entirely upon half-morocco. I read everything, voraciously: I learned how anthologies worked, how the masterpieces among them had been put together, how you balanced the sequential options of chronology, literary contrast, and the tenth-rate pieces done by close friends of the editor. I divined the trick of bibliographical attribution, whereby the skilled anthologizer credited the original source, rather than the previous anthology from which he himself had worked. I noticed how an expensive thin volume could be turned into a cheap fat volume by amplifying it with long sections of junk that happened to be out of copyright. I made out an invaluable list of titled paupers who could be called upon to endorse the anthologizer's choice with tiny masterpieces of prefatorial cliché, usually beginning: 'Here, indeed, are infinite riches in a little room' and ending with a holograph signature.

The idyll could not last: there was a waterfront bar where expatriate anthologizers—they called themselves that, though few among them had ever collated anything more remarkable than privately printed regimental drinking songs or limited-circulation pamphlets called things like *The Best of the Old Eastbournian, 1932-1938*—gathered of an evening to drink and argue recondite theories of anthological technique, and one night I had the misfortune to fall foul of a gigantic ex-Harvard quarterback who claimed to be on the point of closing a two-figure deal for his *Treasury of Mormon Prose*.

I shall not distress you with the details. When I woke up the following morning, my youthful good looks were gone, to be rapidly followed by my Senegalese paramour. Two weeks later, I left the infirmary and returned, far older than my twenty-two years, to England.

Britain, in 1960, was not at all as it had been a few scant years before. A new spirit was abroad, a harsher, grittier, more realistic spirit. It was the Age of Anger, and the whole face of English anthology had changed overnight.

Gone were the elegantly produced collections of ethereal lyrics and robust nineteenth-century narrative verse.

Gone were the leatherbound volumes packed with a thousand pages of India paper bearing the jewelled fragments of English prose from *A Treatise on the Astrolabe* to Hilaire Belloc on mowing. In their place, the new race of angry young anthologizers was churning out paperback collections of bogus radicalese entitled *Whither Commitment?* and *Exercises in Existentialism* and *The Right to Know—Essays on the Obligations of Communicators in a Negative Environment.* As for the more popular market, such classics as *A Knapsackery of Chuckles* or *A Wordsmith's Bouquet* had been thrown out in favour of *The Wit and Wisdom of Macdonald Hobley* and *Dora Gaitskell's Rugger Favourites.*

Ninety per cent of all anthological output was manufactured by the BBC, linked on the one hand to a vaguely similar broadcast and on the other to a wide range of dangle-dollies and jocular tea-towels.

These were, in consequence, bleak years for me. My entire creative life to this point had been wasted, the art of anthology to which I had dedicated myself was no more. Not that I surrendered lightly: by day, I worked as stevedore, cocktail waiter, pump attendant, steeplejack, male model, by night I pursued my muse, working feverishly and without sleep to produce, in the space of five years, *The Connoisseur's Book of Business Poetry, The Big Book of Boer Operetta, A Nosegay of Actuarial Prose,* and, perhaps my own favourite, *We Called It Medicine: A Selection of Middlesex Hospital Correspondence Between the Wars.*

I was thrown out of every publishers in London. It was the same story everywhere, as the sixties rolled inexorably on and television worked its equally inexorable way deeper and deeper into the culture—I was not a Face. For a new breed of anthologizer was abroad: the personality. The great names, names like Michael Barrett, Jimmy Young, Robert and Sheridan Morley, David Frost, Antonia Fraser, Freddie Trueman, Des O'Connor, Henry Cooper and the rest, all represented the New School of English Anthology; they were household words who held the publishing world in enviable thrall.

It was upon this inescapable realization that I finally
threw in the creative sponge. I had reached that nadir
which all anthologizers have at some time or another
plumbed, when you feel you can never skim through a
book again. Worse, my run of bearable jobs had come to an
end with the installation of an automatic car-wash, and I
had nowhere to turn but to a weekly humorous magazine,
where I was employed to manufacture lengths of material
which could be inserted in between pages of advertising in
order to display them to advantage. It was, as can readily, I
think, be imagined, lonely, grim, and unrewarding work,
relieved only by my access to a comprehensive library of
published humour and the constant stream of new
humorous books which paused briefly in the office of the
Literary Editor before being wheeled around the corner to
a Fleet Street bookseller prepared to exchange them for
folding money.

I thus came to read every comic word that had ever been
written. It has left me grey before my time, and I jump at
the slightest sound, but it has produced one strange by-
product, an effect unsettling yet at the same time curiously
thrilling: a year or so ago, when I had been convinced for
the better part of two decades that every creative instinct
within me had shrivelled and died back like a frostbitten
rose, a glimmer of the immortal longings of my youth
returned. On a chill November evening, as I huddled for
warmth among the teetering piles of comedy, a tiny spark
of—shall we call it inspiration—no bigger than a dog-end
falling through the night flashed deep within my head, and,
a second later, hope blew upon it, and it glowed.

This book, then, is the result. Whether, given my time
again, it would have been wiser to have spent the thirty
years in humping barrels, I cannot say. I know only that it
would have been a lot easier.

A.C.

The Kugelmass Episode

WOODY ALLEN

KUGELMASS, A PROFESSOR of humanities at City College, was unhappily married for the second time. Daphne Kugelmass was an oaf. He also had two dull sons by his first wife, Flo, and was up to his neck in alimony and child support.

'Did I know it would turn out so badly?' Kugelmass whined to his analyst one day. 'Daphne had promise. Who suspected she'd let herself go and swell up like a beach ball? Plus she has a few bucks, which is not in itself a healthy reason to marry a person, but it doesn't hurt, with the kind of operating nut I have. You see my point?'

Kugelmass was bald and as hairy as a bear, but he had soul.

'I need to meet a new woman,' he went on. 'I need to have an affair. I may not look the part, but I'm a man who needs romance. I need softness, I need flirtation. I'm not getting any younger, so before it's too late I want to make love in Venice, trade quips at "21", and exchange coy glances over red wine and candlelight. You see what I'm saying?'

Dr Mandel shifted in his chair and said, 'An affair will solve nothing. You're so unrealistic. Your problems run much deeper.'

'And also this affair must be discreet,' Kugelmass continued. 'I can't afford a second divorce. Daphne would really sock it to me.'

'Mr Kugelmass—'

'But it can't be anyone at City College, because Daphne also works there. Not that anyone on the faculty at C.C.N.Y. is any great shakes, but some of those coeds . . .'

'Mr Kugelmass—'

'Help me. I had a dream last night. I was skipping through a meadow holding a picnic basket and the basket was marked "Options". And then I saw there was a hole in the basket.'

'Mr Kugelmass, the worst thing you could do is act out. You must simply express your feelings here, and together we'll analyze them. You have been in treatment long enough to know there is no overnight cure. After all, I'm an analyst, not a magician.'

'Then perhaps what I need is a magician,' Kugelmass said, rising from his chair. And with that he terminated his therapy.

A couple of weeks later, while Kugelmass and Daphne were moping around in their apartment one night like two pieces of old furniture, the phone rang.

'I'll get it,' Kugelmass said. 'Hello.'

'Kugelmass?' a voice said. 'Kugelmass, this is Persky.'

'Who?'

'Persky. Or should I say The Great Persky?'

'Pardon me?'

'I hear you're looking all over town for a magician to bring a little exotica into your life? Yes or no?'

'Sh-h-h,' Kugelmass whispered. 'Don't hang up. Where are you calling from, Persky?'

Early the following afternoon, Kugelmass climbed three flights of stairs in a broken-down apartment house in the Bushwick section of Brooklyn. Peering through the

darkness of the hall, he found the door he was looking for
and pressed the bell. I'm going to regret this, he thought to
himself.

Seconds later, he was greeted by a short, thin, waxy-
looking man.

'You're Persky the Great?' Kugelmass said.

'The Great Persky. You want a tea?'

'No, I want romance. I want music. I want love and
beauty.'

'But not tea, eh? Amazing. OK, sit down.'

Persky went to the back of the room, and Kugelmass
heard the sounds of boxes and furniture being moved
around. Persky reappeared, pushing before him a large
object on squeaky roller-skate wheels. He removed some
old silk handkerchiefs that were lying on its top and blew
away a bit of dust. It was a cheap-looking Chinese cabinet,
badly lacquered.

'Persky,' Kugelmass said, 'what's your scam?'

'Pay attention,' Persky said. 'This is some beautiful
effect. I developed it for a Knights of Pythias date last year,
but the booking fell through. Get into the cabinet.'

'Why, so you can stick it full of swords or something?'

'You see any swords?'

Kugelmass made a face and, grunting, climbed into the
cabinet. He couldn't help noticing a couple of ugly
rhinestones glued onto the raw plywood just in front of his
face. 'If this is a joke,' he said.

'Some joke. Now, here's the point. If I throw any novel
into the cabinet with you, shut the doors, and tap it three
times, you will find yourself projected into that book.'

Kugelmass made a grimace of disbelief.

'It's the emess,' Persky said. 'My hand to God. Not just a
novel, either. A short story, a play, a poem. You can meet
any of the women created by the world's best writers.
Whoever you dreamed of. You could carry on all you like
with a real winner. Then when you've had enough you give
a yell, and I'll see you're back here in a split second.'

'Persky, are you some kind of outpatient?'

'I'm telling you it's on the level,' Persky said.

Kugelmass remained skeptical. 'What are you telling me—that this cheesy homemade box can take me on a ride like you're describing?

'For a double sawbuck.'

Kugelmass reached for his wallet. 'I'll believe this when I see it,' he said.

Persky tucked the bills in his pants pocket and turned toward his bookcase. 'So who do you want to meet? Sister Carrie? Hester Prynne? Ophelia? Maybe someone by Saul Bellow? Hey, what about Temple Drake? Although for a man your age she'd be a workout.'

'French. I want to have an affair with a French lover.'

'Nana?'

'I don't want to have to pay for it.'

'What about Natasha in *War and Peace*?'

'I said French. I know! What about Emma Bovary? That sounds to me perfect.'

'You got it Kugelmass. Give me a holler when you've had enough.' Persky tossed in a paperback copy of Flaubert's novel.

'You sure this is safe?' Kugelmass asked as Persky began shutting the cabinet doors.

'Safe. Is anything safe in this crazy world?' Persky rapped three times on the cabinet and then flung open the doors.

Kugelmass was gone. At the same moment, he appeared in the bedroom of Charles and Emma Bovary's house at Yonville. Before him was a beautiful woman, standing alone with her back turned to him as she folded some linen. I can't believe this, thought Kugelmass, staring at the doctor's ravishing wife. This is uncanny. I'm here. It's her.

Emma turned in surprise. 'Goodness, you startled me,' she said. 'Who are you?' She spoke in the same fine English translation as the paperback.

It's simply devastating, he thought. Then, realizing that it was he whom she had addressed, he said, 'Excuse me. I'm Sidney Kugelmass. I'm from City College. A professor of humanities. C.C.N.Y.? Uptown. I—oh, boy!'

Emma Bovary smiled flirtatiously and said, 'Would you like a drink? A glass of wine, perhaps?'

She is beautiful, Kugelmass thought. What a contrast with the troglodyte who shared his bed! He felt a sudden impulse to take this vision into his arms and tell her she was the kind of woman he had dreamed of all his life.

'Yes, some wine,' he said hoarsely. 'White. No, red. No, white. Make it white.'

'Charles is out for the day,' Emma said, her voice full of playful implications.

After the wine, they went for a stroll in the lovely French countryside. 'I've always dreamed that some mysterious stranger would appear and rescue me from the monotony of this crass rural existence,' Emma said, clasping his hand. They passed a small church. 'I love what you have on,' she murmured. 'I've never seen anything like it around here. It's so . . . so modern.'

'It's called a leisure suit, ' he said romantically. 'It was marked down.' Suddenly he kissed her. For the next hour they reclined under a tree and whispered together and told each other deeply meaningful things with their eyes .Then Kugelmass sat up. He had just remembered he had to meet Daphne at Bloomingdale's. 'I must go,' he told her. 'But don't worry, I'll be back.'

'I hope so,' Emma said.

He embraced her passionately, and the two walked back to the house. He held Emma's face cupped in his palms, kissed her again, and yelled, 'OK, Persky! I got to be at Bloomingdale's by three-thirty.'

There was an audible pop, and Kugelmass was back in Brooklyn.

'So? Did I lie?' Persky asked triumphantly.

'Look, Persky, I'm right now late to meet the ball and chain at Lexington Avenue, but when can I go again? Tomorrow?'

'My pleasure. Just bring a twenty. And don't mention this to anybody.'

'Yeah. I'm going to call Rupert Murdoch.'

Kugelmass hailed a cab and sped off to the city. His heart danced on point. I am in love, he thought, I am the possessor of a wonderful secret. What he didn't realize was that at this moment students in various classrooms across the country were saying to their teachers. 'Who is this character on page 100? A bald Jew is kissing Madame Bovary?' A teacher in Sioux Falls, South Dakota, sighed and thought, Jesus, these kids, with their pot and acid. What goes through their minds!

Daphne Kugelmass was in the bathroom-accessories department at Bloomingdale's when Kugelmass arrived breathlessly. 'Where've you been?' she snapped. 'It's four-thirty.'

'I got held up in traffic,' Kugelmass said.

Kugelmass visited Persky the next day, and in a few minutes was again passed magically to Yonville. Emma couldn't hide her excitement at seeing him. The two spent hours together, laughing and talking about their different backgrounds. Before Kugelmass left,they made love. 'My God, I'm doing it with Madame Bovary!' Kugelmass whispered to himself. 'Me, who failed freshman English.'

As the months passed, Kugelmass saw Persky many times and developed a close and passionate relationship with Emma Bovary. 'Make sure and always get me into the book before page 120,' Kugelmass said to the magician one day. 'I always have to meet her before she hooks up with this Rodolphe character.'

'Why?' Persky asked. 'You can't beat his time?'

'Beat his time. He's landed gentry. Those guys have nothing better to do than flirt and ride horses. To me, he's one of those faces you see in the pages of *Women's Wear Daily*. With the Helmut Berger hairdo. But to her he's hot stuff.'

'And her husband suspects nothing?'

'He's out of his depth. He's a lacklustre little paramedic

who's thrown in his lot with a jitterbug. He's ready to go to sleep by ten, and she's putting on her dancing shoes. Oh, well . . . See you later.'

And once again Kugelmass entered the cabinet and passed instantly to the Bovary estate at Yonville. 'How you doing, cupcake?' he said to Emma.

'Oh, Kugelmass,' Emma sighed. 'What I have to put up with. Last night at dinner, Mr Personality dropped off to sleep in the middle of the dessert course. I'm pouring my heart out about Maxim's and the ballet, and out of the blue I hear snoring.'

'It's OK, darling. I'm here now.' Kugelmass said, embracing her. I've earned this, he thought, smelling Emma's French perfume and burying his nose in her hair. I've suffered enough. I've paid enough analysts. I've searched till I'm weary. She's young and nubile, and I'm here a few pages after Leon and just before Rodolphe. By showing up during the correct chapters, I've got the situation knocked.

Emma, to be sure, was just as happy as Kugelmass. She has been starved for excitement, and his tales of Broadway life, of fast cars and Hollywood and TV stars, enthralled the young French beauty.

'Tell me again about O.J. Simpson,' she implored that evening, as she and Kugelmass strolled past Abbé Bournisien's church.

'What can I say? The man is great. He sets all kinds of rushing records. Such moves. They can't touch him.'

'And the Academy Awards?' Emma said wistfully. 'I'd give anything to win one.'

'First you've got to be nominated.'

'I know. You explained it. But I'm convinced I can act. Of course, I'd want to take a class or two. With Strasberg maybe. Then, if I had the right agent—'

'We'll see, we'll see. I'll speak to Persky.'

That night, safely returned to Persky's flat, Kugelmass brought up the idea of having Emma visit him in the big city.

'Let me think about it,' Persky said. 'Maybe I could work it. Stranger things have happened.' Of course neither of them could think of one.

'Where the hell do you go all the time?' Daphne Kugelmass barked at her husband as he returned home late that evening. 'You got a chippie stashed somewhere?'

'Yeah, sure, I'm just the type,' Kugelmass said wearily. 'I was with Leonard Popkin. We were discussing Socialist agriculture in Poland. You know Popkin. He's a freak on the subject.'

'Well, you've been very odd lately,' Daphne said. 'Distant. Just don't forget about my father's birthday. On Saturday?'

'Oh, sure, sure,' Kugelmass said, heading for the bathroom.

'My whole family will be there. We can see the twins. And Cousin Hamish. You should be more polite to Cousin Hamish—he likes you.'

'Right, the twins,' Kugelmass said, closing the bathroom door and shutting out the sound of his wife's voice. He leaned against it and took a deep breath. In a few hours he told himself, he would be back in Yonville again, with his beloved. And this time, if all went well, he would bring Emma back with him.

At three-fifteen the following afternoon, Persky worked his wizardry again. The two spent a few hours at Yonville with Binet and then remounted the Bovary carriage. Following Persky's instructions, they held each other tightly, closed their eyes, and counted to ten. When they opened them, the carriage was just drawing up at the side door of the Plaza Hotel, where Kugelmass had optimistically reserved a suite earlier in the day.

'I love it! It's everything I dreamed it would be,' Emma said as she swirled joyously around the bedroom, surveying the city from their window. 'There's F.A.O. Schwarz. And there's Central Park, and the Sherry is which one? Oh, there—I see. It's too divine.'

On the bed there were boxes from Halston and Saint Laurent. Emma unwrapped a package and held up a pair of black velvet pants against her perfect body.

'The slacks suit is by Ralph Lauren,' Kugelmass said. 'You'll look like a million bucks in it. Come on sugar, give us a kiss.'

'I've never been so happy!' Emma squealed as she stood before the mirror. 'Let's go out on the town. I want to see *Chorus Line* and the Guggenheim and this Jack Nicholson character you always talk about. Are any of his flicks showing?'

'I cannot get my mind around this,' a Stanford professor said. 'First a strange character named Kugelmass, and now she's gone from the book. Well, I guess the mark of a classic is that you can reread it a thousand times and always find something new.'

The lovers passed a blissful weekend. Kugelmass had told Daphne he would be away at a symposium in Boston and would return Monday. Savoring each moment, he and Emma went to the movies, had dinner in Chinatown, passed two hours at a discothèque, and went to bed with a TV movie. They slept till noon on Sunday, visited SoHo, and ogled celebrities at Elaine's. They had caviar and champagne in their suite on Sunday night and talked until dawn. That morning, in the cab taking them to Persky's apartment. Kugelmass thought, it was hectic, but worth it. I can't bring her here too often, but now and then it will be a charming contrast with Yonville.

At Persky's Emma climbed into the cabinet, arranged her new boxes of clothes neatly around her, and kissed Kugelmass fondly. 'My place next time,' she said with a wink. Persky rapped three times on the cabinet. Nothing happened.

'Hmm,' Persky said, scratching his head. He rapped again, but still no magic. 'Something must be wrong,' he mumbled.

'Persky, you're joking!' Kugelmass cried. 'How can it not work?'

'Relax, relax. Are you still in the box, Emma?'

'Yes.'

Persky rapped again—harder this time.

'I'm still here, Persky.'

'I know, darling. Sit tight.'

'Persky, we *have* to get her back,' Kugelmass whispered. 'I'm a married man, and I have a class in three hours. I'm not prepared for anything more than a cautious affair at this point.'

'I can't understand it,' Persky muttered. 'It's such a reliable little trick.'

But he could do nothing. 'It's going to take a little while,' he said to Kugelmass. 'I'm going to have to strip it down. I'll call you later.'

Kugelmass bundled Emma into a cab and took her back to the Plaza. He barely made it to his class on time. He was on the phone all day, to Persky and to his mistress. The magician told him it might be several days' before he got to the bottom of the trouble.

'How was the symposium?' Daphne asked him that night.

'Fine, fine,' he said, lighting the filter end of a cigarette.

'What's wrong? You're as tense as a cat.'

'Me? Ha, that's a laugh. I'm as calm as a summer night. I'm just going to take a walk.' He eased out the door, hailed a cab, and flew to the Plaza.

'This is no good,' Emma said. 'Charles will miss me.'

'Bear with me sugar,' Kugelmass said. He was pale and sweaty. He kissed her again, raced to the elevators, yelled at Persky over a pay phone in the Plaza lobby, and just made it home before midnight.

'According to Popkin, barley prices in Kraków have not been this stable since 1971,' he said to Daphne, and smiled wanly as he climbed into bed.

The whole week went like that.

On Friday night, Kugelmass told Daphne there was another symposium he had to catch, this one in Syracuse. He hurried back to the Plaza, but the second weekend there was nothing like the first. 'Get me back into the novel or marry me,' Emma told Kugelmass. 'Meanwhile, I want to get a job or go to class, because watching TV all day is the pits.'

'Fine. We can use the money,' Kugelmass said. 'You consume twice your weight in room service.'

'I met an Off Broadway producer in Central Park yesterday, and he told me I might be right for a project he's doing,' Emma said.

'Who is this clown?' Kugelmass asked.

'He's not a clown. He's sensitive and kind and cute. His name's Jeff Something-or-Other, and he's up for a Tony.'

Later that afternoon, Kugelmass showed up at Persky's drunk.

'Relax,' Persky told him. 'You'll get a coronary.'

'Relax. The man says relax. I've got a fictional character stashed in a hotel room, and I think my wife is having me tailed by a private shamus.'

'OK, OK. We know there's a problem.' Persky crawled under the cabinet and started banging on something with a large wrench.

'I'm like a wild animal,' Kugelmass went on. 'I'm sneaking around town, and Emma and I have had it up to here with each other. Not to mention a hotel tab that reads like a defense budget.'

'So what should I do? This is the world of magic,' Persky said. 'It's a nuance.'

'Nuance, my foot. I'm pouring Dom Pérignon and black eggs into this little mouse, plus her wardrobe, plus she's enrolled at the Neighborhood Playhouse and suddenly needs professional photos. Also, Persky, Professor Fivish Kopkind, who teaches Comp Lit and who has always been jealous of me, has identified me as the sporadically appearing character in the Flaubert book. He's threatened to go to Daphne. I see ruin and alimony; jail. For adultery with Madame Bovary, my wife will reduce me to beggary.'

'What do you want me to say? I'm working on it night and day. As far as your personal anxiety goes, that I can't help you with. I'm a magician, not an analyst.'

By Sunday afternoon, Emma had locked herself in the bathroom and refused to respond to Kugelmass's entreaties. Kugelmass stared out the window at the Wollman Rink and contemplated suicide. Too bad this is a low floor, he thought, or I'd do it right now. Maybe if I ran away to Europe and started life over . . . Maybe I could sell the *International Herald Tribune*, like those young girls used to.

The phone rang. Kugelmass lifted it to his ear mechanically.

'Bring her over,' Persky said. 'I think I got the bugs out of it.'

Kugelmass's heart leaped. 'You're serious?' he said. 'You got it licked?'

'It was something in the transmission. Go figure.'

'Persky, you're a genius. We'll be there in a minute. Less than a minute.'

Again the lovers hurried to the magician's apartment, and again Emma Bovary climbed into the cabinet with her boxes. This time there was no kiss. Persky shut the doors, took a deep breath, and tapped the box three times. There was the reassuring popping noise, and when Persky peered inside, the box was empty. Madame Bovary was back in her novel. Kugelmass heaved a great sigh of relief and pumped the magician's hand.

'It's over,' he said. 'I learned my lesson. I'll never cheat again, I swear it.' He pumped Persky's hand again and made a mental note to send him a necktie.

Three weeks later, at the end of a beautiful spring afternoon, Persky answered his doorbell. It was Kugelmass, with a sheepish expression on his face.

'OK, Kugelmass,' the magician said. 'Where to this time?'

'It's just this once,' Kugelmass said. 'The weather is so lovely, and I'm not getting any younger. Listen, you've read *Portnoy's Complaint*? Remember The Monkey?'

'The price is now twenty-five dollars, because the cost of living is up, but I'll start you off with one freebie, due to all the trouble I caused you.'

'You're good people,' Kugelmass said, combing his few remaining hairs as he climbed into the cabinet again. 'This'll work all right?'

'I hope. But I haven't tried it much since all that unpleasantness.'

'Sex and romance,' Kugelmass said from inside the box. 'What we go through for a pretty face.'

Persky tossed in a copy of *Portnoy's Complaint* and rapped three times on the box. This time, instead of a popping noise there was a dull explosion, followed by a series of crackling noises and a shower of sparks. Persky leaped back, was seized with a heart attack, and dropped dead. The cabinet burst into flames, and eventually the entire house burned down.

Kugelmass, unaware of this catastrophe, had his own problems. He had not been thrust into *Portnoy's Complaint*, or into any other novel, for that matter. He had been projected into an old textbook, *Remedial Spanish*, and was running for his life over a barren, rocky terrain as the word *tener* ('to have')—a large and hairy irregular verb—raced after him on its spindly legs.

The Quarrel with Ramlogan

V.S. NAIPAUL

'I SUPPOSE,' GANESH wrote in *The Years of Guilt*, 'I had always, from the first day I stepped into Shri Ramlogan's shop, considered it as settled that I was going to marry his daughter. I never questioned it. It all seemed preordained.'

What happened was this.

One day when Ganesh called Ramlogan was wearing a clean shirt. Also, he looked freshly washed, his hair looked freshly oiled; and his movements were silent and deliberate as though he were doing a *puja*. He dragged up the small bench from the corner and placed it near the table; then sat on it and watched Ganesh eat, all without saying a word. First he looked at Ganesh's face, then at Ganesh's plate, and there his gaze rested until Ganesh had eaten the last handful of rice.

'Your belly full, sahib?'

'Yes, my belly full.' Ganesh wiped his plate clean with an extended index finger.

'It must be hard for you, sahib, now that your father dead.'

Ganesh licked his finger. 'I don't really miss him, you know.'

'No, sahib, don't tell me. I *know* is hard for you. Supposing, just supposing—I just putting this up to you as a superstition, sahib—but just supposing you did want to get married, it have nobody at all to fix up things for you.'

'I don't even know if I want to get married.' Ganesh rose from the table, rubbing his belly until he belched his appreciation of Ramlogan's food.

Ramlogan rearranged the roses in the vase. 'Still, you is a educated man, and you could take care of yourself. Not like me, sahib. Since I was five I been working, with nobody looking after me. Still, all that do something for me. Guess what it do for me, sahib.'

'Can't guess. Tell me what it do.'

'It give me cha'acter and sensa values, sahib. That's what it give me. Cha'acter and sensa values.'

Ganesh took the brass jar of water from the table and went to the Demerara window to wash his hands and gargle.

Ramlogan was smoothing out the oilcloth with both hands and dusting away some crumbs, mere specks. 'I know,' he said apologetically, 'that for a man like you, educated and reading books night and day, shopkeeping is a low thing. But I don't care what people think. You, sahib, answer me this as a educated man: you does let other people worry you?'

Ganesh, gargling, thought at once of Miller and the row at the school in Port of Spain, but when he spat out the water into the yard he said, 'Nah. I don't care what people say.'

Ramlogan pounded across the floor and took the brass jar from Ganesh. 'I go put this away, sahib. You sit down in the hammock. Ooops! Let me dust it for you first.'

When he had seated Ganesh, Ramlogan started to walk up and down in front of the hammock.

'People can't harm me,' he said, holding his hands at his back. 'All right, people don't like me. All right, they stop

coming to my shop. That harm me? That change my
cha'acter? I just go to San Fernando and open a little stall in
the market. No, don't stop me, sahib. Is exactly what I
would do. Take a stall in the market. And what happen?
Tell me, what happen?'

Ganesh belched again, softly.

'What happen?' Ramlogan gave a short crooked laugh.
'Bam! In five years I have a whole chain of grocery shop.
Who laughing then? Then you go see them coming round
and begging, "Mr Ramlogan"—that's what it go be then,
you know: *Mister* Ramlogan—"Mr Ramlogan, gimme this,
gimme that, Mr Ramlogan." Begging me to go up for
elections and a hundred and one stupid things.'

Ganesh said, 'You ain't have to start opening stall in San
Fernando market now, thank God.'

'That is it, sahib. Just just as you say. Is all God work.
Count my property now. Is true I is illiterate, but you just
sit down in that hammock and count my property.'

Ramlogan was walking and talking with such unusual
energy that the sweat broke and shone on his forehead.
Suddenly he halted and stood directly in front of Ganesh.
He took away his hands from behind his back and started to
count off his fingers. 'Two acres near Chaguanas. Good
land, too. Ten acres in Penal. You never know when I could
scrape together enough to make the drillers put a oil-well
there. A house in Fuente Grove. Not much, but is
something. Two three houses in Siparia. Add up all that
and you find you looking at a man worth about twelve
thousand dollars, cool cool.'

Ramlogan passed his hand over his forehead and behind
his neck. 'I know is hard to believe, sahib. But is the gospel
truth. I think is a good idea, sahib, for you to married Leela.'

'All right,' Ganesh said.

He never saw Leela again until the night of their wedding,
and both he and Ramlogan pretended he had never seen
her at all, because they were both good Hindus and knew it

was wrong for a man to see his wife before marriage.

He still had to go to Ramlogan's, to make arrangements for the wedding, but he remained in the shop itself and never went to the back room.

'You is not like Soomintra damn fool of a husband,' Ramlogan told him. 'You is a modern man and you must have a modern wedding.'

So he didn't send the messenger around to give the saffron-dyed rice to friends and relations and announce the wedding. 'The old-fashion,' he said. He wanted printed invitations on scalloped and gilt-edged cards. 'And we must have nice wordings, sahib.'

'But you can't have nice wordings on a thing like a invitation.'

'You is the educated man, sahib. You could think of some.'

'R.S.V.P.?'

'What that mean?'

'It don't mean nothing, but it nice to have it.'

'Let we have it then, man, sahib! You is a modern man, and too besides, it sound as pretty wordings.'

Ganesh himself went to San Fernando to get the cards printed. The printer's shop was, at first sight, a little disappointing. It looked black and bleak and seemed to be manned only by a thin youth in ragged khaki shorts who whistled as he operated the hand-press. But when Ganesh saw the cards go in blank and come out with his prose miraculously transformed into all the authority of type, he was struck with something like awe. He stayed to watch the boy set up a cinema hand-bill. The boy, whistling without intermission, ignored Ganesh altogether.

'Is on this sort of machine they does print books?' Ganesh asked.

'What else you think it make for?'

'You print any good books lately?'

The boy dabbed some ink on the roller. 'You ever hear of Trinidad people writing books?'

'I writing a book.'

The boy spat into a bin full of ink-stained paper. 'This must be a funny sort of shop, you know. The number of people who come in here and ask me to print the books they writing in invisible ink, man!'

'What you name?'

'Basdeo.'

'All right, Basdeo, boy. The day go come when I go send you a book to print.'

'Sure, man. Sure. You write it and I print it.'

Ganesh didn't think he liked Basdeo's Hollywood manner, and he instantly regretted what he had said. But so far as this business of writing books was concerned, he seemed to have no will: it was the second time he had committed himself. It all seemed preordained.

'Yes, they is pretty invitation cards,' Ramlogan said, but there was no joy in his voice.

'But what happen now to make your face long long as mango?'

'Education, sahib, is one hell of a thing. When you is a poor illiterate man like me, all sort of people does want to take advantage on you.'

Ramlogan began to cry. 'Right now, right right now, as you sitting down on that bench there and I sitting down on this stool behind my shop counter, looking at these pretty pretty cards, you wouldn't believe what people trying to do to me. Right now it have a man in Siparia trying to rob my two house there, all because I can't read, and the people in Penal behaving in a funny way.'

'What they doing so?'

'Ah, sahib. That is just like you. I know you want to help me, but is too late now. All sort of paper with fine fine writing they did make me sign and everything, and now—now everything lost.'

Ganesh had not seen Ramlogan cry so much since the funeral. He said, 'Well, look. If is the dowry you worried about, you could stop. I don't want a big dowry.'

'Is the shame, sahib, that eating me up. You know how with these Hindu weddings everybody does know how much the boy get from the girl father. When, the morning after the wedding the boy sit down and they give him a plate of kedgeree, with the girl father having to give money and keep on giving until the boy eat the kedgeree, everybody go see what I give you, and they go say, "Look, Ramlogan marrying off his second and best daughter to a boy with a college education, and this is all the man giving." Is that what eating me up, sahib. I know that for you, educated and reading books night and day, it wouldn't mean much, but for me, sahib, what about my cha'acter and sensa values?'

'You must stop crying and listen. When it come to eating the kedgeree, I go eat quick, not to shame you. Not too quick, because that would make people think you poor as a church-rat. But I wouldn't take much from you.'

Ramlogan smiled through his tears. 'Is just like you, sahib, just what I did expect from you. I wish Leela did see you and then she woulda know what sort of man I choose for she husband.'

'I wish I did see Leela too.'

'Smatterer fact, sahib, I know it have some modern people nowadays who don't even like waiting for money before they eat the kedgeree.'

'But is the custom, man.'

'Yes, sahib, the custom. But still I think is a disgrace in these modern times. Now, if it was *I* was getting married, I wouldn't want any dowry and I woulda say, "To hell with the kedgeree, man."'

As soon as the invitations were out Ganesh had to stop visiting Ramlogan altogether, but he wasn't alone in his house for long. Dozens of women descended on him with their children. He had no idea who most of them were; sometimes he recognized a face and found it hard to believe that the woman with the children hanging about her was the same cousin who was only a child herself when he first went to Port of Spain.

The children treated Ganesh with contempt.

A small boy with a running nose said to him one day, 'They tell me is you who getting married.'

'Yes, is me.'

The boy said, 'Ahaha!' and ran away laughing and jeering.

The boy's mother said, 'Is something we have to face these days. The children getting modern.'

Then one day Ganesh discovered his aunt among the women, she who had been one of the principal mourners at his father's funeral. He learnt that she had not only arranged everything then, but had also paid for it all. When Ganesh offered to pay back the money she became annoyed and told him not to be stupid.

'This life is a funny thing, eh,' she said. 'One day somebody dead and you cry. Two days later somebody married, and then you laugh. Oh, Ganeshwa boy, at a time like this you want your own family around you, but what family you have? Your father, he dead; your mother, she dead too.'

She was so moved she couldn't cry; and for the first time Ganesh realized what a big thing his marriage was.

Ganesh thought it almost a miracle that so many people could live happily in one small house without any sort of organization. They had left him the bedroom, but they swarmed over the rest of the house and managed as best they could. First they had made it into an extended picnic site; then they had made it into a cramped camping site. But they looked happy enough and Ganesh presently discovered that the anarchy was only apparent. Of the dozens of women who wandered freely about the house there was one, tall and silent, whom he had learnt to call King George. It might have been her real name for all he knew: he had never seen her before. King George ruled the house.

'King George got a hand,' his aunt said.

'A hand?'

'She got a hand for sharing things out. Give King George a little penny cake and give she twelve children to share it out to, and you could bet your bottom dollar that King George share it fair and square.'

'You know she, then?'

'Know she! Is I who take up King George. Mark you, I think I was very lucky coming across she. Now I take she everywhere with me.'

'She related to us?'

'You could say so. Phulbassia is a sort of cousin to King George and you is a sort of cousin to Phulbassia.'

The aunt belched, not the polite after-dinner belch, but a long stuttering thing. 'Is the wind,' she explained without apology. 'It have a long time now—since your father dead, come to think of it—I suffering from this wind.'

'You see a doctor?'

'Doctor? They does only make up things. One of them tell me—you know what?—that I have a lazy liver. Is something I asking myself a long time now: how a liver could be lazy, eh?'

She belched again, said, 'You see?' and rubbed her hands over her breasts.

Ganesh thought of this aunt as Lady Belcher and then as The Great Belcher. In a few days she had a devastating effect on the other women in the house. They all began belching and rubbing their breasts and complaining about the wind. All except King George.

Ganesh was glad when the time came for him to be anointed with saffron. For those days he was confined to his room, where his father's body had lain that night, and where now The Great Belcher, King George, and a few other anonymous women gathered to rub him down. When they left the room they sang Hindi wedding songs of a most pessimistic nature, and Ganesh wondered how Leela was putting up with her own seclusion and anointing.

All day long he remained in his room, consoling himself

with *The Science of Thought Review*. He read through all the
numbers Mr Stewart had given him, some of them many
times over. All day he heard the children romping,
squealing, and being beaten; the mothers beating,
shouting, and thumping about on the floor.

On the day before the wedding, when the women had
come in to rub him down for the last time, he asked The
Great Belcher, 'I never think about it before, but what
those people outside eating? Who paying for it?'

'You.'

He almost sat up in bed, but King George's strong arm
kept him down.

'Ramlogan did say that we mustn't get you worried
about that.' The Great Belcher said. 'He say your head hot
with enough worries already. But King George looking
after everything. She got a account with Ramlogan. He go
settle with you after the wedding.'

'Oh God! I ain't even married the man daughter yet, and
already he start!'

Fourways was nearly as excited at the wedding as it had
been at the funeral. Hundreds of people, from Fourways
and elsewhere, were fed at Ramlogan's. There were
dancers, drummers, and singers, for those who were not
interested in the details of the night-long ceremony. The
yard behind Ramlogan's shop was beautifully illuminated
with all sorts of lights, except electric ones; and the
decorations—mainly fruit hanging from coconut-palm
arches—were pleasing. All this for Ganesh, and Ganesh
felt it and was pleased. The thought of marriage had at first
embarrassed him, then, when he spoke with his aunt, awed
him; now he was simply thrilled.

All through the ceremony he had to pretend, with
everyone else, that he had never seen Leela. She sat at his
side veiled from head to toe, until the blanket was thrown
over them and he unveiled her face. In the mellow light
under the pink blanket she was as a stranger. She was no

longer the giggling girl simpering behind the lace curtains. Already she looked chastened and impassive, a good Hindu wife.

Shortly afterwards it was over, and they were man and wife. Leela was taken away and Ganesh was left alone to face the kedgeree-eating ceremony the next morning.

Still in all his bridegroom's regalia, satin robes, and tasselled crown, he sat down on some blankets in the yard, before the plate of kedgeree. It looked white and unpalatable, and he knew it would be easy to resist any temptation to touch it.

Ramlogan was the first to offer money to induce Ganesh to eat. He was a little haggard after staying awake all night, but he looked pleased and happy enough when he placed five twenty-dollar bills in the brass plate next to the kedgeree. He stepped back, folded his arms, looked from the money to Ganesh to the small group standing by, and smiled.

He stood smiling for nearly two minutes; but Ganesh didn't even look at the kedgeree.

'Give the boy money, man,' Ramlogan cried to the people around. 'Give him money, man. Come on, don't act as if you is all poor poor as church-rat.' He moved among them, laughing, and rallying them. Some put down small amounts in the brass plate.

Still Ganesh sat, serene and aloof, like an over-dressed Buddha.

A little crowd began to gather.

'The boy have sense, man.' Anxiety broke into Ramlogan's voice. 'When you think a college education is these days?'

He put down another hundred dollars. 'Eat, boy, eat it up. I don't want you to starve. Not yet, anyway.' He laughed, but no one laughed with him.

Ganesh didn't eat.

He heard a man saying, 'Well, this thing was bound to happen some day.'

People said, 'Come on, Ramlogan. Give the boy money,

man. What you think he sitting down there for? To take
out his photo?'

Ramlogan gave a short, forced laugh, and lost his
temper. 'If he think he going to get any more money from
me he damn well mistaken. Let him don't eat. Think, I care
if he starve? Think I care?'

He walked away.

The crowd grew bigger; the laughter grew louder.

Ramlogan came back and the crowd cheered him.

He put down two hundred dollars on the brass plate and,
before he rose, whispered to Ganesh, 'Remember your
promise, sahib, Eat, boy; eat, son; eat, sahib; eat, pundit
sahib. I beg you, eat.'

A man shouted, 'No! I not going to eat!'

Ramlogan stood up and turned around. 'You, haul your
tail away from here quick, quick, before I break it up for
you. Don't meddle in what don't concern you.'

The crowd roared.

Ramlogan bent down again to whisper. 'You see, sahib,
how you making me shame.' This time his whisper
promised tears. 'You see, sahib, what you doing to my
cha'acter and sensa values.'

Ganesh didn't move.

The crowd was beginning to treat him like a hero.

In the end Ganesh got from Ramlogan: a cow and a
heifer, fifteen hundred dollars in cash, and a house in
Fuente Grove. Ramlogan also cancelled the bill for the food
he had sent to Ganesh's house.

The ceremony ended at about nine in the morning; but
Ramlogan was sweating long before then.

'The boy and I was only having a joke,' he said again and
again at the end. 'He done know long time now what I was
going to give him. We was only making joke, you know.'

Princess Daisy

CLIVE JAMES

TO BE A really lousy writer takes energy. The average novelist remains unread not because he is bad but because he is flat. On the evidence of *Princess Daisy*, Judith Krantz deserves her high place on the best-seller lists. This is the second time she has been up there. The first time was for a book called *Scruples*, which I will probably never get around to reading. But I don't resent the time I have put into reading *Princess Daisy*. As a work of art it has the same status as a long conversation between two not very bright drunks, but as best-sellers go it argues for a reassuringly robust connection between fiction and the reading public. If cheap dreams get no worse than this, there will not be much for the cultural analyst to complain about. *Princess Daisy* is a terrible book only in the sense that it is almost totally inept. Frightening it isn't.

In fact, it wouldn't even be particularly boring if only Mrs Krantz could quell her artistic urge. 'Above all,' said Conrad, 'to make you see.' Mrs Krantz strains every nerve to make you see. She pops her valves in the unrelenting effort to bring it all alive. Unfortunately she has the opposite of a pictorial talent. The more detail she piles on, the less clear things become. Take the meeting of Stash and Francesca. Mrs Krantz defines Prince Alexander Vassili-vitch Valensky, alias Stash, as 'the great war hero and incomparable polo-player'. Stash is Daisy's father. Francesca Vernon, the film star, is her mother. Francesca possesses 'a combination of tranquillity and pure sensuality in the composition of the essential triangle of eyes and mouth'. Not just essential but well-nigh indispensable, one would have thought. Or perhaps that's what she means.

This, however, is to quibble, because before Stash and Francesca can generate Daisy they first have to meet, and theirs is a meeting of transfigurative force, as of Apollo catching up with Daphne. The scene is Deauville, 1952. Francesca the film star, she of the pure sensuality, is a reluctant spectator at a polo game—reluctant, that is, until she claps eyes on Stash. Here is a description of her eyes, together with the remaining component of the essential triangle, namely her mouth. 'Her black eyes were long and widely spaced, her mouth, even in repose, was made meaningful by the grace of its shape: the gentle arc of her upper lip dipped in the centre to meet the lovely pillow of her lower lip in a line that had the power of an embrace.'

And this is Stash, the great war hero and incomparable polo-player: 'Valensky had the physical presence of a great athlete who has punished his body without pity throughout his life and the watchful, fighting eyes of a natural predator. His glance was bold and his thick brows were many shades darker than his blonde hair, cropped short and as coarse as the coat of a hastily brushed dog . . . His nose, broken many times, gave him the air of a roughneck . . . Not only did Valensky never employ unnecessary force on the bit and reins but he had been born, as some men are, with an instinct for establishing a communication between himself and his pony which made it seem as if the animal was merely an extension of his mind, rather than a beast with a will of its own.'

Dog-haired, horse-brained and with a bashed conk, Stash is too much for Francesca's equilibrium. Her hat flies off.

> 'Oh no!' she exclaimed in dismay, but as she spoke, Stash Valensky leaned down from his pony and scooped her up in one arm. Holding her easily, across his chest, he urged his mount after the wayward hat. It had come to rest two hundred yards away, and Valensky, leaving Francesca mounted, jumped down from his saddle, picked the hat up by its ribbons and carefully replaced it on her head. The stands rang with laughter and applause.
>
> Francesca heard nothing of the noise the spectators made. Time, as she knew it, had stopped. By instinct, she remained silent and waiting, passive against Stash's soaking-wet polo shirt. She could smell his sweat and it confounded her with desire. Her mouth filled with saliva. She wanted to sink her teeth into his tan neck, to bite him until she could taste his blood, to lick up the rivulets of sweat which ran down to his open collar. She wanted him to fall to the ground with her in his arms, just as he was, flushed, steaming, still breathing heavily from the game, and grind himself into her.

But this is the first of many points at which Mrs Krantz's minus capability for evocation leaves you puzzled. How did Stash get the hat back on Francesca's head? Did he remount, or is he just very tall? If he did remount, couldn't that have been specified? Mrs Krantz gives you all the details you don't need to form a mental picture, while carefully withholding those you do. Half the trick of pictorial writing is to give only the indispensable points and let the reader's imagination do the rest. Writers who not only give the indispensable points but supply all the concrete details as well can leave you feeling bored with their brilliance—Wyndham Lewis is an outstanding example.

But a writer who supplies the concrete details and leaves out the indispensable points can only exhaust you. Mrs Krantz is right to pride herself on the accuracy of her research into every department of the high life. What she says is rarely inaccurate, as far as I can tell. It is, however, almost invariably irrelevant.

Any way, the book starts with a picture of Daisy ('Her dark eyes, not quite black, but the colour of the innermost heart of a giant purple pansy, caught the late afternoon light and held it fast . . .') and then goes on to describe the meeting of her parents. It then goes on to tell you a lot about what her parents got up to before they met. Then it goes on to tell you about *their* parents. The book is continually going backwards instead of forwards, a canny insurance against the reader's impulse to skip. At one stage I tried skipping a chapter and missed out on about a century. From the upper West Side of New York I was suddenly in the Russian Revolution. That's where Stash gets his fiery temperament from—Russia.

'At Chez Mahu they found that they were able only to talk of unimportant things. Stash tried to explain polo to Francesca but she scarcely listened, mesmerized as she was with the abrupt movements of his tanned hands on which light blonde hair grew, the hands of a great male animal.' A bison? Typically, Mrs Krantz has failed to be specific at the exact moment when specificity would be a virtue. Perhaps Stash is like a horse not just in brain but in body. This would account for his tendency to view Francesca as a creature of equine provenance. 'Francesca listened to Valensky's low voice, which had traces of an English accent, a brutal man's voice which seemed to vibrate with an underlying tenderness, as if he were talking to a newborn foal . . .'

There is a lot more about Stash and Francesca before the reader can get to Daisy. Indeed, the writer herself might never have got to Daisy if she (i.e. Mrs Krantz) had not first wiped out Stash and Francesca. But before they can be killed, Mrs Krantz must expend about a hundred and fifty pages on various desperate attempts to bring them alive. In World War Two the incomparable polo-player becomes the great war hero. Those keen to see Stash crash, however, are doomed to disappointment, since before Stash can win medals in his Hurricane we must hear about his first love affair. Stash is 14 years old and the Marquise Claire de Champery is a sex-pot of a certain age. 'She felt the congestion of blood rushing between her primly pressed together thighs, proof positive that she had been right to provoke the boy.' Stash, meanwhile, shows his customary tendency to metamorphose into an indeterminate life-form. 'He took her hand and put it on his penis. The hot sticky organ was already beginning to rise and fill. It moved under her touch like an animal.' A field mouse? A boa constrictor?

Receiving the benefit of Stash's extensive sexual education, Francesca conceives twins. One of the twins turns out to be Daisy and the other her retarded sister, Danielle. But first Stash has to get to the clinic. 'As soon as the doctor telephoned, Stash raced to the clinic at 95 miles an hour.' Miserly as always with the essentials, Mrs Krantz trusts the reader to supply the information that Stash is attaining this speed by some form of motorized transport.

Stash rejects Danielle, Francesca flees with Danielle and Daisy. Stash consoles himself with his collection of jet aircraft. Mrs Krantz has done a lot of research in this area but it is transparently research, which is not the same thing as knowledge. Calling a Junkers 88 a Junker 88 might be a misprint, but her rhapsody about Stash's prize purchase of 1953 is a dead giveaway. ' He tracked down and bought the most recent model available of the Lockheed XP-80, known as the Shooting Star, a jet which for many years could out-manoeuvre and outperform almost every other aircraft in the world.' USAF fighter aircraft carried 'X' numbers only before being accepted for service. By 1953 the Shooting Star was known as the F-80, had been in service for years, and was practically the slowest thing of its type in the sky. But Mrs Krantz is too fascinated by that 'X' to let it go. She deserves marks, however, for her determination to catch up on the arcane nomenclature of boys' toys.

Stash finally buys a farm during a flying display in 1967. An old Spitfire packs up on him. 'The undercarriage of the 27-year-old plane stuck and the landing gear could not be released.' Undercarriage and landing gear are the same thing—her vocabularies have collided over the Atlantic. Also an airworthy 27-year-old Spitfire in 1967 would have been a very rare bird indeed: no wonder the undercarriage got in the road of the landing gear. But Mrs Krantz goes some way towards capturing the excitement of machines and should not be mocked for her efforts. Francesca, incidentally, dies in a car crash, with the make of car unspecifed.

One trusts that Mrs Krantz's documentation of less particularly masculine activities is as meticulous as it is undoubtedly exhaustive, although even in such straight-forward matters as food and drink she can sometimes be caught making the elementary mistake of piling on the fatal few details too many. Before Stash gets killed he takes Daisy to lunch every Sunday at the Connaught. After he gets killed he is forced to give up this practice, although there is no real reason why he should not have continued, since he is no more animated before his prang than after. Mrs Krantz has researched the Connaught so heavily that she must have made herself part of the furniture. It is duly noted that the menu has a brown and gold border. It is unduly noted that the menu has the date printed at the bottom. Admittedly such a thing would not happen at the nearest branch of the Golden Egg, but it is not necessarily the mark of a great restaurant. Mrs Krantz would probably hate to hear it said, but she gives the impression of having been included late amongst the exclusiveness she so admires. There is nothing wrong with gusto, but when easy familiarity is what you are trying to convey, gush is to be avoided.

Full of grand meals served and consumed at chapter length, *Princess Daisy* reads like *Buddenbrooks* without the talent. Food is important to Mrs Krantz: so important that her characters keep turning into it, when they are not turning into animals. Daisy has a half-brother called Ram, who rapes her, arouses her sexually, beats her up, rapes her again, and does his best to wreck her life because she rejects his love. His passion is understandable, when you consider Daisy's high nutritional value. 'He gave up the struggle and devoured her lips with his own, kissing her as if he were dying of thirst and her mouth were a moist fruit.' A mango? Daisy fears Ram but goes for what he dishes out. 'Deep within her something sounded, as if the string of a great cello had been plucked, a note of remote, mysterious but unmistakable warning.' Boing.

Daisy heeds the warning and lights out for the USA, where she becomes a producer of television commercials in order to pay Danielle's hospital bills. She pals up with a patrician girl called Kiki, whose breasts quiver in indignation—the first breasts to have done that for a long, long time. At such moments one is reminded of Mrs Krantz's true literary ancestry, which stretches all the way back to Elinor Glyn, E. M. Hull and Gertrude Atherton. She is wasting a lot of her time and too much of ours trying to be John O'Hara. At the slightest surge of congested blood between her primly pressed together thighs, all Mrs Krantz's carefully garnered social detail gives way to eyes like twin dark stars, mouths like moist fruit and breasts quivering with indignation.

There is also the warm curve of Daisy's neck where the jaw joins the throat. Inheriting this topographical feature from her mother, Daisy carries it around throughout the novel waiting for the right man to kiss it *tutto tremante*. Ram will definitely not do. A disconsolate rapist, he searches hopelessly among the eligible young English ladies—Jane Bonham-Carter and Sabrina Guiness are both considered —before choosing the almost inconceivably well-connected Sarah Fane. Having violated Sarah in his by now standard manner, Ram is left with nothing to do except blow Daisy's secret and commit suicide. As Ram bites the dust, the world learns that the famous Princess Daisy, star of a multi-million-dollar perfume promotion, has a retarded sister. Will this put the kibosh on the promotion, not to mention Daisy's love for the man in charge, the wheeler-dealer head of Supracorp, Pat Shannon ('larky bandit', 'freebooter' etc)?

Daisy's libido, dimmed at first by Ram's rape, has already been reawakened by the director of her commercials, a ruthless but prodigiously creative character referred to as North. Yet North finally lacks what it takes to reach the warm curve of Daisy's neck. Success in that area is reserved for Shannon. He it is, who undoes all the damage and fully arouses her hot blood. 'It seemed a long time before Shannon began to imprint a blizzard of tiny kisses at the point where Daisy's jaw joined her throat, that particularly warm curve, spendthrift with beauty, that he had not allowed himself to realize had haunted him for weeks. Daisy felt fragile and warm to Shannon, as if he'd trapped a young unicorn [horses again—C.J.], some strange mythological creature. Her hair was the most intense source of light in the room, since it reflected the moonlight creeping through the windows, and by its light he saw her eyes, open, rapt and glowing; twin dark stars.'

Shannon might think he's got hold of some kind of horse, but as far as Daisy's concerned she's a species of cetacean. 'It was she who guided his hands down the length of her body, she who touched him wherever she could reach, as playfully as a dolphin, until he realized that her fragility was strength, and that she wanted him without reserve.'

Daisy is so moved by this belated but shatteringly complete experience that she can be forgiven for what she does next. 'Afterward, as they lay together, half asleep, but unwilling to drift apart into unconsciousness, Daisy farted, in a tiny series of absolutely irrepressible little pops that seemed to her to go on for a minute.' It takes bad art to teach us how good art gets done. Knowing that the dithyrambs have gone on long enough, Mrs Krantz has tried to undercut them with something earthy. Her tone goes wrong, but her intention is worthy of respect. It is like one of those clumsy attempts at naturalism in a late-medieval painting—less pathetic than portentous, since it adumbrates the great age to come. Mrs Krantz will never be much of an artist but she has more than a touch of the artist's ambition.

Princess Daisy is not to be despised. Nor should it be deplored for its concern with aristocracy, glamour, status, success and things like that. On the evidence of her prose, Mrs Krantz has not enough humour to write tongue-in-cheek, but other people are perfectly capable of reading that way. People don't get their morality from their reading matter: they bring their morality to it. The assumption that ordinary people's lives could be controlled and limited by what entertained them was always too condescending to be anything but fatuous.

Mrs Krantz, having dined at Mark's Club, insists that it is exclusive. There would not have been much point to her dining there if she did not think that. A bigger snob than she might point out that the best reason for not dining at Mark's Club is the chance of finding Mrs Krantz there. It takes only common sense, though, to tell you that on those terms exclusiveness is not just chimerical but plain tedious. You would keep better company eating Kentucky Fried Chicken in a launderette. But if some of this book's readers find themselves day-dreaming of the high life, let us be grateful that Mrs Krantz exists to help give their vague aspirations a local habitation and a name. They would dream anyway, and without Mrs Krantz they would dream unaided.

To pour abuse on a book like this makes no more sense than to kick a powder-puff. *Princess Daisy* is not even reprehensible for the three million dollars its author was paid for it in advance. It would probably have made most of the money back without a dime spent on publicity. The only bad thing is the effect on Mrs Krantz's personality.

Until lately she was a nice Jewish lady harbouring the usual
bourgeois fancies about the aristocracy. But now she gives
interviews extolling her own hard head. 'Like so many of
us,' she told the *Daily Mail* on 28 April, 'I happen to believe
that being young, beautiful and rich is more desirable than
being old, ugly and destitute.' Mrs Krantz is 50 years old,
but to judge from the photograph on the back of the book
she is engaged in a series of hard-fought delaying actions
against time. This, I believe, is one dream that intelligent
people ought not to connive at, since the inevitable result
of any attempt to prolong youth is a graceless old age.

Leonard as a Lover

CYRA McFADDEN

KATE'S ATTEMPT TO take her psychiatrist friend Leonard as a lover couldn't have turned out worse if Sam Peckinpah had written her life script. But it looked great in the planning stage, while she was still conceptualizing it, and she trucked off to Tiburon that awful day in a warm glow of anticipation. She was feeling just terrific. For one thing, she was wearing her new proletarian, chic overalls, which were dynamite. For another, she had decided to play the whole scene off the wall, to just go with the flow. Everybody knew, in these days of heightened consciousness, that the rational mind was a screw-up; the really authentic thing to do was to act on your impulses.

How could she have dreamed that two hours later she'd be gorging compulsively on refined sugar at the Swedish bakery, weeping into her coffee, and wondering how to get even with Leonard for doing that absolutely unbelievable number on her?

Omens and portents were everywhere, if she'd just stopped to notice them. For one thing, Tiburon was crawling with tourist types, in drip-dry coordinates, and their no-class wives, who all looked like runners-up for Miss Disneyland of 1955. For another, when she finally found a parking place in front of Tiburon Vintners, another VW bus tried to back into it while she was backing and filling.

Kate won, but not before the other driver, whose bumper sticker read 'One World, One Spirit, One Humanity,' had given her the finger. Then she got the pant leg of her overalls caught in the bus door, a blow because they were just back from Meader's. Kate hadn't dared wash them because she was afraid the Esso patch would run.

And finally, when she got to Leonard's office in the back of a remodeled ark he shared with a head shop, Sunshine, Leonard's receptionist, was still at her desk. Kate had hoped she'd be off on her yogurt break.

At last Sunshine padded out in her beaded moccasins, made for her 'by this native American craftsman who's one thirty-second Cherokee,' and Kate stopped pretending to read *Psychology Today* and restlessly paced Leonard's office, which was wittily decorated with positively Jungian primitive African masks and a collection of shrunken heads.

Leonard emerged from his inner sanctum a few minutes later escorting a boy of about seven. The boy was carrying something Kate recognized, incredulously, as one of those plastic dog messes from the sidewalk stands in Chinatown. As she stared, he thrust it at Leonard.

'Nummy num num!' Leonard said enthusiastically, pretending to take a bite. Then he steered the kid out the door a bit more firmly than seemed absolutely necessary. 'And remember,' he told him, waving, 'stay loose.'

Kate couldn't help blowing her cool and asking what *that* was all about, and when Leonard told her that Kevin had 'this mind and body dichotomy thing,' and that Leonard was trying to get him in touch with himself, starting with feces, her throat closed.

So they got off to a bad start, and things went steadily

downhill from there. Kate suggested lunch, but they couldn't agree where to go; she liked El Burro, but Leonard was 'enchilada'd out' and had also 'O.D.'d on tostadas compuestas' the night before. He manipulated her into agreeing on Sam's Deck, which Kate didn't like because the last time she'd gone there, a gull had dumped on her shrimp Louie.

Worst of all, when they were sitting on the sunny deck at last, he couldn't stop talking about his own trip, rapping at her in this very hyper way about how he was into corporal punishment, the latest breakthrough in child psychology. He said he'd had amazing results just acting out his anger with his patients. He was also big on video feedback ('fantastic'), role-playing ('fantastic') and Japanese hot tubs, which made meaningful human interaction 'practically inevitable'.

Her anxieties mounting as Leonard ordered another Wallbanger (did she have enough cash in her Swedish carpenter's tool kit to cover the tab?), Kate wondered how a man who had spent three weekends at Esalen and knew Werner Erhard personally could be so insensitive. She kept trying to tell Leonard about Harvey's hangups and how repressed she was because of them, but Leonard wouldn't really pay attention. Although he kept saying, 'I hear you, I hear you,' he wasn't listening, and once, when she confessed a particularly intimate dissatisfaction with Harvey, he murmured absently, '*That's* cool . . .'

Her self-image disintegrating rapidly, Kate decided to lay her body on the line. 'Leonard,' she said, raising her voice, 'I'm sorry to dump on you like this, but I'm on a really heavy trip right now, you know? Like, I can't get my act together.' She paused significantly. 'Leonard, I *need* you. I want you to help me get clear.'

Leonard leaned across the table and gave Kate his full attention for the first time. At least she thought he did; he was wearing acid glasses, so it was hard to tell.

'Listen,' he said sincerely, 'I know exactly where you're coming from.' He covered her hand warmly with his, crushing the piece of hamburger bun she'd been nervously shredding.

'Why don't you come to my place on Bolinas for the weekend?' His turquoise ring bit into her knuckles as he began to chant seductively. 'Wholistic nutrition... hypnosis . . . bio-feedback . . . massage . . .' Kate was beginning to hyperventilate when he added in another voice entirely, 'Friday night through Sunday noon. One hundred and fifty bucks if you crash in the dorm. Extra charge for the hot tub. I take Master Charge, American Express, all your major credit cards.'

Kate had seldom felt such overwhelming affection for her husband, good old Harvey, as she did when she was back in her Mill Valley tract house that afternoon, cooking her nuclear family a gourmet dinner to expiate her guilt and wondering how she could manage to plant a dead horse in Leonard's waterbed. But while she was furiously mashing chicken livers, which reminded her unpleasantly of Kevin's plastic turd, Harvey called to say he wouldn't be home for dinner and not to wait up.

She knew better, of course, but she felt an alarming little pang of suspicion. The fourth time this week, and was Harvey really *that* far behind on his flow charts?

Jeeves in the Springtime

P. G. WODEHOUSE

'JEEVES,' I SAID, coming away from the window.

'Sir?' said Jeeves. He had been clearing the breakfast things, but at the sound of the young master's voice he cheesed it courteously.

'It's a topping morning, Jeeves.'

'Decidedly, sir.'

'Spring and all that.'

'Yes sir.'

'In the spring, Jeeves, a livelier iris gleams upon the burnished dove.'

'So I have been informed, sir.'

'Right-o! Then bring me my whangee, my yellowest shoes, and the old green Homburg. I'm going into the park to do pastoral dances.'

'Very good, sir.'

I don't know if you know that sort of feeling you get on these days round about the end of April and the beginning of

May, when the sky's a light blue with cotton-wool clouds and there's a bit of a breeze blowing form the west? Kind of uplifted feeling. Romantic, if you know what I mean. I'm not much of a ladies' man, but on this particular morning it seemed to me that what I really wanted was some charming girl to buzz up and ask me to save her from assassins or something. So that it was a bit of an anti-climax when I merely ran into young Bingo Little, looking perfectly foul in a crimson satin tie decorated with horseshoes.

'Hallo, Bertie.' said Bingo.

'My God, man!' I gargled. 'The cravat! The gent's neckwear! Why? For what reason?'

'Oh, the tie?' He blushed. 'I—er—I was given it.'

He seemed embarrassed, so I dropped the subject. Always the gentleman. We toddled along a bit, and sat down on a couple of chairs by the Serpentine. Conversation languished. Bingo was staring straight ahead of him in a glassy sort of manner.

'I say, Bertie,' he said, after a pause of about an hour and a quarter.

'Hallo!'

'Do you like the name Mabel?'

'No.'

'No?'

'No.'

'You don't think there's a kind of music in the word, like the wind rustling gently through the treetops?'

'No.'

He seemed disappointed for a moment; then cheered up.

'Of course, you wouldn't. You always were a fat-headed worm without any soul, weren't you?'

'Just as you say. Who is she? Tell me all.'

For I realized now that poor old Bingo was going through it once again. Ever since I have known him—and we were at school together—he has been perpetually falling in love with someone, generally in the spring, which seems to act on him like magic. At school he had the finest collection of

actresses' photographs of anyone of his time; and at
Oxford his romantic nature was a byword.

'You'd better come along and meet her at lunch,' he said,
looking at his watch.

'A ripe suggestion,' I said. 'Where are you meeting her?
At the Ritz?'

'Near the Ritz.'

He was geographically accurate. About fifty yards east of
the Ritz there is one of those blighted tea-and-bun shops
you see dotted about all over London, and into this, if you'll
believe me, young Bingo dived like a homing rabbit; and
before I had time to say a word we were wedged in at a
table, on the brink of a silent pool of coffee left there by an
early luncher.

I'm bound to say I couldn't quite follow the development
of the scenario. Bingo, while not absolutely rolling in the
stuff, has always had a fairish amount of the ready. Apart
from what he got from his uncle old Mortimer Little;
you've probably heard of Little's Liniment (It Limbers Up
The Legs): he ran that till he turned it into a company and
retired with a pile—I say, apart from what he got from the
above, who gave him a pretty decent allowance, Bingo
being his only relative and presumably his heir, I knew that
Bingo had finished up the jumping season well on the right
side of the ledger, having collected a parcel over the
Lincolnshire. Why, then, was he lunching the girl at this
Godforsaken eatery? It couldn't be because he was hard up.

Just then the waitress arrived. Rather a pretty girl.

'Aren't we going to wait——?' I started to say to Bingo,
thinking it somewhat thick that, in addition to asking a girl
to lunch with him in a place like this, he should fling himself
on the foodstuffs before she turned up, when I caught
sight of his face, and stopped.

The man was goggling. His entire map was suffused
with a rich blush. He looked like the Soul's Awakening
done in pink.

'Hallo, Mabel!' he said, with a sort of gulp.

'Hallo!' said the girl.

'Mabel,' said Bingo, 'this is Bertie Wooster, a pal of mine.'

'Pleased to meet you,' she said. 'Nice morning.'

'Fine,' I said.

'You see I'm wearing the tie,' said Bingo.

'It suits you beautiful,' said the girl.

Personally, if anyone had told me that a tie like that suited me, I should have risen and struck them on the mazzard, regardless of their age and sex; but poor old Bingo simply got all flustered with gratification, and smirked in the most gruesome manner.

'Well, what's it going to be today?' asked the girl, introducing the business touch into the conversation.

Bingo studied the menu devoutly.

'I'll have a cup of cocoa, cold veal and ham pie, slice of fruit cake, and a macaroon. Same for you, Bertie?'

I gazed at the man, revolted. That he could have been a pal of mine all these years and think me capable of insulting the old tum with this sort of stuff cut me to the quick.

'Or how about a bit of hot steak-pudding, with a sparkling limado to wash it down?' said Bingo.

You know the way love can change a fellow is really frightful to contemplate. This bird before me. who spoke in this absolutely careless way of macaroons and limado, was the man I had seen in happier days telling the head-waiter at Claridge's exactly how he wanted the *chef* to prepare the *sole frit au gourmet aux champignons*, and saying he would jolly well sling it back if it wasn't just right. Ghastly! Ghastly!

A roll and butter and a small coffee seemed the only things on the list that hadn't been specially prepared by the nastier-minded members of the Borgia family for people they had a particular grudge against, so I chose them, and Mabel hopped it.

'Well?' said Bingo, rapturously.

I took it that he wanted my opinion of the female poisoner who had just left us.

'Very nice,' I said.

He seemed dissatisfied.

'You don't think she's the most wonderful girl you ever saw?' he said, wistfully.

'Oh, absolutely!' I said, to appease the blighter. 'Where did you meet her?'

'At a Subscription dance at Camberwell.'

'What on earth were you doing at a Subscription dance at Camberwell?'

'Your man Jeeves asked me if I would buy a couple of tickets. It was in aid of some charity or other.'

'Jeeves? I didn't know he went in for that sort of thing.'

'Well, I suppose he has to relax a bit every now and then. Anyway, he was there, swinging a dashed efficient shoe. I hadn't meant to go at first, but I turned up for a lark. Oh, Bertie, think what I might have missed!'

'What might you have missed?' I asked, the old lemon being slightly clouded.

'Mabel, you chump. If I hadn't gone I shouldn't have met Mabel.'

'Oh, ah!'

At this point Bingo fell into a species of trance, and only came out of it to wrap himself round the pie and macaroon.

'Bertie,' he said, 'I want your advice.'

'Carry on.'

'At least, not your advice, because that wouldn't be much good to anybody. I mean, you're a pretty consummate old ass, aren't you? Not that I want to hurt your feelings, of course.'

'No, no, I see that.'

'What I wish you would do is to put the whole thing to that fellow Jeeves of yours, and see what he suggests. You've often told me that he has helped other pals of yours out of messes. From what you tell me, he's by way of being the brains of the family.'

'He's never let me down yet.'

'Then put my case to him.'

'What case?'

'My problem.'

'What problem?'

'Why, you poor fish, my uncle, of course. What do you think my uncle's going to say to all this? If I sprang it on him cold, he'd tie himself in knots on the hearth-rug.'

'One of these emotional johnnies, eh?'

'Somehow or other his mind has got to be prepared to receive the news. But how?'

'Ah!'

'That's a lot of help, that "ah!" You see, I'm pretty well dependent on the old boy. If he cut off my allowance, I should be very much in the soup. So you put the whole binge up to Jeeves and see if he can't scare up a happy ending somehow. Tell him my future is in his hands, and that, if the wedding bells ring out, he can rely on me, even unto half my kingdom. Well, call it ten quid. Jeeves would exert himself with ten quid on the horizon, what?'

'Undoubtedly,' I said.

I wasn't in the least surprised at Bingo wanting to lug Jeeves into his private affairs like this. It was the first thing I would have thought of doing myself if I had been in any hole of any description. Most fellows, no doubt, are all for having their valets confine their activities to creasing trousers and what not without trying to run the home; but it's different with Jeeves. Right from the first day he came to me, I have looked on him as a sort of guide, philosopher, and friend. He is a bird of the ripest intellect, full of bright ideas. If anybody could fix things for poor old Bingo, he could.

I stated the case to him that night after dinner.

'Jeeves.'

'Sir?'

'Are you busy just now?'

'No, sir.'

'I mean, not doing anything in particular?'

'No, sir, It is my practice at this hour to read some improving book: but, if you desire my services, this can easily be postponed, or indeed, abandoned altogether.

'Well, I want your advice. It's about Mr Little.'

'Young Mr Little, sir, or the elder Mr Little, his uncle,

who lives in Pounceby Gardens?'

Jeeves seemed to know everything. Most amazing thing. I'd been pally with Bingo practically all my life, and yet I didn't remember ever having heard that his uncle lived anywhere in particular.

'How did you know he lived in Pounceby Gardens?' I said.

'I am on terms of some intimacy with the elder Mr Little's cook, sir. In fact, there is an understanding.'

I'm bound to say that this gave me a bit of a start. Somehow I'd never thought of Jeeves going in for that sort of thing.

'Do you mean you're engaged?'

'It may be said to amount to that, sir.'

'Well, well!'

'She is a remarkably excellent cook, sir,' said Jeeves, as though he felt called on to give some explanation. "What was it you wished to ask me about Mr Little?'

I sprang the details on him.

'And that's how the matter stands, Jeeves,' I said. 'I think we ought to rally round a trifle and help poor old Bingo put the thing through. Tell me about old Mr Little. What sort of a chap is he?'

'A somewhat curious character, sir. Since retiring from business he has become a great recluse, and now devotes himself almost entirely to the pleasures of the table.'

'Greedy hog, you mean?'

'I would not, perhaps, take the liberty of describing him in precisely those terms, sir. He is what is usually called a gourmet. Very particular about what he eats, and for that reason sets a high value on Miss Watson's services.'

'The cook?'

'Yes, sir.'

'Well, it looks to me as though our best plan would be to shoot young Bingo on to him after dinner one night. Melting mood, I mean to say, and all that.'

'The difficulty is, sir, that at the moment Mr Little is on a diet, owing to an attack of gout.'

'Things begin to look wobbly.'

'No, sir, I fancy that the elder Mr Little's misfortune may be turned to the younger Mr Little's advantage. I was speaking only the other day to Mr Little's valet, and he was telling me that it has become his principal duty to read to Mr Little in the evenings. If I were in your place, sir, I should send young Mr Little to read to his uncle.'

'Nephew's devotion, you mean? Old man touched by kindly action, what?'

'Partly that, sir. But I would rely more on young Mr Little's choice of literature.'

'That's no good. Jolly old Bingo has a kind face, but when it comes to literature he stops at the *Sporting Times.*'

'That difficulty may be overcome. I would be happy to select books for Mr Little to read. Perhaps I might explain my idea further?'

'I can't say I quite grasp it yet.'

'The method which I advocate is what, I believe, the advertisers call Direct Suggestion, sir, consisting as it does of driving an idea home by constant repetition. You may have had experience of the system?'

'You mean they keep on telling you that some soap or other is the best, and after a bit you come under the influence and charge round the corner and buy a cake?'

'Exactly, sir. The same method was the basis of all the most valuable propaganda during the world war. I see no reason why it should not be adopted to bring about the desired result with regard to the subject's views on class distinctions. If young Mr Little were to read day after day to his uncle a series of narratives in which marriage with young persons of an inferior social status was held up as both feasible and admirable, I fancy it would prepare the elder Mr Little's mind for the reception of the information that his nephew wishes to marry a waitress in a tea-shop.'

'*Are* there any books of that sort nowadays? The only ones I ever see mentioned in the papers are about married couples who find life grey, and can't stick each other at any price.'

'Yes, sir, there are a great many, neglected by the reviewers but widely read. You have never encountered *All for Love,* by Rosie M. Banks?'

'No.'

'Nor *A Red, Red Summer Rose,* by the same author?'

'No.'

'I have an aunt, sir, who owns an almost complete set of Rosie M. Banks. I could easily borrow as many volumes as young Mr Little might require. They make very light, attractive reading.'

'Well, it's worth trying.'

'I should certainly recommend the scheme, sir.,'

'All right, then. Toddle round to your aunt's tomorrow and grab a couple of the fruitiest. We can but have a dash at it'

'Precisely, sir.'

Bingo reported three days later that Rosie M. Banks was the goods and beyond a question the stuff to give the troops. Old Little had jibbed somewhat at first at the proposed change of literary diet, he not being much of a lad for fiction and having stuck hitherto exclusively to the heavier monthly reviews; but Bingo had got chapter one of *All for Love* past his guard before he knew what was happening, and after that there was nothing to it. Since then they had finished *A Red, Red Summer Rose, Madcap Myrtle,* and *Only a Factory Girl* and were halfway through *The Courtship of Lord Strathmorlick.*

Bingo told me all this in a husky voice over an egg beaten up in sherry. The only blot on the thing from his point of view was that it wasn't doing a bit of good to the old vocal chords, which were beginning to show signs of cracking under the strain. He had been looking his symptoms up in a medical dictionary, and he thought he had got 'clergyman's throat'. But against this you had to set the fact that he was making an undoubted hit in the right quarter, and also that after the evening's reading he always stayed on to dinner;

and, from what he told me, the dinners turned out by old
Little's cook had to be tasted to be believed. There were
tears in the old blighter's eyes as he got on the subject of
the clear soup. I suppose to a fellow who for weeks had
been tackling macaroons and limado it must have been like
Heaven.

Old Little wasn't able to give any practical assistance at
these banquets, but Bingo said that he came to the table
and had his whack of arrowroot, and sniffed the dishes, and
told stories of *entrées* he had had in the past, and sketched out
scenarios of what he was going to do to the bill of fare in the
future, when the doctor put him in shape; so I suppose he
enjoyed himself, too, in a way. Anyhow, things seemed to
be buzzing along quite satisfactorily, and Bingo said he had
got an idea which, he thought, was going to clinch the thing.
He wouldn't tell me what it was, but he said it was a pippin.

'We make progress, Jeeves,' I said.

'That is very satisfactory, sir.'

'Mr Little tells me that when he came to the big scene in
Only a Factory Girl, his uncle gulped like a stricken bull-pup.'

'Indeed, sir?'

'Where Lord Claude takes the girl in his arms, you know,
and says—'

'I am familiar with the passage, sir, It is distinctly
moving. It was a great favourite of my aunt's.'

'I think we're on the right track.'

'It would seem so, sir.'

'In fact, this looks like being another of your successes.
I've always said, and always shall say, that for sheer brain,
Jeeves, you stand alone. All the other great thinkers of the
age are simply in the crowd, watching you go by.'

'Thank you very much, sir. I endeavour to give
satisfaction.'

About a week after this, Bingo blew in with the news that
his uncle's gout had ceased to trouble him, and that on the
morrow he would be back at the old stand working away

with knife and fork as before.

'And, by the way,' said Bingo, 'he wants you to lunch with him tomorrow.'

'Me? Why me? He doesn't know I exist.'

'Oh, yes, he does. I've told him about you.'

'What have you told him?'

'Oh, various things. Anyhow, he wants to meet you. And take my tip, laddie—you go! I should think tomorrow would be something special.'

I don't know why it was, but even then it struck me that there was something dashed odd— almost sinister, if you know what I mean—about young Bingo's manner. The old egg had the air of one who has something up his sleeve.

'There is more in this than meets the eye,' I said. 'Why should your uncle ask a fellow to lunch whom he's never seen?'

'My dear old fathead, haven't I just said that I've been telling him all about you—that you're my best pal—at school together, and all that sort of thing?'

'But even then—and another thing. Why are you so dashed keen on my going?'

Bingo hesitated for a moment.

'Well, I told you I'd got an idea. This is it. I want you to spring the news on him. I haven't the nerve myself.'

'What! I'm hanged if I do!'

'And you call yourself a pal of mine!'

'Yes, I know; but there are limits.'

'Bertie,' said Bingo, reproachfully, 'I saved your life once.'

'When?'

'Didn't I? It must have been some other fellow, then. Well, anyway, we were boys together and all that. You can't let me down.'

'Oh, all right,' I said. 'But, when you say you haven't nerve enough for any dashed thing in the world. you misjudge yourself. A fellow who—'

'Bung-oh!' said young Bingo. 'One-thirty tomorrow, Don't be late.'

I'm bound to say that the more I contemplated the binge, the less I liked it. It was all very well for Bingo to say that I was slated for a magnificent lunch; but what good is the best possible lunch to a fellow if he is slung out into the street on his ear during the soup course? However, the word of a Wooster is his bond and all that sort of rot, so at one-thirty next day I tottered up the steps of No. 16, Pounceby Gardens, and punched the bell. And half a minute later I was up in the drawing-room, shaking hands with the fattest man I have ever seen in my life.

The motto of the Little family was evidently 'variety'. Young Bingo is long and thin and hasn't had a superfluous ounce on him since we first met; but the uncle restored the average and a bit over. The hand which grasped mine wrapped it round and enfolded it till I began to wonder if I'd ever get it out without excavating machinery.

'Mr Wooster, I am gratified—I am proud—I am honoured.'

It seemed to me that young Bingo must have boosted me to some purpose.

'Oh, ah!' I said.

He stepped back a bit, still hanging on to the good right hand.

'You are very young to have accomplished so much!'
I couldn't follow the train of thought. The family, especially my Aunt Agatha, who has savaged me incessantly from childhood up, have always rather made a point of the fact that mine is a wasted life, and that, since I won a prize at my first school for the best collection of wild flowers made during the summer holidays, I haven't done a dam' thing to land me on the nation's scroll of fame. I was wondering if he couldn't have got me mixed up with someone else, when the telephone-bell rang outside in the hall, and the maid came in to say that I was wanted. I buzzed down, and found it was young Bingo.

'Hallo!' said young Bingo. 'So you've got there? Good man! I knew I could rely on you. I say, did my uncle seem pleased to see you?'

'Absolutely all over me. I can't make it out.'

'Oh, that's all right. I just rang up to explain. The fact is, old man, I know you won't mind, but I told him you were the author of those books I've been reading to him.'

'What!'

'Yes, I said, that "Rosie M. Banks" was your pen-name, and you didn't want it generally known, because you were a modest, retiring sort of chap. He'll listen to you now. Absolutely hang on your words. A brightish idea, what? I doubt if Jeeves in person could have thought up a better one than that. Well, pitch it strong, old lad, and keep steadily before you the fact that I must have my allowance raised. I can't possibly marry on what I've got now. If this film is to end with the slow fade-out on the embrace, at least double is indicated. Well, that's that. Cheerio!'

And he rang off. At that moment the gong sounded, and the genial host came tumbling downstairs like the delivery of a ton of coals.

I always look back to that lunch with a sort of aching regret. It was the lunch of a lifetime, and I wasn't in a fit state to appreciate it. Subconsciously, if you know what I mean, I could see it was pretty special, but I had got the wind up to such a frightful extent over the ghastly situation in which young Bingo had landed me that its deeper meaning never really penetrated. Most of the time I might have been eating sawdust for all the good it did me.

Old Little struck the literary note right from the start.

'My nephew has probably told you that I have been making a close study of your books of late?' he began.

'Yes. He did mention it. How—er—how did you like the bally things?'

He gazed reverently at me.

'Mr Wooster, I am not ashamed to say that the tears came into my eyes as I listened to them. It amazes me that a man as young as you can have been able to plumb human nature so surely to its depths; to play with so unerring a hand on the quivering heartstrings of your reader; to write novels so true, so human, so moving, so vital!'

'Oh, it's just a knack,' I said.

The good old persp. was bedewing my forehead by this time in a pretty lavish manner. I don't know when I've been so rattled.

'Do you find the room a trifle warm?'

'Oh no, no, rather not. Just right.'

'Then it's the pepper. If my cook has a fault—which I am not prepared to admit—it is that she is inclined to stress the pepper a trifle in her made dishes. By the way, do you like her cooking?'

I was so relieved that we had got off the subject of my literary output that I shouted approval in a ringing baritone.

'I am delighted to hear it, Mr Wooster. I may be prejudiced, but to my mind that woman is a genius.'

'Absolutely!' I said.

'She has been with me many years, and in all that time I have not known her guilty of a single lapse from the highest standard. Except once, in the winter of 1917, when a purist might have condemned a certain mayonnaise of hers as lacking in creaminess. But one must make allowances. There had been several air-raids about that time, and no doubt the poor woman was shaken. But nothing is perfect in this world, Mr Wooster, and I have had my cross to bear. All these years I have lived in constant apprehension lest some evilly-disposed person might lure her from my employment. To my certain knowledge she has received offers, lucrative offers, to accept service elsewhere. You may judge of my dismay, Mr Wooster, when only this morning the bolt fell. She gave notice!'

'Good Lord!'

'Your consternation does credit, if I may say so, to the heart of the author of *A Red, Red Summer Rose*. But I am thankful to say the worst has not happened. The matter has been adjusted. Jane is not leaving me.'

'Good egg!'

'Good egg, indeed—though the expression is not familiar to me. I do not remember having come across it in your books. And, speaking of your books, may I say that what has impressed me about them even more than the moving poignancy of the actual narrative is your philosophy of life. If there were more like you, Mr Wooster, London would be a better place.'

This was dead opposite to my Aunt Agatha's philosophy of life, she having always rather given me to understand that it is the presence in it of fellows like me that makes London more or less of a plague-spot; but I let it go.

'Let me tell you, Mr Wooster, that I appreciate your splendid defiance of the outworn fetishes of a purblind social system. I appreciate it! *You* are big enough to see that rank is but the guinea stamp and that, in the magnificent words of Lord Bletchmore in *Only a Factory Girl*, "Be her origin ne'er so humble, a good woman is the equal of the finest lady on earth!" '

I sat up.

'I say! Do you think that?'

'I do, Mr Wooster. I am ashamed to say that there was a time when I was like other men, a slave to the idiotic convention which we call Class Distinction. But, since I read your books—'

I might have known it. Jeeves had done it again.

'You think it's all right for a bloke in what you might call a certain social position to marry a girl of what you might describe as the lower classes?'

'Most assuredly I do, Mr Wooster.'

I took a deep breath, and slipped him the good news.

'Young Bingo—your nephew, you know—wants to marry a waitress,' I said.

'I honour him for it.'

'You don't object?'

'On the contrary.'

I took another deep breath, and shifted to the sordid side of the business.

'I hope you won't think I'm butting in, don't you know,' I said, 'but—er—well, how about it?'

'I fear I do not quite follow you.'

'Well, I mean to say, his allowance and all that. The money you're good enough to give him. He was rather hoping that you might see your way to jerking up the total a bit.'

Old Little shook his head regretfully.

'I fear that can hardly be managed. You see, a man in my position is compelled to save every penny. I will gladly continue my nephew's existing allowance, but beyond that I cannot go. It would not be fair to my wife.'

'What! But you're not married?'

'Not yet. But I propose to enter upon that holy state almost immediately. The lady who for years has cooked so well for me honoured me by accepting my hand this very morning.' A cold gleam of triumph came into his eye. 'Now let 'em try to get her away from me!' he muttered, defiantly.

'Young Mr Little has been trying frequently during the afternoon to reach you on the telephone, sir,' said Jeeves that night, when I got home.

'I'll bet he has,' I said. I had sent poor old Bingo an outline of the situation by messenger-boy shortly after lunch.

'He seemed a trifle agitated.'

'I don't wonder. Jeeves,' I said, 'brace up and bite the bullet. I'm afraid I've bad news for you.'

'Sir?'

'That scheme of yours—reading those books to old Mr Little and all that—has blown out a fuse.'

'They did not soften him?'

'They did. That's the whole bally trouble. Jeeves, I'm sorry to say that *fiancée* of yours— Miss Watson, you know—the cook, you know—well, the long and the short of it is that she's chosen riches instead of honest worth, if you know what I mean.'

'Sir?'

'She's handed you the mitten and gone and got engaged to old Mr Little!'

'Indeed, sir?'

'You don't seem much upset?'

'The fact is, sir, I had anticipated some such outcome.'

I stared at him. 'Then what on earth did you suggest the scheme for?'

'To tell you the truth, sir, I was not wholly averse from a severance of my relations with Miss Watson. In fact, I greatly desired it. I respect Miss Watson exceedingly, but I have seen for a long time that we were not suited. Now the other young person with whom I have an understanding—'

'Great Scott, Jeeves! There isn't another?'

'Yes, sir.'

'How long has this been going on?'

'For some weeks, sir. I was greatly attracted by her when I first met her at a Subscription dance at Camberwell.'

'My sainted aunt! Not—'

Jeeves inclined his head gravely.

'Yes, sir. By an odd coincidence it is the same young person that young Mr Little—I have placed the cigarettes on the small table. Good night, sir.'

Strictly from Hunger

S. J. PERELMAN

I

YES I WAS excited, and small wonder. What boy wouldn't be, boarding a huge, mysterious, puffing steam train for golden California? As Mamma adjusted my reefer and strapped on my leggings, I almost burst with impatience. Grinning redcaps lifted my luggage into the compartment and spat on it. Mamma began to weep into a small pillow-case she had brought along for the purpose.

'Oh, son, I wish you hadn't become a scenario writer!' she sniffled.

'Aw, now, Moms,' I comforted her, 'it's no worse than playing the piano in a call-house.' She essayed a brave little smile, and, reaching into her reticule, produced a flat package which she pressed into my hands. For a moment I was puzzled, then I cried out with glee.

'Jelly sandwiches! Oh, Moms!'

'Eat them all, boy o' mine,' she told me, 'they're good for boys with hollow little legs.' Tenderly she pinned to my lapel the green tag reading 'To Plushnick Productions, Hollywood, California.' The whistle shrilled and in a moment I was chugging out of Grand Central's dreaming spires followed only by the anguished cries of relatives who would now have to go to work. I had chugged only a few feet when I realized that I had left without the train, so I had to run back and wait for it to start.

As we sped along the glorious fever spots of the Hudson I decided to make a tour of inspection. To my surprise I found that I was in the only passenger car of the train; the other cars were simply dummies snipped out of cardboard and painted to simulate coaches. Even 'passengers' had been cunningly drawn in coloured crayons in the 'window', as well as ragged tramps clinging to the blinds below and drinking Jamaica ginger. With a rueful smile I returned to my seat and gorged myself on jelly sandwiches.

At Buffalo the two other passenges and I discovered to our horror that the conductor had been left behind. We finally decided to divide up his duties; I punched the tickets, the old lady opposite me wore a conductor's hat and locked the washroom as we came into stations, and the young man who looked as if his feet were not mates consulted a Hamilton watch frequently. But we missed the conductor's earthy conversation and it was not until we had exchanged several questionable stories that we began to forget our loss.

A flicker of interest served to shorten the trip. At Fort Snodgrass, Ohio, two young and extremely polite road-agents boarded the train and rifled us of our belongings. They explained that they were modern Robin Hoods and were stealing from the poor to give to the rich. They had intended to rape all the women and depart for Sherwood Forest, but when I told them that Sherwood Forest as well as the women were in England, their chagrin was comical in the extreme. They declined my invitation to stay and take a chance on the train's pool, declaring that the engineer had fixed the run and would fleece us, and got off at South Bend with every good wish.

The weather is always capricious in the Middle West, and although it was midsummer, the worst blizzard in Chicago's history greeted us on our arrival. The streets were crowded with thousands of newsreel cameramen trying to photograph one another bucking the storm on the Lake Front. It was a novel idea for the newsreels and I wished them well. With only two hours in Chicago I would be unable to see the city, and the thought drew me into a state of composure. I noted with pleasure that a fresh coat of grime had been given to the Dearborn Street station, though I was hardly vain enough to believe that it had anything to do with my visit. There was the usual ten-minute wait while the porters withdrew with my portable typewriter to a side room and flailed it with hammers, and at last I was aboard the 'Sachem', crack train of the B.B.D. & O. lines.

It was as if I had suddenly been transported into another world. 'General Crook', in whom I was to make my home for the next three days, and his two neighbours, 'Lake Tahoe' and 'Chief Malomai', were everything that the word 'Pullman' implies; they were Pullmans. Uncle Eben, in charge of 'General Crook', informed me that the experiment of air-cooling the cars had been so successful that the road intended trying to heat them next winter.

'Ah suttinly looks fo'd to dem roastin' ears Ah's gwine have next winter he, he, he!' he chuckled, rubbing soot into my hat.

The conductor told me he had been riding on trains for so long that he had begun to smell like one, and sure enough, two brakemen waved their lanterns at him that night and tried to tempt him down a siding in Kansas City. We became good friends and it came as something of a blow when I heard next morning that he had fallen off the train during the night. The fireman said that we had circled about for an hour trying to find him but that it had been impossible to lower a boat because we did not carry a boat.

The run was marked by only one incident out of the ordinary. I had ordered breaded veal cutlet the first evening, and my waiter, poking his head into the kitchen, had repeated the order. The cook, unfortunately, understood him to say '*dreaded* veal cutlet', and resenting the slur, sprang at the waiter with drawn razor. In a few seconds I was the only living remnant of the shambles, and at Topeka I was compelled to wait until a new shambles was hooked on and I proceeded with dinner.

It seemed only a scant week or ten days before we were pulling into Los Angeles. I had grown so attached to my porter that I made him give me lock of his hair. I wonder if he still has the ten-cent piece I gave him? There was a gleam in his eye which could only have been insanity as he leaned over me. Ah, Uncle Eben, faithful old retainer, where are you now? Gone to what obscure ossuary? If this should chance to meet your kindly gaze, drop me a line care of *Variety*, won't you? They know what to do with it.

II

The violet hush of twilight was descending over Los Angeles as my hostess, Violet Hush, and I left the suburbs headed toward Hollywood. In the distance a glow of huge piles of burning motion-picture scripts lit up the sky. The crisp tang of frying writers and directors whetted my appetite. How good it was to be alive, I thought, inhaling deep lungfuls of carbon monoxide. Suddenly our powerful Gatti-Gazazza slid to a stop in the traffic.

'What is it, Jenkin?' Violet called anxiously through the speaking-tube to the chauffeur (played by Lyle Talbot).

A *suttee* was in progress by the roadside, he said—did we wish to see it? Quickly Violet and I elbowed our way through the crowd. An enormous funeral pyre composed of thousands of feet of film and scripts, drenched with Chanel Number Five, awaited the torch of Jack Holt, who was to act as master of ceremonies. In a few terse words Violet explained this unusual custom borrowed from the Hindus and never paid for. The worst disgrace that can befall a producer is an unkind notice from a New York reviewer. When this happens, the producer becomes a pariah in Hollywood. He is shunned by his friends, thrown into bankruptcy, and like a Japanese electing hara-kiri, he commits *suttee*. A great bonfire is made of the film, and the luckless producer, followed by directors, actors, technicians, and the producer's wives, immolate themselves. Only the scenario writers are exempt. These are tied between the tails of two spirited Caucasian ponies, which are then driven off in opposite directions. The custom is called 'a conference'.

Violet and I watched the scene breathlessly. Near us Harry Cohn, head of Columbia Studios, was being rubbed with huck towels preparatory to throwing himself into the flames. He was nonchalantly smoking a Rocky Ford five-center, and the man's courage drew a tear to the eye of even the most callous. Weeping relatives besought him to eschew his design, but he stood adamant. Adamant Eve, his plucky secretary, was being rubbed with crash towels preparatory to flinging herself into Cohn's embers. Assistant directors busily prepared spears, war-bonnets and bags of pemmican which the Great Chief would need on his trip to the 'Happy Hunting Grounds'. Wampas and beads to placate the Great Spirit (played by Will Hays) were piled high about the stoical tribesman.

Suddenly Jack Holt (played be Edmund Lowe) raised his hand for silence. The moment had come. With bowed head Holt made a simple invocation couched in one-syllable words so that even the executives might understand. Throwing his five-center to a group of autograph-hunters, the great man poised himself for the fatal leap. But from off-scene came the strident clatter of coconut shells, and James Agee, Filmdom's fearless critic, wearing the uniform of a Confederate guerrilla and the whiskers of General Beauregard, galloped in on a foam-flecked pinto. It was he whose mocking review had sent Cohn into Coventry. It was a dramatic moment as the two stood pitted against each other—Cohn against Agee, the Blue against the Grey.

But with true Southern gallantry Agee was the first to extend the hand of friendship.

'Ah reckon it was an unworthy slur, suh,' he said in manly tones. 'Ah-all thought you-all's pictuah was lousy but it opened at the Rialto to sensational grosses, an' Ah-all 'pologizes. Heah, have a yam.' And he drew a yam from his tunic. Not to be outdone in hospitality, Cohn drew a yam from his tunic, and soon they were exchanging yams and laughing over the old days.

When Violet and I finally stole away to our waiting motor, we felt that we were somehow nearer to each other. I snuggled luxuriously into the buffalo lap-robe Violet had provided against the treacherous night air and gazed out at the gleaming neon lights. Soon we would be in Beverly Hills, and already the quaint native women were swarming alongside in their punts urging us to buy their cunning beadwork and mangoes. Occasionally I threw a handful of coppers to the Negro boys, who dived for them joyfully. The innocent squeals of the policemen as the small blackamoors pinched them were irresistible. Unable to resist them, Violet and I were soon pinching each other till our skins glowed. Violet was good to the touch, with a firm fleshy texture like a winesap or pippin. It seemed but a moment before we were sliding under the porte-cochère of her home, a magnificent rambling structure of beaver-board patterned after an Italian ropewalk of the sixteenth century. It had recently been remodelled by a family of wrens who had introduced chewing-gum into the left wing, and only three or four obscure Saxon words could do it justice.

I was barely warming my hands in front of the fire and watching Jimmy Fidler turn on a spit when my presence on the Pacific Slope made itself felt. The news of my arrival had thrown international financial centres into an uproar, and sheaves of wires, cables, phone messages and even corn began piling up. An ugly rumour that I might reorganize the motion-picture industry was being bruited about in the world's commodity markets. My brokers,

Whitelipped & Trembling, were beside themselves. The New York Stock Exchange was begging them for assurances of stability, and Threadneedle Street awaited my next move with drumming pulses. Film shares ricocheted sharply, although wools and meats were sluggish, if not downright sullen. To the reporters who flocked around me I laughingly disclaimed that this was a business trip. I was simply a scenario writer to whom the idea of work was abhorrent. A few words murmured into the transatlantic telephone, the lift of an eyebrow here, the shrug of a shoulder there, and equilibrium was soon restored. I washed sparsely, curled my moustache with a heated hairpin, flicked a drop of Sheik Lure on my lapel, and rejoined my hostess.

After a copious dinner, melting-eyed beauties in lacy black underthings fought with each other to serve my kümmel. A hurried apology, and I was curled up in bed with the Autumn, 1927, issue of *The Yale Review*. Halfway through an exciting symposium on St Thomas Aquinas' indebtedness to Professors Whitehead and Spengler, I suddenly detected a stowaway blonde under the bed. Turning a deaf ear to her heartrending entreaties and burning glances, I sent her packing. Then I treated my face to a feast of skin food, buried my head in the pillow and went bye-bye.

III

Hollywood Boulevard! I rolled the rich syllables over on my tongue and thirstily drank in the beauty of the scene before me. On all sides nattily attired boulevarders clad in rich stuffs strolled nonchalantly, inhaling cubebs and exchanging epigrams stolen from Martial and Wilde. Thousands of scantily draped but none the less appetizing extra girls milled past me, their mouths a scarlet wound and their eyes clearly defined in their faces. Their voluptuous curves set my blood on fire, and as I made my way down Mammary Lane, a strange thought began to invade my brain: I realized that I had not eaten breakfast yet. In a Chinese eatery cunningly built in the shape of an old shoe I managed to assuage the inner man with a chopped glove salad topped off with frosted cocoa. Charming platinum-haired hostesses in red pyjamas and peaked caps added a note of colour to the surroundings, whilst a gypsy orchestra played selections from Victor Herbert's operettas on musical saws. It was a bit of old Vienna come to life, and the sun was a red ball in the heavens before I realized with a start that I had promised to report at the Plushnick Studios.

Commandeering a taxicab, I arrived at the studio just in time to witness the impressive ceremony of changing the guard. In the central parade ground, on a snowy white charger, sat Max Plushnick, resplendent in a producer's uniform, his chest glittering with first mortgage liens, amortizations, and estoppels. His personal guard, composed of picked vice-presidents of the Chase National Bank, was drawn up stiffly about him in a hollow square.

But the occasion was not a happy one. A writer had been caught trying to create an adult picture. The drums rolled dismally, and the writer, his head sunk on his chest, was led out amid a ghastly silence. With the aid of a small step-ladder Plushnick slid lightly from his steed. Sternly he ripped the epaulettes and buttons from the traitor's tunic, broke his sword across his knee, and in a few harsh words demoted him to the mail department.

'And now,' began Plushnick, 'I further condemn you to eat . . .'

'No, no!' screamed the poor wretch, falling to his knees and embracing Plushnick's jack boots, 'not that, not that!'

'Stand up, man,' ordered Plushnick, his lip curling, 'I condemn you to eat in the studio restaurant for ten days and may God have mercy on your soul.' The awful words rang out on the still evening air and even Plushnick's hardened old mercenaries shuddered. The heartrending cries of the unfortunate were drowned in the boom of the sunset gun.

*

In the wardrobe department I was photographed, fingerprinted, and measured for the smock and Windsor tie which was to be my uniform. A nameless fear clutched at my heart as two impressive turnkeys herded me down a corridor to my supervisor's office. For what seemed hours we waited in an ante-room. Then my serial number was called, the leg-irons were struck off, and I was shoved through a door into the presence of Diana ffrench-Mamoulian.

How to describe what followed? Diana ffrench-Mamoulian was accustomed to having her way with writers, and my long lashes and peachblow mouth seemed to whip her to insensate desire. In vain, time and again, I tried to bring her attention back to the story we were discussing, only to find her gem-encrusted fingers straying through my hair. When our interview was over, her cynical attempt to 'date me up' made every fibre of my being cry out in revolt.

'P-please,' I stammered, my face burning, 'I—I wish you wouldn't . . . I'm engaged to a Tri Kappa at Goucher—'

'Just one kiss,' she pleaded, her breath hot against my neck. In desperation I granted her boon, knowing full well that my weak defences were crumbling before the onslaught of this love tigree. Finally she allowed me to leave, but only after I had promised to dine at her penthouse apartment and have an intimate chat about the script. The basket of slave bracelets and marzipan I found awaiting me on my return home made me realize to what lengths Diana would go.

I was radiant that night in blue velvet tails and a boutonniere of diamonds from Cartier's, my eyes starry and the merest hint of cologne at my ear-lobes. An inscrutable Oriental served the Lucullan repast and my vis-à-vis was as effervescent as the wine.

'Have a bit of wine, darling?' queried Diana solicitously, indicating the roast Long Island aeroplane with apple-sauce, I tried to turn our conversation from the personal note, but Diana would have none of it. Soon we were exchanging gay bantam over the mellow Vouvray, laughing as we dipped fastidious fingers into the Crisco parfait for which Diana was famous. Our meal finished, we sauntered into the rumpus room and Diana turned on the radio. With a savage snarl the radio turned on her and we slid over the waxed floor in the intricate maze of the jackdaw strut. Without quite knowing why, I found myself hesitating before the plate of liqueur candies Diana was pressing on me

'I don't think I should—really, I'm a trifle faint—'

'Oh, come on,' she urged masterfully, 'After all, you're old enough to be your father—I mean I'm old enough to be my mother. . . .' She stuffed a brandy bonbon between my clenched teeth. Before long I was eating them thirstily, reeling about the room and shouting snatches of coarse drunken doggerel. My brain was on fire, I tell you. Through the haze I saw Diana ffrench-Mamoulian, her nostrils dilated, groping for me. My scream of terror only egged her on, overturning chairs and tables in her bestial pursuit. With superhuman talons she tore off my collar and suspenders, I sank to my knees, choked with sobs, hanging on to my last shirt-stud like a drowning man. Her Svengali eyes were slowly hypnotizing me; I fought like a wounded bird—and then, blissful unconsciousness.

When I came to, the Oriental servant and Diana were battling in the centre of the floor. As I watched, Yen Shee Gow drove a well-aimed blow to her mid-section, followed it with a right cross to the jaw. Diana staggered and rolled under a table. Before my astonished eyes John Chinaman stripped the mask from his face and revealed the features of Blanche Almonds, a little seamstress I had long wooed unsuccessfully in New York. Gently she bathed my temples with Florida water and explained how she had followed me, suspecting Diana ffrench-Mamoulian's intentions. I let her rain kisses over my face and lay back in her arms as beaming Ivan tucked us in and cracked his whip over the prancing bays. In a few seconds our sleigh was skimming over the hard crust toward Port Arthur and

freedom, leaving Plushnick's discomfited officers gnashing
one another's teeth. The wintry Siberian moon glowed
over the tundras, drenching my hair with moonbeams for
Blanche to kiss away. And so, across the silvery steppes
amid the howling of wolves, we rode into a new destiny,
purified in the crucible that men call Hollywood.

Flag of Inconvenience

KEITH WATERHOUSE

Cunard is attempting to transfer cruise liners to foreign flags of convenience, enabling it to hire cheaper foreign crews. Guardian

Number One Boy Him Log. Day One.
This plenty big day for me-fella. This most plenty big day since me-fella come belong big-boat-him-have-many-chimney as assistant head steward in the Louis XIV Starlight Grill Room on top deck below more top deck, plenty-big-swank passengers only.

Big-fella-strong-with-scrambled-egg-on-cap, him call me-fella up to him stateroom. Him say:

Ah, there you are, Louis XIV Starlight Grill Room Number Two Boy. How you-fella get on along big boat him ride big waves?

Me-fella say: OK, Boss.

Big-fella-strong him say: Mister First Officer Boss him been keep beady eye on you, Number Two Boy, and him say you good boy. How you like be Number One Boy? Job pay plenty glass beads enough along more than coolie minimum. You better take damn job chop-chop.

Me-fella say: Boss, what happen to Number One Boy, him plenty belong-nice to plenty-big-swank passengers, him cook them kai-kai along them table, him add Worcester sauce, double cream and Remy Martin firewater, then light him match and make him go up like him volcano.

Big-fella-strong him say: Him-fella have no more idea of how to flambé a Steak Diane than him back behind of me-fella sit-upon. Him damn near set Louis XIV Starlight Grill room on fire today some time after big ball come up in sky. Plenty-big-swank passenger Mr McGregor him had to come down along below sick-bay with singed eyebrows, and plenty-big-swank passenger McGregor him woman, Mrs McGregor, she-him have hysterics. Him come too big for him boots, that him trouble.

Me-fella say: Me-fella find plenty-big-swank passenger Boss McGregor him woman more small boot narrow fitting, P.D.Q.

Big-fella-strong him say; not plenty-big-swank passenger Mr McGregor him woman, you bloody fool Number Two Boy, it Number One Boy who come too big for him boots.

Me-fella say: Boss, Number One Boy him no wear boots. Number One Boy him wear evening-dress loincloth and black tie.

Big-fella-strong him say: Not any more him doesn't. Evening-dress loincloth and black tie is Number One Boy uniform and Number One Boy him not bloody Number One Boy much damn more along today after them Louis XIV Starlight Grill Room second sitting run all about them lifeboats chop-chop shouting, 'Fire, fire!' Now do you want Number One Boy job, Number Two Boy, or not?

So me-fella are come be Maitre d'belong Louis XIV Starlight Grill Room.

Number One Boy Him Log. Day Two.
Me-fella look in glass-it-look-back. Me-fella pretty damn tip-top smart in velveteen loincloth with blue silk cummerbund. Me-fella boss boy now. Me-fella call all

together them no-good serve-hot-roll-with-tongs-and-fold-pink-napkin-in-shape-of-swan boys belong Louis XIV Starlight Grill Room, and tell all them we turn over new broom P.D.Q. chop-chop bloody now. That mean no more become legless on silver polish long before big ball in sky him sink in water and last plenty-big-swank passenger him have coffee along enough him after-dinner mints.

Them no-good serving-boys mutter rhubarb-rhubarb but them speak no bad pidgin agin me-fella.

By-m-by, plenty-big-swank passenger Yankee Boss Mister Zmansky, him-fella come sit in Crowsnest Bar belong Louis XIV Starlight Grill Room. Him-fella order him drink from Wine Boy and eat plenty cheese footballs. When by-m-by him drink come on silver salver balanced on Wine Boy him head, him-fella clap him hands and call out to me-fella: sir, would you step over here a moment?

Me-fella say: Yes sir, Mr Yankee Boss Zmansky, sir?

Him-fella point at drink on silver salver balanced on Wine Boy him head and say: Would you call that a very dry martini on the rocks with a twist of lemon?

Me-fella look at drink on silver salver on Wine Boy him head and say: No sir, Mr Yankee Boss Zmansky, sir. Him tube of lighter fuel.

Him-fella say: OK. Now will you tell me what I have to do to get a dry martini around here?

Me-fella say: Sir, Mr Big-fella Belong Papa-him-on-top's Own Country must tell stupid Wine Boy, fetch plenty juniper berry juice with him dash of vermouth clink-clink and him twist of yellow fruit fall from tree pretty damn quick, shaken not stirred. Otherwise stupid Wine Boy fetch glass of pink paraffin with him olive.

Wine Boy hit me-fella on head with him silver salver and say: Me-fella not stupid. Him-fella Mr Big Yankee Boss Zmansky give me-fella plenty big tip so me-fella fetch him-fella Ronsonol from no-good serving boys them personal cellar.

Mr Yankee Boss Zmansky him say: Jesus!

Number One Boy Him Log. Day Two And One More Day
Me-fella bow-and-scrape to plenty-big-swank-passengers
them come for first when-big-ball-in-sky-all-above sitting.
Plenty-big-toff passenger Sir Ffitch-Ffrench, him bang
him table with him spoon and tell me-fella to get across
along-him-fella and him-fella woman with belong-what-
name list of kai-kai.

Him-fella point at belong-what-name list under *Volaille*
and say: Head Waiter, is this Coq au vin à la bourguignonne
fresh or frozen?

Me-fella say: Sir Boss Mister Big-shot Ffitch-Ffrench,
until soon before Number One Boy him get chop, all bird-
from-sky on belong-what-name list from freezer. Him bad
man, Lord Boss Mister Ffitch-Ffrench sir. Him get drunk
on Brasso and come too big for him boots.

Him-fella say: Never mind all that, Head Waiter. My wife
merely wishes to know if the chicken is fresh?

Me-fella say: Sir Mrs Boss Ffitch-Ffrench him woman,
all bird-from-sky on belong-what-name list him now so
fresh that him not dead yet. Cookie come up along from
down galley and cut bird-from-sky's throat at plenty-big-
swank passengers them table, then him-fella pluck him
bird-from-sky feathers while me-fella simmer mushrooms
and baby onions in red jump-on-grape-water and bird-
from-sky blood. Served with fried croutons and a selection
of today's freshly-prepared vegetables from him trolley.

Mrs Sir Ffitch-Ffrench him woman say: How absolutely
revolting. We shall have the Chateaubriand.

Me-fella say: Yes sir, madam, how you like him cook?

Him Woman say: Rare.

Me-fella tell no-good serving boy go down below along
galley and tell Cookie him cook Chateaubriand not plenty
much for bigshot passengers and him women chop-chop
P.D.Q. By-m-by him-fella come back with big silver dish-
belong-keep-hot.

Me-fella take off him lid and show Chateaubriand to Sir
Boss Ffitch-Ffrench and him woman. Him woman say:
Aaaarrrrrgggghhhh! It's a raw pig! Oh my God, I'm going
to faint!

Me-fella say to no-good serving boy; You-fella bad no-good serving boy, you-fella been at him surgical spirit.

No-good serving boy him say: Me-fella sober as him-wear-wig-and-say-them-jury-have-rightly-found-you-fella-guilty. Cookie him run out of Chateaubriand, so him-fella think Sir Mighty Boss Ffitch-Ffrench and him woman them like Cochon de la Saint-Fortunat, done not plenty much chop-chop.

Me-fella say: Him-fella bad Cookie.

By-m-by him-fella Cookie come along up from down below into Louis XIV Starlight Grill Room and try to kill me-fella with him meat-axe.

Number One Boy Him Log. Day Two And Two More Day

All no-good serving boys drunk on plenty dry martinis with him twist of lemon. Me-fella serve all kai-kai to all plenty-big-swank passengers.

Me-fella run off him feet.

When him-fella eat him main course, by-m-by Mr Yankee Boss Zmansky clap him hands and tell me-fella what him-fella want for him pudding.

Something snap.

Me-fella pick up steak-knife from Table 43 and hold him at Yankee Boss Mister Zmansky him throat. Me-fella say: You bad man, Mr Boss sir! You-fella cannibal! You-fella eat d'agneau aux primeurs with all them trimmings and now you-fella want me-fella kill Lascar deckhand and boil him in pot. You cruel Mister Zmansky sir!

Him-fella shout: What's gotten into you? All I asked for was a goddam Baked Alaska! OK fella, him-fella continue, I've had enough of this, I'm going straight to the captain.

Number One Boy Him Log. No More Day

Big-fella-strong-with-scrambled-egg-on-cap, him give me-fella new job swab him deck. Big-fella-strong him plenty kind man, him-fella not make me-fella take him job. Him-fella say me-fella can take him or leave him.

The Love Nest

RING LARDNER

'I'LL TELL YOU what I'm going to do with you, Mr Bartlett,'
said the great man. 'I'm going to take you right out to my
home and have you meet the wife and family; stay to
dinner and all night. We've got plenty of room and extra
pajamas, if you don't mind them silk. I mean that'll give you
a chance to see us just as we are. I mean you can get more
that way than if you sat here a whole week, asking me
questions.'

'But I don't want to put you to a lot of trouble,' said Bartlett.

'Trouble!' The great man laughed. 'There's no trouble
about it. I've got a house that's like a hotel. I mean a big
house with lots of servants. But anyway I'm always glad to
do anything I can for a writing man, especially a man that
works for Ralph Doane. I'm very fond of Ralph. I mean I
like him personally besides being a great editor. I mean I've
known him for years and when there's anything I can do
for him, I'm glad to do it. I mean it'll be a pleasure to have
you. So if you want to notify your family—'

'I haven't any family,' said Bartlett.

'Well, I'm sorry for you! And I bet when you see mine, you'll wish you had one of your own. But I'm glad you can come and we'll start now and so as to get there before the kiddies are put away for the night. I mean I want you to be sure and see the kiddies. I've got three.'

'I've seen their pictures,' said Bartlett. 'You must be very proud of them. They're all girls, aren't they?'

'Yes, sir; three girls. I wouldn't have a boy. I mean I always wanted girls. I mean girls have got a lot more zip to them. I mean they're a lot zippier. But let's go! The Rolls is downstairs and if we start now we'll get there before dark. I mean I want you to see the place while it's still daylight.'

The great man—Lou Gregg, president of Modern Pictures, Inc.—escorted his visitor from the magnificent office by a private door and down a private stairway to the avenue, where the glittering car with its glittering chauffeur waited.

'My wife was in town today,' said Gregg as they glided northward, 'and I hoped we could ride out together, but she called up about two and asked would I mind if she went on home in the Pierce. She was through with her shopping and she hates to be away from the house and the kiddies any longer than she can help. Celia's a great home girl. You'd never know she was the same girl now as the girl I married seven years ago. I mean she's different. I mean she's not the same. I mean her marriage and being a mother has developed her. Did you ever see her? I mean in pictures?'

'I think I did once,' replied Bartlett. 'Didn't she play the young sister in *The Cad*?'

'Yes, with Harold Hodgson and Marie Blythe.'

'I thought I'd seen her. I remember her as very pretty and vivacious.'

'She certainly was! And she is yet! I mean she's even prettier, but of course she ain't a kid, though she looks it. I mean she was only seventeen in that picture and that was ten years ago. I mean she's twenty-seven years old now. But I never met a girl with as much zip as she had in those

days. It's remarkable how marriage changes them. I mean
nobody would ever have thought Celia Sayles would turn
out to be a sit-by-the-fire. I mean she still likes a good time,
but her home and kiddies come first. I mean her home and
kiddies come first.'

'I see what you mean,' said Bartlett.

An hour's drive brought them to Ardsley-on-Hudson
and the great man's home.

'A wonderful place!' Bartlett exclaimed with a heroic
semblance of enthusiam as the car turned in at an *arc de
triomphe* of a gateway and approached a white house that
might have been mistaken for the Yale Bowl.

'It ought to be! said Gregg. 'I mean I've spent enough on
it. I mean these things cost money.'

He indicated with a gesture the huge house and
Urbanesque landscaping.

'But no amount of money is too much to spend on home.
I mean it's a good investment if it tends to make your family
proud and satisfied with their home. I mean every nickel
I've spent here is like so much insurance; it insures me of a
happy wife and family. And what more can a man ask!'

Bartlett didn't know, but the topic was forgotten in the
business of leaving the resplendent Rolls and entering the
even more resplendent reception hall.

'Forbes will take your things,' said Gregg. 'And, Forbes,
you may tell Dennis that Mr Bartlett will spend the night.'
He faced the wide stairway and raised his voice.
'Sweetheart!' he called.

From above came the reply in contralto: 'Hello,
sweetheart!'

'Come down, sweetheart. I've brought you a visitor.'

'All right sweetheart, in just a minute.'

Gregg led Bartlett into a living-room that was five laps to
the mile and suggestive of an Atlantic City auction sale.

'Sit there,' said the host, pointing to a balloon-stuffed
easy chair, 'and I'll see if we can get a drink. I've got some
real old Bourbon that I'd like you to try. You know I come
from Chicago and I always liked Bourbon better than

Scotch. I mean I always preferred it to Scotch. Forbes,' he addressed the servant, 'we want a drink. You'll find a full bottle of that Bourbon in the cupboard.'

'It's only half full, sir,' said Forbes.

'Half full! That's funny! I mean I opened it last night and just took one drink. I mean it ought to be full.'

'It's only half full,' repeated Forbes, and went to fetch it.

'I'll have to investigate,' Gregg told his guest. 'I mean this ain't the first time lately that some of my good stuff has disappeared. When you keep so many servants, it's hard to get all honest ones. But here's Celia!'

Bartlett rose to greet the striking brunette who at this moment made an entrance so Delsarte as to be almost painful. With never a glance at him, she minced across the room to her husband and took a half interest in a convincing kiss.

'Well, sweetheart,' she said when it was at last over.

'This is Mr Bartlett, sweetheart,' said her husband. 'Mr Bartlett, meet Mrs Gregg.'

Bartlett shook his hostess's proffered two fingers.

'I'm so pleased!' said Celia in a voice reminiscent of Miss Claire's imitation of Miss Barrymore.

'Mr Bartlett,' Gregg went on, 'is with *Mankind*, Ralph Doane's magazine. He is going to write me up; I mean us.'

'No, you mean you,' said Celia. 'I'm sure the public is not interested in great men's wives.'

'I am sure you are mistaken, Mrs Gregg,' said Bartlett politely. 'In this case at least. You are worth writing up aside from being a great man's wife.'

'I'm afraid you're a flatterer, Mr Bartlett,' she returned. 'I have been out of the limelight so long that I doubt if anybody remembers me. I'm no longer an artist; merely a happy wife and mother.'

'And I claim, sweetheart,' said Gregg, 'that it takes an artist to be that.'

'Oh, no, sweetheart!' said Celia. 'Not when they have you for a husband!'

The exchange of hosannahs was interrupted by the

arrival of Forbes with the tray.

'Will you take yours straight or in a high-ball?' Gregg inquired of his guest. 'Personally I like good whisky straight. I mean mixing it with water spoils the flavor. I mean whisky like this, it seems like a crime to mix it with water.'

'I'll have mine straight,' said Bartlett, who would have preferred a high-ball.

While the drinks were being prepared, he observed his hostess more closely and thought how much more charming she would be if she had used finesse in improving on nature. Her cheeks, her mouth, her eyes and lashes had been, he guessed, far above the average in beauty before she had begun experimenting with them. And her experiments had been clumsy. She was handsome in spite of her efforts to be handsomer.

'Listen, sweetheart,' said her husband. 'One of the servants has been helping himself to this Bourbon. I mean it was a full bottle last night and I only had one little drink out of it. And now it's less than half full. Who do you suppose has been at it?'

'How do I know, sweetheart? Maybe the groceryman or the iceman or somebody.'

'But you and I and Forbes are the only ones that have a key. I mean it was locked up.'

'Maybe you forgot to lock it.'

'I never do. Well, anyway, Bartlett, here's a go!'

'Doesn't Mrs Gregg indulge?' asked Bartlett.

'Only a cocktail before dinner,' said Celia. 'Lou objects to me drinking whisky, and I don't like it much anyway.'

'I don't object to you drinking whisky, sweetheart. I just object to you drinking to excess. I mean I think it coarsens a woman to drink. I mean it makes them coarse.'

'Well, there's no argument, sweetheart. As I say, I don't care whether I have it or not.'

'It certainly is great Bourbon!' said Bartlett, smacking his lips and putting his glass back on the tray.

'You bet it is!' Gregg agreed. 'I mean you can't buy that kind of stuff any more. I mean it's real stuff. You help yourself when you want another. Mr Bartlett is going to stay all night, sweetheart. I told him he could get a whole lot more of a line on us that way than just interviewing me in the office. I mean I'm tongue-tied when it comes to talking about my work and my success. I mean it's better to see me out here as I am, in my home, with my family. I mean my home life speaks for itself without me saying a word.'

'But, sweetheart,' said his wife, 'what about Mr Latham?'

'Gosh! I forgot all about him! I must phone and see if I can call it off. That's terrible! You see,' he explained to Bartlett, 'I made a date to go up to Tarrytown tonight, to K. I. Latham's, the sugar people. We're going to talk over the new club. We're going to have a golf club that will make the rest of them look like a toy. I mean a real golf club! They want me to kind of run it. And I was to go up there tonight and talk it over. I'll phone and see if I can postpone it.'

'Oh, don't postpone it on my account!' urged Bartlett. 'I can come out again some other time, or I can see you in town.'

'I don't see how you *can* postpone it sweetheart,' said Celia. 'Didn't he say old Mr King was coming over from White Plains? They'll be mad at you if you don't go.'

'I'm afraid they would resent it, sweetheart. Well, I'll tell you. You can entertain Mr Bartlett and I'll go up there right after dinner and come back as soon as I can. And Bartlett and I can talk when I get back. I mean we can talk when I get back. How is that?'

'That suits me,' said Bartlett.'

'I'll be as entertaining as I can,' said Celia, 'but I'm afraid that isn't very entertaining. However, if I'm too much of a bore, there's plenty to read.'

'No danger of my being bored' said Bartlett.

'Well, that's all fixed then,' said the relieved host. 'I hope you'll excuse me running away. But I don't see how I can get out of it. I mean with old King coming over from White Plains. I mean he's an old man. But listen sweetheart—where are the kiddies? Mr Bartlett wants to see them.'

'Yes, indeed!' agreed the visitor.

'Of course you'd say so!' Celia said. 'But we *are* proud of them! I suppose all parents are the same. They all think their own children are the only children in the world. Isn't that so, Mr Bartlett? Or haven't you any children?'

'I'm sorry to say I'm not married.'

'Oh, you poor thing! We pity him, don't we, sweetheart? But why aren't you, Mr Bartlett? Don't tell me you're a woman hater!'

'Not now, anyway,' said the gallant Bartlett.

'Do you get that, sweetheart? He's paying you a pretty compliment.'

'I heard it, sweetheart. And now I'm sure he's a flatterer. But I must hurry and get the children before Hortense puts them to bed.'

'Well,' said Gregg when his wife had left the room, 'would you say she's changed?'

'A little, and for the better. She's more than fulfilled her early promise.'

'I think so,' said Gregg. 'I mean I think she was a beautiful girl and now she's an even more beautiful woman. I mean wifehood and maternity have given her a kind of a—well, you know—I mean a kind of a pose. I mean a pose. How about another drink?'

They were emptying their glasses when Celia returned with two of her little girls.

'The baby's in bed and I was afraid to ask Hortense to get her up again. But you'll see her in the morning. This is Norma and this is Grace. Girls, this is Mr Bartlett.'

The girls received this news calmly.

'Well, girls,' said Bartlett.

'What do you think of them, Bartlett?' demanded their father. 'I mean what do you think of them?'

'They're great!' replied the guest with creditable warmth.

'I mean aren't they pretty?'

'I should say they are!'

'There, girls! Why don't you thank Mr Bartlett?'

'Thanks,' murmured Norma.

'How old are you, Norma?' asked Bartlett.

'Six,' said Norma.

'Well,' said Bartlett. 'And how old is Grace?'

'Four,' replied Norma.

'Well,' said Bartlett. 'And how old is baby sister?'

'One and a half,' answerd Norma.

'Well,' said Bartlett.

As this seemed to be final, 'Come, girls,' said their mother. 'Kiss daddy good night and I'll take you back to Hortense.'

'I'll take them,' said Gregg. 'I'm going upstairs anyway. And you can show Bartlett around. I mean before it gets any darker.'

'Good night, girls,' said Bartlett, and the children murmured a good night.

'I'll come and see you before you're asleep,' Celia told them. And after Gregg had led them out, 'Do you really think they're pretty?' she asked Bartlett.

'I certainly do. Especially Norma. She's the image of you,' said Bartlett.

'She looks a little like I used to,' Celia admitted. 'But I hope she doesn't look like me now. I'm too old looking.'

'You look remarkably young!' said Bartlett. 'No one would believe you were the mother of three children.'

'Oh, Mr Bartlett. ! But I mustn't forget I'm to "show you around." Lou is so proud of our home!'

'And with reason,' said Bartlett.

'It *is* wonderful! I call it our love nest. Quite a big nest, don't you think? Mother says it's too big to be cosy; she says she can't think of it as a home. But I always say a place is whatever one makes of it. A woman can by happy in a tent if they love each other. And miserable in a royal palace without love. Don't you think so, Mr Bartlett?'

'Yes, indeed.'

'Is this really such wonderful Bourbon? I think I'll just take a sip of it and see what it's like. It can't hurt me if it's so good. Do you think so, Mr Bartlett?'

'I don't believe so.'

'Well then, I'm going to taste it and if it hurts me it's your fault.'

Celia poured a whisky glass two-thirds full and drained it at a gulp.

'It *is* good, isn't it?' she said. 'Of course I'm not much of a judge as I don't care for whisky and Lou won't let me drink it. But he's raved so about this Bourbon that I did want to see what it was like. You won't tell on me, will you, Mr Bartlett?'

'Not I!'

'I wonder how it would be in a high-ball. Let's you and I have just one. But I'm forgetting I'm supposed to show you the place. We won't have time to drink a high-ball and see the place too before Lou comes down. Are you so crazy to see the place?'

'Not very.'

'Well, then, what do you say if we have a high-ball? And it'll be a secret between you and I.'

They drank in silence and Celia pressed a button by the door.

'You may take the bottle and tray,' she told Forbes. 'And now,' she said to Bartlett, 'we'll go out on the porch and see as much as we can see. You'll have to guess the rest.'

Gregg, having changed his shirt and collar, joined them.

'Well,' he said to Bartlett, 'have you seen everything?'

'I guess I have, Mr Gregg,' lied the guest readily. 'It's a wonderful place!'

'We like it. I mean it suits us. I mean it's my idea of a real home. And Celia calls it her love nest.'

'So she told me,' said Bartlett.

'She'll always be sentimental,' said her husband.

He put his hand on her shoulder, but she drew away.

'I must run up and dress,' she said.

'Dress!' exclaimed Bartlett, who had been dazzled by her flowered green chiffon.

'Oh, I'm not going to really dress,' she said. 'But I couldn't wear this thing for dinner!'

'Perhaps you'd like to clean up a little, Bartlett,' said Gregg. 'I mean Forbes will show you your room if you want to go up.'

'It might be best,' said Bartlett.

Celia, in a black lace dinner gown, was rather quiet during the elaborate meal. Three or four times when Gregg addressed her, she seemed to be thinking of something else and had to ask, 'What did you say, sweetheart?' Her face was red and Bartlett imagined that she had 'sneaked' a drink or two besides the two helpings of Bourbon and the cocktail that had preceded dinner.

'Well, I'll leave you,' said Gregg when they were in the living-room once more. 'I mean the sooner I get started, the sooner I'll be back. Sweetheart, try and keep your guest awake and don't let him die of thirst. *Au revoir*, Bartlett. I'm sorry, but it can't be helped. There's a fresh bottle of the Bourbon, so go to it. I mean help yourself. It's too bad you have to drink alone.'

'It *is* too bad, Mr Bartlett,' said Celia when Gregg had gone.

'What's too bad?' asked Bartlett.

'That you have to drink alone. I feel like I wasn't being a good hostess to let you do it. In fact, I refuse to let you do it. I'll join you in just a little wee sip.'

'But it's so soon after dinner!'

'It's never too soon! I'm going to have a drink myself and if you don't join me, you're a quitter.'

She mixed two life-sized high-balls and handed one to her guest.

'Now we'll turn on the radio and see if we can't stir things up. There! No, No! Who cares about the old baseball! Now! This is better! Let's dance.'

'I'm sorry, Mrs Gregg, but I don't dance.'

'Well, you're an old cheese! To make me dance alone! "All alone, yes, I'm all alone." '

There was no affectation in her voice now and Bartlett was amazed at her unlabored grace as she glided around the big room.

'But it's no fun alone,' she complained. 'Let's shut the damn thing off and talk.'

'I love to watch you dance,' said Bartlett.

'Yes, but I'm no Pavlowa,' said Celia as she silenced the radio. 'And besides, it's time for a drink.'

'I've still got more than half of mine.'

'Well, you had that wine at dinner, so I'll have to catch up with you.'

She poured herself another high-ball and went at the task of 'catching up'.

'The trouble with you, Mr— now isn't that a scream! I can't think of your name.'

'Bartlett.'

'The trouble with you, Barker–do you know what's the trouble with you? You're too sober. See? You're too damn sober! That's the whole trouble, see? If you weren't so sober, we'd be better off. See? What I can't understand is how you can be so sober and me so high.'

'You're not used to it.'

'Not used to it! That's the cat's pajamas! Say, I'm like this half the time, see? If I wasn't, I'd die!'

'What does your husband say?'

'He don't say because he don't know. See, Barker? There's nights when he's out and there's nights when I'm out myself. And there's other nights when we're both in and I pretend I'm sleepy and I go up-stairs. See? But I don't go to bed. See? I have a little party all by myself. See? If I didn't, I'd die!'

'What do you mean, you'd die?'

'You're dumb, Barker! You may be sober, but you're dumb! Did you fall for all that apple sauce about the happy home and the contented wife? Listen, Barker—I'd give anything in the world to be out of this mess. I'd give anything to never see him again.'

'Don't you love him any more? Doesn't he love you? Or what?'

'Love! I never did love him! I didn't know what love was! And all his love is for himself!'

'How did you happen to get married?'

'I was a kid; that's the answer. A kid and ambitious. See? He was a director then and he got stuck on me and I thought he'd make me a star. See, Barker? I married him to get myself a chance. And now look at me!'

'I'd say you were fairly well off.'

'Well off, am I? I'd change places with the scum of the earth just to be free? See, Barker? And I could have been a star without any help if I'd only realized it. I had the looks and I had the talent. I've got it yet. I could be a Swanson and get myself a marquis; maybe a prince! And look what I did get! A self-satisfied, self-centred——! I thought he'd *make* me! See, Barker? Well, he's made me all right; he's made me a chronic mother and it's a wonder I've got any looks left.

'I fought at first. I told him marriage didn't mean giving up my art, my life work. But it was no use. He wanted a beautiful wife and beautiful children for his beautiful home. Just to show us off. See? I'm part of his chattels. See, Barker? I'm just like his big diamond or his cars or his horses. And he wouldn't stand for his wife "lowering" herself to act in pictures. Just as if pictures hadn't made him!

'You go back to your magazine tomorrow and write about our love nest. See, Barker? And be sure and don't get mixed and call it a baby ranch. Babies! You thought little Norma was pretty. Well, she is. And what is it going to get her? A rich —— of a husband that treats her like a ——! That's what it'll get her if I don't interfere. I hope I don't last long enough to see her grow up, but if I do, I'm going to advise her to run away from home and live her own life. And *be* somebody! Not a *thing* like I am! See, Barker?'

'Did you ever think of a divorce?'

'Did I ever think of one! Listen—but there's no chance. I've got nothing on him, and no matter what he had on me, he'd never let the world know it. He'd keep me here and torture me like he does now, only worse. But I haven't done anything wrong, see? The men I might care for, they're all scared of him and his money and power. See, Barker? And the others are just as bad as him. Like fat old Morris, the hotel man, that everybody thinks he's a model husband. The reason he don't step out more is because he's too stingy. But I could have him if I wanted him. Every time he gets near enough to me, he squeezes my hand. I guess he thinks it's a nickel, the tight old—! But come on, Barker. Let's have a drink. I'm running down.'

'I think it's about time you were running up—upstairs,' said Bartlett. 'If I were you, I'd try to be in bed and asleep when Gregg gets home.'

'You're all right, Barker. And after this drink I'm going to do just as you say. Only I thought of it before you did, see? I think if it lots of nights. And tonight you can help me out by telling him I had a bad headache.'

Left alone, Bartlett thought a while, then read, and finally dozed off. He was dozing when Gregg returned.

'Well, well, Bartlett,' said the great man, 'did Celia desert you?'

'It was perfectly all right, Mr Gregg. She had a headache and I told her to go to bed.'

'She's had a lot of headaches lately; reads too much, I guess. Well, I'm sorry I had this date. It was about a new golf club and I had to be there. I mean I'm going to be president of it. I see you consoled yourself with some of the Bourbon. I mean the bottle doesn't look as full as it did.'

'I hope you'll forgive me for helping myself so generously,' said Bartlett. 'I don't get stuff like that every day!'

'Well, what do you say if we turn in? We can talk on the way to town tomorrow. Though I guess you won't have much to ask me. I guess you know all about us. I mean you know all about us now.'

'Yes, indeed, Mr Gregg. I've got plenty of material if I can just handle it.'

Celia had not put in an appearance when Gregg and his guest were ready to leave the house next day.

'She always sleeps late,' said Gregg. 'I mean she never

wakes up very early. But she's later than usual this morning. Sweetheart!' he called up the stairs.

'Yes, sweetheart,' came the reply.

'Mr Bartlett's leaving now. I mean he's going.'

'Oh, good-by, Mr Bartlett. Please forgive me for not being down to see you off.'

'You're forgiven, Mrs Gregg. And thanks for your hospitality.'

'Good-by, sweetheart!'

'Good-by, sweetheart!'

Conference Purposes

MALCOLM BRADBURY

IT IS A long, thin chamber preserved only for conference purposes; as a result a certain dignity, a spacious seriousness has been attempted. On two sides there are long glass windows, giving onto the distractingly good views; to prevent these being distracting, white slatted Venetian blinds have been hung, and these are dropped now, and will clatter ceaselessy throughout the afternoon's deliberations. The other two walls are pure and white and undecorated, conscious aids to contemplation, save that in one spot a large abstract painting, conceived by a nakedly frantic sensibility, opens a large, obsessive hole into inner chaos. The architect and his design consultant, a man of many awards, have exercised themselves considerably in conceiving and predicating the meetings that would come to be held here. For the long central space of the room, they have chosen an elaborate, table-like construct which has a bright orange top and many thin, brushed-chrome legs; they have surrounded this with a splendid vista of forty white vinyl high-backed chairs. Three more chairs with somewhat higher backs and the university's crest embossed into the vinyl designate the head of the table. On the floor is a serious, undistracting brown carpet; on the ceiling, an elaborate acoustical muffle. Minnehaha Ho, Professor Marvin's secretary, has been diligent during the morning; she has put before every place a large, leather-edged blotter, a notepad, and copies of the department's prospectus and the university's calendar and regulations, their covers all backed out in the official design colours of the university, which are indigo and puce. In the original master-plan, Danish grey-glass ashtrays had been provided for each place; but the room has seen a fair incidence of sit-ins, and the ashtrays have been stolen, and replaced by many one-ounce Player's Whiskey tobacco tins, retrieved from the wastepaper basket of Dr Zachery. Someone has sprayed the room with scented deodorant, and emptied these ashtrays. All stands in its committee dignity; the meeting, then, is ready to begin.

When the party from the cafeteria arrives, Professor Marvin, who is always early, is there already, in the central high chair, his back to one of the windows. A row of pens is in his top pocket; an annotated agenda lies between his two hairy hands on the blotter before him. To the left of his left hand is a stack of files, the record of all recent past meetings, bound in hard-loop bindings; to the right of his right hand is a small carafe of water. On his left sits Minnehaha Ho, who will take the minutes; on his right sits his administrative assistant, Benita Pream, who has before her many more files, and a small alarm clock. At the top of the long row of chairs where the faculty sit there is, on Marvin's left, Professor Debison, a man rarely seen, except in meetings such as this. His field is Overseas Studies, and overseas is where he most often is , as the fresh BOAC and SAS tags on his worn brown briefcase, laid on the table before him, indicate. Dr Zachery, by custom, takes the place opposite; he goes up the long room and sits down. It is his boast that on one such occasion he read the entirety of

Talcott Parsons' *The Social System*, no mean feat; he has now prepared for the afternoon by placing here a backfile of bound volumes of the *British Journal of Sociology*; he is head-down at once, flicking over pages with practised hand and putting in slips to mark articles relevant to his micro-sociological scheme of things. Beside him, resting informally across a chair, there is already present one of the six student representatives, who always sit together as a caucus; he passes time usefully by inspecting photographs of female crotches in a magazine. The room fills up; the sociologists and social psychologists, sophisticates of meetings, readers of Goffman who all know intimately the difference between a group and an encounter, who are expert in the dynamics of interaction, come in and pick their places with care, examining existing relationships, angles of vision, even the cast of the light. Finally the elaborate social construct is ready. Marvin sits at the head of the table, in that curious state of suspended animation appropriate to the moment before the start of a meeting. Outside, pile-drivers thump, and dumper-trucks roar; inside is a severe, expectant curiosity.

Then the alarm clock of Benita Pream, the administrative assistant, pings; Professor Marvin coughs very loudly and waves his arms. He looks up and down the long table, and says: 'Can we now come to order, gentlemen?' Immediately the silence breaks; many arms go up, all round the table; there is a jabber of voices. 'May I point out, Mr Chairperson, that of the persons in this room you are addressing as "gentlemen", seven are women?' says Melissa Todoroff. 'May I suggest the formulation "Can we come to order, persons?" or perhaps "Can we come to order, colleagues?"' 'Doesn't the phrase itself suggest we're somehow normally in a state of *dis*order?' asks Roger Fundy. 'Can I ask whether under Standing Orders of Senate we are bound to terminate this meeting in three and a half hours? And, if so, whether the Chairman thinks an agenda of thirty-four items can be seriously discussed under those limitations, especially since my colleagues will presumably want to take tea?' 'On a point of information, Mr Chairman, may I point out that the tea interval is not included within the three and a half hour limitation, and also draw Dr Petworth's attention to the fact that we have concluded discussion of longer agendas in shorter times?' 'Here?' asks someone. 'May I ask if it is the wish of this meeting that we should have a window open?' The meeting has started; and it is always so. It has often been remarked, by Benita Pream, who services several such departmental meetings, that those in History are distinguished by their high rate of absenteeism, those in English by the amount of wine consumed afterwards, and those in Sociology by their contentiousness. The pile-drivers thump outside; the arguments within continue. The sociologists, having read Goffman, know there is a role of Chairman, and a role of Argumentative Person, and a role of Silent Person; they know how situations are made, and how they can be leaked, and how dysphoria can be induced; they put their knowledge to the test in such situations as this. Benita Pream's alarm has pinged at 14.00 hours, according to her own notes; it is 14.20 before the meeting has decided how long it is to continue, and whether it is quorate, and if it should have the window open, and 14.30 before Professor Marvin has managed to sign the minutes of the last meeting, so that they can begin on item 1 of the agenda of this one, which concerns the appointment of external examiners for finals: 'An uncontentious item, I think,' says Professor Marvin.

It is 15.05 before the uncontentious item is resolved. Nobody likes the two names proposed by Professor Marvin. But their dissents are founded on such radically different premises that no two other names can be proposed from the meeting and agreed upon. A working party is suggested, to bring names to the next meeting; no one can agree on the membership of the working party. A select committee of the department is proposed, to suggest names for the members of the working party; no one can agree on the membership of the select committee. A recommendation that Senate be asked to nominate the members of the select committee who will nominate the members of the working party who will make proposals for nominations so that the departmental meeting can nominate the external examiners is defeated, on the grounds that this would be external interference from Senate in the affairs of the department: even though, as the chair points out, the department cannot in any case nominate external examiners, but only recommend names to Senate, who will nominate them. A motion that the names of the two external examiners originally recommended be put again is put, and accepted. The names are put again, and rejected. A motion that there be no external examiners is put, and rejected. Two ladies in blue overalls come in with cups of tea and a plate of biscuits, and place cups in front of all the people present. A proposal that, since the agenda is moving slowly, discussion continue during tea is put and accepted, with one abstainer, who takes his cup of tea outside and drinks it there. The fact that tea has come without an item settled appears to have some effect: a motion that Professor Marvin be allowed to make his own choice of external examiners, acting on behalf of the department, is put and accepted. Professor Marvin promptly indicates that he will recommend to Senate the two names originally mentioned, an hour before; and then he moves onto the next item.

'A rather contentious item,' he says, introducing a proposal that the number of student representatives be increased from six to eight. The six students already there, most of them in sweatshirts, breathe hard, look fierce, lean their heads together; they separate to discover that there has been no discussion, and that the item, presumably in weariness, has been passed immediately. The tea-ladies come in to remove the cups. Trading on success, the student representatives propose that membership of the department meeting be further expanded, to include representatives from the tea-ladies. The motion is put and passed. Benita Pream, the administrative assistant, intervenes here, whispering first in Marvin's ear, then addressing the meeting; she states that under regulations the tea-ladies are not entitled to membership of department meetings. The meeting passes a recommendation urging Senate to change regulations in order to permit tea-ladies to serve on department meetings. The resolution and the preceding one are both ruled out of order from the chair, on the ground that neither refers to any item on the agenda of the meeting. A resolution that items not on the agenda of the meeting be allowed is proposed, but is ruled out of order on the grounds that it is not on the agenda of the meeting. A resolution that the chair be held out of order because it has allowed two motions to come to the vote which are not, according to standing orders, on the agenda of the meeting is refused from the chair, on the grounds that the chair cannot allow motions to come to the vote which are not, according to standing orders, on the agenda of the meeting. Outside it rains a great deal, and the level of the lake rises considerably.

'Are all your meetings this boring?' asks Melissa Todoroff, who will later be discovered not to be entitled to be in the meeting at all, since she is only a visitor, and will be asked to leave, and will do so, shouting. 'Don't worry,' whispers Howard, 'this is just a preliminary skirmish. It will warm up later.' It warms up, in fact, shortly after 17.05, when it is beginning to go dark, and when Professor Marvin reaches item 17, which is concerned with Visiting Speakers. 'A non-controversial item, I think,' says Professor Marvin. 'A few proposed names here, I think we can accept them.' Roger Fundy raises his hand and says, 'Can I ask the chair under whose auspices the invitation to Professor Mangel was issued?' The chair looks bewildered: it says, 'Professor Mangel? As far as I know, Dr Fundy, no invitation has been issued to Professor Mangel.' 'Can I draw the chair's attention to the departmental memo, circulated this very morning, which states that Professor Mangel has been asked here to give a lecture?' 'I sent out no such departmental memo,' says the chair. 'I have here a

copy of the departmental memo which the chair says it did
not send out,' says Roger Fundy. 'Perhaps the chair would
like to see it.' The chair would; it inspects the memo, and
turns to Minnehaha Ho. 'It was on the dictaphone,' says
Miss Ho, with wide oriental eyes, 'so I sent it out.' 'It was on
the dictaphone so you sent it out?' murmurs Professor
Marvin, 'I didn't put it on the dictaphone.' 'Can I ask the
Chairperson,' says Melissa Todoroff, 'if that person is
aware that this invitation will be seen by all non-
Caucasians and women on this campus as a deliberate
insult to their genetic origins?' 'This is trouble, man,' says
one of the student representatives, 'he's a racist and a
sexist.' Professor Marvin looks around in some mystifica-
tion. 'Professor Mangel is to my knowledge neither a racist
nor a sexist, but a very well-qualified geneticist,' he says.
'However, since we have not invited him here the
question seems scarcely to arise on this agenda.' 'In view of
the opinion of the chair that Mangel is neither a racist nor a
sexist,' says Howard, 'would that mean that the chair
would be prepared to invite him to this campus, if his name
were proposed?' 'It isn't proposed,' says Marvin. 'The point
is that Professor Mangel's work is fascist, and we've no
business to confirm that by inviting him here,' says Moira
Millikin. 'I had always thought the distinguishing mark of
fascism was its refusal to tolerate free enquiry, Dr
Millikin,' says Marvin, 'but the question needs no
discussion, since there's no proposal to invite this man. I
doubt if we could ever agree on such an invitation. It would
be an issue.'

'May I ask why?' asks Dr Zacher, the *British Journal of
Sociology* forgotten. 'Why?' asks Fundy. 'Do you know what
the consequences of inviting that man would be? One
doesn't tolerate . . .' 'But that is just what one does,' says Dr
Zachery. 'One tolerates. May I propose, and I think this is
in order, since the agenda permits us to make suggestions
for visiting speakers, that we issue a formal invitation from
this department to Professor Mangel, to come and speak to
this department?' There is much noise around the table;

Howard sits silent, so silent that Flora Beniform leans over
to him and murmurs, 'Don't I see a hand at work here?'
'Ssshh,' says Howard, 'this is a serious issue.' 'You wish to
put that as a motion?' asks Marvin, looking at Zachery. 'I do,'
says Zachery, 'and I should like to speak to my motion. I
observe, among some of my younger colleagues, perhaps
less experienced in recent history than some of us, a real
ignorance of the state of affairs we are discussing.
Professor Mangel and myself have a background in
common; we are both Jewish, and both grew up in Nazi
Germany, and fled here from the rise of fascism. I think we
know the meaning of this term. Fascism, and the associated
genocide, arose because a climate developed in Germany in
which it was held that all intellectual activity conform with
an accepted, approved ideology. To make this happen, it
was necessary to make a climate in which it became virtually
impossible to think, or exist, outside the dominant
ideological construct. Those who did were isolated, as now
some of our colleagues seek to isolate Professor Mangel.'
There are many murmurs round the table from the
sociologists, all of whom are deeply conscious of having
definitions of fascism they too could give, if asked. 'May I
continue?' asks Zachery. 'Fascism is therefore an elegant
sociological construct, a one-system world. Its opposite is
contingency or pluralism or liberalism. That means a chaos
of opinion and ideology; there are people who find that
hard to endure. But in the interests of it, I think we must
ask Professor Mangel to come here and lecture.'
    'Then you'll get your chaos all right, if he does,' says
Fundy. 'You know what the radical feeling is about this.
You know what uproar and violent protest there always is
when someone like Jensen or Eysenck is invited to lecture
at a university. The same will happen with Mangel.'
'Justified violence and protest,' says Moira Millikin. 'I'm
extremely disturbed, Mr Chairman,' says Dr Macintosh,
'to see so many of my colleagues stopping us from inviting
someone we haven't even invited.' But now there is much
shouting across the table, and Professor Marvin has to

stand, and bang his wodge of files down hard onto the desk
in front of him, before something like silence returns.
'Gentlemen!' he shouts. 'Persons!' 'Oh, Howard, Howard,
is this you?' whispers Flora. 'Flora,' whispers back Howard.
'Stop taking the plane to bits once it's left the ground.'
'You're playing games,' whispers Flora. 'I've not spoken,'
says Howard. Professor Marvin, now, has resumed his
seat. He waits for full quietness, and then he says: 'Well, Dr
Zachery has proposed a motion, which is now on the table,
that we in this department of Social Studies issue an
invitation to Professor Mangel to came and lecture here.
Does that motion have a seconder?' 'Go on, Flora,'
whispers Howard; Flora puts her hand up. 'Oh,' says
Marvin, 'well, let me briefly note that this issue could
become a bone of severe contention, and remind the
department of the experience of other universities who
have ventured in this unduly charged area, before I put the
motion to the vote. Let us be cautious in our actions,
cautious but just. Now may we vote. Those in favour?' The
hands go up around the table; Benita Pream rises to count
them. 'And those against?' Another group of hands, some
waving violently, go up; Benita Pream rises once more to
count these. She writes the results down on a piece of
paper, and slips this over the table top to Marvin, who looks
at it. 'Well,' he says, 'this motion has been carried. By eleven
votes to ten. I'm sure that's just, but I'm afraid we've
committed ourselves to a real bone of contention.' There is
uproar at the table. 'Castrate all sexists,' shouts Melissa
Todoroff; and it is now that, on a point of order from Dr
Petworth, a constitutional spirit dedicated to such
precisions as points of order, it is discovered that Miss
Todoroff is not, as a visitor, formally a member of this
meeting at all, and therefore has been voting without
entitlement, and so she is taken from the room, shouting,
'Sisters, rebel,' and 'Off the pigs'. The table settles;
Howard's hand goes up; 'Mr Chairman,' he says, 'may I
point out that the vote just taken—and passed by only one
vote—is now clearly invalid, since Miss Todoroff's should

not have been cast.' 'I had seen that constitutional point, Dr Kirk,' says Marvin. 'I'm afraid it leaves us in a very difficult position. You see, that applies not only to the last vote, but to all the votes taken throughout the meeting. Unless we can see a way round it, we may have to start this entire meeting from the beginning again.'

There are groans and shouts; Benita Pream, meanwhile, has been fumbling through papers; now she whispers a brief something into the ear of the chair. The chair says: 'Oh, good.' There is still much noise in the room, so Marvin taps the table. 'I feel quite sure,' he says, 'my colleagues will bear with me if I say that it is undesirable to re-run this entire meeting. It now appears that this is the only motion today which was passed on a margin of one vote. With the consent of the meeting, I will assume all other votes satisfactory. Do I have that?' The sociologists, weary from the fray, agree. 'Now our last vote,' says Marvin. 'As your chairman, I have to consider the position here very carefully. Do we happen to know the way Dr Todoroff voted?' 'It seemed to me rather obvious,' says Dr Zachery, 'from her comments on leaving.' 'That's injustice,' says Moira Millikin, 'a ballot should be secret. When one individual's vote can be singled out in this way, the system's wrong.' 'I think there may be another way to answer this,' says Marvin, looking at another note from Benita Pream. 'I think I've resolved it, I hope to the satisfaction of this meeting.' The meeting looks about itself; it does not have the air of a group easily satisfied. 'If Dr Todoroff had voted against the motion,' says Marvin, 'and we simply subtracted her vote, that would leave the voting as eleven to nine, with the motion carried. Do we agree?' The meeting agrees. 'If, on the other hand, she had voted for the motion, and her vote was subtracted, that would give us a tie, at ten ten. But in the event of such a tie, I as chairman would have had to use my casting vote. In the circumstances, and only because of the circumstances, as a pure matter of procedure and not of preference, I would have had to vote for the motion. Either way, therefore, the motion may be presumed to be carried.'

There is once again much uproar. 'Wishy-washy liberal equivocation,' shouts Moira Millikin, while her baby squawks by her chair. 'A crime against mankind,' says Roger Fundy. 'I can only tell you, Dr Fundy,' says Marvin, 'that I do not myself greatly relish the idea of Mangel visiting this campus. Not because what has been said about him seems to me true, but because we as a department do much better without these contentious situations. But this has been forced on me, and there was no other way procedurally for justice to be done.' 'A reactionary reason,' says Moira Millikin, 'Justice!' cried Roger Fundy. 'Democratic justice is clear injustice.' 'You always seem to find it convenient when it is in your favour,' says Marvin. This generates much more uproar, through which come many shouts for the vote to be retaken, and the level of the lake outside continues to rise, and the darkness increases beyond the big windows with their rattling blinds. The dumper-trucks have stopped; the pile-drivers have been put away; but, high in the dark, the lights of the Durkheim Room shine bright. The meeting goes on, and then, at 17.30, there is a loud ping of Benita Pream's alarm clock, and it is over. Or almost over, for even now they have to consider a proposal that, since there has been no tea interval, a notional time should be set for the actual consumption of the tea and the biscuits; it is this spot of notional time that is finally used to justify the fact that the meeting has gone on a few minutes longer in order to consider whether it should go on a few minutes longer. The sociologists rise and disperse; Professor Debison, who has not spoken at all, hurries off to his taxi, which will take him straight to Heathrow; in the corridor outside the Durkheim Room, caucuses huddle and discuss coming upheaval. 'You were very quiet,' says Flora Beniform to Howard, as they leave the room. 'Well,' says Howard, 'some of these bones of contention are very hard to resolve.' 'You've never had that trouble before,' says Flora. 'You want Mangel. You want a fight.'

'Who, me?' asks Howard, innocently, as they get into the lift. They stand there, waiting for the doors to close. 'I've got a babysitter,' says Howard. 'I see,' says Flora, and reaches in her bag, and gets out her diary, and deletes from the page marked with a thread a word that says: 'Provisionally'. 'Secret assignation?' asks Henry Beamish, getting into the lift, his arm sticking out stiffly before him. 'Well, Howard, that was very enjoyable. I'm glad I took the trouble to come. There were some issues there that greatly concerned me.' 'Were there, Henry?' asks Flora. 'What were those?' 'The question of the grant for research into senile delinquency,' says Henry. 'We can really move forward on that one now.' 'Did we discuss that?' asks Flora. 'Flora, you weren't attending,' says Henry, 'it was one of the most important items. I thought we'd have a battle over it, but it went straight through without discussion. I suppose people see its importance. A very uncontentious meeting, I thought.' 'Were you attending?' asks Flora, 'I noticed a certain flurry round the matter of Mangel.' 'I found that terribly predictable,' says Henry. 'The trouble with sociologists is that they usually fail to take genetics seriously. They talk about the balance of nature and nurture, but when it comes down to it they're all on the side of nurture, because they can interfere with that. They can't realize how much we're genetically predetermined.' 'But it is, as the chair says, a bone of contention,' says Flora. 'It'll blow over,' says Henry. 'Will it, Howard?' asks Flora. 'I doubt it,' says Howard. 'There's a lot of passion on this.' 'Oh, God,' says Flora, 'I must admit I was really hoping for just one quiet term. Without an issue, without a sit-in. I know it sounds terribly reactionary. But even though permanent revolution may have its claims, I really think before I die I'd like the peace to write one decent book.' 'But we won't let you,' says Howard. 'No,' says Flora, 'so I see.'

The lift stops at the fifth floor, and they get out, back into Sociology. 'Funny how it came up,' says Henry, 'it was all a bit of an accident.' 'Henry,' says Flora, wearily, 'there are no accidents.' Henry turns and looks at her, puzzled.

'Of course there are,' he says. 'I don't think Howard agrees with you,' says Flora. 'I must go home and work. Take care of yourself, Henry.' 'Of course,' says Henry. The three of them separate, going along three of the four corridors that lead away from the lift, to collect up the briefcases and the books and the new essays, and the new department memos, the accumulated intellectual deposit of the day, which will now need fresh attention. 'Grand girl, Flora,' says Henry, a few minutes later, when Howard comes to the door of his room, to remind him of their appointment. Henry's room, like all rooms, is a matching version of Howard's own, with the Conran desk, the Roneo-Vickers filing cabinet, the gunmetal wastepaper basket, the red desk chair, all in approximately similar places in the rectangle. The difference is that Henry has domesticated the space, and filled it with potted plants, and a bust of Gladstone, and a modernistic silver-frame mirror, and a loose-weave Norwegian rug for the floor, and a machine called a Teasmaid, which links a teapot to a clock, and throws out an intense smell of tea-leaves. 'Are you ready, Henry?' asks Howard. 'I've got a somewhat busy evening. And I've got to take you home for your steak.' 'I think that's about it,' says Henry, 'I shan't get much work done tonight like this. I wonder, Howard, if you would give me a hand to get my raincoat on? The problem is to fit this arm of mine in somewhere.' 'Let's put it over your shoulders,' says Howard, 'and I'll button it up for you at the neck.' They stand in Henry's domestic room, Henry with his chin up, as Howard attends to his coat. Then they pick up their briefcases and walk down the empty corridor towards the lift.

The lift comes quickly, and they get inside. 'I do hope you're not angry with me,' says Henry, as they descend. 'Why should I be?' asks Howard. 'I mean, over the Mangel question,' says Henry, 'I had to vote for him, of course, on principle. It was quite clear to me, though I respect the other point of view. I suppose you voted against.' 'I abstained, actually,' says Howard. 'But I know what you must have thought,' said Henry. 'If only Henry had done the sensible thing, and stayed at home, and then the vote would have gone the other way.' 'Nonsense,' says Howard, 'if you'd stayed at home, we wouldn't have had an issue. Now there'll be trouble, and it will radicalize everyone, and we shall have a good term.' 'Well, I don't think we agree on that,' says Henry. The lift doors open, and they step out into the empty foyer. The Kaakinen waterfall has been turned off for the night; many of the lights are out; the floors are being cleaned by a cleaner with a cleaner. 'No,' says Henry, 'I'm like Flora. I cry for peace. My political days are good and over. I'm not sure I was every really very far in. In any case, politics were fair, in the fifties.' 'That was why nothing got done,' says Howard, 'and there is no peace.' They go out, through the glass doors, into the darkening campus. 'Well, that's my point of view,' says Henry, 'though of course I do respect the other one.' 'Yes,' says Howard, as they stop and stand in the rain, 'well, where shall we go for our drink?' 'Ah,' says Henry, brightening, 'that's what I call a really serious issue. Where do you think?'

Appetites

JAMES JOYCE

MR BLOOM, CHAMPING standing, looked upon his sigh.
Nosey numskull. Will I tell him that horse Lenehan? He
knows already. Better let him forget. Go and lose more. Fool
and his money. Dewdrop coming down again. Cold nose
he'd have kissing a woman. Still they might like. Prickly
beards they like. Dog's cold noses. Old Mrs Riordan with
the rumbling stomach's Skye terrier in the City Arms
hotel. Molly fondling him in her lap. O the big doggy-
bowwowsywowsy!

Wine soaked and softened rolled pith of bread mustard a
moment mawkish cheese. Nice wine it is. Taste it better
because I'm not thirsty. Bath of course does that. Just a bite
or two. Then about six o'clock I can. Six, six. Time will be
gone then. She . . .

Mild fire of wine kindled his veins. I wanted that badly.
Felt so off colour. His eyes unhungrily saw shelves of tins,
sardines, gaudy lobsters' claws. All the odd things people
pick up for food. Out of shells, periwinkles with a pin, off
trees, snails out of the ground the French eat, out of the sea

with bait on a hook. Silly fish learn nothing in a thousand years. If you didn't know risky putting anything into your mouth. Poisonous berries. Johnny Magories. Roundness you think good. Gaudy colour warns you off. One fellow told another and so on. Try it on the dog first. Led on by the smell or the look. Tempting fruit. Ice cones. Cream. Instinct. Orangegroves for instance. Need artificial irrigation. Bleibtreustrasse. Yes but what about oysters? Unsightly like a clot of phlegm. Filthy shells. Devil to open them too. Who found them out? Garbage, sewage they feed on. Fizz and Red bank oysters. Effect on the sexual. Aphrodis. He was in the Red bank this morning. Was he oyster old fish at table. Perhaps he young flesh in bed. No. June has no ar no oysters. But there are people like tainted game. Jugged hare. First catch your hare. Chinese eating eggs fifty years old, blue and green again. Dinner of thirty courses. Each dish harmless might mix inside. Idea for a poison mystery. That archduke Leopold was it? No. Yes, or was it Otto one of those Habsburgs? Or who was it used to eat the scruff off his own head? Cheapest lunch in town. Of course, aristocrats. Then the others copy to be in the fashion. Milly too rock oil and flour. Raw pastry I like myself. Half the catch of oysters they throw back in the sea to keep up the price. Cheap. No one would buy. Caviare. Do the grand. Hock in green glasses. Swell blowout. Lady this. Powdered bosom pearls. The *élite*. *Crème de la crème*. They want special dishes to pretend they're. Hermit with a platter of pulse keep down the stings of the flesh. Know me come eat with me. Royal sturgeon. High sheriff, Coffey, the butcher, right to venisons of the forest from his ex. Send him back the half of a cow. Spread I saw down in the Master of the Rolls' kitchen area. Whitehatted *chef* like a rabbi. Combustible duck. Curly cabbage *à la duchesse de Parme*. Just as well to write it on the bill of fare so you can know what you've eaten too many drugs spoil the broth. I know it myself. Dosing it with Edwards' desiccated soup. Geese stuffed silly for them. Lobsters boiled alive. Do ptake some ptarmigan. Wouldn't mind being a waiter in a

swell hotel. Tips, evening dress, halfnaked ladies. May I
tempt you to a little more filleted lemon sole, miss
Dubedat? Yes, do bedad. And she did bedad. Huguenot
name I expect that. A miss Dubedat lived in Killiney I
remember. *Du, de la*, French. Still it's the same fish, perhaps
old Micky Hanlon of Moore street ripped the guts out of
making money, hand over fist, finger in fishes' gills, can't
write his name on a cheque, think he was painting the
landscape with his mouth twisted. Moooikill A Aitcha Ha.
Ignorant as a kish of brogues, worth fifty thousand
pounds.

Stuck on the pane two flies buzzed, stuck.

Glowing wine on his palate lingered swallowed. Crushing in the winepress grapes of Burgundy. Sun's heat
it is. Seems to a secret touch telling me memory. Touched
his sense moistened remembered. Hidden under wild ferns
on Howth. Below us bay sleeping sky. No sound. The sky.
The bay purple by the Lion's head. Green by Drumleck.
Yellowgreen towards Sutton. Fields of undersea, the lines
faint brown in grass, buried cities. Pillowed on my coat she
had her hair, earwigs in the heather scrub my hand under
her nape, you'll toss me all. O wonder! Coolsoft with
ointments her hand touched me, caressed: her eyes upon
me did not turn away. Ravished over her I lay, full lips full
open, kissed her mouth. Yum. Softly she gave me in my
mouth the seedcake warm and chewed. Mawkish pulp her
mouth had mumbled sweet and sour with spittle. Joy: I ate
it: joy. Young life, her lips that gave me pouting. Soft,
warm, sticky gumjelly lips. Flowers her eyes were, take
me, willing eyes. Pebbles fell. She lay still. A goat. No-one.
High on Ben Howth rhododendrons a nannygoat walking
surefooted, dropping currants. Screened under ferns she
laughed warmfolded. Wildly I lay on her, kissed her; eyes,
her lips, her streched neck, beating, woman's breasts full in
her blouse of nun's veiling, fat nipples upright. Hot I
tongued her. She kissed me. I was kissed. All yielding she
tossed my hair. Kissed, she kissed me.

Me. And me now.

Stuck, the flies buzzed.

His downcast eyes followed the silent veining of the oaken slab. Beauty: it curves, curves are beauty. Shapely goddesses, Venus, Juno: curves the world admires. Can see them library museum standing in the round hall, naked goddesses. Aids to digestion. They don't care what man looks. All to see. Never speaking, I mean to say to fellows like Flynn. Suppose she did Pygmalion and Galatea what would she say first? Mortal! Put you in your proper place. Quaffing nectar at mess with gods, golden dishes, all ambrosial. Not like a tanner lunch we have, boiled mutton, carrots and turnips, bottle of Allsop. Nectar, imagine it drinking electricity: gods' food. Lovely forms of woman sculped Junonian. Immortal lovely. And we stuffing food in one hole and out behind: food, chyle, blood, dung, earth, food: have to feed it like stoking an engine.

Sense of Humour

DAMON RUNYON

ONE NIGHT I am standing in front of Mindy's restaurant on
Broadway, thinking of practically nothing whatever, when
all of a sudden I feel a very terrible pain in my left foot.

In fact, this pain is so very terrible that it causes me to
leap up and down like a bullfrog, and to let out loud cries of
agony, and to speak some very profane language, which is
by no means my custom, although of course I recognize
the pain as coming from a hot foot, because I often
experience this pain before.

Furthermore, I know Joe the Joker must be in the
neighbourhood, as Joe the Joker has the most wonderful
sense of humour of anybody in this town, and is always
around giving people the hot foot, and gives it to me more
times than I can remember. In fact, I hear Joe the Joker
invents the hot foot, and it finally becomes a very popular
idea all over the country.

The way you give a hot foot is to sneak up behind some
guy who is standing around thinking of not much, and stick
a paper match in his shoe between the sole and the upper

along about where his little toe ought to be, and then light the match. By and by the guy will feel a terrible pain in his foot, and will start stamping around, and hollering, and carrying on generally, and it is always a most comical sight and a wonderful laugh to one and all to see him suffer.

No one in the world can give a hot foot as good as Joe the Joker, because it takes a guy who can sneak up very quiet on the guy who is to get the hot foot, and Joe can sneak up so quiet many guys on Broadway are willing to lay you odds that he can give a mouse a hot foot if you can find a mouse that wears shoes. Furthermore, Joe the Joker can take plenty of care of himself in case the guy who gets the hot foot feels like taking the matter up, which sometimes happens, especially with guys who get their shoes made to order at forty bobs per copy and do not care to have holes burned in these shoes.

But Joe does not care what kind of shoes the guys are wearing when he feels like giving out hot foots, and furthermore, he does not care who the guys are although many citizens think he makes a mistake the time he gives a hot foot to Frankie Ferocious. In fact, many citizens are greatly horrified by this action, and go around saying no good will come of it.

This Frankie Ferocious comes from over in Brooklyn, where he is considered a rising citizen in many respects, and by no means a guy to give hot foots to, especially as Frankie Ferocious has no sense of humour whatever. In fact, he is always very solemn, and nobody ever sees him laugh, and he certainly does not laugh when Joe the Joker gives him a hot foot one day on Broadway when Frankie Ferocious is standing talking over a business matter with some guys from the Bronx.

He only scowls at Joe, and says something in Italian, and while I do not understand Italian, it sounds so unpleasant that I guarantee I will leave town inside of the next two hours if he says it to me.

Of course Frankie Ferocious's name is not really Ferocious, but something in Italian like Feroccio, and I hear

he originally comes from Sicily, although he lives in
Brooklyn for quite some years, and from a modest
beginning he builds himself up until he is a very large
operator of merchandise of one kind and another,
especially alcohol. He is a big guy of maybe thirty-odd, and
he has hair blacker than a yard up a chimney, and black eyes,
and black eyebrows, and a slow way of looking at people.

Nobody knows a whole lot about Frankie Ferocious,
because he never has much to say, and he takes his time
saying it, but everybody gives him plenty of room when he
comes around, as there are rumours that Frankie never
likes to be crowded. As far as I am concerned, I do not care
for any part of Frankie Ferocious, because his slow way of
looking at people always makes me nervous, and I am
always sorry Joe the Joker gives him a hot foot, because I
figure Frankie Ferocious is bound to consider it a most
disrespectful action, and hold it against everybody that
lives on the Island of Manhattan.

But Joe the Joker only laughs when anybody tells him he
is out of line in giving Frankie the hot foot, and says it is not
his fault if Frankie has no sense of humour. Furthermore,
Joe says he will not only give Frankie another hot foot if he
gets a chance, but that he will give hot foots to the Prince of
Wales or Mussolini, if he catches them in the right spot,
although Regret, the horse player, states that Joe can have
twenty to one any time that he will not give Mussolini any
hot foots and get away with it.

Anyway, just as I suspect, there is Joe the Joker watching
me when I feel the hot foot, and he is laughing very
heartily, and furthermore, a large number of other citizens
are also laughing heartily, because Joe the Joker never sees
any fun in giving people the hot foot unless others are
present to enjoy the joke.

Well, naturally when I see who it is gives me the hot foot
I join in the laughter, and go over and shake hands with Joe,
and when I shake hands with him there is more laughter,
because it seems Joe has a hunk of Limburger cheese in his
duke, and what I shake hands with is this Limburger.

Futhermore, it is some of Mindy's Limburger cheese, and
everybody knows Mindy's Limburger is very squashy, and
also very loud.

Of course I laugh at this, too, although to tell the truth I
will laugh much more heartily if Joe the Joker drops dead in
front of me, because I do not like to be made the subject of
laughter on Broadway. But my laugh is really quite hearty
when Joe takes the rest of the cheese that is not on my
fingers and smears it on the steering-wheels of some
automobiles parked in front of Mindy's, because I get to
thinking of what the drivers will say when they start
steering their cars.

Then I get talking to Joe the Joker, and I ask him how
things are up in Harlem where Joe and his younger
brother, Freddy, and several other guys have a small
organization operating in beer, and Joe says things are as
good as can be expected considering business conditions.
Then I ask him how Rosa is getting along, this Rosa being
Joe the Joker's ever-loving wife, and a personal friend of
mine, as I know her when she is Rosa Midnight and is
singing in the old Hot Box before Joe hauls off and marries
her.

Well, at this question Joe the Joker starts laughing, and I
can see that something appeals to his sense of humour, and
finally he speaks as follows:

'Why,' he says, 'do you not hear the news about Rosa?
She takes the wind on me a couple of months ago for my
friend Frankie Ferocious, and is living in an apartment over
in Brooklyn, right near his house, although,' Joe says, 'of
course you understand I am telling you this only to answer
your question, and not to holler copper on Rosa.'

Then he lets out another large ha-ha, and in fact Joe the
Joker keeps laughing until I am afraid he will injure himself
internally. Personally, I do not see anything comical in a
guy's ever-loving wife taking the wind on him for a guy
like Frankie Ferocious, so when Joe the Joker quiets down a
bit I ask him what is funny about the proposition.

'Why,' Joe says, 'I have to laugh every time I think of how

the big greaseball is going to feel when he finds out how
expensive Rosa is. I do not know how many things Frankie
Ferocious has running for him in Brooklyn,' Joe says, 'but
he better try to move himself in on the mint if he wishes to
keep Rosa going.'

Then he laughs again, and I consider it wonderful the
way Joe is able to keep his sense of humour even in such a
situation as this, although up to this time I always think Joe
is very daffy indeed about Rosa, who is a little doll,
weighing maybe 90 pounds with her hat on and quite cute.

Now I judge from what Joe the Joker tells me that
Frankie Ferocious knows Rosa before Joe marries her and is
always pitching to her when she is singing in the Hot Box,
and even after she is Joe's ever-loving wife, Frankie
occasionally calls her up, especially when he commences to
be a rising citizen of Brooklyn, although of course Joe does
not learn about these calls until later. And about the time
Frankie Ferocious commences to be a rising citizen of
Brooklyn, things begin breaking a little tough for Joe the
Joker, what with the depression and all, and he has to
economize on Rosa in spots, and if there is one thing Rosa
cannot stand it is being economized on.

Along, about now, Joe the Joker gives Frankie Ferocious
the hot foot, and just as many citizens state at the time, it is a
mistake, for Frankie starts calling Rosa up more than
somewhat, and speaking of what a nice place Brooklyn is to
live in—which it is, at that— and between these boosts for
Brooklyn and Joe the Joker's economy, Rosa hauls off and
takes a subway to Borough Hall, leaving Joe a note telling
him that if he does not like it he knows what he can do.

'Well, Joe,' I say, after listening to his story, 'I always hate
to hear of these little domestic difficulties among my
friends, but maybe this is all for the best. Still, I feel sorry
for you, if it will do you any good,' I say.

'Do not feel sorry for me,' Joe says. 'If you wish to feel
sorry for anybody, feel sorry for Frankie Ferocious, and,'
he says, 'if you can spare a little more sorrow, give it to
Rosa.'

And Joe the Joker laughs very hearty again and starts telling me about a little scatter that he has up in Harlem where he keeps a chair fixed up with electric wires so he can give anybody that sits down in it a nice jolt, which sound very humorous to me, at that , especially when Joe tells me how they turn on too much juice one night and kill Commodore Jake.

Finally Joe says he has to get back to Harlem, but first he goes to the telephone in the corner cigar store and calls up Mindy's and imitates a doll's voice, and tells Mindy he is Peggy Joyce, or somebody, and orders fifty dozen sandwiches sent up at once to an apartment in West 72nd Street for a birthday party, although of course there is no such number as he gives, and nobody there will wish fifty dozen sandwiches if there is such a number.

Then Joe gets in his car and starts off, and while he is waiting for the traffic lights at Fiftieth Street, I see citizens on the sidewalks making sudden leaps, and looking around very fierce, and I know Joe the Joker is plugging them with pellets made out of tin foil, which he fires from a rubber band hooked between his thumb and forefinger.

Joe the Joker is very expert with this proposition, and it is very funny to see the citizens jump, although once or twice in his life Joe makes a miscue and knocks out somebody's eye. But it is all in fun, and shows you what a wonderful sense of humour Joe has.

Well, a few days later I see by the papers where a couple of Harlem guys Joe the Joker is mobbed up with are found done up in sacks over in Brooklyn, very dead indeed, and the coppers say it is because they are trying to move in on certain business enterprises that belong to nobody but Frankie Ferocious. But of course the coppers do not say Frankie Ferocious puts these guys in the sacks, because in the first place Frankie will report them to Headquarters if the coppers say such a thing about him, and in the second place putting guys in sacks is strictly a St Louis idea and to have a guy put in a sack properly you have to send to St Louis for experts in this matter.

Now, putting a guy in a sack is not as easy as it sounds, and in fact it takes quite a lot of practice and experience. To put a guy in a sack properly, you first have to put him to sleep, because naturally no guy is going to walk into a sack wide awake unless he is a plumb sucker. Some people claim the best way to put a guy to sleep is to give him a sleeping powder of some kind in a drink, but the real experts just tap the guy on the noggin with a blackjack, which saves the expense of buying the drink.

Anyway, after the guy is asleep, you double him up like a pocketknife, and tie a cord or a wire around his neck and under his knees. Then you put him in a gunny sack, and leave him some place, and by and by when the guy wakes up and finds himself in the sack, naturally he wants to get out and the first thing he does is to try to straighten out his knees. This pulls the cord around his neck up so tight that after a while the guy is all out of breath.

So then when somebody comes along and opens the sack they find the guy dead, and nobody is responsible for this unfortunate situation, because after all the guy really commits suicide, because if he does not try to straighten out his knees he may live to a ripe old age, if he recovers from the tap on the noggin.

Well, a couple of days later I see by the papers where three Brooklyn citizens are scragged as they are walking peaceably along Clinton Street, the scragging being done by some parties in an automobile who seem to have a machine gun, and the papers state the citizens are friends of Frankie Ferocious, and that it is rumoured the parties with the machine gun are from Harlem.

I judge by this that there is some trouble in Brooklyn, especially as about a week after the citizens are scragged in Clinton Street, another Harlem guy is found done up in a sack like a Virginia ham near Prospect Park, and now who is it but Joe the Joker's brother, Freddy, and I know Joe is going to be greatly displeased by this.

By and by it gets so nobody in Brooklyn will open as much as a sack of potatoes without first calling in the gendarmes, for fear a pair of No. 8 shoes will jump out at them.

Now one night I see Joe the Joker, and this time he is all alone, and I wish to say I am willing to leave him all alone, because something tells me he is hotter than a stove. But he grabs me as I am going past, so naturally I stop to talk to him, and the first thing I say is how sorry I am about his brother.

'Well,' Joe the Joker says, 'Freddy is always a kind of a sap. Rosa calls him up and asks him to come over to Brooklyn to see her. She wishes to talk to Freddy about getting me to give her a divorce,' Joe says, 'so she can marry Frankie Ferocious, I suppose. Anyway,' he says, 'Freddy tells Commodore Jake why he is going to see her. Freddy always likes Rosa, and thinks maybe he can patch it up between us. So,' Joe says, 'he winds up in a sack. They get him after he leaves her apartment. I do not claim Rosa will ask him to come over if she has any idea he will be sacked,' Joe says, 'but,' he says, 'she is responsible. She is a bad-luck doll.'

Then he starts to laugh, and at first I am greatly horrified, thinking it is because something about Freddy being sacked strikes his sense of humour, when he says to me, like this:

'Say,' he says, 'I am going to play a wonderful joke on Frankie Ferocious.'

'Well, Joe,' I say, 'you are not asking me for advice, but I am going to give you some free, gratis, and for nothing. Do not play any jokes on Frankie Ferocious, as I hear he has no more sense of humour than a nanny goat. I hear Frankie Ferocious will not laugh if you have Al Jolson, Eddie Cantor, Ed Wynn and Joe Cook telling him jokes all at once. In fact,' I say, 'I hear he is a tough audience.'

'Oh,' Joe the Joker says, 'he must have some sense of humour somewhere to stand for Rosa. I hear he is daffy about her. In fact, I understand she is the only person in the world he really likes, and trusts. But I must play a joke on him. I am going to have myself delivered to Frankie Ferocious in a sack.'

Well, of course I have to laugh at this myself, and Joe the Joker laughs with me. Personally, I am laughing just at the idea of anybody having themselves delivered to Frankie Ferocious in a sack, and especially Joe the Joker, but of course I have no idea Joe really means what he says.

'Listen,' Joe says, finally. 'A guy from St Louis who is a friend of mine is doing most of the sacking for Frankie Ferocious. His name is Ropes McGonnigle. In fact,' Joe says, 'he is a very dear old pal of mine, and he has a wonderful sense of humour like me. Ropes McGonnigle has nothing whatever to do with sacking Freddy,' Joe says, 'and he is very indignant about it since he finds out Freddy is my brother, so he is anxious to help me play a joke on Frankie.

'Only last night,' Joe says, 'Frankie Ferocious sends for Ropes and tells him he will appreciate it as a special favour if Ropes will bring me to him in a sack. I suppose,' Joe says, 'that Frankie Ferocious hears from Rosa what Freddy is bound to tell her about my ideas on divorce. I have very strict ideas on divorce,' Joe says, 'especially where Rosa is concerned. I will see her in what's-this before I ever do her and Frankie Ferocious such a favour as giving her a divorce.

'Anyway,' Joe the Joker says, 'Ropes tells me about Frankie Ferocious propositioning him, so I send Ropes back to Frankie Ferocious to tell him he knows I am to be in Brooklyn to-morrow night, and furthermore, Ropes tells Frankie that he will have me in a sack in no time. And so he will,' Joe says.

'Well,' I say, 'personally, I see no percentage in being delivered to Frankie Ferocious in a sack, because as near as I can make out from what I read in the papers, there is no future for a guy in a sack that goes to Frankie Ferocious. What I cannot figure out,' I say, 'is where the joke on Frankie comes in.'

'Why,' Joe the Joker says, 'the joke is, I will not be asleep in the sack, and my hands will not be tied, and in each of my hands I will have a John Roscoe, so when the sack is delivered to Frankie Ferocious and I pop out blasting away, can you not imagine his astonishment?'

Well, I can imagine this, all right. In fact when I get to thinking of the look of surprise that is bound to come to Frankie Ferocious's face when Joe the Joker comes out of the sack I have to laugh, and Joe the Joker laughs right along with me.

'Of course,' Joe says, 'Ropes McGonnigle will be there to start blasting with me, in case Frankie Ferocious happens to have any company.'

Then Joe the Joker goes on up the street, leaving me still laughing, from thinking of how amazed Frankie Ferocious will be when Joe bounces out of the sack and starts throwing slugs around and about. I do not hear of Joe from that time to this, but I hear the rest of the story from very reliable parties.

It seems that Ropes McGonnigle does not deliver the sack himself, after all, but sends it by an expressman to Frankie Ferocious's home. Frankie Ferocious received many sacks such as this in his time, because it seems that it is a sort of passion with him to personally view the contents of the sacks and check up on them before they are distributed about the city, and of course Ropes McGonnigle knows about this passion from doing so much sacking for Frankie.

When the expressman takes the sack into Frankie's house, Frankie personally lugs it down into the basement, and there he outs with a big John Roscoe and fires six shots into the sack, because it seems Ropes McGonnigle tips him off to Joe the Joker's plan to pop out of the sack and start blasting

I hear Frankie Ferocious has a very strange expression on his pan and is laughing the only laugh anybody ever hears from him when the gendarmes break in and put the arm on him for murder, because it seems that when Ropes McGonnigle tells Frankie of Joe the Joker's plan, Frankie tells Ropes what he is going to do with his own hands before opening the sack. Naturally, Ropes speaks to Joe the Joker of Frankie's idea about filling the sack full of slugs, and Joe's sense of humour comes right out again.

So, bound and gagged, but otherwise as right as rain in the sack that is delivered to Frankie Ferocious, is by no means Joe the Joker, but Rosa.

Identity Crisis

MICHAEL FRAYN

'THIS IS MR Goldwasser, Your Majesty,' said Riddle, as
Nobbs shook hands with Haugh.

'No, no, no,' smiled Mrs Plushkov with exasperating
patience. 'That's not Goldwasser, Riddle. That's Riddle.'

'For crying out loud,' snarled Riddle. 'He *can't* be.
Goldwasser's Riddle.'

'But my dear Riddle, you forget that Riddle is Plushkov.'

Everyone was standing in the lobby, glaring at each
other, or leaning hopelessly against the walls and staring
dully at the floor. The whole staff of the Institute was tired
and cross. They had been in the corridors all week,
rehearsing for the Official Opening, and they all had that
dreary, crushed feeling in their intestines that comes from
standing around for a long time without knowing exactly
what one is supposed to be doing.

What they were trying to do was to time the various
sections of the visit against a stop-watch, since the Co-
ordinating Committee was advised by the Sub-Committee
on Timing that these occasions always had to be rehearsed

down to the last second. But it was not easy. The 'Balmoral' scissors, the jewelled switch, the gas-fired golden taper, and all the rest of the equipment had not yet arrived from the Empire Ceremonial Supply Company, and there was still no apparatus of any sort in the new wing itself. The missing links were replaced by a variety of more or less unsatisfactory substitutes and hypotheses, as were all the official guests whose hands would have to be shaken on the day, and one or two of the senior staff, like Nunn and Macintosh, who were impressive enough not to be argued with when they said they were too busy to attend. So, for the sake of rehearsals, Rowe was Vulgurian, Riddle was Nunn, and Goldwasser was Macintosh, which meant that Plushkov had to be Riddle and Haugh Goldwasser. No, Riddle had to be Goldwasser, and . . . or was it Rowe who was Goldwasser?

The only point on which everyone was clear was that the principle deficiency, the Queen herself, was being supplied by Nobbs. He was not an ideal surrogate sovereign, or even a willing one, but when the Joint Committee for Understudying had appealed to Heads of Departments to spare someone for the job, Goldwasser had spared Nobbs before anyone else could think.

Now Goldwasser was regretting his generosity. It was bad enough to have Nobbs about the laboratory all day, humping his resentful bag of ill-articulated bones back and forth, catching the corners of desks with his thighs and knocking them slightly out of line. But to spend his days shaking Nobbs's limp hand over and over again, and calling him 'Ma'am', was less agreeable still. As the rehearsals wore on, Goldwasser became increasingly concerned about the hand's remarkable limpness. So far as Goldwasser could tell, it was not exactly a natural limpness. Nobbs kept his hand limp when he shook hands because he had read that the firm grasp he had affected as an adolescent to create the impression of strong character was merely an affectation designed to create the impression of a strong character. But then Nobbs wore a beard because he had read that since it was generally believed that only men with weak chins wore beards, no one with a weak chin would wear a beard for fear of being thought to have a weak chin; therefore, it could be deduced that anyone who wore a beard had in fact a strong chin; and in this way Nobbs grew a beard to hide his weak chin. Or so Goldwasser believed. Altogether there was something about Nobbs that was two-faced—or not so much two-faced as three-faced, with one face watching the other two.

'Let's go right back to the beginning,' said Mrs Plushkov. 'Opening positions, please, everyone.'

There was a weary groan. Goldwasser felt his crushed intestines pack down a little farther.

'Jellicoe,' said Mrs Plushkov to the janitor as they all trooped outside into the forecourt, 'don't slam the car door this time until Nobbs is well clear of it. Remember, you've got seven seconds before she—he—Nobbs is supposed to be on his feet on the pavement. Now, is One ready? Let's take it from—*now.*'

Jellicoe stepped forward and opened an imaginary car door. Nobbs lurched out of the imaginary car.

'Steady, Nobbs,' said Mrs Plushkov.

'Good afternoon,' said Chiddingfold, and led Nobbs across to the guard of honour of laboratory technicians.

'Stop!' cried Mrs Plushkov.

There was a general sigh. Jellicoe took out a pocket mirror and began to examine his moustache. Nobbs sat down on the edge of the pavement. Goldwasser tried to shuffle part of his weight on to a narrow ornamental ledge. He knew what the delay was. The Conversation Committee had gone into emergency session yet again. They would be discussing whether Chiddingfold should be asked to elaborate his greeting with a few conversational remarks. There was a faction which favoured the Director's making some comment on the weather. There was another faction which felt that any comment on the weather would present difficulties in timing, since the exact text could not be decided upon until the day, and that some remark about the royal car would be preferable. 'How many miles to the gallon do you get out of her, ma'am?' was thought to be the most generally acceptable. But finally the committee would face up to the impossibility of putting any of this to Chiddingfold, and would vote to postpone a decision until the next meeting. Goldwasser gazed hopelessly at a patch of ground about one foot square just in front of his shoes.

'Let's go on again, please,' cried Mrs Plushkov. 'From where we stopped.'

Nobbs shambled across to the guard of honour of laboratory technicians.

'For inspection,' shouted the Senior Laboratory Technician, 'port—slide rules!'

'Up, two, three,' called Mrs Plushkov. 'In, two, three. Ragged, very ragged.'

Nobbs barged along the ranks, treading on the right marker's toe, and knocking another man's slide rule out of his hands.

'Steady, Nobbs,' said Mrs Plushkov.

'Ease—cursors!' shouted the Senior Laboratory Technician.

'Three seconds under,' said Mrs Plushkov. 'You were cutting the corners, Nobbs.'

Nobbs lumbered across to the foot of the steps, received a bouquet from Chiddingfold's small daughter, deputized for by Miss Fram, and reeled on into the lobby to meet the assembled staff and guests.

'Stop!' cried Mrs Plushkov. 'Nomenclature Committee around me, please!'

Goldwasser subsided weakly against a wall. The Nomenclature Committeee was his fault. In a light-hearted moment one day he had suggested that calling Nobbs 'Your Majesty' might strictly speaking constitute an act of sedition, and within two days the question was being urgently debated throughout the thirty-seven committees. Almost everyone agreed that a seditious interpretation could be put upon the usage, and that to continue using it might open the Institute to the possibility of prosecution or blackmail. But the practical problem was what to call Nobbs if not Her Majesty. It would be ridiculous, everyone said, to expect people to bow and curtsy to him and call him Nobbs. The original smile had scarcely faded from Goldwasser's face before the Nomenclature Committee had been set up, to compose a formula which would both command respect and correspond more closely to the realities of Nobbs's situation. Various working parties and study groups had so far produced:

Your Humility
Your Servitude
Your Ordinariness
Your Humanity
Your Anonymity
Your Proxyship
Your Beardedness
Your Nobbs
Your Principal Research Assistantship

Once more, Goldwasser knew, the decision would have to be postponed.

'Carry on from where we were,' shouted Mrs Plushkov. 'Go on calling Nobbs "Your Majesty" for to-day. Let me once again ask everyone to use his discretion, and not to talk about this outside the Institute.'

Hands were shaken, at five seconds per hand, then off went everyone on the tour of the establishment, at two feet per second. Into a department. Meet typical Research Assistant (Grade One) and look at typical computer (12 seconds). Ask typical question about computer (say, 5 seconds). Get typical answer (15 seconds). Express appreciation of work done (say, 4 seconds).

On down corridor, at two feet per second, up stairs at two seconds per stair, and into next department. Meet typical Research Assistant (Grade Two) and ask typical personal question (say, 10 seconds). Get typically modest answer (1 second). Comment on pleasantness of view out of window (say, 5 seconds). Deputy-Director explains how fortunate Institute is in this respect (31 seconds). Adds polite joke (3 seconds). Laughter (26 seconds). Public amazement at how informal and charming Nobbs is (4 seconds). Out, striking ill-articulated Nobbs thigh against table and bringing down three files, a bottle of ink, and 140 loose sheets of foolscap manuscript. Recriminations all round (20 minutes).

For Goldwasser the afternoon began to go by in a dream. It was interrupted momentarily when he was caught a sharp blow on the side of the head with a window-pole which was being used as a substitute for the golden taper to light a flame of undying remembrance to those who fell in the Luddite riots. At another point he was conscious of a limp hand being thrust authoritatively into his, and a well-known voice saying 'Wakey wakey, mate.' And there were a few moments of wonderful sitting down when the Special Purposes Committee met to consider once again whether time should be allowed for Nobbs to powder his nose.

Then they were in the new wing, and Rowe, deputizing for Macintosh, was showing Nobbs all the equipment so far installed, which consisted of several office tables and a number of chairs. Almost the last thing Goldwasser was conscious of was Rowe reading off a piece of paper:

'And this is a table, ma'am. What in essence it consists of is a horizontal rectilinear plane surface maintained by four vertical columnar supports, which we call legs. The tables in the laboratory, ma'am, are as advanced in design as one will find anywhere in the world.'

Which was how, when everybody else was standing up for the National Anthem, Goldwasser came to be lying on the floor, sprawling face downwards with great casualness. Nunn, who was keeping an eye on various security aspects from a discreet distance, was not surprised. The case against Goldwasser was open and closed already; he would be in no position to demonstrate his feelings about the National Anthem on the day.

What Nunn was really worrying about now was Nobbs's

thighs. The more he saw of them in action the less he liked them. Were they a secret weapon in the pay of Goldwasser? They didn't appear to be in the pay of Nobbs. He watched them intently as they knocked things off desks and split chairs they came up against. They appeared to pursue their programme of sabotage and disruption quite independently of Nobbs.

Of course, they might be *unconscious* agents of Goldwasser's. It was possible that Nobbs had been brainwashed by Goldwasser without knowing about it. But then so might anyone else in the room. Such things could happen. Nobody who was in security was likely to underestimate what could be done these days with brainwashing techniques. For all Nunn knew, he might have been brainwashed himself. He might well be an unconscious agent of Goldwasser's. His whole campaign against Goldwasser might be the result of a post-hypnotic suggestion implanted by Goldwasser himself. Indeed, his very realization that he might be acting under Gold-wasser's orders, even as Goldwasser took his ease down there on the floor, might itself be a response engineered by Goldwasser.

As soon as the anthem was over he retired to his room and brooded for a long time over a favourite niblick. These were deep waters he was fishing, and in deep waters, there was nothing to do but keep one's eye on the ball and wait for an opening. He took a nap to clear his head and was awakened, greatly refreshed, by the sound of the Director collapsing heavily into his chair in the office next door after finishing the day's rehearsals. The Director, when he went in to see him, looked surprisingly old and tired, and Nunn spent nearly an hour trying to cheer him up by telling him the full medical histories of everyone who had dropped dead while running the marathon.

Here We Go Again

ARTHUR MARSHALL

FOREIGN VISITORS TO our shores, no longer a purely seasonal phenomenon but, like cucumbers and globe artichokes and pineapples, now so fully available on every day of the year that one sometimes tires of them, find themselves faced in London by various perplexities. For example, there is the fact, to which the permanent residents are now sadly accustomed, that the most popular numbered motor buses travel along, at half-hourly intervals, in a communally self-protective pack like wildebeests, nose to tail in clutches of five (I once saw eight No 14s, queen of buses, jammed together in Shaftesbury Avenue at 2.25 p.m., but perhaps they were returning from a reunion lunch at a chic Soho pizza parlour, or were on their way to a matinée). There is also the fact that, unless humans open their mouths to speak, it is no longer possible to tell, from the clothes they are wearing, which person is what. A camouflage of general subfusc and dirty-jeaned drabness covers everybody and we merge into the background. The French, tremendous snobs despite that rather showy and ostentatious Revolution, are for ever peering about for *les milords anglais* whom they still imagine to be bowling along in their Rolls and shrieking insults ('Cow!' 'Villain!') at the chauffeur down a gold-plated speaking-tube, little realizing that that shifty, down-at-heels creature beside them in the bus queue is either a *milord* or just a lord, off to pocket his daily attendance fee at the House.

Then there is the question of surnames. Although brought up in their foreign schools and led, in their English language lessons, to think that every other British person is called either Smith or Brown ('*Que fait Madame Smith?*' 'She is steaming her pudding.' '*Was macht Frau Brown?*' 'She is making jokes and laughing "Ho ho" '), the evidence of their eyes on hoardings and walls, on the backs of bus seats and chalked on pavements, tells them otherwise. I am speaking, of course, of the extensive Wanks family, ever anxious to leave behind them proof that they, or one of their close friends, has been present. On entering an underground station, it is in no way surprising to see, scratched up in the passage-way that leads trackwards, the proud names of Les Wanks, Stan Wanks and Rod Wanks. Sometimes just initials are used—P. H. Wanks, N. R. Wanks. Occasionally there is a generous measure of admiration and praise for the entire, and predominately male, family ('There's nothing like a few good Wanks'). Once again, the poor Frogs find themselves baffled ('*Qui sont ces Wanks?*'). The bearers of this name are, I incline to think, not from the upper-crust and they tend to favour shortened Christian names with rather a lower-crust lilt to them—Len, Perce, Sid. I have yet to see any mention of Peregrine Wanks, Jocelyn Wanks or Osbert Wanks. Perhaps I don't go to the right walls.

There is one perplexity which will not at once offer itself as such to foreign visitors. To be aware of it one needs to have been frequently resident in the capital. It concerns pigeons. In the thousands of miles that I have walked and hours that I have spent and years that I have lived in

London, I have never once seen a *dead* pigeon, apart from those served up on a plate, partly disguised by *les légumes* and masquerading as *poulet*, in wartime restaurants. But among the millions of pigeons that exist in London, many thousands must daily die. Where, then, do they do it? Certainly not on streets or pavements, nor do they come plopping lifelessly out of the sky onto one's nut. Have they I wonder, like elephants, some secret, secluded haunt (screened-off section of the Mansion House roof? A disused ventilator shaft at what was dear old Pontings?) known to them all and to which, at the approach of the dread hour, they flap and, in messy roof-top confusion, turn up their pigeon toes? And what then, there being no vultures (none with wings, anyhow) hereabouts to tidy them up and pick the bones clean?

I peered about for dead pigeons (no dice) on my way through St James's Park, bound for St James's Palace to see, on view as I write, the representative display of gifts lavished on the Queen at her jolly Silver Jubilee. Well aware that many NS readers are territorially denied these treats, I bring from time to time, as you know, news of such matters, in this case in fuller detail than in a recent reference in these pages and for those who missed BBC-2's guided tour. Here again are perplexities galore for foreigners (the queue was stiff with them) who, from some of the gifts, will form a very odd view of Her Majesty's activities. What, for example, does she get up to with a necklace made of teeth, a cowhide (which I take to be the outside of a dead cow rather than a nature-lover's foliage-bedecked Wendyhouse from which secretly to observe cows), and a membership badge of a Welsh Trampoline Club (can there be a Palace rumpus-room with the sovereign bouncing healthfully up and down?). Then what can overseas visitors, not to speak of ourselves or the recipient herself, possibly make of two miniature chairs fashioned from tin cans, a red, white and blue felt donkey, a tinsel sash, an 18th-century pewter syringe ('This may

hurt you a little'), a carving of two Maoris kissing and a
large sago pot?

Members of the royal family clearly have little time for
reading, even if their inclinations actually led that way, and
therefore, as the donors obviously realized, almost any
book comes as a delightful novelty. One can picture the
unfamiliar objects being passed excitedly from hand to
hand at breakfast, and striking passages read out. Certain
of the volumes presented lend themselves admirably to
this treatment—*History of Sidcup Cricket Club, Caring for Textiles*
and *East Gwilliambury in the 19th Century*. Purely visual
pleasures have not been neglected and photographs and
paintings have come pouring in. During that spare five
minutes before the next Ambassador presents his
credentials (and whatever can they be? Do they ever forget
them? '*Where* are your credentials?'), Her Majesty can feast
her eyes on Sherwood Forest, an oil platform, the
Ilfracombe Corps of Drums, Stockton-on-Tees, 'a picture
of two people reading *The Times*' and Queen Victoria done
in needlework.

One item I at first found very worrying, 'a Greetings
telegram in stainless steel'. Could this be some new Post
Office wheeze to bump up the already outrageous price
('We also have them in burnished gold'), or a clever method
of preventing them being blown away at the front door as
you sign for them, in which case telegrams made of lead
might be even better? However, I now see that this
extremely unusual gift comes from the Lord Mayor and
Citizens of Sheffield, clearly advertising home products.
Another item that I don't quite follow comes from
Members of the Diplomatic Corps, who decided to hand
over 'a dinner table' (something to put that sago pot on at
last). How has the Queen been managing hitherto, one
wonders? Plastic telly-trays perched on her knees? Indeed,
there are indications, that when donors decide to club
together, they rather lose their heads—the people of
Newfoundland (a book containing 300,000 signatures), the

Shell Co. Ltd. (snaps of fireworks), the California Historical Society ('a printed resolution').

What anxious discussions as to a suitable present went on, I ask myself, in the Vatican? I was once in St Peter's Square on Easter Day and got blessed, along with a million others, by the Pope. He appeared to us high up at a very non-grand window that looked to belong to a housemaid's bedroom. One almost expected to see long black stockings hanging out to dry. It was a pleasing little ceremony and one that our Archbishop, the clergy being so woefully uncolourful, might well copy from some attic window in Lambeth Palace. His Holiness seemed a delightfully simple, modest personality and his gift to the Queen is in keeping with it. Just a bible: and a secondhand one at that.

Suicide

PHILIP ROTH

I AM REMINDED at this joyous little juncture of when we lived in Jersey City, back when I was still very much my mother's papoose, still very much a sniffer of her body perfumes and a total slave to her *kugel* and *grieben* and *ruggelech*—there was a suicide in our building. A fifteen-year-old boy named Ronald Nimkin, who had been crowned by the women in the building 'José Iturbi the Second' hanged himself from the shower head in his bathroom. 'With those golden hands!' the women wailed, referring of course to his piano playing—'With that talent!' Followed by, 'You couldn't look for a boy more in love with his mother than Ronald!'

I swear to you, this is not bullshit or a screen memory, these are the very words these women use. The great dark operatic themes of human suffering and passion come rolling out of those mouths like the prices of Oxydol and Del Monte canned corn! My own mother, let me remind you, when I returned this past summer from my adventure in Europe, greets me over the phone with the following

salutation: 'Well, how's my lover?' Her *lover* she calls me,
while her husband is listening on the other extension! And it
never occurs to her, if I'm her lover, who is he, the
schmegeggy she lives with? No, you don't have to go digging
where these people are concerned—they wear the old
unconscious on their *sleeves*!

Mrs Nimkin, weeping in our kitchen: 'Why? Why? Why
did he do this to us?' Hear? Not what might *we* have done to
him, oh no, never that—why did he do this *to us*? To us! Who
would have given our arms and legs to make him happy and
a famous concert pianist into the bargain! Really, can they
be this blind? Can people be so abysmally stupid and live?
Do you *believe* it? Can they actually be equipped with all the
machinery, a brain, a spinal cord, and the four apertures for
the ears and eyes—equipment, Mrs Nimkin, nearly as
impressive as color TV—and still go through life without a
single clue about the feelings and yearnings of anyone
other than themselves? Mrs Nimkin, you shit, I remember
you, I was only six, but I remember you, and what killed
your Ronald, the concert-pianist-to-be is obvious: YOUR
FUCKING SELFISHNESS AND STUPIDITY! 'All the lessons we
gave him,' weeps Mrs Nimkin . . . Oh look, look, why do I
carry on like this? Maybe she means well, surely she
must—at a time of grief, what can I expect of these simple
people? It's only because in her misery she doesn't know
what else to say that she says that God-awful thing about
all the lessons they gave to somebody who is now a corpse.
What are they, after all, these Jewish women who raised us
up as children? In Calabria you see their suffering
counterparts sitting like stones in the churches, swallow-
ing all that hideous Catholic bullshit; in Calcutta they beg
in the streets, or if they are lucky, are off somewhere in a
dusty field hitched up to a plow . . . Only in America, Rabbi
Golden, do these peasants, our mothers, get their hair dyed
platinum at the age of sixty, and walk up and down Collins
Avenue in Florida in pedalpushers and mink stoles— and
with opinions on every subject under the sun. It isn't their
fault they were given a gift like speech—look, if cows could

talk, they would say things just as idiotic. Yes, yes, maybe that's the solution then: think of them as cows, who have been given the twin miracles of speech and mah-jongg. Why not be charitable in one's thinking, right, Doctor?

My favorite detail from the Ronald Nimkin suicide: even as he is swinging from the shower head, there is a note pinned to the dead young pianist's short-sleeved shirt—which is what I remember most about Ronald: this tall emaciated teen-age catatonic, swimming around all by himself in those oversized short-sleeved sport shirts, and with their lapels starched and ironed back so fiercely they looked to have been bulletproofed . . . And Ronald himself, every limb strung so tight to his backbone that if you touched him, he would probably have begun to hum . . . and the fingers, of course, those long white grotesqueries, seven knuckles at least before you got down to the nicely gnawed nail, those Bela Lugosi hands that my mother would tell me—and tell me—*and tell me*—because nothing is ever said once—nothing!—were 'the hands of a born pianist'.

Pianist! Oh, that's one of the words they just love, almost as much as *doctor*, Doctor. And *residency*. And best of all, *his own office. He opened his own office in Livingston.* 'Do you remember Seymour Schmuck, Alex?' she asks me, or Aaron Putz or Howard Shlong, or some yo-yo I am supposed to have known in grade school twenty-five years ago, and of whom I have no recollection whatsoever. 'Well, I met his mother on the street today, and she told me that Seymour is now the biggest brain surgeon in the entire Western Hemisphere. He owns six different split-level ranch-type houses made all of fieldstone in Livingston, and belongs to the boards of eleven synagogues, all brand-new and designed by Marc Kugel, and last year with his wife and his two little daughters, who are so beautiful that they are already under contract to Metro, and so brilliant that they should be in college—he took them all to Europe for an eighty-million-dollar tour of seven thousand countries, some of them you never even heard of, that they made them just to honor Seymour, and on top of that, he's so important, Seymour, that in every single city in Europe that they visited he was asked by the mayor himself to stop and do an impossible operation on a brain in hospitals that they also built for him right on the spot, and—listen to this—where they pumped into the operating room during the operation the theme song from *Exodus* so everybody should know what religion he is—and that's how big your friend Seymour is to-day! *And how happy he makes his parents!'*

And you, the implication is, when are *you* going to get married already? In Newark and the surrounding suburbs this apparently is the question on everybody's lips: WHEN IS ALEXANDER PORTNOY GOING TO STOP BEING SELFISH AND GIVE HIS PARENTS, WHO ARE SUCH WONDERFUL PEOPLE, GRANDCHILDREN? 'Well,' says my father, the tears brimming up in his eyes, 'well,' he asks, *every single time I see him,* 'is there a serious girl in the picture, Big Shot? Excuse me for asking, I'm only your father, but since I'm not going to be alive forever, and you in case you forgot carry the family name, I wonder if maybe you could let me in on the secret.'

Yes, shame, shame, on Alex P., the only member of his graduating class who hasn't made grandparents of his Mommy and his Daddy. While everybody else has been marrying nice Jewish girls, and having children, and buying houses, and (my father's phrase) *putting down roots,* while all the other sons have been carrying forward the family name, what he has been doing is—chasing cunt. And *shikse* cunt, to boot! Chasing it, sniffing it, lapping it, *shtupping* it, but above all, *thinking about it.* Day and night, at work and on the street—thirty-three years old and still he is roaming the streets with his eyes popping. A wonder he hasn't been ground to mush by a taxicab, given how he makes his way across the major arteries of Manhattan during the lunch hour. Thirty-three, and still ogling and daydreaming about every girl who crosses her legs opposite him in the subway! Still cursing himself for speaking not a word to the succulent pair of tits that rode twenty-five floors alone with him in an elevator! Then cursing himself for the opposite as well! For he has been known to walk up to thoroughly respectable-looking girls in the street, and despite the fact that since his appearance on Sunday morning TV his face is not entirely unknown to an enlightened segment of the public—despite the fact that he may be on his way to his current mistress' apartment for his dinner—he has been known on one or two occasions to mutter, 'Look, would you like to come home with me?' *Of course* she is going to say 'No.' Of course she is going to scream, 'Get out of here, you!' or answer curtly, 'I have a nice home of my own, thank you, with a husband in it.' What is he doing to himself, this fool! this idiot! this furtive *boy*! This sex maniac! He simply cannot—*will* not—control the fires in his putz, the fevers in his brain, the desire continually burning within for the new, the wild, the unthought-of, and, if you can imagine such a thing, *the undreamt-of.* Where cunt is concerned he lives in a condition that has neither diminished nor in any significant way been refined from what it was when he was fifteen years old and could not get up from his seat in the classroom without hiding a hard-on beneath his three-ring notebook. Every girl he sees turns out (hold your hats) to be carrying around between her legs—a real cunt. Amazing! Astonishing! Still can't get over the fantastic idea that when you are looking at a girl, you are looking at somebody who is guaranteed to have on her—a cunt! *They all have cunts!* Right under their dresses! Cunts—for fucking! And, Doctor, Your Honor, whatever your name is—it seems to make no difference how much the poor bastard actually gets, for he is dreaming about tomorrow's pussy even while pumping away at today's!

Do I exaggerate? Am I doing myself in only as a clever way of showing off? Or boasting perhaps? Do I really experience this restlessness, this horniness, as an affliction—or as an accomplishment? Both? Could be. Or is it only a means of evasion? Look, at least I don't find myself still in my early thirties locked into a marriage with some

nice person whose body has ceased to be of any genuine
interest to me—at least I don't have to get into bed every
night with somebody who by and large I fuck out of
obligation instead of lust. I mean, the nightmarish
depression some people suffer at bedtime . . . On the other
hand, even I must admit that there is maybe, from a certain
perspective, something a little depressing about my
situation, too. Of course you can't have everything, or so I
understand—but the question I am willing to face is: have I
anything? How much longer do I go on conducting these
experiments with women? How much longer do I go on
sticking this thing into the holes that come available to
it—first this hole, then when I tire of this hole, that hole
over there . . . and so on. When will it end? Only *why*
should it end! To please a father and mother? To conform
to the norm? Why on earth should I be so defensive about
being what was honorably called some years ago, a
bachelor? After all, that's all this is, you know—bachelor-
hood. So what's the crime? Sexual freedom? In this day and
age? Why should *I* bend to the bourgeoisie? Do I ask them
to bend to me? Maybe I've been touched by the tarbrush of
Bohemia a little—is that so awful? Whom am I harming
with my lusts? I don't blackjack the ladies, I don't twist
arms to get them into bed with me. I am, if I may say so, an
honest and compassionate man; let me tell you, as men go I
am . . . But why must I explain myself! *Excuse* myself! Why
must I justify with my Honesty and Compassion my
desires! So I have desires—only they're endless. Endless!
And that, that may not be such a blessing, taking for the
moment a psychoanalytic point of view . . . But then all the
unconscious can do anyway, so Freud tells us, is *want. And
want! And* WANT! Oh, Freud, do I know! This one has a nice
ass, but she talks too much. On the other hand, this one
here doesn't talk at all, at least not so that she makes any
sense—but, boy, can she suck! What cock know-how!
While here is a honey of a girl, with the softest, pinkest,
most touching nipples I have ever drawn between my lips,
only she won't go down on me. Isn't that odd? And yet—go

understand people—it is her pleasure while being boffed to have one or the other of my forefingers lodged snugly up her anus. What a mysterious business it is! The endless fascination of these apertures and openings! You see, I just can't stop! Or tie myself to any *one*. I have affairs that last as long as a year, a year and a half, months and months of love, both tender and voluptuous, but in the end—it is as inevitable as death—time marches on and lust peters out. In the end, I just cannot take that step into marriage. But why should I? *Why?* Is there a law saying Alex Portnoy has to be somebody's husband and father? Doctor, they can stand on the window ledge and threaten to splatter themselves on the pavement below, they can pile the Seconal to the ceiling—I may have to live for weeks and weeks on end in terror of these marriage-bent girls throwing themselves beneath the subway train, but I simply cannot, I simply *will* not, enter into a contract to sleep with just one woman for the rest of my days. Imagine it: suppose I were to go ahead and marry A, with her sweet tits and so on, what will happen when B appears, whose are even sweeter—or, at any rate, newer? Or C, who knows how to move her ass in some special way I have never experienced; or D, or E, or F. I'm trying to be honest with you, Doctor—because with sex the human imagination runs to Z, and then beyond! Tits and cunts and legs and lips and mouths and tongues and assholes! How can I give up what I have never even had, for a girl, who delicious and provocative as once she may have been, will inevitably grow as familiar to me as a loaf of bread? For love? What love? Is that what binds all these couples we know together—the ones who even bother to let themselves be bound? Isn't it something more like weakness? Isn't it rather convenience and apathy and guilt? Isn't it rather fear and exhaustion and inertia, gutlessness plain and simple, far far more than that 'love' that the marriage counselors and the songwriters and the psychotherapists are forever dreaming about? Please, let us not bullshit one another about 'love' and its duration. Which is why I ask:

how can I marry someone I 'love' knowing full well that
five, six, seven years hence I am going to be out on the
streets hunting down the fresh new pussy—all the while
my devoted wife, who has made me such a lovely home, et
cetera, bravely suffers her loneliness and rejection? How
could I face her terrible tears? I couldn't. How could I face
my adoring children? And then the divorce, right? The *child*
support. The *alimony*. The *visitation* rights. Wonderful
prospect, just wonderful. And as for anybody who kills
herself because I prefer not to be blind to the future, well,
she is her worry—she has to be! There is surely no need or
justification for anybody to threaten suicide just because I
am wise enough to see what frustrations and recriminations lie ahead . . . Baby, please, don't howl like that
please—somebody is going to think you're being strangled
to death. Oh baby (I hear myself pleading, last year, this
year, every year of my life!), you're going to be all right,
really, truly you are; you're going to be just fine and dandy
and much better off, so please, you bitch come back inside
this room *and let me go*! 'You! You and your filthy cock!' cries
the most recently disappointed (and self-appointed) bride-
to-be, my strange, lanky, and very batty friend, who used
to earn as much in an hour posing for underwear ads as her
illiterate father would earn in a week in the coal mines of
West Virginia: 'I thought you were supposed to be a
superior person, you muff-diving, mother-fucking son of a
bitch!' This beautiful girl, who has got me all wrong, is
called The Monkey, a nickname that derives from a little
perversion she once engaged in shortly before meeting me
and going on to grander things. Doctor, I had never had
anybody like her in my life, she was the fulfillment of my
most lascivious adolescent dreams—but marry her, can she
be serious? You see, for all her preening and perfumes, she
has a low opinion of herself, and simultaneously—and here
is the source of much of our trouble—a ridiculously high
opinion of me. And simultaneously, a very *low* opinion of
me! She is one confused Monkey, and, I'm afraid, not too
very bright. 'An intellectual!' she screams. 'An educated,

spiritual person! You mean, miserable hard-on you, you care more about the niggers in Harlem that you don't even know, than you do about me, who's been sucking you off for a solid year!' Confused, heartbroken, and also out of her mind. For all this comes to me from the balcony of our hotel room in Athens, as I stand in the doorway, suitcases in hand, begging her to *please* come back inside so that I can catch a plane out of that place. Then the angry little manager, all olive oil, mustache, and outraged respectability, is running up the staircase waving his arms in the air—and so, taking a deep breath, I say, 'Look, you want to jump, jump!' and out I go—and the last words I hear have to do with the fact that it was only out of love for me ('*Love!*' she screams) that she allowed herself to do the degrading things I forced quote unquote upon her.

Which is not the case, Doctor! Not the case at all! Which is an attempt on this sly bitch's part to break me on the rack of guilt—and thus get herself a husband. Because at twenty-nine that's what she wants, you see—but that does not mean, you see, that I have to oblige. 'In September, you son of a bitch, I am going to be thirty years old!' Correct Monkey, correct! Which is precisely why it is you and not me who is responsible for your expectations and your dreams! Is that clear? *You!* 'I'll tell the world about you, you cold-hearted prick! I'll tell them what a filthy pervert you are, and the dirty things you made me do!'

The cunt! I'm lucky really that I came out of that affair *alive*. If I have!

Earth to Earth

YES, YES AND yes! Don't get me wrong, for goodness' sake. I
am heart and soul with you. I agree that Man is wickedly
defrauding the Earth-Mother of her ancient dues by not
putting back into the soil as much nourishment as he takes
out. And that modern plumbing is, if you like, a running
sore in the body politic. And that municipal incinerators are
genocidal rather than germicidal . . . And that cremation
should be made a capital crime. And that dust bowls created
by the greedy plough . . .

. . . Yes, yes and yes again. *But!*

Elsie and Roland Hedge—she a book-illustrator, he an
architect with suspect lungs—had been warned against Dr
Eugen Steinpilz. 'He'll bring you no luck,' I told them. 'My
little finger says so decisively.'

'You too?' asked Elsie indignantly. (This was at Brixham,
South Devon, in March 1940.) 'I suppose you think that
because of his foreign accent and his beard he must be a
spy?'

'No,' I said coldly, 'that point hadn't occurred to me. But I won't contradict you.'

The very next day Elsie deliberately picked a friendship—I don't like the phrase, but that's what she did—with the Doctor, an Alsatian with an American passport, who described himself as a *Naturphilosoph*; and both she and Roland were soon immersed in Steinpilzerei up to the nostrils. It began when he invited them to lunch and gave them cold meat and two rival sets of vegetable dishes—potatoes (baked), carrots (creamed), bought from the local fruiterer; and potatoes (baked) and carrots (creamed), grown on compost in his own garden.

The superiority of the latter over the former in appearance, size and especially flavour came as an eye-opener to Elsie and Roland. Yes, and yes, I know just how they felt. Why shouldn't I? When I visit the market here in Palma, I always refuse La Torre potatoes, because they are raised for the early English market and therefore reek of imported chemical fertilizer. Instead I buy Son Sardina potatoes, which taste as good as the ones we used to get in England fifty years ago. The reason is that the Son Sardina farmers manure their fields with Palma kitchen-refuse, still available by the cartload—this being too backward a city to afford effective modern methods of destroying it.

Thus Dr Steinpilz converted the childless and devoted couple to the Steinpilz method of composting. It did not, as a matter of fact, vary greatly from the methods you read about in the *Gardening Notes* of your favourite national newspaper, except that it was far more violent. Dr Steinpilz had invented a formula for producing extremely fierce bacteria, capable (Roland claimed) of breaking down an old boot or the family Bible or a torn woollen vest into beautiful black humus almost as you watched. The formula could not be bought, however, and might be communicated under oath of secrecy only to members of Eugen Steinpilz Fellowship—which I refused to join. I won't pretend therefore to know the formula myself, but one night I overheard Elsie and Roland arguing in their garden as to whether the planetary influences were favourable; and they also mentioned a ram's horn in which, it seems, a complicated mixture of triturated animal and vegetable products—technically called 'the Mother'—was to be cooked up. I gather also that a bull's foot and a goat's pancreas were part of the works, because Mr Pook the butcher afterwards told me that he had been puzzled by Roland's request for these unusual cuts. Milkwort and penny-royal and bee-orchid and vetch certainly figured among the Mother's herbal ingredients; I recognized these one day in a gardening basket Elsie had left at the post office.

The Hedges soon had their first compost heap cooking away in the garden, which was about the size of a tennis court and consisted mostly of well-kept lawn. Dr Steinpilz, who supervised, now began to haunt the cottage like the smell of drains; I had to give up calling on them. Then, after the Fall of France, Brixham became a war-zone whence everyone but we British and our Free French or Free Belgians allies were extruded. Consequently Dr Steinpilz had to leave; which he did with very bad grace, and was killed in a Liverpool air-raid the day before he should have sailed back to New York. But that was far from closing the ledger. I think Elsie must have been in love with the Doctor, and certainly Roland had a hero-worship for him. They treasured a signed collection of all his esoteric books, each called after a different semi-precious stone, and used to read them out aloud to each other at meals, in turns. Then to show that this was a practical philosophy, not just a random assemblage of beautiful thoughts about nature, they began composting in a deeper and even more religious way than before. The lawn had come up, of course; but they used the sods to sandwich layers of kitchen waste, which they mixed with the scrapings from an abandoned pigsty, two barrowfuls of sodden poplar leaves from the recreation ground, and a sack of rotten turnips. Looking over the hedge, I caught the fanatic gleam in Elsie's eye as she turned the hungry bacteria loose on the heap, and could not repress a premonitory shudder.

So far, not too bad, perhaps. But when serious bombing started and food became so scarce that housewives were fined for not making over their swill to the national pigs, Elsie and Roland grew worried. Having already abandoned their ordinary sanitary system and built an earth-closet in the garden, they now tried to convince neighbours of their duty to do the same, even at the risk of catching cold and getting spiders down the neck. Elsie also sent Roland after the slow-moving Red Devon cows as they lurched home along the lane at dusk, to rescue the precious droppings with a kitchen shovel; while she visited the local ash-dump with a packing case mounted on wheels, and collected whatever she found there of an organic nature—dead cats, old rags, withered flowers, cabbage stalks and such household waste as even a national wartime pig would have coughed at. She also saved every drop of their bath-water for sprinkling the heaps; because it contained, she said, valuable animal salts.

The test of a good compost heap, as every illuminate knows, is whether a certain revolting-looking, if beneficial, fungus sprouts from it. Elsie's heaps were grey with this crop, and so hot inside that they could be used for haybox cookery; which must have saved her a deal of fuel. I call them 'Elsie's heaps', because she now considered herself Dr Steinpilz's earthly delegate; and loyal Roland did not dispute this claim.

A critical stage in the story came during the Blitz. It will be remembered that trainloads of Londoners, who had been evacuated to South Devon when war broke out, thereafter de-evacuated and re-evacuated and re-de-evacuated themselves, from time to time, in a most disorganized fashion. Elsie and Roland, as it happened, escaped having evacuees billeted on them, because they had no spare bedroom; but one night an old naval pensioner came knocking at their door and demanded lodging for the night. Having been burned out of Plymouth, where everything was chaos, he had found

himself walking away and blundering along in a daze until
he fetched up here, hungry and dead-beat. They gave him a
meal and bedded him on the sofa; but when Elsie came
down in the morning to fork over the heaps, she found him
dead of heart-failure.

Roland broke a long silence by coming, in some
embarrassment, to ask my advice. Elsie, he said, had
decided that it would be wrong to trouble the police about
the case; because the police were so busy these days, and
the poor old fellow had claimed to possess neither kith nor
kin. So they'd read the burial service over him and, after
removing his belt-buckle, trouser buttons, metal spectacle-
case and a bunch of keys, which were irreducible, had laid
him reverently in the new compost heap. Its other
contents, he added, were a cartload of waste from the
cider-factory, salvaged cow-dung, and several basketfuls
of hedge clippings. Had they done wrong?

'If you mean "will I report you to the Civil Authorities?"
the answer is no,' I assured him. 'I wasn't looking over the
hedge at the relevant hour, and what you tell me is only
hearsay.' Roland shambled off satisfied.

The War went on. Not only did the Hedges convert the
whole garden into serried rows of Eugen Steinpilz
memorial heaps, leaving no room for planting the potatoes
or carrots to which the compost had been prospectively
devoted, but they scavenged the offal from the Brixham
fish-market and salvaged the contents of the bin outside
the surgical ward at the Cottage Hospital. Every spring, I
remember Elsie used to pick big bunches of primroses and
put them straight on the compost, without even a last
wistful sniff; virgin primroses were supposed to be
particularly relished by the fierce bacteria.

Here the story becomes a little painful for members, say,
of a family reading circle; I will soften it as much as possible.
One morning a policeman called on the Hedges with a
summons, and I happened to see Roland peep anxiously out
of the bedroom window, but quickly pull his head in again.
The policeman rang and knocked and waited, then tried the

back door; and presently went away. The summons was for a blackout offence, but apparently the Hedges did not know this. Next morning he called again, and when nobody answered, forced the lock of the back door. They were found dead in bed together having taken an overdose of sleeping tablets. A note on the coverlet ran simply:

> Please lay our bodies on the heap nearest the pigsty Flowers by request Strew some on the bodies, mixed with a little kitchen waste, and then fork the earth lightly over.
>
> E.H.; R.H.

George Irks, the new tenant, proposed to grow potatoes and dig for victory. He hired a cart and began throwing the compost into the River Dart, 'not liking the look of them toadstools', as he subsequently explained. The five beautifully clean human skeletons which George unearthed in the process were still awaiting identification when the War ended.

Red-blooded $^3/_4$rose

PAUL JENNINGS

THERE WAS ONCE an article in the *Observer* by Dr Bronowski in which he said that mathematics ought to be taught as a language. At the time I had fantasies of passages like this:

'It is time (the Government)^2 up to the situation. On $>$ 1 issue $\dfrac{\text{the country}}{2}$, and unless they treat the Opposition as = in hammering out a bipartisan policy they will not get to $\sqrt{\text{our troubles}}$. All the omens $\cdot$ 2 trouble in the Middle East . . .'*

But of course that wasn't the idea at all. Years ago I got off the mathematics train at Quadratic Equations—a neat, airy little station with trellis, ivy, roses, a sunlit platform. There was just a hint of weirdness now and then—the

---

* Crib for art students, beatniks, peasants:

(*The Government*)^2: *the Government squared.*

$>$ 1: *more than one.*

= : *equals.*

$\sqrt{\text{our troubles}}$: *the root of our troubles.*

$\cdot$ 2: *point two recurring.*

stationmaster made clicking noises in his throat, there was an occasional far-off harmonious humming in the sky, strange bells rang; one knew the frontier was not far away, where the line crosses into the vast country of Incomprehensibility, the jagged peaks of the Calculus Mountains standing up, a day's journey over its illimitable plains.

The train thundered off into those no doubt exhilarating spaces, but without me. I sniffed the mountainy air a little, then I crossed the line by the footbridge and went back in a fusty suburban train to my home town, Contemptible Ignorance. This train had no engine; it was simply a train of carriages rolling gently down through the warm orchards of Amnesia Hill.

The only language we speak in that town is, well, language (we're not *mad* about it like those people at Oxford; we know the world is infinite and real, language is about it, it isn't *it*). But we have got typewriters, and they introduce mathematics into language in their own way. Even without those figures on the top row, 1 to 9 (all you need) there is something *statistical* about the typewriter as it sits there. It contains instantaneously the entire alphabet, the awful pregnant potentiality of everything. I am certain most readers of this article will have read somewhere or other a reference to the odds against a monkey's sitting at a typewriter and writing *Hamlet*.

For some reason philosophical writers about chance, design and purpose are led irresistibly to this analogy. Nobody ever suggests the monkey's writing *Hamlet* with a pen, as Shakespeare did. With a pen the monkey would get distracted, draw funny faces, found a school of poetry of its own. There's something about having the whole alphabet in front of it, on a machine, that goads the monkey to go on, for *millions* of years (but surely evolution would be quicker?), persevering after heartbreaking setbacks; think of getting the whole of *King Lear* right until it came to the lines over the dead body of Cornelia, which would come out:

Thou'lt come no more
Never, never, never, never, ever,
or, on *my* typewriter—
Necer, neved, lever, nexelm vrevney.

The typewriter knows very well how to mix language
and mathematics, the resources between A and Z and 1 and
9, in its own sly way. Mine likes to put ¾ instead of the
letter p. How brilliantly this introduces a nuance, a *frisson* of
chance and doubt into many words that begin so well with
this confident, explosive consonant! How often is one
disappointed by a watery ¾ale ale! How often does some
much-publicized meeting of statesmen result in the
signing of something that the typists of both sides know is
just a ¾act! How many ¾apists one knows! How many
people praised for their courage are not so much plucky as
just ¾*lucky.*

Most of all, is not the most common form of social
occasion to-day the cocktail ¾arty? One always goes
expecting a real party, but nine times out of ten turns out
to be a ¾arty; all the people there have some sort of
connection with the '¾' arts such as advertising, films,
news ¾apers—although there is often a real ¾ainter or
two. After a few ¾ink gins one of the ¾ainters makes a
¾ass at one of those strange silent girls, with long hair and
sullen ¾outing lips, that one always sees at ¾arties
(doubtless he thinks she will be ¾liable). There may be some
V.I.¼, (on my typewriter the capital ¾ is a ¼)* as the chief
guest—an M.¼., or a fashionable ¾reacher (nothing so
grand as the ¼rime Minister, of course. Guests like that
are only at real parties, given by Top ¼eople); but at a
¾arty it is always difficult to get the interesting guest to
himself, to ¾in him down in an argument, because of the
¾rattle going on all round.

Of course this isn't mathematical language in Dr
Bronowski's sense. But you've got to admit it's figurative.

* That's mathematics for you. I have an obscure feeling it should be either ⁹⁄₁₆
or 1½.

The Soldier in White

JOSEPH HELLER

YOSSARIAN RAN RIGHT into the hospital, determined to remain there forever rather than fly one mission more than the thirty-two missions he had. Ten days after he changed his mind and came out, the colonel raised the missions to forty-five and Yossarian ran right back in, determined to remain in the hospital forever rather than fly one mission more than the six missions more he had just flown.

Yossarian could run into the hospital whenever he wanted to because of his liver and because of his eyes; the doctors couldn't fix his liver condition and couldn't meet his eyes each time he told them he had a liver condition. He could enjoy himself in the hospital, just as long as there was no one really very sick in the same ward. His system was sturdy enough to survive a case of someone else's malaria or influenza with scarcely any discomfort at all. He could come through other people's tonsilectomies without suffering any postoperative distress, and even endure their hernias and hemorrhoids with only mild nausea and revulsion. But that was just about as much as he could go through without getting sick. After that he was ready to bolt. He could relax in the hospital, since no one there expected him to do anything. All he was expected to do in the hospital was die or get better, and since he was perfectly all right to begin with, getting better was easy.

Being in the hospital was better than being over Bologna or flying over Avignon with Huple and Dobbs at the controls and Snowden dying in back.

There were usually not nearly as many sick people inside the hospital as Yossarian saw outside the hospital, and there were generally fewer people inside the hospital who were seriously sick. There was a much lower death rate inside the hospital then outside the hospital, and a much healthier death rate. Few people died unnecessarily. People knew a lot more about dying inside the hospital and made a much neater, more orderly job of it. They couldn't dominate Death inside the hospital, but they certainly made her behave. They had taught her manners. They couldn't keep Death out, but while she was in she had to act like a lady. People gave up the ghost with delicacy and taste inside the hospital. There was none of that crude, ugly ostentation about dying that was so common outside the hospital. They did not blow up in mid-air like Kraft or the dead man in Yossarian's tent, or freeze to death in the blazing summertime the way Snowden had frozen to death after spilling his secret to Yossarian in the back of the plane.

'I'm cold,' Snowden had whimpered. 'I'm cold.'

'There, there,' Yossarian had tried to comfort him. 'There, there.'

They didn't take it on the lam weirdly inside a cloud the way Clevinger had done. They didn't explode into blood and clotted matter. They didn't drown or get struck by lightning, mangled by machinery or crushed in landslides. They didn't get shot to death in hold-ups, strangled to death in rapes, stabbed to death in saloons, bludgeoned to death with axes by parents or children or die summarily by some

*

other act of God. Nobody choked to death. People bled to
death like gentlemen in an operating room or expired
without comment in an oxygen tent.There was none of
that tricky now-you-see-me-now-you-don't business so
much in vogue outside the hospital, none of that now-I-
am-and-now-I-ain't. There were no famines or floods.
Children didn't suffocate in cradles or iceboxes or fall
under trucks. No one was beaten to death. People didn't
stick their heads into ovens with the gas on, jump in front
of subway trains or come plummeting like dead weights
out of hotel windows with a *whoosh!*, accelerating at the rate
of sixteen feet per second to land with a hideous *plop!* on the
sidewalk and die disgustingly there in public like an alpaca
sack full of hairy strawberry ice cream, bleeding, pink toes
awry.

All things considered, Yossarian often preferred the
hospital, even though it had its faults. The help tended to
be officious, the rules, if heeded, restrictive, and the
management meddlesome. Since sick people were apt to be
present, he could not always depend on a lively young
crowd in the same ward with him, and the entertainment
was not always good. He was forced to admit that the
hospitals had altered steadily for the worse as the war
continued and one moved closer to the battlefront, the
deterioration in the quality of the guests becoming most
marked within the combat zone itself where the effects of
booming wartime conditions were apt to make themselves
conspicuous immediately. The people got sicker and sicker
the deeper he moved into combat, until finally in the
hospital that last time there had been the soldier in white,
who could not have been any sicker without being dead,
and he soon was.

The soldier in white was constructed entirely of gauze,
plaster and a thermometer, and the thermometer was
merely an adornment left balanced in the empty dark hole
in the bandages over his mouth early each morning and late
each afternoon by Nurse Cramer and Nurse Duckett right
up to the afternoon Nurse Cramer read the thermometer

and discovered he was dead. Now that Yossarian looked
back, it seemed that Nurse Cramer, rather than the
talkative Texan, had murdered the soldier in white; if she
had not read the thermometer and reported what she had
found, the soldier in white might still be lying there alive
exactly as he had been lying there all along, encased from
head to toe in plaster and gauze with both strange, rigid
legs elevated from the hips and both strange arms strung
up perpendicularly, all four bulky limbs in casts, all four
strange useless limbs hoisted up in the air by taut wire
cables and fantastically long lead weights suspended darkly
above him. Lying there that way might not have been
much of a life, but it was all the life he had, and the decision
to terminate it, Yossarian felt, should hardly have been
Nurse Cramer's.

The soldier in white was like an unrolled bandage with a
hole in it or like a broken block of stone in a harbor with a
crooked zinc pipe jutting out. The other patients in the
ward, all but the Texan, shrank from him with a
tenderhearted aversion from the moment they set eyes on
him the morning after the night he had been sneaked in.
They gathered soberly in the farthest recess of the ward
and gossiped about him in malicious, offended undertones,
rebelling against his presence as a ghastly imposition and
resenting him malevolently for the nauseating truth of
which he was bright reminder. They shared a common
dread that he would begin moaning.

'I don't know what I'll do if he does begin moaning,' the
dashing young fighter pilot with the golden mustache had
grieved forlornly. 'It means he'll moan during the night,
too, because he won't be able to tell time.'

No sound at all came from the soldier in white all the
time he was there. The ragged round hole over his mouth
was deep and jet black and showed no sign of lip, teeth,
palate or tongue. The only one who ever came close
enough to look was the affable Texan, who came close
enough several times a day to chat with him about more
votes for the decent folk, opening each conversation with

the same unvarying greeting: 'What do you say, fella? How you coming along?' The rest of the men avoided them both in their regulation maroon corduroy bathrobes and unraveling flannel pajamas, wondering gloomily who the soldier in white was, why he was there and what he was really like inside.

'He's all right, I tell you,' the Texan would report back to them encouragingly after each of his social visits. 'Deep down inside he's really a regular guy. He's just feeling a little shy and insecure now because he doesn't know anybody here and can't talk. Why don't you all just step right up to him and introduce yourselves? He won't hurt you.'

'What the goddam hell are you talking about?' Dunbar demanded. 'Does he even know what you're talking about?'

'Sure he knows what I'm talking about. He's not stupid. There ain't nothing wrong with him.'

'Can he hear you?'

'Well, I don't know if he can hear me or not, but I'm sure he knows what I'm talking about.'

'Does that hole over his mouth ever move?'

'Now, what kind of crazy question is that?' the Texan asked uneasily.

'How can you tell if he's breathing if it never moves?'

'How can you tell it's a he?'

'Does he have pads over his eyes underneath that bandage over his face?'

'Does he ever wiggle his toes or move the tips of his fingers?'

The Texan backed away in mounting confusion. 'Now, what kind of a crazy question is that? You fellas must all be crazy or something. Why don't you just walk right up to him and get acquainted? He's a real nice guy, I tell you.'

The soldier in white was more like a stuffed and sterilized mummy than a real nice guy. Nurse Duckett and Nurse Cramer kept him spick-and-span. They brushed his bandages often with a whiskbroom and scrubbed the plaster casts on his arms, legs, shoulders, chest and pelvis with soapy water. Working with a round tin of metal polish, they waxed a dim gloss on the dull zinc pipe rising from the cement on his groin. With damp dish towels they wiped the dust several times a day from the slim black rubber tubes leading in and out of him to the two large stoppered jars, one of them, hanging on a post beside his bed, dripping fluid into his arm constantly through a slit in the bandages while the other, almost out of sight on the floor, drained the fluid away through the zinc pipe rising from his groin. Both young nurses polished the glass jars unceasingly. They were proud of their housework. The more solicitous of the two was Nurse Cramer, a shapely, pretty sexless girl with a wholesome unattractive face. Nurse Cramer had a cute nose and a radiant, blooming complexion dotted with fetching sprays of adorable freckles that Yossarian detested. She was touched very deeply by the soldier in white. Her virtuous, pale-blue, saucerlike eyes flooded with leviathan tears on unexpected occasions and made Yossarian mad.

'How the hell do you know he's even in there?' he asked her.

'Don't you dare talk to me that way!' she replied indignantly.

'Well, how do you? You don't even know if it's really him.'

'Who?'

'Whoever's supposed to be in all those bandages. You might really be weeping for somebody else. How do you know he's even alive?'

'What a terrible thing to say!' Nurse Cramer exclaimed. 'Now, you get right into bed and stop making jokes about him.'

'I'm not making jokes. Anybody might be in there. For all we know, it might even be Mudd.'

'What are you talking about?' Nurse Cramer pleaded with him in a quavering voice.

'Maybe that's where the dead man is.'

'What dead man?'

'I've got a dead man in my tent that nobody can throw out. His name is Mudd.'

Nurse Cramer's face blanched and she turned to Dunbar desperately for aid. 'Make him stop saying things like that,' she begged.

'Maybe there's no one inside,' Dunbar suggested helpfully. 'Maybe they just sent the bandages here for a joke.'

She stepped away from Dunbar in alarm. 'You're crazy,' she cried, glancing about imploringly. 'You're both crazy.'

Nurse Duckett showed up then and chased them all back to their own beds while Nurse Cramer changed the stoppered jars for the soldier in white. Changing the jars for the soldier in white was no trouble at all, since the same clear fluid was dripped back inside him over and over again with no apparent loss. When the jar feeding the inside of his elbow was just about empty, the jar on the floor was just about full, and the two were simply uncoupled from their respective hoses and reversed quickly so that the liquid could be dripped right back into him. Changing the jars was no trouble to anyone but the men who watched them changed every hour or so and were baffled by the procedure.

'Why can't they hook the two jars up to each other and eliminate the middleman?' the artillery captain with whom Yossarian had stopped playing chess inquired. 'What the hell do they need him for?'

'I wonder what he did to deserve it,' the warrant officer with malaria and a mosquito bite on his ass lamented after Nurse Cramer had read her thermometer and discovered that the soldier in white was dead.

'He went to war,' the fighter pilot with the golden mustache surmised.

'We all went to war,' Dunbar countered.

'That's what I mean,' the warrant officer with malaria continued. 'Why him? There just doesn't seem to be any logic to this system of rewards and punishment. Look what happened to me. If I had gotten syphillis or a dose of clap for my five minutes of passion on the beach instead of this damned mosquito bite, I could see some justice. But malaria? *Malaria?* Who can explain malaria as a consequence of fornication?' The warrant officer shook his head in numb astonishment.

'What about me?' Yossarian said. 'I stepped out of my tent in Marrakech one night to get a bar of candy and caught your dose of clap when that Wac I never even saw before hissed me into the bushes. All I really wanted was a bar of candy, but who could turn it down?'

'That sounds like my dose of clap, all right,' the warrant officer agreed. 'But I've still got somebody else's malaria. Just for once I'd like to see all these things sort of straightened out, with each person getting exactly what he deserves. It might give me some confidence in this universe.'

'I've got somebody else's three hundred thousand dollars,' the dashing young fighter captain with the golden mustache admitted. 'I've been goofing off since the day I was born. I cheated my way through prep school and college, and just about all I've been doing ever since is shacking up with pretty girls who think I'd make a good husband. I've got no ambition at all. The only thing I want to do after the war is marry some girl who's got more money than I have and shack up with lots more pretty girls. The three hundred thousand bucks was left to me before I was born by a grandfather who made a fortune selling on an international scale. I know I don't deserve it, but I'll be damned if I give it back. I wonder who it really belongs to.'

'Maybe it belongs to my father,' Dunbar conjectured. 'He spent a lifetime at hard work and never could make enough money to even send my sister and me through college. He's dead now, so you might as well keep it.'

'Now, if we can just find out who my malaria belongs to we'd be all set. It's not that I've got anything against malaria. I'd just as soon goldbrick with malaria as with anything else. It's only that I feel an injustice has been committed. Why should I have somebody else's malaria and you have my dose of clap?'

'I've got more than your dose of clap,' Yossarian told him. 'I've got to keep flying combat missions because of that dose of yours until they kill me.'

'That makes it even worse. What's the justice in that?'

'I had a friend named Clevinger two and a half weeks ago who used to see plenty of justice in it.'

'It's the highest kind of justice of all,' Clevinger had gloated, clapping his hands with a merry laugh. 'I can't help thinking of the *Hippolytus* of Euripedes, where the early licentiousness of Theseus is probably responsible for the asceticism of the son that helps bring about the tragedy that ruins them all. If nothing else, that episode with the Wac should teach you the evil of sexual immorality.'

'It teaches me the evil of candy.'

'Can't you see that you're not exactly without blame for the predicament you're in?' Clevinger had continued with undisguised relish. 'If you hadn't been laid up in the hospital with venereal disease for ten days back there in Africa, you might have finished your twenty-five missions in time to be sent home before Colonel Nevers was killed and Colonel Cathcart came to replace him.'

'And what about you?' Yossarian had replied. 'You never got clap in Marrakech and you're in the same predicament.'

'I don't know,' confessed Clevinger, with a trace of mock concern. 'I guess I must have done something very bad in my time.'

'Do you really believe that?'

Clevinger laughed. 'No, of course not. I just like to kid you along a little.'

There were too many dangers for Yossarian to keep track of. There was Hitler, Mussolini and Tojo, for example, and they were all out to kill him. There was Lieutenant Scheisskopf with his fanaticism for parades and there was the bloated colonel with his big fat mustache and his fanaticism for retribution, and they wanted to kill him, too. There was Appleby, Havermeyer, Black and Korn.

There was Nurse Cramer and Nurse Duckett, who he was
almost certain wanted him dead, and there was the Texan
and the C.I.D. man, about whom he had no doubt. There
were bartenders, bricklayers and bus conductors all over
the world who wanted him dead, landlords and tenants,
traitors and patriots, lynchers, leeches and lackeys,
and they were all out to bump him off. That was the
secret Snowden had spilled to him on the mission to
Avignon—they were out to get him; and Snowden had
spilled it all over the back of the plane.

There were lymph glands that might do him in. There
were kidneys, nerve sheaths and corpuscles. There were
tumors of the brain. There was Hodgkin's disease,
leukemia, amyotropical lateral sclerosis. There was fertile
red meadows of epithelial tissue to catch and coddle a
cancer cell. There were diseases of the skin, diseases of the
bone, diseases of the lung, diseases of the stomach,
diseases of the heart, blood and arteries. There were
diseases of the head, diseases of the neck, diseases of the
chest, diseases of the intestines, diseases of the crotch.
There even were diseases of the feet. There were billions of
conscientious body cells oxidating away day and night like
dumb animals at their complicated job of keeping him alive
and healthy, and every one was a potential traitor and foe.
There were so many diseases that it took a truly diseased
mind to even think about them as often as he and Hungry
Joe did.

Hungry Joe collected lists of fatal diseases and arranged
them in alphabetical order so that he could put his finger
without delay on any one he wanted to worry about. He
grew very upset whenever he misplaced some or when he
could not add to his list, and he would go rushing in a cold
sweat to Doc Daneeka for help.

'Give him Ewing's tumor,' Yossarian advised Doc
Daneeka, who would come to Yossarian for help in
handling Hungry Joe, 'and follow it up with melanoma.
Hungry Joe likes lingering diseases, but he likes the
fulminating ones even more.'

Doc Daneeka had never heard of either. 'How do you manage to keep up on so many diseases like that?' he inquired with high professional esteem.

'I learn about them at the hospital when I study the *Reader's Digest*.'

Yossarian had so many ailments to be afraid of that he was sometimes tempted to turn himself into the hospital for good and spend the rest of his life stretched out there inside an oxygen tent with a battery of specialists and nurses seated at one side of his bed twenty-four hours a day waiting for something to go wrong and at least one surgeon with a knife poised at the other, ready to jump forward and begin cutting away the moment it became necessary. Aneurisms, for instance; how else could they ever defend him in time against an aneurism of the aorta? Yossarian felt much safer inside the hospital than outside the hospital, even though he loathed the surgeon and his knife as much as he had ever loathed anyone. He could start screaming inside a hospital and people would at least come running to try to help; outside the hospital they would throw him in prison if he ever started screaming about all the things he felt everyone ought to start screaming about, or they would put him in the hospital. One of the things he wanted to start screaming about was the surgeon's knife that was almost certain to be waiting for him and everyone else who lived long enough to die. He wondered often how he would ever recognize the first chill, flush, twinge, ache, belch, sneeze, stain, lethargy, vocal slip, loss of balance or lapse of memory that would signal the inevitable beginning of the inevitable end.

He was afraid also that Doc Daneeka would still refuse to help him when he went to him again after jumping out of Major Major's office, and he was right.

'You think you've got something to be afraid about?' Doc Daneeka demanded, lifting his delicate immaculate dark head up from his chest to gaze at Yossarian irascibly for a moment with lachrymose eyes. 'What about me? My precious medical skills are rusting away here on this lousy

island while other doctors are cleaning up. Do you think I
enjoy sitting here day after day refusing to help you? I
wouldn't mind it so much if I could refuse to help you back
in the States or in some place like Rome. But saying no to
you here isn't easy for me, either.'

'Then stop saying no. Ground me.'

'I can't ground you,' Doc Daneeka mumbled. 'How many
times do you have to be told?'

'Yes you can. Major Major told me you're the only one in
the squadron who *can* ground me.'

Doc Daneeka was stunned. 'Major Major told you that?
When?'

'When I tackled him in the ditch.'

'Major Major told you that? In a ditch?'

'He told me in his office after we left the ditch and
jumped inside. He told me not to tell anyone he told me, so
don't start shooting your mouth off.'

'Why that dirty, scheming liar!' Doc Daneeka cried. 'He
wasn't supposed to tell anyone. Did he tell you how I could
ground you?'

'Just by filling out a little slip of paper saying I'm on the
verge of nervous collapse and sending it to Group. Dr
Stubbs grounds men in his squadron all the time, so why
can't you?'

'And what happens to the men after Stubbs does ground
them?' Doc Daneeka retorted with a sneer. 'They go right
back on combat status, don't they? And he finds himself
right up the creek. Sure, I can ground you by filling out a
slip saying you're unfit to fly. But there's a catch.'

'Catch-22?'

'Sure. If I take you off combat duty, Group has to
approve my action, and Group isn't going to. They'll put
you right back on combat status, and then where will I be?
On my way to the Pacific Ocean, probably. No, thank you.
I'm not going to take any chances for you.'

'Isn't it worth a try?' Yossarian argued. 'What's so hot
about Pianosa?'

'Pianosa is terrible. But it's better than the Pacific Ocean.

I wouldn't mind being shipped someplace civilized where I might pick up a buck or two in abortion money every now and then. But all they've got in the Pacific is jungles and monsoons. I'd rot there.'

'You're rotting here.'

Doc Daneeka flared up angrily. 'Yeah? Well, at least I'm going to come out of this war alive, which is a lot more than you're going to do.'

'That's just what I'm trying to tell you, goddammit. I'm asking you to save my life.'

'It's not my business to save lives,' Doc Daneeka retorted sullenly.

'What is your business?'

'I don't know what my business is. All they ever told me was to uphold the ethics of my profession and never give testimony against another physician. Listen. You think you're the only one whose life is in danger? What about me? Those two quacks I've got working for me in the medical tent still can't find out what's wrong with me.'

'Maybe it's Ewing's tumor,' Yossarian muttered sarcastically.

'Do you really think so?' Doc Daneeka exclaimed with fright.

'Oh, I don't know,' Yossarian answered impatiently. 'I just know I'm not going to fly any more missions. They wouldn't really shoot me, would they? I've got fifty-one.'

'Why don't you at least finish the fifty-five before you take a stand?' Doc Daneeka advised. 'With all your bitching, you've never finished a tour of duty even once.'

'How the hell can I? The colonel keeps raising them every time I get close.'

'You never finish your missions because you keep running into the hospital or going off to Rome. You'd be in a much stronger position if you had your fifty-five finished and then refused to fly. Then maybe I'd see what I could do.'

'Do you promise?'

'I promise.'

'What do you promise?'

'I promise that maybe I'll think about doing something to help if you finish your fifty-five missions and if you get McWatt to put my name on his flight log again so that I can draw my flight pay without going up in a plane. I'm afraid of airplanes. Did you read about that airplane crash in Idaho three weeks ago? Six people killed. It was terrible. I don't know why they want me to put in four hours' flight time every month in order to get my flight pay. Don't I have enough to worry about without worrying about being killed in an airplane crash too?'

'I worry about airplane crashes also,' Yossarian told him. 'You're not the only one.'

'Yeah, but I'm also pretty worried about that Ewing's tumor,' Doc Daneeka boasted. 'Do you think that's why my nose is stuffed all the time and why I always feel so chilly? Take my pulse.'

Yossarian also worried about Ewing's tumor and melanoma. Catastrophes were lurking everywhere, too numerous to count. When he contemplated the many diseases and potential accidents threatening him, he was positively astounded that he had managed to survive in good health for as long as he had. It was miraculous. Each day he faced was another dangerous mission against mortality. And he had been surviving them for twenty-eight years.

The Luck of the Irish

BERNARD LEVIN

Friday, October 31st

This must be the fourteenth time I have been to Wexford. The thirteenth? The fifteenth? Just as, at Wexford itself, the days and nights blur into each other with less distinction made between them than at any other place on earth with the exception of Las Vegas, so memories of my annual visits have become one extended memory. It is not just a matter of assigning particular moments to particular years, like Americans, back home after doing Europe in three weeks, unable to agree whether the place with the Eiffel Tower was Brussels or London; I have long since stopped trying to remember which was The Year of the Grape-Lady, The Year of the Police Raid, The Year of the Disastrous *Oberon*, The Year There Was No Boat.

But I can remember at once that 1979 was The Year of the Missing Lemon Juice. The Theatre Royal in Wexford holds 440; it was completely full that night, so there are, allowing for a few who have already died (it is not true, though it might well have been, that some died of laughter at the time), hardly more than four hundred people who now share, to the end of their lives, an experience from which the rest of the world, now and for ever, is excluded. When the last of us dies, the experience will die with us, for although it is already enshrined in legend, no one who was not an eye witness will ever really understand what we felt. Certainly I am aware that these words cannot convey more than the facts, and the facts, as so often and most particularly in this case, are only part, and a small part, too, of the whole truth. But I must try.

The opera that night was *La Vestale*, by Spontini. It has been described as 'a poor man's *Norma*', since it tells, in music and drama much inferior to Bellini's, of a vestal virgin who betrays her charge for love. It was revived for Maria Callas, but otherwise figures rarely in the repertoire of the world's leading opera houses. But it is part of Wexford's business to revive operas which other opera houses and festivals unjustly neglect, and I have been repeatedly surprised in a most pleasant manner to discover much of interest and pleasure in some of them; Lalo's *Le Roi d'Ys*, for instance, or Prokoviev's *The Gambler*, or Bizet's *Les Pêcheurs des Perles*. (The Year of the Disastrous *Oberon* was a notable exception, though even then mainly because of the terrible production rather than the opera itself. The Year of the Grape-Lady was the year I found myself lolling in an armchair after a gigantic lunch, while the most beautiful woman in Ireland dropped luscious black grapes, one by one, into my mouth. The Year There Was No Boat was the year in which Mr Fletcher, who runs the lunch-cruising excursion from nearby New Ross was refitting his vessel and therefore not operating the cruise. Of The Year of the Police Raid I shall speak in due course.)

Well, in 1979 it was *La Vestale*. The set for Act I of the opera consisted of a platform laid over the stage, raised about a foot at the back and sloping evenly to the footlights. This was meant to represent the interior of the Temple where burned the sacred flame, and had therefore to look like marble; the designer had achieved a convincing alternative by covering the raised stage in Formica. But the Formica was slippery; to avoid the risk of a performer taking a tumble, designer and stage manager had between them discovered that an ample sprinkling of lemon juice would make the surface sufficiently sticky to provide a secure foothold. The story now forks; down one road there lies the belief that the member of the stage staff whose duty it was to sprinkle the lifesaving liquid, and who had done so without fail at rehearsal and at the earlier performances (this was the last one of the Festival), had simply forgotten. Down the other branch in the road is a much more attractive rumour: that the theatre charlady, inspecting the premises in the afternoon, had seen to her horror and indignation that the stage was covered in the remains of some spilt liquid, and, inspired by professional pride, had thereupon set to and given it a good scrub and polish all over.

The roads now join again, for apart from the superior charm of the second version, it makes no difference what the explanation was. What matters is what happened.

What happened began to happen very early. The hero of the opera strides on to the stage immediately after the curtain has gone up. The hero strode; and instantly fell flat on his back. There was a murmur of sympathy and concern from the audience for his embarrassment and for the possibility that he might have been hurt; it was the last such sound that was to be heard that night and it was very soon to be replaced by sounds of a very different nature.

The hero got to his feet, with considerable difficulty, and, having slid some way down the stage in falling, proceeded to stride up-stage to where he should have been in the first place; he had, of course, gone on singing throughout, for the music had not stopped. Striding up-stage, however, was plainly more difficult than he had reckoned on, for every time he took a step and tried to follow it with another, the foot with which he had taken the first proceeded to slide down-stage again, swiftly followed by its companion: he may not have known it but he was giving a perfect demonstration of what is called *marcher sur place*, a graceful manoeuvre normally used in mime, and seen at its best in the work of Marcel Marceau.

Finding progress uphill difficult, indeed impossible, the hero wisely decided to abandon the attempt and stay where he was, singing bravely on, no doubt calculating that, since the stage was brightly lit, the next character to enter would notice him and adjust his own movements accordingly. So it proved, in a sense at least, for the next character to enter was the hero's trusted friend and confidant, who, seeing his hero further down-stage than he was supposed to be, loyally decided to join him there. Truth to tell, he had little choice, for from the moment he had stepped on to the stage he had begun to slide downhill, arms semaphoring, like Scrooge's clerk on the way home to his Christmas dinner. His downhill progress was arrested by his fetching up against his friend with a thud; this, as it happened, was not altogether inappropriate, as the opera called for them to embrace in friendly greeting at that point. It did not, however, call for them, locked in each other's arms and propelled by the impetus of the friend's descent, to career helplessly further down-stage with the evident intention of going straight into the orchestra pit with vocal accompaniment—for the hero's aria had, on the arrival of his companion, been transformed into a duet.

On the brink of ultimate disaster they managed to arrest their joint progress to destruction and, working their way along the edge of the stage like mountaineers seeking a route round an unbridgeable crevasse, most gallantly began, with infinite pain and by a form of progress most aptly described in the title of Lenin's famous pamphlet, *Four Steps Forward, Three Steps Back*, to climb up the terrible hill. It speedily became clear that the hazardous ascent was not being made simply from a desire to retain dramatic credibility; it had a much more practical object. The only structure breaking the otherwise all too smooth surface of the stage was a marble pillar, a yard or so high, on which there burned the sacred flame of the rite. This pillar was embedded firmly in the stage, and it had obviously occurred to both mountaineers at once that if they could only reach it it would provide a secure base for their subsequent operations, since if they held on to it for dear life they would at any rate be safe from any further danger of sliding downhill and/or breaking their necks.

It was soon borne in upon them that they had undertaken a labour of truly Sisyphean proportions, and would have been most heartily pardoned by the audience if they had abandoned the librettist's words at this point, and fitted to the music instead the old moral verse:

> *The heights by great men reached and kept,*
> *Were not attained by sudden flight;*
> *But they, while their companions slept,*
> *Were toiling upwards in the night.*

By this time the audience—all 440 of us—were in a state of such abandon with laughter that several of us felt that if this were to continue a moment longer we would be in danger of doing ourselves a serious internal mischief; little did we know that the fun was just beginning, for shortly after Mallory and Irvine reached their longed-for goal, the chorus entered, and instantly flung themselves *en masse* into a very freely choreographed version of *Les Patineurs*, albeit to the wrong music. The heroine herself, the priestess Giulia, with a survival instinct strong enough to suggest that she would be the one to get close to should any reader of these lines happen to be shipwrecked along with the Wexford opera company, skated into the wings and kicked her shoes off and then, finding on her return that this had hardly improved matters, skated back to the wings and removed her tights as well.

Now, however, the singing never having stopped for a moment, the chorus had come to the same conclusion as had the hero and his friend, namely that holding on to the holy pillar was the only way to remain upright and more or less immobile. The trouble with this conclusion was that

there was only one such pillar on the stage, and it was a
small one; as the cast crowded round it, it seemed that
there would be some very unseemly brawling among those
seeking a hand-hold, a foothold, even a bare finger-hold, on
this tiny island of security in the terrible sea of
impermanence. By an instinctive understanding of the
principles of co-operation, however, they decided the
matter without bloodshed; those nearest the pillar
clutched it, those next nearest clutched the clutchers, those
farther away still clutched those, and so on until, in a kind
of daisy-chain that snaked across the stage, everybody was
accommodated.

The condition of the audience was now one of fully
extended hysteria, which was having the most extraordinary effect—itself intensifying the audience's condition—on the orchestra. At Wexford, the orchestra pit runs
under the stage; only a single row of players—those at the
edge of the pit nearest the audience, together, of course,
with the conductor—could see what was happening on the
stage. The rest realized that *something* out of the ordinary
was going on up there, and would have been singularly dull
of wit if they had not, for many members of the audience
were now slumped on the floor weeping helplessly, in the
agony of their mirth, and although the orchestra at
Wexford cannot see the stage, it can certainly see the
auditorium.

Theologians tell us that the delights of the next world
are eternal. Perhaps; but what is certain is that all earthly
ones, alas, are temporary, and duly, after giving us a
glimpse of the more enduring joy of Heaven that must
have strengthened the devout in their faith and caused
instant conversion among many of the unbelievers, the
entertainment came to an end when the first act of the
opera did so, amid such cheering as I had never before
heard in an opera house, and can never hope to hear again.
In the interval before Act II, a member of the production
staff walked back and forth across the stage, sprinkling it
with the precious nectar, and we knew that our happiness

was at an end. But he who, after such happiness, would have demanded more, would be greedy indeed, and most of us were content to know that, for one crowded half-hour, we on honeydew had fed, and drunk the milk of Paradise.

Hotel Superbe v The Filthistan Trio

BEACHCOMBER

THE ACTION IN which the Hotel Superbe is endeavouring, for purposes of publicity, to recover damages from the Filthistan Trio was begun yesterday before Mr Justice Cocklecarrot in Court 4 of the Probate and Fisheries Division.

Cocklecarrot, in his opening address to the jury, began, amid frequent laughter:

'This curious case turns on the unorthodox activities of three Persian visitors to this country—'

Whereupon Kazbulah interrupted thus:

'May I please your lordship's grace, I object to the word unorthodox in connection with see-saw. There is nothing in our religion to say that see-saw is unorthodox.'

Cocklecarrot: Objection sustained. I was not using the word unorthodox in a religious sense. It is possible that expert authorities on the game of see-saw might describe the actual method employed in your case—I refer to the laying of the plank on the belly of one of you—as unorthodox.

Rizamughan: In Persia this form of see-saw is exceedingly common, O judge, yes.

Cocklecarrot: But we are here concerned with what you were doing in England.

Ashura: He is right, O Rizamughan.

Cocklecarrot: You must not talk like that in this court. I am not here to be criticized.

Ashura: Not even favourably, O judge?

There was no reply.

Cocklecarrot then resumed:

'Whether or not the use of the belly—'

Foreman of the Jury: M'lud, one of our number, a sworn juror, Mr Muffler, objects strongly to the public utterance of the word belly. He suggests that stomach is the word.

Cocklecarrot: Really, sir, I am the best judge of what words can or cannot be used in this court.

Rizamughan: We have no objection to the word stomach, O judge.

Cocklecarrot: You have not been asked to express any opinion, Mr Rizamughan.

Ashura: Is not a law court a rendezvous of free expression of opinion, O lordship?

Cocklecarrot: Certinly not.

Kazbulah: But is not your excellency freely expressing his opinion?

Cocklecarrot (with angry patience): I happen to be supreme here. I am, so to speak, above the law. I *am* the law. Your attitude is contempt of court.

Ashura: Oh, yes.

Cocklecarrot: Yes what?

Ashura: We have great contempt of court.

(Cocklecarrot then bowed his head in his hands and there was silence.)

Mr Justice Cocklecarrot, in another address to the jury, said yesterday: ·

'We have here a case of three grown-up men playing the

childish game of see-saw in the lounge of a restaurant, and playing it in such an unusual manner that ferrets were loosed apparently without any definite object. What we have to decide is at what precise moment and to what precise extent see-saw played by two Persians seated on a plank balanced on the belly of a third, and involving the peregrination of ferrets, may be said to contravene any accepted code of behaviour, or any written or unwritten law of the land. There is no precedent for such a case. The nearest parallel is the case of Ibstock *versus* Prancing, in which an antique dealer sought to restrain a night-watchman from filling the holes on a miniature golf-course with diminutive turtles. But the cases are not very similar—' At that moment the three Persians cried repeatedly, 'Rashmiak!' Nobody knew what they meant, and after a hasty consultation with counsel the court rose with a bad grace, Cocklecarrot having ordered that the meaning of this word should be discovered.

Mr Justice Cocklecarrot continued his fourth address today. He said: 'This case seems to me to fall under two headings. It is really two cases. First, there is the question of the see-saw playing in the lounge, and then the question of the ferrets. I am tempted to say that it is a ferretable maze of intrigue—' (Laughter).

Rizamughan: There was no vegetable.

Ashura: And no maze.

Kazbulah: And no intrigues.

Cocklecarrot: You gentlemen must really restrain your-selves. You are not in Persia now. If there are any more of these interruptions I shall have to take the steps which the law allows in cases of this nature.

Rizamughan: But, O lord, this is a court of law, and we are the culprits.

Cocklecarrot: The defendants.

Ashura: Halt, O lord, we are not defendants. We are free men.

Cocklecarrot (with weary patience): Your interests are being looked after by your counsel. He will speak for you when the time comes.

Kazbulah: He will be too late, O lord, thou thyself having got at the jury.

Cocklecarrot: This is monstrous! Mr Snapdriver, kindly keep your clients in order. The court will now adjourn for twenty minutes. The case will then proceed normally—I hope.

A pretty girl at the back of the court: What a hope!

The case of the Hotel Superbe *v.* the Filthistan Trio was bogged down yesterday for many hours, owing to the discovery of a misplaced comma in the Puisne Warrant (*ex delicto* and *quasi ex delicto, Post Moselle ergo propter Moselle*). The Clerk of Arraigns and Torts pointed out that a stay of refringement might be granted, as in the case of the Burlington Tortoise Farms, Ltd., *v.* Mrs Amber Duckforth and Betty the Parrot, but that, if this were so, or not, the obligation of wrongful assumption of partial liability would fall like a ton of rock on the plaintiffs, slander of title and fraudulent competition being assumed *in toto* wherever proven or non-proven unless, howbeit and albeit, collusion or collusions could be adduced from the behaviour of those who happened to be there at the time of the offence, the offence, for present purposes, being assumed to have been committed, or to have been about to be committed by some parson or parsons unknown.

'Malpractice!' cries the uninstructed reader.

'Not necessarily!' retorts the Law, and sends the uninstructed reader hotfoot to the famous case of the Billericay Bilberry-Canning Syndicate *v.* Heckmondwyke Football Accessories, the Bank of Honduras, and Professor Felix Burtaway.

There the matter rests at present, as the actress said when she smeared the stockbroker's face with decayed vegetable refuse.

Another important technical detail held up the hearing of
the case yesterday. The words fee simple, a term used in
the Law of Real Property, had crept into the brief of Mr
Honeyweather Gooseboote. There followed a long
argument as to whether, in the registration of deeds of
conveyancing, the abstract of title is an abstract of the
deeds themselves or of public record.

Mr Snapdriver: It is immaterial,this case not being
concerned with a deed of conveyancing.

Mr Gooseboote: I yield that point. Nevertheless the
question arises, am I justified in assuming that a term
which occurs in my brief can be ignored at will—see Vesey
468 Wodenholme *v.* Cherry-pip.

Cocklecarrot: Come, come, Mr Gooseboote, the words fee
simple in your brief quite clearly refer to some other case.
The Statute de Davis (51 Edw.III c.19,1334), dealing with
tenants in fee tail, by a clerk's error, is precedent enough
for you. Or do you hold it to be sporadic?

Mr Snapdriver: I suggest, M'lud, that livery of seisin covers
it, as in Mrs Gullet *v.* HMS Contemptible.

Mr Gooseboote: But I find in my brief also the apparently
meaningless phrase 'inter alia'.

Cocklecarrot (sarcastically): Are you sure you have your
brief in court—or is it the script of a music-hall turn?

(Loud laughter, fruit-throwing, and cat-calls.)

The case was adjourned yesterday owing to an accident as
unfortunate as it was unforeseen. Mr Honeyweather
Gooseboote, counsel for the prosecution, while leaning
over to whisper to Mr Tinklebury Snapdriver, counsel for
the defence, dislocated his elbow. Mr Snapdriver, in trying
to rectify the damage, got the elbow stuck in his mouth,
and could not withdraw it. Mr Gooseboote left the court,
walking sideways,with his elbow clamped tightly between
Mr Snapdriver's jaws. The sight of the two learned counsel
shuffling gingerly towards the exit, to all intents and
purposes chained to each other by these unusual bonds,

was too much for the public. Loud and prolonged laughter filled the court for twenty minutes.

Mr Honeyweather Gooseboote today read an appeal from his clients, the management of the Hotel Superbe, asking whether it would not be possible to do something to expedite the hearing of the case. Mr Justice Cocklecarrot said, 'This is most irregular. The law must take its course. The unfortunate incident of the trapping of one learned counsel's elbow in the mouth of another learned counsel has held matters up somewhat. There have also been technical difficulties, and misunderstandings, but—'

At that moment a cry rang out. Mr Gooseboote, in leaning forward to speak to Mr Snapdriver, had somehow got the latter's elbow in his mouth again, and was unable to dislodge it. Officials tugged in vain, and once more the two learned counsel had to leave the court, the one sideways, and the other chained to him by the imprisoned elbow. Mr Justice Cocklecarrot said, 'If you two gentlemen cannot manage to keep your elbows out of each other's mouths you will have to surrender your briefs to less unfortunate practitioners. Such ludicrous clumsiness can do nothing but bring down upon the Law the ridicule of the public Press.'

A doctor was called, and after examining the two counsel said that in his opinion the accident was a manifestation of certain psychic forces of which medicine as yet knew nothing. He said it was a clear case of Gumford's disease.

The case of the Hotel Superbe *v.* the Filthistan Trio was about to continue today—if I may use the word of a case which can hardly be said to have begun—when a police official, by order of Mr Justice Cocklecarrot, approached the two learned counsel, to request them to sit far apart, in order to avoid accidents. But *hélas*, it was too late. Once more, for the third and presumably lucky time, Mr Honeyweather Gooseboote, in bowing to Mr Tinklebury Snapdriver, had got the latter's elbow (including coat-sleeve and shirt-sleeve) stuck in his jaws, and was unable to dislodge the offending morsel.

There was uproar in the court. The fire brigade was summoned, and many junior narks heaved and tugged in the best Metropolitan Police tug-of-war traditions. When the fire brigade arrived, expanding ladders were run up, water poured in great volumes all over everything, shrieking women were carried in and out, windows were smashed with hatchets and ambulance men practised first aid on a half-drowned charwoman. Hysterical members of the public clambered on to the judge's dias, poised themselves uneasily, and dived on to horse blankets held below by a posse of bookies. Doubtful characters 'saved' important documents and bits of furniture, which were piled on taxis and driven away into the unknown.

Mr Justice Cocklecarrot then pointed out that there was no fire, and the court rose shakily.

Mr Honeyweather Gooseboote: Your name is Kazbulah?

Kazbulah: O lord, yes, it is my name please.

Mr Gooseboote: You must answer yes or no.

Kazbulah: Yes or no.

Cocklecarrot: The learned counsel means that you must say yes or no.

Kazbulah: My gracious worship, I did indeed say yes or no.

Mr Tinklebury Snapdriver: No, no. You must answer either yes or no to all questions.

Kazbulah: Even so. Very well, I say either yes or no to your questions, O lord.

Mr Gooseboote: Is—your—name Kazbulah?

Kazbulah: Either yes or no. I reply even as bidden, oh, please.

Mr Snapdriver: I don't really see how the thing can be put more clearly to him.

Mr Gooseboote: Anyhow, we know it's his name. It's a mere formality—

Cocklecarrot: Mr Gooseboote, you will kindly remember that the law rests on legal formalities. The procedure must be adhered to. We know his name, but we are bound to go through all this rub—all this. We cannot take it as read. Lunch will now be taken. The court will rise.

Mr Gooseboote: M'lud, I should like to call Mr Groundswell, the proprietor of the Hotel Superbe.

Cocklecarrot: Call away! You don't tell me we are actually getting on with this case! Why, we've only been at it a mere three weeks or so!

Gooseboote: Now, Mr Groundswell!

Cocklecarrot: Mr Snapdriver, kindly keep your distance. We don't want any more elbow stuff.

Gooseboote: Now, Mr Groundswell, tell us what happened on the day in question.

Groundswell: Ough ough wurgh wurgh ough erph ough wurgh wurgh erph ough—

Snapdragon: This is not a foreign national anthem. My client was last night stung on the roof of the mouth by a hornet.

Cocklecarrot: Well, is there an interpreter?

Gooseboote: M'lud, it's not a foreign language. You can't have an interpreter for noises due to a sting in the mouth.

Cocklecarrot: Well, then, you must cross-examine someone else, Mr Gooseboote. How long will he be in this state?

Snapdriver: The doctor says about a month, m'lud, failing further calamities.

Cocklecarrot (gloomily): Oh.

An atmosphere of tension was noticeable in the court today. Every time Mr Snapdriver even glanced towards Mr Gooseboote there was a universal intake of breath which sounded like high tide at Dungeness. At one point, when the two learned counsel leaned towards each other, Mr Justice Cocklecarrot uttered an involuntary cry: the elbow specialist, who is in constant attendance sprang to his feet and whipped out his gibboscope and his mometer; a police officer drew his luncheon in mistake for his truncheon; the Clerk of the Arraigns and the Puisne Serjaunte-at-Arms closed in tenderly but menacingly: the public shouted warnings.

The relaxation and relief after the false alarm were such that several ladies fainted, and a small commercial traveller went off into shrieking hysterics. A quantity of flock fell from the roof, prompting Cocklecarrot to ask who was tearing mattresses to pieces up there. By the time calm was restored, and the elbow specialist had diagnosed ulnitis and compound cubititis, it was found that in the general mix-up and to-and-fro caused by the mattress-tearing up aloft, Mr Gooseboote's elbow was again firmly wedged between Mr Snapdriver's jaws.

There the elbow rests at present.

Mr Justice Cocklecarrot said yesterday: 'In all my years of experience at the Bar, I have never before known a case to be held up because the elbow of the counsel for the prosecution was jammed between the jaws of the counsel for the defence. How such a ludicrous accident occurred, it is not for me to say. I can only express mild astonishment that two grown men could be the victims of such a monstrous piece of idiocy. The elbow, I am glad to say, has now been removed, and the two counsel will, I understand be ready to take their places in court tomorrow. The medical report speaks of shock sustained by them both. I should like to take this opportunity of saying that when the elbow of one counsel gets stuck in the jaws of another, if anybody is entitled to suffer from shock, I should think it is the unfortunate judge who is trying the case. It will be my task in future to ensure that a distance separates the two protagonists sufficient to make a repetition of this ridiculous incident impossible.'

The Funeral of the Year

TOM STOPPARD

I

'TO SEE LONDON on the morning of a state funeral is to see London at her best,' said the ninth earl as the coach swung round out of the Serpentine Road into Park Lane, 'provided one goes nowhere near the proceedings. On our right is the house of the Duke of Wellington, on our left a statue of Achilles, both reminders of the importance of boots. Over there, a statue of Byron, not a badly dressed fellow though often dishevelled. Across there, Londonderry House, where the English genius for settling matters of public concern over private luncheons reached its finest flower. How very appropriate that it should be overshadowed by an hotel for Americans, and how significant that the monument to Mammon should have turned out, quite inadvertently, to be ecclesiastical in its effect— a trinity of conjoined towers, the First Church of Christ Tourist. And now this is Curzon Street, so named after the first earl, George Nathaniel Curzon, Marquess of Kedleston, who is revered throughout India to this day as a Viceroy whose concern for his collars was such that he sent his laundry to London—'

'Falcon, why are you going on so?'

'Merely defining our context, my dear lady. It is necessary to define one's context at all times.'

'A police cell is quite enough context for one day, darling.'

'Were it not for Sir Mortimer it might have had to suffice for several months.'

'Who *is* Sir Mortimer?'

'He is a merchant prince whom I employ to look after my interests. A useful fellow, though somewhat forward.'

'Well, he seems to have some influence, bless him. It was horrible—I thought it would be cosy and romantic, being punted about under the willows and the moon and everything . . . That blanket smelled of horses.'

'It was a horse blanket. Clarges Street, passing the Ministry of Education (of which there is too much nowadays) over whose portals is carved the legend *Thou shalt not pass with less than forty per cent*. Oh dear, I wish my man were here.'

'What man?'

'Moon. He should be recording me with Boswellian indiscrimination.'

'My husband.'

'Why so he is. You shall be re-united in a few moments unless he has already left for my residence.'

'What do you mean, Falcon?—I don't want to go home, I want to see the funeral.'

'What an extraordinary desire. Don't you want to have a bath and some breakfast and a long lie-in till luncheon? That seems to me the sensible course after a night in the cells.'

'No, I don't, Falcon. I want to see the funeral—you said you were invited.'

'So I was. But I'm sending one of the servants. Funerals depress me so, they distort the meaning of honour.'

The ninth earl raised his stick and beat it against the roof of the coach.

'O'Hara, turn back!'

He mused sadly. 'The most honourable death I have ever heard of was that of Colonel Kelly of the Foot Guards who died in an attempt to save his boots from the Customs House fire. Colonel Kelly's boots were the envy of the town, they shone so. His friends hearing of his death rushed in their grief to buy the services of the valet who had the secret of the inimitable blacking. Now *that* is a tribute to an officer and a gentleman, much more sincere than all the panoply of a state funeral, for it was a tribute despite itself, inspired by the self-interest . . . Poor Colonel Kelly.'

'He sounds like a bit of an idiot to me. I've heard of people dying in fires to save their *pearls* or something.'

'How vulgar.'

'Or their relatives.'

'How suburban.'

'I don't think that's very nice, Falcon.'

'South Street, home of George Brummell called Beau. When Brummell was living abroad in reduced circumstances he ordered a snuff-box costing more than his annual income. It was he who was the first to reach Colonel Kelly's bootblack, by the way. You see, he understood that substance is ephemeral but style is eternal . . . which may not be a solution to the realities of life but it is a workable alternative.'

Jane pressed against him as they wheeled back into Park Lane and headed south.

Lord Malquist brooded on. 'As an attitude it is no more fallacious than our need to identify all our ills with one man so that we may kill him and all our glory with another so that we may line the streets for him. What a nonsense it all is.'

Jane said, 'I want to see it anyway.'

'You'd think the streets would be lined with jeering Indians and miners and war widows . . . But it's nothing to do with what he did or didn't do, when you come down to it.'

He was a monument and when a monument falls the entire nation is enlisted to augment official grief.'

'I don't know *what* you're talking about, Falcon—I want to see the bands and the soldiers.'

The ninth earl was silent for some while and then remarked: 'K. J. Key who was captain of Surrey, kept a pair of gold scissors in his waistcoat for cutting his return ticket.'

'Poor O'Hara,' said Jane. 'He must be getting awfully wet.'

The greys jogged handsomely down Park Lane shining with rain, and O'Hara huddled himself in the dripping cloak of mustard yellow, his hat pulled low, his pipe jutting damply between the two.

'You must give him whisky in hot milk when he gets home,' said Jane.

'My grandfather used to horsewhip his servants by day and offer them a drink before he went to bed, in case the revolution occurred during the night.'

'Poor O'Hara,' said Jane. 'I bet he hates you.'

'One must keep a dialogue of tension between the classes, otherwise how is one to distinguish between them? Socialists treat their servants with respect and then wonder why they vote Conservative. So unintelligent.'

He yawned behind his gloved hand. The coach swung round Hyde Park Corner past the memorials to the Machine Gun Corps and the Artillery, and started to climb Constitution Hill.

Jane squealed.

'Golly!—what's that?'

'Rollo!'

A lion was crouched on the wall of Buckingham Palace Gardens, a pink bird in its mouth. It leapt down into the road in front of the coach and ran up the hill.

'Chase him, O'Hara!'

O'Hara's whip cracked and the horses heaved into a gallop.

'Falcon, what *was* it?'

'Rollo—poor thing, he's been lost for days.'

'He was eating something.'

'I know, he has a weakness for flamingos. Her Majesty will not be amused I fear. On the last occasion she was distinctly unamused . . . Oh, dear, this is going to require all Sir Mortimer's delicacy.'

He waited under the trees until the rain stopped, and then urged the donkey forward again. The donkey sneezed. They were wet and cold but the Risen Christ hardly noticed that. Now that he was alone again he felt a great peace and a conviction that took away his burdens of doubt and fear and choice. The donkey's burden was not so nebulous but it protected him from the weather to some extent.

When they turned into the road the Risen Christ was gratified but not surprised to see that people were crowded thick on either side. He composed his features into an expression of modest disdain similar to the donkey's, and they plodded on together.

Jasper Jones rode into the Square, his eyes as hard as flints. The rain had stopped but wet shined his leather chaps and drops of water fell from the brim of his hat. The horse was dulled dark as boot polish from the rain.

Jasper walked his horse into the Square and did not allow himself to acknowledge the stares of the people who watched him go by. Many of them recognized him and told each other, 'Look, there he goes, the Hungriest Gun in the West man with the porkiest beans straight out of the can.'

He sneered under his hat, and rode across into the open space where the fountains were and when the horse lowered its head to drink he slipped off its back and looked around and saw Long John Slaughter leaning against the stone pedestal under George IV.

'Slaughter!'

Long John turned.

'Hello, Jasper,' he said.

'I've been looking for you,' said Jasper Jones.

Everything was suddenly quiet. They stood facing each other across twenty yards of empty ground. Jasper's eyes were hard as silver dollars. He took a step forward and nicked his calf with the spur.

'I told you to keep your cotton pickin' hands off my gal, Slaughter.'

Long John looked around but most of the people were watching the other way. He licked his lips and smiled nervously.

'Oh, leave off, will you?' he said. 'I want to watch the funeral.'

'You'll get one of your own, Slaughter. I've got a message from her and I'm deliverin' it through a forty-five. So draw.'

Long John licked his lips again.

'Listen, don't be like that. She doesn't care for you anyway.'

Jasper Jones grated, 'You yeller coyote—draw.' His eyes were hard as the Rocky Mountains.

'No, I don't want to,' said Long John. 'I'm finished with all that.'

'Then you've got five till I shoot you down like dawg,' drawled Jasper Jones. He stood easy, his right hand close by his hip.

'You must be off your rocker.'

'One.'

'Jasper?'

'Two.'

Long John licked his lips. The wall was behind him.

'Three.'

'It's not fair!' He started to cry. 'It jest ain't fair, I'm tired of all this, I'm tired of ridin' an' shootin' and runnin'—you cain't run away from yerself, my pappy tol' me that!—I'm tired, I wanna hang up my guns!'

'Four.'

Slaughter wept. 'Wanna settle down, git me a woman, few kids, bit o' land to plough—'

'Five.'

With a sob Slaughter went for his gun. It fell on the ground and bounced and there was a roar from a .45 as Jasper outdrew him and shot himself in the leg. Jasper cursed and sat down. Fast as a rattlesnake Long John scooped up his gun and shot Jasper in the stomach and started to run across the Square past Jasper who was dying on his knees. A mountain lion with a flamingo in its mouth streaked across in front of him and seemed to leap over the backs of the crowd; and beyond, a pink coach was rattling down the Mall towards him. Slaughter ran towards it shouting, 'Jane! Jane!' and he had reached the edge of the pavement when Jasper Jones, rolling onto his stomach with his gun held in both hands, took careful aim at the middle of Slaughter's back and shot him through the head.

The excitement of the chase brought a rosy flush to Jane's cheek. Her eyes danced merrily as she smiled at the handsome aristocrat at her side. 'Ah, my dear Jane,' he said, his eyes twinkling, 'you seem to be enjoying yourself.'

It was true. Yet she could but sigh. A shadow passed over her exquisite features and her soft ripe bosom heaved.

'Too late, too late!' a voice cried within her. 'Ah, would that we had met when we were free!'

For him she would have gladly turned her back on Society and escaped with him to some perfect spot away from all this, but she knew deep down in her heart that this would not bring them happiness. They were duty bound to live out their roles in this hollow masquerade even as they recoiled from the hypocritical conventions that kept them apart. No, all they could do was to snatch a few precious moments together.

It was a dull rainy morning but her heart sang as the horses galloped along. The coach rocked violently and she laid her hand on her companion's arm. He smiled roguishly down at her.

She leaned forward in excitement as the coach burst into the Square, thrilled to see the crowds around her. It was as if all the common people of the town had gathered there. She smiled and waved at them—and suddenly she gasped.

'Look!' she cried and pointed to where a man came running towards the coach with a pistol in his hand. She knew him at once, and seized her companion's arm with a soft cry. She closed her eyes and heard a shot ring out.

When she opened her eyes the man was falling headlong into the road as the coach swept up the side of the Square.

Jane leaned back and felt her knee being patted calmingly. She could but admire his insouciance. She smiled bravely and glanced up at him roguishly and was pressed to him as the coach turned the corner.

The horses had slowed down and now moved quite gently down the slope between the people. Looking up, Jane saw a sight the like of which she had never encountered. She stared and involuntarily clutched Lord Malquist's hand as all the blood drained from her cheeks.

'Falcon,' she breathed, 'what is it?'

At that moment the door was flung open and her hand flew to her mouth.

'My husband!' she cried.

Bech Enters Heaven

JOHN UPDIKE

WHEN HENRY BECH was an impressionable pre-adolescent
of thirteen, more bored than he would admit with the
question of whether or not the 1936 Yankees could wrest
the pennant back from Detroit, his mother one May
afternoon took him out of school, after consultation with
the principal; she was a hardened consulter with the
principal. She had consulted when Henry entered the first
grade, when he came back from the second with a bloody
nose, when he skipped the third, when he was given a 65 in
Penmanship in the fifth, and when he skipped the sixth.
The school was P.S. 87, at Seventy-seventh and
Amsterdam—a bleak brick building, whose interior
complexity of smells and excitement, especially during a
snowstorm or around Hallowe'en, was transcendent.
None but very young hearts could have withstood the daily
strain of so much intrigue, humour, desire, personality,
mental effort, emotional current, of so many achingly
important nuances of prestige and impersonation. Bech,
rather short for his age, yet with a big nose and big feet that

promised future growth, was recognized from the first by his classmates as an only son, a mother's son more than a father's, pampered and bright though not a prodigy (his voice had no pitch, his mathematical aptitude was no Einstein's); naturally he was teased. Not all the teasing took the form of bloody noses; sometimes the girl in the adjacent desk-seat tickled the hair on his forearms with her pencil, or his name was flaunted through the wire fence that separated the sexes at recess. The brownstone neighbourhoods that supplied students to the school were in those years still middle-class, if by middle-class is understood not a level of poverty (unlike today's poor, they had no cars, no credit and delivery arrangements with the liquor store) but of self-esteem. Immersed in the Great Depression, they had kept their families together, kept their feet from touching bottom, and kept their faith in the future—their children's future more than their own. These children brought a giddy relief into the sanctum of the school building, relief that the world, or at least this brick cube carved from it, had survived another day. How fragile the world felt to them!—as fragile as it seems sturdy to today's children, who wish to destroy it. Predominately Jewish, Bech's grammar school classes had a bold bright dash of German Gentiles, whose fathers also kept a small shop or plied a manual craft, and some Eastern Europeans, whose fey manners and lisped English made them the centres of romantic frenzy and wild joking attacks. At this time Negroes, like Chinese, were exotic oddities, created, like zebras, in jest. All studied, by the light of yellowish overhead globes and of the 48-star flag nailed above the blackboard, penmanship, the spice routes, the imports and exports of the three Guianas, the three cases of percentage, and other matters of rote given significance by the existence of breadlines and penthouses, just as the various drudgeries of their fathers were given dignity, even holiness by their direct connection with food and survival. Although he would have been slow to admit this also, little Bech loved the school; he cherished his citizenship in its ragged population, was enraptured by the freckled chin and cerulean eyes of Eva Hassel across the aisle, and detested his mother's frequent interference in his American education. Whenever she appeared outside the office of the principal (Mr Linnehan, a sore-lidded spoiled priest with an easily mimicked blink and stammer), he was teased in the cloakroom or down on the asphalt at recess; whenever she had him skipped a grade, he became all the more the baby of the class. By the age of thirteen, he was going to school with girls that were women. That day in May, he showed his anger with his mother by not talking to her as they walked from the scarred school steps, down Seventy-eighth, past a mock-Tudor apartment house like some evilly enlarged and begrimed fairy-tale chalet, to Broadway and Seventy-ninth and the IRT kiosk with its compounded aroma of hot brakes, warm bagels, and vomit.

Extraordinarily, they took a train *north*. The whole drift of their lives was *south* — south to Times Square and to the Public Library, south to Gimbels, south to Brooklyn where his father's two brothers lived. North, there was nothing but Grant's Tomb, and Harlem, and Yankee Stadium, and Riverdale where a rich cousin, a theatre manager, inhabited an apartment full of glass furniture and an array of leering and scribbled photographs. North of that yawned the foreign vastness, first named New York State but melting westward into other names, other states, where the *goyim* farmed their farms and drove their roadsters and swung on their porch swings and engaged in the countless struggles of moral heroism depicted continuously in the Hollywood movies at the Broadway RKO. Upon the huge body of the United States, swept by dust storms and storms of Christian conscience, young Henry knew that his island of Manhattan existed like a wart; relatively, his little family world was an immigrant enclave, the religion his family practised was a tolerated affront, and the language of this religion's celebration was a backwards-running archaism. He and his kin and their kindred were huddled in shawls within an overheated back room while outdoors a huge and beautiful wilderness rattled their sashes with wind and painted the panes with frost; and all the furniture they had brought with them from Europe, the foot-stools and phylacteries, the copies of Tolstoy and Heine, the ambitiousness and defensiveness and love, belonged to this stuffy back room.

Now his mother was pointing him north, into the cold. Their reflections shuddered in the black glass as the express train slammed through local stops, wan islands of light where fat coloured women waited with string shopping bags. Bech was always surprised that these frozen vistas did not shatter as they pierced them; perhaps it was the multi-levelled sliding, the hurtling metal precariously switched aside from collision, more than the odours and subterranean claustrophobia, that made the boy sick on subways. He figured that he was good for eight stops before nausea began. It had just begun when she touched his arm. High, high on the West Side they emerged, into a region where cliffs and windy hilltops seemed insecurely suppressed by the asphalt grid. A boistrous shout of spring rolled upwards from the river, and unexpected bridges of green metal arched seraphically overhead. Together they walked, the boy and his mother, he in a wool knicker suit that scratched and sang between his legs, she in a tremulous hat of shining black straw, up a broad pavement bordered with cobblestones and trees whose bark was scabbed brown and white like a giraffe's neck. This was the last year when she was taller than he; his sideways glance reaped a child's cowing impression of, beneath the unsteady flesh of her jaw, the rose splotches at the side of her neck that signalled excitement or anger. He had better talk. 'Where are we going?'

'So,' she said, 'the cat found his tongue.'

'You know I don't like you coming into the school.'

'Mister Touch-Me-Not,' she said, 'so ashamed of his mother he wants all his blue-eyed *shikses* to think he came out from under a rock, I suppose. Or better yet lives in a tree like Siegfried.'

Somewhere in the past she had wormed out of him his admiration of the German girls at school. He blushed. 'Thanks to you,' he told her, 'they're all two years older than me.'

'Not in their empty golden heads, they're not so old. Maybe in their pants, but that'll come to you soon enough. Don't hurry the years, soon enough they'll hurry you.'

Homily, flattery, and humiliation: these were what his mother applied to him, day after day, like a sculptor's pats. It deepened his blush to hear her mention Eva Hassel's pants. Were they what would come to him soon enough? This was her style, to mock his reality and stretch his expectations. 'Mother, don't be fantastic.'

'Ai, nothing fantastic. There's nothing one of those golden girls would like better than fasten herself to some smart little Jewish boy. Better that than some sausage-grinding Fritz who'll go to beer and beating her before he's twenty-five. You keep your nose in your books.'

'That's where it was. Where are you taking me?'

'To see something more important than where to put your *putz*.'

'Mother, don't be vulgar.'

'Vulgar is what I call a boy who wants to put his mother under a rock. His mother and his people and his brain, all under a rock.'

'Now I understand. You're taking me to look at Plymouth Rock.'

'Something like it. If you have to grow up American, at least let's not look only at the underside. Arnie' – the Riverdale cousin – 'got two tickets from Josh Glazer, to I don't know quite what it is. We shall see.'

The hill beneath their feet flattened; they arrived at a massive building of somehow unsullied granite, with a paradoxical look of having been here forever yet having been rarely used. Around its top ran a ribbon of carved names: PLATO . NEWTON . AESCHYLUS . LEONARDO . AQUINAS . SHAKESPEARE . VOLTAIRE . COPERNICUS . ARISTOTLE . HOBBES . VICO . PUSHKIN . LINNAEUS . RACINE

and infinitely on, around cornices and down the receding
length of the building's two tall wings. Courtyard followed
courtyard, each at a slightly higher level than the last.
Conical evergreens stood silent guard; an unseen fountain
played. For entrance, there was a bewildering choice of
bronze doors. Bech's mother pushed one and encountered
a green-uniformed guard; she told him, 'My name is
Hannah Bech and this is my son Henry. These are our
tickets, it says right here this is the day, they were obtained
for us by a close associate of Josh Glazer's, the playwright.
Nobody forewarned me it would be such a climb from the
subway, that's why I'm out of breath like this.' The guard,
then another guard, for they several times got lost,
directed them (his mother receiving and repeating a full set
of directions each time) up a ramifying series of marble
stairways into the balcony of an auditorium whose ceiling,
the child's impression was, was decorated with plaster toys
– scrolls, masks, seashells, tops, and stars.

A ceremony was already in progress. Their discussions
with the guards had consumed time. The bright stage far
below them supported a magical tableau. On a curved dais
composed of six or seven rows a hundred persons, mostly
men, were seated. Though some of the men could be seen
to move – one turned his head, another scratched his knee –
their appearance in sum had an iron unity; they looked
engraved. Each face, even at the distance of the balcony,
displayed the stamp of extra precision that devout
attention and frequent photography etch upon a visage;
each had suffered the crystallization of fame. Young Henry
saw that there were other types of Heaven, less agitated
and more elevated than the school, more compact and less
tragic than Yankee Stadium, where the scattered players,
fragile in white, seemed about to be devoured by the
dragon-shaped crowd. He knew, even before his mother,
with the aid of a diagram provided on her programme,
began to name names, that under his eyes was assembled
the flower of the arts in America, its rabbis and chieftains,
souls who while still breathing enjoyed their immortality.

The surface of their collective glory undulated as one or another would stand, shuffle outwards from his row, seize the glowing lectern, and speak. Some rose to award prizes; others rose to accept them. They applauded one another with a polite rustle eagerly echoed and thunderously amplified by the anonymous, perishable crowd on the other side of the veil, a docile cloudy multitude stretching backwards from front rows of corsaged loved ones into the dim regions of the balcony where mere spectators sat, where little Bech stared dazzled while his mother busily bent above the identifying diagram. She located, and pointed out to him, with that ardour for navigational detail that had delayed their arrival here, Emil Nordquist, the Bard of the Prairie, the beetle-browed celebrant in irresistible *vers libre* of shocked corn and Swedish dairymaids; John Kingsgrant Forbes, New England's dapper novelist of manners; Hannah Ann Collins, the wispy, mystical poet of impacted passion from Alabama, the most piquant voice in American verse since the passing of the Amherst recluse; the massive Jason Honeygale, Tennessee's fabled word-torrent; hawk-eyed Torquemada Langguth, lover and singer of California's sheer cliffs and sere unpopulated places; and Manhattan's own Josh Glazer, Broadway wit, comedywright, lyricist, and Romeo. And there were squat bald sculptors with great curved thumbs; red-bearded painters like bespattered prophets; petite, gleaming philosophers who piped Greek catchwords into the microphone; stooped and drawling historians from the border states; avowed Communists with faces as dry as paper and black ribbons dangling from their *pinces-nez*; atonal composers delicately exchanging awards and reminiscences of Paris, the phrases in French nasally cutting across their speech like accented trombones; sibylline old women with bronze faces – all of them unified, in the eyes of the boy Bech, by not only the clothy dark mass of their clothes and the brilliance of the stage but by their transcendence of time: they had attained the haven of lasting accomplishment and exempted themselves from the nagging nuisance of growth and its twin (which he precociously felt in himself even then, especially in his teeth), decay. He childishly assumed that, though unveiled every May, they sat like this eternally, in the same iron arrangement, beneath this domed ceiling of scrolls and stars.

At last the final congratulation was offered, and the final modest acceptance enunciated. Bech and his mother turned to re-navigate the maze of staircases. They were both shy of speaking, but she sensed, in the abstracted way he clung to her side, neither welcoming nor cringing from her touch when she reached to reassure him in the crowd, that his attention had been successfully turned. His ears were red, showing that an inner flame had been lit. She had set him on a track, a track that must be—Mrs Bech ignored a sudden qualm, like a rude jostling from behind—the right one.

Bech never dared hope to join that pantheon. Those faces of the thirties, like the books he began to read, putting aside baseball statistics forever, formed a world impossibly high and apart, an immutable text graven on the stone brow—his confused impression was—of Manhattan. In middle age, it would startle him to realize that Louis Bromfield, say, was no longer considered a sage, that van Vechten, Cabell, and John Erskine had become as obscure as the famous gangsters of the same period, and that an entire generation had grown to wisdom without once chuckling over a verse by Arthur Guiterman or Franklin P. Adams. When Bech received, in an envelope not so unlike those containing solicitations to join the Erotica Book Club or the Associated Friends of Apache Education, notice of his election to a society whose title suggested that of a merged church, with an invitation to its May ceremonial, he did not connect the honour with his truant afternoon of over three decades ago. He accepted, because in his fallow middle years he hesitated to decline any invitation, whether it was to travel to Communist Europe or to smoke marijuana. His working day was brief, his living day was long, and there always lurked the hope that around the corner of some impromptu acquiescence he would encounter, in a flurry of apologies and excitedly mis-aimed kisses, his long-lost mistress, Inspiration. He took a taxi north on the appointed day. By chance he was let off at a side entrance in no way reminiscent of the august frontal approach he had once ventured within the shadow of his mother. Inside the bronze door, Bech was greeted by a mini-skirted secretary who, licking her lips and perhaps unintentionally bringing her pelvis to within an inch of his, pinned his name in plastic to his lapel and, as a tantalizing afterthought, the tip of her tongue exposed in playful concentration, adjusted the knot of his necktie. Other such considerate houris were supervising arrivals, separating antique *belle-lettrists* from their overcoats with philatelic care, steering querulously nodding poetesses towards the elevator, administering the distribution of gaudy heaps of name tags, admission cards, and coded numerals.

His girl wore a button that said GOD FREAKS OUT.

Bech asked her, 'Am I supposed to do anything?'

She said, 'When your name is announced, stand.'

'Do I take the elevator?'

She patted his shoulders and tugged one of his earlobes. 'I think you're a young enough body,' she judged, 'to use the stairs.'

He obediently ascended a thronged marble stairway and found himself amid a cloud of murmuring presences; a few of the faces were familiar—Tory Ingersoll, a tireless old fag, his prim features rigid in their carapace of orangish foundation, who had in recent years plugged himself into hipsterism and become a copious puffist and anthologist for the 'new' poetry, whether concrete, non-associative, neo-gita, or plain protest; Irving Stern, a swarthy, ruminative critic of Bech's age and background, who for all his strenuous protests of McLuhanite openness had never stopped squinting through the dour goggles of Leninist

aesthetics, and whose own prose style tasted like aspirin
tablets being chewed; Mildred Belloussovsky-Dommergues, her name as polyglot as her marriages, her weight-
lifter's shoulders and generous slash of a wise whore's
mouth perversely dwindled in print to a trickle of elliptic
dimeters; Char Ecktin, the revolutionary young dramatist
whose foolish smile and high-pitched chortle consorted
oddly with the facile bitterness of his dénouements—but
many more were half-familiar, faces dimly known, like
those of bit actors in B movies, or like those faces which
emerge from obscurity to cap a surprisingly enthusiastic
obituary, or those names which figure small on title pages,
as translator, co-editor, or 'as told to', faces whose air of
recognizability might have been a matter of ghostly family
resemblance, or of a cocktail party ten years ago, or a P.E.N.
meeting, or of a moment in a bookstore, an inside flap
hastily examined and then resealed into the tight bright
row of the unpurchased. In this throng Bech heard his
name softly called, and felt his sleeve lightly plucked. But
he did not lift his eyes for fear of shattering the spell, of
disturbing the penumbral decorum and rustle around him.
They came to the end of their labyrinthine climb, and were
ushered down a dubiously narrow corridor. Bech
hesitated, as even the dullest steer hesitates in the
slaughterer's chute, but the pressure behind moved him
on, outwards, into a spotlit tangle of groping men and
scraping chairs. He was on a stage. Chairs were arranged in
curved tiers. Mildred Belloussovsky-Dommergues waved
an alabaster, muscular arm: 'Yoo-hoo, Henry, over here.
Come be a B with me.' She even spoke now—so thoroughly
does art corrupt the artist—in dimeters. Willingly he made
his way upwards towards her. Always, in his life, no matter
how underfurnished in other respects, there had been a
woman to shelter beside. The chair beside her bore his
name. On the seat of the chair was a folded programme.
On the back of the programme was a diagram. The diagram
fitted a memory, and looking outward, into the populated
darkness that reached backwards into a balcony, beneath a

ceiling dimly decorated with toylike protrusions of plaster, Bech suspected, at last, where he was. With the instincts of a literary man he turned to printed matter for confirmation; he bent over the diagram and, yes, found his name, his number, his chair. He was here. He had joined that luminous, immutable tableau. He had crossed to the other side.

Now that forgotten expedition with his mother returned to him, and their climb through those ramifications of marble, a climb that mirrored, but profanely, the one he had just taken within sacred precincts; and he deduced that this building was vast twice over, an arch-like interior meeting in this domed auditorium where the mortal and the immortal could behold one another, through a veil that blurred and darkened the one and gave to the other a supernatural visibility, the glow and precision of Platonic forms. He studied his left hand — his partner in numerous humble crimes, his delegate in many furtive investigations —and saw it partaking, behind the flame-blue radiance of his cuff, joint by joint, to the quicks of his fingernails, in the fine articulation found less in reality than in the Promethean anatomical studies of Leonardo and Raphael.

Bech looked around; the stage was filling. He seemed to see, down front, where the stage light was most intense, the oft-photographed (by Steichen, by Karsh, by Cartier-Bresson) profile and vivid cornsilk hair of—it couldn't be—Emil Nordquist. The Bard of the Prairie still lived! He must be a hundred. No, well, if in the mid-thirties he was in his mid-forties, he would be only eighty now. While Bech, that pre-adolescent, was approaching fifty: time had treated him far more cruelly.

And now, through the other wing of the stage, from the elevator side, moving with the agonized shuffle-step of a semi-paralytic but still sartorially formidable in double-breasted chalkstripes and a high starched collar, entered John Kingsgrant Forbes, whose last perceptive and urbane examination of Beacon Hill mores had appeared in World War II, during the paper shortage. Had Bech merely imagined his obituary?

'Arriveth our queen,' Mildred Belloussovsky-Dommergues sardonically murmured on his left, with that
ambiguous trace of a foreign accent, the silted residue of
her several husbands. And to Bech's astonishment in came,
supported on the courtly arm of Jason Honeygate, whose
epic bulk had shrivelled to folds of veined hide draped over
stegosaurian bones, the tiny tottering figure of Hannah
Ann Collins, wearing the startled facial expression of the
blind. She was led down front, where the gaunt figure of
Torquemada Langguth, his spine bent nearly double, his
falconine crest now white as an egret's, rose to greet her
and feebly to adjust her chair.

Bech murmured leftwards, 'I thought they were all
dead.'

Mildred airily answered, 'We find it easier, not to die.'

A shadow plumped brusquely down in the chair on
Bech's right; it was—O, monstrous!—Josh Glazer. His
proximity seemed to be a patron's, for he told Bech windily,
'Jesus Christ, Bech, I've been plugging you for years up
here, but the bastards always said, "Let's wait until he
writes another book, that last one was such a flop." Finally I
say to them, "Look. The son of a bitch, he's *never* going to
write another book," so they say, "OK, let's let him the hell
in." Welcome aboard, Bech. Christ I've been a raving fan of
yours since the Year One. When're you gonna try a
comedy, Broadway's dead on its feet.' He was deaf, his hair
was dyed black, and his teeth were false too, for his blasts
of breath carried with them a fetid smell of trapped alcohol
and of a terrible organic something that suggested to
Bech—touching a peculiar fastidiousness that was all that
remained of his ancestors' orthodoxy—the stench of
decayed shellfish. Bech looked away and saw everywhere
on this stage dissolution and riot. The furrowed skulls of
philosophers lolled in a Bacchic stupor. Wicked smirks
flickered back and forth among faces enshrined in
textbooks. Eustace Chubb, America's poetic conscience
throughout the Cold War, had holes in his socks and

mechanically chaffed a purple sore on his shin. Anatole
Husač, the Father of Neo-Figurism, was sweating out a
drug high, his hands twitching like suffocating fish. As the
ceremony proceeded, not a classroom of trade-school
dropouts could have been more impudently inattentive.
Mildred Belloussovsky-Dommergues persistently tickled
the hairs on Bech's wrist with the edge of her programme;
Josh Glazer offered him a sip from a silver flask signed by
the Gershwin brothers. The leonine head   that of a great
lexicographer—directly in front of Bech drifted sideways
and emitted illegible snores. The Medal for Modern Fiction
was being awarded to Kingsgrant Forbes; the cello-shaped
critic (best known for his scrupulous editorship of the six
volumes of Hamlin Garland's correspondence) began his
speech, 'In these sorry days of so-called Black Humour, of
the fictional apotheosis of the underdeveloped,' and a
Negro in the middle of Bech's row stood, spoke a single
black expletive, and, with much scraping of chairs, made
his way from the stage. A series of grants was bestowed.
One of the recipients, a tiptoeing fellow in a mauve jump
suit, hurled paper streamers towards the audience and
bared his chest to reveal painted there a psychedelic pig
labelled Milhaus; at this, several old men, an Arizona
naturalist and a New Deal muralist, stamped off, and for a
long time could be heard buzzing for the elevator. The
sardonic hubbub waxed louder. Impatience set in.
'Goddammit,' Josh Glazer breathed to Bech, 'I'm paying a
limousine by the hour downstairs. Jesus and I've got a
helluva cute little fox waiting for me at the Plaza.'

At last the time came to introduce the new members.
The citations were read by a far-sighted landscape painter
who had trouble bringing his papers, the lectern light, and
his reading glasses into mutual adjustment at such short
focus. 'Henry Bech,' he read, pronouncing it 'Betch', and
Bech confusedly stood. The spotlights dazzled him; he had
the sensation of being microscopically examined, and of
being strangely small. When he stood, he had expected to
rear into a man's height, and instead rose no taller than a child.

'A native New Yorker,' the citation began, 'who has chosen to sing of the continental distances—'

Bech wondered why writers in official positions were always supposed to 'sing'; he couldn't remember the last time he had even hummed.

'—a son of Israel loyal to Melville's romanticism—'

He went around telling interviewers Melville was his favourite author, but he hadn't got a third of the way through *Pierre*.

'—a poet in prose whose polish precludes pre- pro- pardon me, these are new bifocals—'

Laughter from the audience. Who was out there in that audience?

'—let me try again: whose polish precludes prolifigacy—'

His mother was out there in that audience!

'—a magician of metaphor—'

She was there, right down front, basking in the reflected stagelight, an orchid corsage pinned to her bosom.

'—and a friend of the human heart.'

But she had died four years ago, in a nursing home in Riverdale. As the applause washed in, Bech saw that the old lady with the corsage was applauding only politely, she was not his mother but somebody else's, maybe of the boy with the pig on his stomach, though for a moment, a trick of the light, something determined and expectant in the tilt of her head, something hopeful. . . . The light in his eyes turned to warm water. His applause ebbed away. He sat down. Mildred nudged him. Josh Glazer shook his hand, too violently. Bech tried to clear his vision by contemplating the backs of the heads. They were blank: blank shabby backs of a cardboard tableau lent substance only by the credulous, by old women and children. His knees trembled, as if after an arduous climb. He had made it, he was here, in Heaven. Now what?

The Fall of the House of Hazelstone

TOM SHARPE

TO KOMMANDANT VAN Heerden the transition of Miss Hazelstone from the mistress of Jacaranda House to the inmate of Fort Rapier Mental Hospital was a sad affair. As he watched the stretcher on which the old lady lay carried for the last time past the portraits of her ancestors in the fern-infested hall, he knew that an epoch was ending. No longer would Jacaranda House stand supreme in the eyes of Zululand society, the symbol of all that was best in the British occupation of Africa and an emblem of an aristocratic way of life. No more garden parties, no more grand balls, no more of those dinner parties for which Miss Hazelstone had such a reputation, nothing of importance would happen within these walls. The house would stand empty and sepulchral until the white ants or the demolition men cleared it away to make room for a new suburb. As Kommandant van Heerden turned off the lights and the house stood dark under the moon, he was filled with a great sense of loss. The old arrogance on which he had relied to sharpen his servility was gone. He was a free man,

and the architect of his own freedom. It was the last thing
that he wanted.

It was a cortège which passed up the drive and out the
contorted gates, a funeral cortège of motorcycles and
police cars accompanying the ambulance in which Miss
Hazelstone slept the sleep of the heavily sedated. In the
driver's seat of the leading car sat Konstabel Els, happy in
the knowledge that he had earned his just reward, and
behind him in the darkness Kommandant van Heerden
wondered at the strangeness of fate which had made a
creature like Els the instrument of the fall of the house of
Hazelstone.

It was not as if Els was clever, the Kommandant thought,
as the procession wound its way through the unlighted
streets of Piemburg, nor was there anything vaguely
intentional about his activities which would explain their
effect. Els was merely chance, random and trivial in its
ways.

'Entropy made man,' the Kommandant said to himself
and opened the window. The car had begun to smell quite
intolerable.

'Els,' said the Kommandant, 'you need a bath.'

'Me, sir?' said Els.

'You, Els. You stink.'

'Not me, sir. That's Toby.'

'Who the hell's Toby?'

'The Dobermann, sir. He's a bit high.'

'You mean you've got the carcase of a rotting dog in the
car?' shouted the Kommandant.

'Oh no, sir,' said Els. 'He's in the boot.'

The Kommandant was about to say that he wasn't going
to share his car with a putrefying Dobermann, when they
passed through the gates of Fort Rapier and drove up the
drive to the hospital.

In the moonlight the buildings of Fort Rapier looked much
as they had done when the garrison occupied the barracks.
A few bars had been added here and there to convert an
establishment which had been designed to keep people out

into one that served to keep them in, but the atmosphere had not altered. Irrationality had kept its hold on the place.

'Old traditions die hard,' the Kommandant thought as the car stopped at the edge of the parade ground. He stepped out and patted a field gun that had once seen service at Paardeberg where his grandfather had slept through its bombardment and which now stood like an iron pensioner overlooking the lunacies of another generation.

While Miss Hazelstone was taken into a ward reserved for the criminally insane, Kommandant van Heerden explained her case to the Superintendent, Dr Herzog, who had been summoned from his bed to deal with the case.

'Couldn't you have waited till morning?' he asked grumpily. 'I didn't get to bed until one.'

'I haven't been to bed at all,' said the Kommandant, 'and in any case this is an emergency. Miss Hazelstone is something of a celebrity and her committal may arouse public comment.'

'She certainly is, and it certainly will,' said the doctor. 'She happens to be the chief benefactress of this hospital.'

'She has evidently been providing for her own future which will be to remain here until she decides to die,' said the Kommandant.

'Who has diagnosed her?' asked Dr Herzog.

'I have,' said the Kommandant.

'I wouldn't have thought you were qualified to.'

'I know a criminal lunatic when I see one. The police surgeon and her own doctor will be up in the morning, and committal papers will arrive in due course.'

'It seems rather irregular,' said the doctor.

'As a matter of fact, it is irregular,' said the Kommandant. 'But if you really want to know, we have pretty incontrovertible evidence that she has murdered someone. I won't go into details but I can assure you that we have enough evidence to have her tried for murder. I think you understand that the trial of such a prominent person would not be in the public interest.'

'Good God,' said the doctor, 'what is Zululand coming
to? First her brother and now Miss Hazelstone.

'Quite,' said the Kommandant. 'It's a reflection on our
times.'

Having ensured that Miss Hazelstone would be allowed
no visitors and that she would have no access to the Press
or to her lawyers, the Kommandant took his leave. Dawn
had broken when he crossed the great parade ground, and a
few grey figures had emerged from the wards and were
shuffling about sadly in the early sunlight.

'To think it had to end like this,' the Kommandant
thought and his mind dwelt not so much on Miss
Hazelstone as on the Imperial splendour that had once
marched red-coated and supreme across the square. He
stood for a moment imagining the regiments that had
passed the saluting base on which Miss Hazelstone's
grandfather had stood before going to their deaths on
Majuba Hill and Spion Kop and then he turned away and
climbed into his reeking car.

When Miss Hazelstone woke to find herself in bed in a
ward, she had difficulty understanding where she was. The
decor and the row of beds brought back to her memories of
her boarding school but her companions were hardly the gay
carefree girls of her youth. Not that they were really gay,
she thought lying back and studying the ceiling, merely
expectant, which passed for gaiety. There was nothing
remotely gay or expectant about the figures she could see
now. Withdrawn into remote provinces of their own
imaginations the patients wandered listlessly among the
obstacles presented by reality. Miss Hazelstone looked at
them and was tempted to follow their example. Only a
sense of pride prevented her. 'Such lack of style,' she said to
herself, and sitting on the edge of her bed looked round for
her clothes.

In the days that followed she clung grimly to her
arrogance, firmly rejecting the unreal worlds the other

patients pressed on her.

'You may be,' she told a patient who introduced himself as Napoleon, 'though I doubt it. I am Miss Hazelstone of Jacaranda House,' and even the staff learnt that it was unwise to address her simply as Hazelstone.

'Miss Hazelstone to you,' she snapped at a sister who made the mistake.

'One must keep up appearances,' she told Dr von Blimenstein, the psychiatrist who had been assigned to deal with the new patient, and who was trying vainly to get Miss Hazelstone to recognize the sexual origins of her illness. Dr von Blimenstein was so wildly eclectic in her approach that it was difficult to tell which school of psychology she most favoured. She was known to prescribe electric-shock therapy in unlimited doses to the black patients, but with whites placed particular stress on sexual guilt as the cause of psychoses. She was so successful in this approach that she had once even managed to cure a keeper at the Durban Snake Park of his anxiety neurosis about snakes. His phobia had, he claimed, been brought on by his having been bitten on forty-eight separate occasions by snakes as venomous and varied as puff-adders, cobras, Gabon vipers, ringhals and asps, each of which had brought him to the verge of death. Dr von Blimstein had convinced the poor man that his fears were purely sexual in origin and resulted from a feeling of inadequacy brought on by the realization that his penis was neither so long nor so potent as a mature python and had sent him back to work at the Snake Park where three weeks later he had been bitten, this time with fatal results, by a black mamba whose length he had been trying to measure by comparing it with his own erect member which he knew to be six inches long. 'Nine feet three inches,' he had just concluded, laying the mamba's head against his *glans penis*. It was practically the last thing he could conclude, as the mamba with a ferocity fully justified by the absurd comparison plunged its fangs into its symbolic counterpart. After that Dr von Blimenstein had turned away from psychoanalysis and had favoured a more behaviourist approach.

With Miss Hazelstone she decided there was no danger of such tragic results and she had encouraged the patient to record her dreams so that these could be examined for the symbolic meaning which would explain all her problems. The trouble was that Miss Hazelstone never dreamt and the concocted dreams that she supplied the doctor with were down-to-earth in the extreme. They were for one thing punctuated with phalluses and vaginas which no amount of symbolic interpretation could turn into anything else.

'How about snakes, or steeples?' Miss Hazelstone inquired when the doctor explained how difficult it was.

'I've never heard of people having dreams about penises before,' said the doctor.

'Probably wish-fulfilment dreams,' Miss Hazelstone said and went on to describe a dream in which a creature called Els had struggled with a black dog on a lawn.

'Extraordinary,' said von Blimenstein, 'absolutely archetypal,' and had begun to talk about the Shadow struggling with Instinctual Libido.

'Yes, it struck me like that at the time,' said Miss Hazelstone cryptically. After several weeks of these dreams the doctor had begun to think she would be able to write a monograph on 'The Policeman Archetype in South African Psychology' using this material.

For Miss Hazelstone these interviews provided a break from the boredom of life in Fort Rapier.

'Madness is so monotonous,' she told the doctor. 'You would think that fantasies would be more interesting, but really one has to conclude that insanity is a poor substitute for reality.'

Then again, when she looked around her, there didn't seem to be any significant difference between life in the mental hospital and life in South Africa as a whole. Black madmen did all the work, while white lunatics lounged about imagining they were God.

'I'm sure the Almighty has more dignity,' Miss Hazelstone said to herself, as she watched the shuffling figures moving aimlessly about the grounds. 'And I'm sure He hasn't delusions of grandeur.'

The news that his sister had finally been found and was now an inmate in Fort Rapier Mental Hospital came as no surprise to the Bishop of Barotseland.

'She was never very sane,' he told the Kommandant who came to see him personally to break the news, and demonstrated once more that lack of family loyalty the Kommandant found so deplorable in one who belonged to such an illustrious line, by adding, 'The best place for her. She should have been certified years ago.' The Bishop was shedding all his illusions, it seemed, and certainly he had ceased to feel kindly towards his sister and had stopped thinking she was merely mildly eccentric. 'I have a great admiration for Miss Hazelstone,' said the Kommandant coldly. 'She was a remarkable woman and Zululand will be the poorer for her passing.'

'You speak of her as though she were already dead,' said the Bishop, whose thoughts about mortality were markedly more frequent since he had moved into Bottom. 'I suppose in a way she has gone to a better life.'

'She won't be leaving there until she is dead,' said the Kommandant grimly. 'By the way, your trial starts next week so if you have anything to say in your defence you had better start thinking about it now,' and the Kommandant had gone away convinced that Jonathan Hazelstone deserved his fate.

The Bishop, left alone in his cell, decided that there was really nothing he could do to add to the confession he had made. It seemed to him a perfectly adequate defence in itself. Nobody on earth could possibly believe he had committed the crimes he had admitted to, and he doubted if any but an expert on High Church ritual could disentangle criminal offences from ecclesiastical practices. No judge

worth his salt could ever condemn him for latitudinarian-
ism. The Bishop lay down on the mat on the floor of his cell
which served as his bed and looked forward to the verdict
he was sure would free him.

'It probably won't even come to that,' he thought
cheerfully. 'The judge will throw the prosecution case out
of court.'

As usual with the Bishop of Barotseland's prognostications
events were to prove him entirely wrong. The Judge
chosen to hear the case was Justice Schalkwyk, whose
mother had died in a British concentration camp and who
was noted both for his deafness and his loathing for all
things British. The attorney for the defence, Mr Leopold
Jackson, was likewise handicapped physically by a cleft
palate which made his speeches almost inaudible, and who
was in any case known for his tendency to defer to the
authority of judges. He had been chosen to conduct the
defence by the accused man's heirs, distant cousins who
lived in a poor section of Capetown and who hoped by
speeding the course of justice to avoid any further
unwelcome publicity which would besmirch the family
name. Mr Jackson was only allowed to see his client a few
days before the trial began, and then only in the presence of
Konstabel Els.

The interview took place in Bottom and was marked by
an almost complete misunderstanding from the start.

'You thay you've thigned a confethion. Motht unfortunate,' said Mr Jackson.

'It was made under duress,' said the Bishop.

'It wasn't,' said Els. 'It was made in here.'

'Under dureth,' said Mr Jackson. 'Then it won't thtand
up.'

'I don't expect it to,' said the Bishop.

'It can't,' said Els. 'Confessions never do.'

'How wath it forthed out of you?'

'I was made to stand up.'

'You weren't,' said Els. 'I let you sit down.'

'So you did,' said the Bishop.

'Tho it wathn't made under dureth,' said Mr Jackson.

'I told you just now. It was made in here,' said Els.

'It was partly made under duress,' said the Bishop.

'Don't listen to him,' said Els. 'I know where it was made. It was made in here.'

'Wath it made in here?' asked Mr Jackson.

'Yeth,' said the Bishop, lapsing into legal jargon.

'There you are. I told you it was,' said Els.

'There theemth to be thome confuthion,' said Mr Jackson. 'What did you confeth to?'

'Genuflexion with a rubber prick,' said Els hurriedly forestalling lesser crimes.

'Genuflecthion with a what?' Mr Jackson asked.

'He means a rubric, I think,' said the Bishop.

'I don't. I mean a rubber prick,' said Els indignantly.

'Thoundth a thrange thort of offenth,' said Mr Jackson.

'You're telling me,' said Els.

'I thought thith wath a capital cathe,' said Mr Jackson.

'It is,' said Els, 'I'm enjoying it no end.'

'Genuflecthing ithn't a crime under Thouth African law.'

'It is with a rubber prick,' said Els.

'There was some other crimes in my confession,' said the Bishop.

'Thuthch ath?'

'Murder,' said the Bishop.

'Lesbianism,' said Els.

'Lethbianithm? Thatth impothible. A man can't commit lethbianithm. Are you thure you've got the right cathe?'

'Positive,' said Els.

'Would you mind allowing my client to thpeak for himthelf?' Mr Jackson asked Els.

'I'm just trying to help,' said Els aggrieved.

'Now then,' Mr Jackson went on, 'ith it true that you have admitted to being a lethbian?'

'As a matter of fact, yes,' said the Bishop.

'And a murderer?'

'It does seem strange, doesn't it?' said the Bishop.

'It thoundth fantathtic. What elth did you confeth?'

The Bishop hesitated. He did not want Mr Jackson to object to his confession before it was read out in court. Everything depended on the absurdity of the document and Mr Jackson did not look like a lawyer who would understand that.

'I think I would prefer the case to go forward as it is,' he said, and excusing himself on the ground that he was tired, ushered the attorney out of the cell.

'Thee you on the day,' Mr Jackson said cheerily, and left Bottom.

It was not due to Mr Jackson however, that Jonathan Hazelstone's confession never reached the court in its unabridged version. It was thanks rather to the conscientiousness of Luitenant Verkramp who, eager for praise, had sent a copy of the confession to BOSS in Pretoria. The head of the Bureau of State Security found the document on his desk one morning and read the thing through with a growing sense of disbelief. It wasn't that he was unused to reading extravagant confessions. After all the Security Branch existed to manufacture them and he could boast that it had a reputation in this respect second to none. One hundred and eighty days in solitary confinement and days of standing up without sleep while being questioned had the tendency to produce some pretty damning admissions from the suspects, but the confession that Verkramp had sent him made all previous ones look positively tame.

'The man's out of his mind,' he said after ploughing though a catalogue of crimes that included necrophilia, flagellation and liturgy, but it was not certain which man he was referring to. After a conference with leading members of the Government, BOSS decided to intervene in the interests of Western civilization incarnate in the Republic of South Africa and using the powers bestowed

on it by Parliament, ordered the suppression of nine-tenths
of the confession. Judge Schalkwyk was to try, convict, and
condemn the prisoner, with no opportunity to appeal, on
charges of murdering one Zulu cook and twenty-one
policemen. No other charges were to be preferred and no
evidence prejudicial to State security was to be presented in
court. Grumbling furiously, the old Judge was forced in
accordance with South African law to obey. Jonathan
Hazelstone was to be hanged, there must be no miscarriage
of justice, but he was after all to be hanged for a lamb.

The trial took place in Piemburg and in the very courtroom
in which the accused's father had made such a great
reputation.

'The old order changeth,' Jonathan murmured to his
lawyer as he took his seat in the dock. Mr Jackson was not
amused.

'It hardly becometh you to make mockery of my defect,'
he said. 'Bethideth from what I have heard you would do
better to thay "The wortht ith yet to come." '

Mr Jackson for once was right. The discovery that his
confession had been expurgated came as the real shock of
the trial to the Bishop. In the adjournment that followed
the announcement that he was only to be tried for murder,
Jonathan consulted with his attorney.

'I thould plead inthanity. It theemth your only chanth,'
was Mr Jackson's advice.

'But I'm entirely innocent. I had nothing to do with the
murder of twenty-one policemen.'

'I darethay but it ith an unfortunate fact that you have
confethed to killing them.'

'I was forced to. Why on earth should I want to murder
them?'

'I have no idea,' said Mr Jackson. 'My clienth motiveth are
alwayth a mythtery to me. The point ith that the evidenth
againtht you theemth pretty concluthive. You had the
opportunity and the weaponth were found in your

pothethion. Furthermore you have admitted in a thigned confethion to having killed them. I thuggetht you change your plea from not guilty to guilty but inthane.'

'I'm not inthane,' shouted the Bishop.

'I haven't come here to be inthulted,' said Mr Jackson.

'I'm thorry,' said the Bishop. 'I mean I'm sorry.'

'I shall change the plea,' said Mr Jackson finally. 'Inthanity it ith.'

'I suppose so,' said the Bishop.

'It'th better than being hanged,' said Mr Jackson. They went back into the courtroom.

The trial proceeded rapidly. By the end of the afternoon the prosecution's case had been presented and Mr Jackson had made no attempt at a reasoned defence. He was relying on the leniency of the court in the face of the accused's obvious insanity.

In his summing-up to a jury handpicked from close relatives of the murdered policemen, Judge Schalkwyk spoke with a brevity and degree of impartiality quite unusual for him.

'You have heard it said,' he mumbled, though it was certain that thanks to his own deafness he hadn't, 'by the prosecuting counsel that the accused committed these crimes. You have seen the accused's confession with your own eyes, and you have heard the defence counsel's plea that his client is insane. Now you may think that there is something to be said for the hypothesis that a man who murders twenty-one policemen and then signs a confession saying that he has done so is manifestly not of his right mind. It is my duty however to point out to you that to plead insanity in the light of the overwhelming evidence against him is not the action of an insane person. It is a highly rational action and one that indicates a degree of perception only to be found in an intelligent and healthy mind. I think therefore that you can disregard the question of insanity altogether in your deliberations. You need only concern yourselves with the matter of guilt. There is in my mind no shadow of doubt that the defendant committed the murders of which he is accused. He possessed, as we have heard from the expert evidence presented by the prosecution, both the opportunity and the means. He was found in possession of the murder weapons and in the act of disposing of them. His wallet and handkerchief were found at the scene of the crime, and he has given no adequate explanation of how they got there. Finally, he has admitted in a signed confession that he was responsible for the murders. I think I need say no more. You and I both know that the defendant is guilty. Now go away and come back and say so.'

The jury filed out of the courtroom. Two minutes later they returned. Their verdict was unanimous. Jonathan Hazelstone was guilty of murder twenty-one and a quarter times over.

In passing sentence Judge Schalkwyk allowed himself to depart from the lack of bias he had shown in his summing-up. He took into account a previous conviction which concerned a motoring offence. The convicted man had failed to give adequate notice of intention to make a left-hand turn at the intersection and as the Judge pointed out, this threatened the very existence of the South African constitution which was based on a series of consistent moves to the right.

'You are a threat to the values of Western civilization,' said the Judge, 'and it is the duty of this court to stamp Communism out,' and he ordered the prisoner to be taken from the court and hanged by the neck until he was dead. He was about to leave the courtroom when Mr Jackson asked to have a word with him in private.

'I would like to draw your Honour'th attention to a privilege which belongth to the Hazelthtone family,' he gurgled.

'The Hazelstone family doesn't have any privileges any more, I'm glad to say,' said the Judge.

'It'th a prerogative of long thtanding. It dateth back to the dayth of Thir Theophiluth.

'Long standing, what do you mean? There's no question

of his standing long. He'll be hanged shortly.'

'I mean the privilege of being hanged in Piemburg Prithon. It wath conferred on the family for perpetuity,' Mr Jackson tried to explain.

'Mr Jackson,' the Judge shouted, 'you are wasting my time and that of this court, not to mention that of your client who has little enough left of it as it is. Perpetuity means the quality of preserving something from oblivion. The quality of the sentence I have just passed is in intent quite the opposite. I think I need say no more, and I should advise you to do the same.'

Mr Jackson made one last effort. 'Can my client be hanged in Piemburg Prithon?' he shouted.

'Of course he can,' the Judge yelled. 'He has to be. It's a long-standing privilege of the Hazelstone family.'

'Thank you,' said Mr Jackson. As the court was cleared Jonathan Hazelstone was taken back to his cell in a state of numbed shock.

The Eyes of Texas are Upon You

ALEX ATKINSON

I DID NOT spend much time in Oklahoma, partly on principle (it is a dry State) and partly because I arrived on Will Rogers' birthday and the shops were shut.

Oklahoma was at one time considered to be so useless that it was thoughtfully turned into a dumping ground for Indians, who were marched up from the South by the Army and died like flies on the way, thus demonstrating once again the superiority of the white race, who finished the trip as fresh as daisies. Unfortunately, some time later a lot of oil was discovered under the Osage Indian Reservation, and it began to look as though money was going to find its way into the wrong hands. Suitable arrangements were hastily made, however, and I have no doubt that the Indians got some kind of compensation, such as the right to sell home-made shawls to trippers. (As a matter of fact at more than one stage of my journey through the States I heard reckless talk about letting all Indians vote in elections. Naturally I made no comment, but I hope they know what they're doing.)

I hope Rogers and Hammerstein know what they're doing, too, because most of the elephants' eyes I have seen were higher than any corn I encountered in Oklahoma. The scenery consists mainly of medders, each with a bright golden haze, and oil-derricks. In these parts a man is judged not so much by the number of washing-machines he buys for his wife in an average year as by the size of the oil derrick in his back yard. If you are particularly sensitive to the jibes of your neighbours you can buy a lightweight plastic do-it-yourself derrick which can be erected in next to no time. All you need is screw driver. They come in a pleasing variety of pastel shades, and for an extra fifty dollars they can be fitted with a lifelike gusher. Things have got so bad in Oklahoma City now that you can hardly cross the road for derricks. As for Cadillacs, these are so plentiful that there were times when I kept thinking I was in Kuwait.

From Oklahoma I made my way into the trackless deserts of Nevada. This was hard, wild country, with here and there a cairn marking the last resting place of some unfortunate fellow who got separated from the herd while doing crowd work on location. I saw several shallow depressions made by the flying saucers which land here from time to time, and I saw Reno, where I was approached five minutes after checking in at my hotel by a free-lance Marriage Guidance Counsellor who entreated me to sit down quietly and think the whole thing over before I wrecked two lives.

'My good fellow,' I said suavely, 'what brings me here is this: I want to see the evening sun go down over the snow-tipped Sierra Nevada.'

Within the hour he had spread this all over the town, and I was pointed out for the rest of my visit as the mad Englishman. It seems that there are people who have spent exactly six weeks in Reno without so much as setting eyes on the Sierra Nevada.

Reno is a wide-open town, and I was told that this was due to the silvermining that goes on in the vicinity. 'Where you have miners,' they said, 'you're *bound* to have gambling and high life. It's an historical fact.' 'I suppose you're right,' I said, recalling the riotous nights I used to spend in the Lancashire coalfields in my youth, eating chipped potatoes until all hours and playing pontoon for matches.

Superficially, Las Vegas is something like Reno, but on closer inspection it proves to be even more like Blackpool during Wakes Week. It is also wider open than Reno, probably because it's closer to the Equator. There are fruit-machines everywhere (I found one in my boot-cupboard) and nothing ever closes, even if the sheriff comes in with a posse and takes away the floor-show in a wagon. If ever a town was an embodiment of the old saw 'Americans know how to live,' this is it. I spent three whole days and nights smoking king-size cigarettes and shooting craps in an establishment as big as St Paul's, called the Diamond Studded Dollar, and that's a thing you couldn't do in Runcorn. There was also some kind of cabaret turn going on—Yehudi Menuhin, or Zsa Zsa Gabor, or someone like that—and every now and again the foundations of the place were shaken by an atomic explosion.

'Don't you ever feel,' I asked a croupier, 'rather like those people who were dancing on the eve of Waterloo?'

'No,' said the croupier, 'I feel fine. Only thing is, my feet hurt.'

It was shortly after this that I happened to come across Texas—more or less by accident, really, owing to some mix-up about trains.

The truth is, I had thought I might glance at it as we passed through if I happened to be awake, for I had heard it was not without interest, if inclined to be flat. However, finding myself set down on a remote wayside halt in a sort of field, and being assured that this was in fact Texas, I decided to occupy myself with a tour of investigation. There was some time to wait before the next train, and I felt it would be churlish simply to sit in the waiting-room.

Nobody, by the way, could fail to be fascinated by American trains. For one thing, they are the only trains I know which go grinding and clanking through the very hearts of towns, at street level, preceded by a man with a red flag. This gives rise to a peculiarity of American town-planning: on one side of the tracks you will see the well-to-do hanging about waiting for the jewellers' shops to open, while on the other side the poor will be grubbing for scraps in the trash-cans. Then again, the trains always start from some vast echoing temple with a carillon and a misleading name. (In New York they have a station called Pennsylvania, and in Philadelphia they presumably have one called Kansas City, and so it goes on.) You can telephone from a train if you are an accredited executive,* and even if you are not you can take a bath in a train, or post a letter, or play deck tennis in the Lounge Hall, or get married, or enjoy a session of square-dancing in the Rumpus Coach, or order a grey flannel suit. The back of each train is open to the sky, with a railing. These draughty *patios* are for the convenience of passengers who happen to be running for President. They are allowed to have the train stopped at every cross-roads so that they can lean over the rail and promise a handful of innocent bystanders that they're going to introduce piped water and raise the price of hogs.

The sleeping arrangements are sensational, the bunks being placed one above another along each side of the coach, and hidden behind curtains. Nobody is ever quite certain which bunk is which, so that a great part of the night is taken up with people in dressing-gowns lurching up and down the centre aisle, opening and closing curtains until the whole train is in an uproar. To add to the din, the engine-driver sounds his siren on the slightest provocation, and if he hasn't a siren he tolls a bell instead. In the day-coach the travelling salesmen, in their two-tone shoes, are whooping it up with root beer and draw poker, while the box-cars and cattle-trucks are loud with the snores of hoboes, escaped convicts, bums, bank-robbers, thimble-

* Anyone higher than the boy who fills the inkwells is an executive. He has a suite.

riggers, migratory roustabouts and missing persons, some
with prices on their heads. One way and another it's just
about as lively as the night boat from Holyhead to Dun
Laoghaire.

The coaches have sunshine roofs. They are pressurized,
dustproof, pollen-proof, air-conditioned, sterilized, oblong,
mothproof, shrink-resisting, stabilized, rustproof and
antiseptic. The staff includes a resident manicurist, first-
and second-class dentists, peanut vendors, the editor of the
Train Newspaper, and a porter who wakes you with a glass
of iced water at three in the morning to warn you that your
station is less than five hundred miles away.

It was through the helpful enthusiasm of one such
minion that I found myself standing on this lonely platform
watching the train's rear light disappearing up an *arroyo*.

'Look here,' I said angrily to a man with a green eyeshade,
who was tapping out messages for Western Union in the
ticket-office, 'this doesn't look much like San Francisco to
me. I thought there was supposed to a bridge?'

'San Francisco?' said the man with the eyeshade
suspiciously. 'What's that?'

Then, as I simultaneously heard the lowing of distant
shorthorns and noticed that the man was tall and lean and
wore high heels, the truth dawned on me. This was the
Lone Star State, birthplace of Ken Maynard, Ginger
Rogers and Dwight D. Eisenhower!

Without much more ado I asked him to keep an eye on
my baggage, and stepped outside to look the place over.

Perhaps I can best give you some idea of the extent of
Texas if I tell you that it is very considerably smaller than
Australia and British Somaliland put together. As things
stand at present there is nothing much the Texans can do
about this, and I noticed that they are inclined to shy away
from the subject in ordinary conversation, muttering
defensively about the size of oranges. Roughly speaking,
Texas is the strip of land that separates Oklahoma from
Mexico. It is chiefly used for pasture, although it produces
more helium and mohair than any other State. ('Texas

Leads the World in Mohair!' is a familiar cry in the streets
of Laredo.) Other products include spinach, pecan nuts,
fuller's earth, oil, and shrimps.

The dry-as-dust historical background is as follows.
Texas broke away from Mexican rule after the slaughter of
Davy Crockett in the Mission San Antonio de Valero. (The
Mission San Antonio de Valero being too long a name for
anyone to remember, they changed it to the Alamo. Even a
child could remember the Alamo.) Texas then blossomed
out as an independent nation under its able ruler Sam
Houston, who presently, in a fit of depression, suggested
that the place should become a Crown Colony of Great
Britain. This charming development having been avoided
in the nick of time, Texas finally agreed to join the Union
on its own terms, one of which was that it should be freely
acknowledged and admitted, once and for all, preferably in
an amendment to the Constitution, that Texas has the
prettiest girls in the world, not to mention the longest dark
brown man-made navigable underground collapsible
viaduct. Since then Texas and the US have gotten along
splendidly.

Texans, quite apart from being tall and lean, turned out
to be short and stout, hospitable, stingy to a degree,
generous to a fault, even-tempered, cantankerous, doleful,
and happy as the day is long. The men wear bootlace
neckties on account of the pioneer influence (the pioneers
always carried a spare pair), and the women, on account of
the Spanish influence, hanker after *haciendas* and turn up at
the Saturday afternoon rodeos in *mantillas*. In the south
they also drink a good deal of *tequila*, which is a spirit made
from the juice of the cactus. It has to be taken with a pinch
of salt.

I called on a Texan I had previously met in New York.
(We had both been entertained by two gentlemen in a bar
on Sixth Avenue, and the Texan had succeeded in buying a
brick of solid gold from them at a bargain price—much to
my chagrin, for I'd set my heart on it.) He had a typical
Texan ranch-house, with a log fire in every room,

Chippendale ironing boards, Staffordshire china, a view of the Gulf, monogrammed scatter rugs, a wife like last year's Miss Rheingold and a daughter like next year's. His convertible was brand new, but he had had it impregnated with a special concoction to make it smell of very old leather and spaniels. It was fitted with a shower, a herb garden, a folding boudoir, an ashtray, and an electric device for sharpening scythes, which was new to me, and didn't work.

I suppose Texas is principally famous for the statue of Popeye in Crystal City. It is a momentous work, certainly, but I must say I saw several other things which seemed worthy of mention. In San Antonio, for example, there are poverty-stricken Mexicans of the most picturesque and photogenic nature imaginable, while a little to the south lies a farm called the King Ranch, ruled over by semi-feudal barons and noticeably smaller than metropolitan France.

Texas is certainly a region of superlatives. In the university I saw the largest collection of mystery stories in existence, and in Pecos County I saw the deepest hole. In Jacksonville I was introduced to the ugliest dog in the world, in Dallas I used the bluntest knife, in Austin I slept on the hardest bed, and on Robinson Boulevard, El Paso, I heard the oldest joke. Also, Texans wear far bigger hats than anybody else, and one can't help wondering why.

All the same, Texas is a pretty little place, and I don't care who hears me say it, within reason. I'm glad I was able to fit it in. I shall long remember the sound of mission bells wafting across the *mesas* full of cotton, the millionaires playing pitch and toss for chains of hotels in the cocktail bars of Houston, the pearl-grey Stetsons of the bootblacks in Dallas, the cowhands singing all night long in the streets of Fort Worth, and the stripper in the Amarillo night-spot who had to do her act behind a barbed-wire entanglement on paynights. And, just to be on the safe side, I shall **remember the Mission San Antonio de Valero.**

A Woman of a Certain Class

PAUL DEHN

I HAVE ONLY kept silent so long because the English gentleman in me shies, like one of my own hunters, at the idea of betraying a woman. But when Miss Nancy Mitford explicitly states that by a person's vocabulary you may recognize his or her class, and implicitly suggests that by her own vocabulary—*e.g.*, the use of 'writing-paper' for 'notepaper'—we may recognize her as upper-class (U) rather than lower-middle-class (non-U), my *noblesse* refuses to *oblige.*

If language is (as I devoutly believe) an historical indicator of social status, then Miss Mitford's status as revealed by her language is open to the ghastliest misgiving. Since my own reputation as an etymologist has always been modestly confined to a limited academic circle, I prefer to emphasize this misgiving by quotation from the more widely accepted, historically incontrovertible Oxford English Dictionary.

Miss Mitford says that 'They have a very lovely *home*' is non-U for 'They've a very nice *house*' (U).

House [con. with verbal root *hud-* of *hydan*—to HIDE, from Indo-European stem *keudh-*] 1. A building for human habitation. b. The portion of a building occupied by one tenant or family. 2. A place of worship; a temple; a church. b. An inn, tavern 1550. 3. A building for the keeping of cattle, birds, plants, goods, etc., 1503. c. A boarding-house attached to a public school . . . f. A place of business.

Home [Old English *ham*] 1 A village or town. 2. A dwelling-place, house, abode; the fixed residence of a family or household; one's own house; the dwelling in which one habitually lives, or which one regards as one's proper abode. The place of one's dwelling or nurturing, with its associations 1460.

You see? There were these Indo-European Mitfords skulking in Christian churches or hiding in their portions of buildings (designed for cattle and birds and plants and goods) which they later turned into taverns, boarding-houses and places of business—while we Old English Dehns were dwelling and being nurtured (from about 1460 onwards) in whole villages, towns, fixed residences and proper abodes with associations. We may even, without knowing it, have harboured an Abou Ben Mitford in one of our granaries. After what fashion, you may ask, can he have lived there? Listen.

'U-speakers,' says Miss Mitford, 'eat *luncheon* in the middle of the day and *dinner* in the evening. Non-U speakers have their *dinner* in the middle of the day.'

Now *luncheon*, as any fool etymologist knows, is an expanded form of the older word *lunch* (derived from LUMP on the analogy of hump, hunch, bump, bunch). It means: 'A piece, a thick piece'.

Luncheon. 1. = LUNCH. 2. A repast taken between two meal-times, *esp.* in the morning. Still so applied by those who dine at midday. With others, *luncheon* denotes a less ceremonious meal than dinner.

Dinner [Middle English *diner*]. The chief meal of the day, eaten originally, and still by many, about midday; but now, by the fashionable classes, in the evening.

Under *Dinner*, note the pejorative antithesis between 'originally' (*i.e.*, traditionally) and 'now' (fashionably, ephemerally). We Dehns have always kept up our mediaeval family practice of 'dining at midday', while the Mitfords (slightingly referred to in the O.E.D. as 'others') less ceremoniously gnaw and chumble their thick pieces between two civilized meal-times. What do they actually eat? '*Greens*', says Miss Mitford, 'is non-U for U *vegetables*.'

> **Greens.** Green vegetables such as are boiled for the table 1725.
> **Vegetable.** 1. A living organism belonging to the lower of the two series of organic beings; a growth devoid of animal life. 2. An edible herb or root used for human consumption and commonly eaten, either cooked or raw, with meat or other articles of food 1767.

Mark that 'commonly'. Half a century after my family had first eaten decently cooked greens, these upstart Mitfords arrived by caravan from God knows where behind the Karakorams and began commonly chewing roots, raw growths devoid of life, and low, living organisms. It makes one sick.

What else do they eat between meals? '*Sweet*,' says Miss Mitford, 'is non-U for U *pudding*.'

> **Sweet** [Middle English]. 1. That which is sweet to the taste; something having a sweet taste. b. A sweet food or drink.
> **Pudding** [Middle English *poding*, deriv. unkn.]. I. 1. The stomach or one of the entrails of a pig, sheep or other animal, stuffed with minced meat, suet, seasoning, etc., boiled and kept till needed; a kind of sausage. 2. Bowels, entrails, guts. II. 1. A preparation

of food of a soft or moderately firm consistency, in which the ingredients, animal or vegetable, are either mingled in a farinaceous basis, or are enclosed in a farinaceous crust, and cooked by boiling or steaming. Preparations of batter, milk and eggs, rice, sago, suitably seasoned and cooked by baking, are now also called puddings.

It will not, I assure you, be pleasant—as I traditionally eat my sweet food and drink my sweet drink—to think of these hirsute, half-naked, Transcaucasian Mitfords spooning up great helpings of batter, rice and suitably seasoned sago or (at worst) of guts, entrails and even bowels cooked by steaming. And where, I should like to know, did they find the pigs whose stomachs they stuffed and kept (under their straw pallets?) till needed? In one of our family sties, no doubt. Tartar nomads who live furtively in portions of buildings designed for cattle are not immune from such temptations.

What do they do when they have finished their savage meal? '*Serviette*,' says Miss Mitford, 'is exaggeratedly non-U usage for *napkin*.'

Now the O.E.D. is quite right in saying of *serviette*: 'latterly considered vulgar'. Naturally it was so considered —by the sort of Mongolian immigrants who reached England latterly enough to be ignorant that we born-and-bred, dyed-in-the-wool Englishmen were using the word as early (says the O.E.D.) as 1489. It means, and meant then, 'a table-napkin'. And how disturbing to find that the word *napkin*, if not preceded by the cumbersome prefix *table-*, can mean 'an infant's diaper'. It must be small comfort for Miss Mitford to know that her ancestors were at least civilized enough to *provide* their infants with diapers when she has to weigh such knowledge against the unspeakably nauseous use of these same diapers to . . . to . . . but, no. One's gorge heaves. Quick! My serviette!

Did they wash? Not, it appears, until 1656. '*Toilet*,' says Miss Mitford, is 'non-U for *lavatory*'.

Toilet. A dressing-room; in U.S. *esp.,* a dressing-room furnished with bathing facilities.

Lavatory. An apartment with apparatus for washing the hands and face; now often combined with water-closets, etc. 1656. A laundry 1661. A place for washing gold 1727.

It was in 1495, some months after Columbus' return from America, that my family installed the first New World 'toilet' at Dehn Towers. Even then it was far in advance of the primitive 'apparatus' occasionally to be found in those portions of buildings inhabited by the vagabond Mitfords. We have called it the Toilet for four-and-a-half centuries. After 1727 we had a Lavatory, too, of course, but only for washing gold.

A very painful composite-picture now emerges of the Mitford sect—which I hope will finally put paid to their fantastic social pretensions. I see them, these huge, swart, hispid gipsies, after their mid-morning meal of lumps— stomachs distended with suet and entrails, their mouths streaming with raw roots and lower organisms whose tell-tale traces they have been unable to wipe away with a hastily snatched-up baby's diaper. They rush to the washing-apparatus combined with water-closet in that portion of the cow-byre which tribal custom forbids them to call 'home'. And what do they find? Nothing but writing-paper.

It's amazing that the line isn't extinct. But then barbarians are notoriously hardy.

Scoop

ALEXANDER FRATER

The Zimbabwe Government this week announced the formation of a new national news agency to be known as the Zimbabwe Inter African News Agency. —The Times.

THE GLEAMING MERCEDES sped down the dusty, rutted road, its grinning chauffeur proceeding with his right elbow planted on the horn and his left leg dangling idly through a hole in the floor. This had been made, he thought, by an unswept landmine the previous week, but it allowed a cooling breeze to whistle up his fine frogged trousers and caused his jacket, tricked out with shiny Death's Head buttons and heavy gold epaulettes, to flap and billow. The windscreen had been stolen the night before and its absence made his eyes water; later he would visit one of the unattended car parks in the city to find a replacement of approximately the same size, but now, tearing across a dry river bed, there was a thunderous report and a bell-like clang as the exhaust fell off. He glanced around at the back seat, wondering whether the sudden lurch and clamour had been noted, but the boss, frowning heavily and giving little grunts of interest, seemed deeply immersed in a book called JANET AND JOHN FIND OUT ABOUT JOURNALISM. Minutes later they squealed to a halt before the office and the chauffeur sprang out and swung open the rear door. The boss put the book in his shiny new briefcase and sighed. Then, his movements slow and deliberate, he loosened his tie, rolled up his sleeves, placed a green eye-shade on his head and stuck a pencil behind his ear. 'You're fired,' he said, and then he got out.

The editor had arrived.

As he walked into his agency, the News Desk personnel sprang to attention. Nodding at them, he threw himself down behind his desk and tossed a few dog biscuits to the office bat, a ferocious carnivore that hung upside down, snarling, from the framed portrait of President Banana. 'So what's new?' he said.

His star reporter, Mwanga, cleared his throat. Mwanga was young and keen and wore a battered fedora on the back of his head. 'I have a great story, mboss,' he said, eagerly. 'About a man who mbit a lion.'

The editor looked up. Janet and John had mentioned something along very similar lines. 'Tell me more,' he said.

'He ran amok,' said Mwanga, 'due to his wife having congress with a traffic warden in the mback of my cousin Hugh's Ndatsun Cedric.'

The editor pondered a moment. 'You'd have to open your tailgate in the Cedric,' he said. 'Otherwise your feet would stick out the window. And if they mbumped the knobs they could inadvertently open the mboot or start the mblinkers going.' He pursed his lips and blew a kiss at the bat. 'The lion wasn't in the Cedric too, was it? You're not telling me that the man, his vision impaired because his head was under the seat, gave the lion a love mbite in error, are you?'

'No, sir,' said Mwanga. 'A Volkswagen camper would be needed for that sort of arrangement. Well, mbeast that size.'

'Quite so. So fill me in on the story, Mwanga, then you

can mbang it out and we'll get it on the tapes. Be on the world's mbreakfast tables tomorrow morning, carrying our ndateline, your mby-line.'

'The lion has been stuffed,' said Mwanga, ' and turned into a cocktail cabinet. It belongs to the wronged husband—who is actually my cousin Hugh, a trader in mbells and ngongs—and when he was told of the incident he had two large gins and a cigar, then he began frothing at the mouth and clamped it around the lion's ear.'

There was a silence. The editor sighed. 'So Hugh got plastered and mbit a piece of furniture. Can you imagine my friend Rees-Mogg shaking with excitement and screaming at them to hold the presses when he reads that?'

Mwanga shuffled his feet and hung his head. 'Nice little human interest item,' he muttered. 'Needs a witty treatment, of course.'

The editor leant forward and addressed his staff in ringing tones. 'What I want,' he proclaimed, 'are major natural disasters of the kind Janet and John recommend— earthquakes, volcanic eruptions, tidal waves and so forth. I want planes crashing into mountains and trains crowded with pilgrims plunging into foaming gorges. I want people trapped on the roofs of mblazing skyscrapers. I want it raining lizards. I want Siamese quins and three-headed ngoats. I want prison riots and epidemics; you remember what Janet says on page 36? "There is nothing the intrepid journos of Fleet Street like mbetter, mboys and ngirls, than a jolly good outbreak of plague or an epidemic of killer flu." I want corruption in high places. I want wars. I want murder, famine and armed insurrection. I want *scoops!*'

The newsmen shifted about, looking miserable. One of them muttered, 'I hear there is a midwife at Bulawayo who tears up telephone directories.'

The editor bared his teeth in a terrible sneer.

Mr Ndongo, the news editor, murmured, 'At Shabani public library you can get spanking magazines and German mbondage literature behind the Reference Section.'

The editor's sneer ran from ear to ear.

The atmosphere around the News Desk was heavy with despair. Suddenly, though, they were distracted by a pounding at the door. Mwanga opened it cautiously and the chauffeur fell through. His uniform was stained with sweat and his peaked cap, embellished with a Screaming Eagle, was on back to front and rammed hard down over his rolling eyes. 'Mboss!' he gasped, collapsing on a chair. 'I've ngot a story!'

'Oh, Mafeking's been relieved, has it?' Mwanga muttered sourly. 'Or is there news from Rorke's Drift?'

The chauffeur ignored him. 'I was wandering around the Parliament House car park,' he said, breathlessly, 'looking for some new components for the Merc. I spotted this nice mbig ngreen 300 SL and went to work on it with my screwdriver and monkey wrench. Well, I had just removed the tinted windscreen when I happened to notice something inside.'

A hush lay over the News Desk. The editor's face wore an expression of keen interest. 'Ngo on,' he said.

'On the front seat was a pile of ndocuments.' He paused. 'I had a little look and couldn't mbelieve my eyes.'

'Let me see,' said the editor.

The chauffeur reached down into the front of his shirt. He produced four hubcaps, a push-button radio, two sheepskin seat covers, various cassettes, a tartan travelling rug—and a brown manila folder which, wordlessly, he handed to the editor.

The editor flicked it open. 'Ngood Ngod,' he murmured, after a moment.

'What is it?' said Mr Ndongo.

'The Zimbabwe Tobacco Growers' Association have formed a secret consortium to mbuy the London *Times*,' he said. 'Ian Smith is to be editor, Bishop Abel Muzorewa will run the Sports Desk and the Rev. Ndabaningi Sithole the Terrorist's Page. That is to consist of news, gossip and useful tips for guerrillas everywhere—how, for example, to walk undetected through a police checkpoint with a hand grenade in your mouth. There is to be a Smoking

Correspondent too, who will write pithy and trenchant pieces about the virtues of Zimbabwe tobacco three times a week and who will probably replace Mbernard Levin.'

'Ndid I ndo well, mboss?' the chauffeur murmured. 'Am I taken on again?'

The editor nodded. 'You have ndone very well,' he said. 'That is the kind of spirit and enterprise I want to see around here. Yes, I am taking you on again, but I have a new job for you. From now on you will take charge of the News Desk.'

'But what about me?' said Mr Ndongo, a highly respected figure with three weeks' Overseas Experience.

The editor examined him. 'Can you ndrive, Ndongo?'

'Why, yes, mboss, of course. I've been knocking around in the old Ndaimler for twenty years now.'

'Then you shall be my new chauffeur. Come with me. We must get down to Parliament House to check this story out.'

The door closed behind them. The stunned reporters heard the Mercedes start up and move uncertainly away. There was a muffled crash as, cannonading repeatedly off the pavement, it lost its suspension; then it accelerated around a corner and was gone.

How To Be Topp

GEOFFREY WILLANS

I HAVE SAID there only one peom in the english language e.g. The Brook which chater chater as it flo my dear it is obviously a girlie just like fotherington-tomas. However there are other peoms which creep in from time to time there is one which go

> *Har fleag har fleag har fleag onward*
> *Into the er rode the 600.*

There are as well lars porsena of clusium elegy in country churchyard loss of the royal george and chevy chase. Anything to do with dafodils is also grate favourite of english masters but then nothing is beyond them they will even set burns (rabbie) who is uterly weedy.

It is farely easy to be topp in english and sometimes you may find yourself even getting interested. If that happens of course you can always draw junctions and railway lines on your desk viz

EXPRESSION

Sometimes english masters make you *read* peoms chiz chiz chiz. you have to sa the weedy words and speke them beaitfully as if you knew what they meant. Fotherington-tomas thinks this is absolutely super and when he sa he wander lonely as a cloud you think he will flote out of the window. Some cads roters and swots love to read they beg for the chance and put their hands up saing sir sir sir please sir as if they are in agony. English masters who are always perverse then sa molesworth go on CHIZ.

SIR THE BURIAL SIR OF SIR JOHN MOORE SIR AT CORUNNA SIR
(*A titter from 2B they are wet and i will tuough them up after.*)

> Notadrumwaheardnotafuneralnote
> shut up peason larffing
> As his corse
> As his corse
> what is a corse sir? gosh is it
> to the rampart we carried
> (*whisper you did not kno your voice was so lovely*)
> Not a soldier discharged his farewell shot.
> *PING!*
> Shut up peason i know sir he's blowing peas at me
> Oer the grave where our hero we buried.

(*A pause a grave bow i retire and Egad! peason hav placed a dainty pin upon mine seat.* Fie!)

Occasionally you can work a wizard wheeze that the english master reads. This is not so difficult becos all masters like to show how it should be done. They look very grave turn the pages and announce

THE RETURN OF THE CHIFF-CHAFF

The class palpitate with excitement at the prospect of so exciting a story. Master slowly and sadly cast his eye to the ceiling and then down to the book while pupils prepare

hugh dumps of ammunition, train guns and ease atomic
catapults.

MAGISTER (*in a deep sad voice*): The chiff-chaff, the common
warbler of his moorland district, was now abundant,
more so than anywhere else in England. (*BONK*) two or
three were flitting about (eeeauowoooo—*WAM*) within a
few feet of my head give me that peashooter
molesworth and a dozen at least were singing within
hearing (*ur-ur-ur-ur-ur-ur*) chiff-chaffing near and if this
noise continues i shall stop reading and give you some
parsing far, their notes sounding strangely loud at that
still, sequestered spot. (*CRASH BONK WAM WHIZZ*)

Listening to that insistent sound I was reminded of
Warde Fowler's words please sir, molesworth is
strangling me stand on your chair molesworth CRASH
words about the sweet season which brings new life and
hope to men there is no need to cry fotherington-tomas
and now a BONK and BANG is CRASH on it by that same
bird's ur-ur-ur-ur-ur-ur eeeauowooo—

(*MAGISTER continues nothing can stop him while the ELEVES
disport themselves merily each small one to his own inclinations. It is
thus indeed that n. molesworth acquired that grate love for english
literature which was such a comfort to him in later years hem-hem.*)

What it all amounts to is that english is chiefly a matter of
marksmanship. You can always come topp if you lay the
rest of the class out but as auden sa so witily no cracked
shot can hit every time. Ho fie lo egad and away for it is the
BELL and it tolleth for me cheers cheers cheers.

Blacked Up

THOMAS BERGER

'LADIES AND GENTLEMEN,' Reinhart began, drunk as a lord, and then brayed in laughter, for their titles might be many, but never those two. He began again to himself, while the persons of the audience stirred respectfully: 'Whores, pimps, cutthroats, degenerates, and fiends,' an address that better suited his drunken compulsion towards the truth. 'Uh,' he went on, 'you may smoke.' Several people instantly lighted brown-paper cigarettes that exuded a sweetish aroma, and two felonious types, propped against the left wall, took the liberty to drain a flat pint of maroon liquid.

Reinhart bowed slightly from the waist, which motion caused the turban to pitch forward and strike the top rim of his sunglasses. He adjusted the headdress, being careful not to brush the fake mustache attached to his upper lip with library paste, which was pulling his mouth into a sneer as it dried—a purely physical phenomenon, for this was the first time he had been the cynosure of a roomful of moral lepers and consequently had never felt less disdainful.

The Maker, priceless man, as good as his word, had given a hundred cents' value for every dollar; not only had he collected an audience and, tapping the cleaner's power cable, brought light; he also found boxes, kegs, stacked newspapers, stools, and even a chair or two, for there had not been a seat in the house. He posted the wall-notices he had earlier characterized as essential, adding one that read: GOD IS WACHING YOU. He directed his scouts in a quick policing-up of the store: there were rats to rout, fallen plaster to sweep, and a grocery counter, dating from Big Ruthie days, to find under a Matterhorn of trash. It was behind this counter that Reinhart now supported himself, knee against the lower shelf where stood his half-empty fifth of gin, another provision of the Maker's.

Splendor, who was personally responsible for Reinhart's debut as orator, had proved a complete washout.

'Splendor, Splendor,' Reinhart had called down to him on the couch. 'Are you sick?'

The nonchemical interne had revolved agate eyes in the light of the torch, moaning 'Very.' He rolled against the wall, face to it, the way people show defeat in novels. His turban lay in the debris of the floor.

'You don't have stage fright?' asked Reinhart. 'Not you. Why, I can recall your Debating Contest speech before the whole high school. I believe you defended war, while that little skinny girl Angelica Slimp took the opposing view.'

'I cribbed most of that from Henry Five, by William Shakespeare,' Splendor admitted with a faint smile. ' "Once more into the breach, dear friends." Ah, but I feel very grisly at present.'

'Hey,' Reinhart cried, 'you can't sleep now. It's after eight and the people will be coming soon.' He took the light off Splendor's face and directed it upon the leprous wall.

'Nobody's coming, Carlo. Nobody cares. You strive, and for what? You find the electricity turned off.'

'But we're fixing that, and the Maker's collecting an audience, and you'll be just great. I thought your idea was pretty punk until tonight. Now I'm enthusiastic. Really!

Hahaha.' Reinhart turned and kicked an old carton through the back window.

With the flashlight on him again, Splendor said irrelevantly: 'You don't know what it's like not being respectable. Your mother didn't run off with Henry Bligh.'

But in sympathy Reinhart fervently wished she had, and he said, 'I'm sorry.'

'My parents used to play cards every Friday night. One evening Seneca Bligh and my father sat there three hours waiting for their partners—who actually had long departed to St Louis by Greyhound bus. Well, you've seen my father.'

'I've met Mrs Bligh as well,' Reinhart answered. 'But it was fortunate that you are grown up and not a little child on whom such a thing would be crushing—that you have your plans and ideas and can't be fazed.'

'True,' Splendor said very weakly. Big Ruthie's sofa had very high ends, and he hung between them like a vacant hammock.

'Anyhow,' Reinhart went on, 'what is respectability? Pretty boring if you ask me and furthermore a false category. What we want is a celebration of life, because we've only got one.'

'True. But now Dr Goodykuntz writes that the tuition fee I already paid doesn't cover the genuine parchment diploma with seal of fourteen-carat gold.'

'How much?'

'Twenty-five dollars, and it's unethical to practise without it. Why can't we postpone the meeting until next week?'

'Splendor, Splendor,' chided Reinhart. 'Are you losing your faith in Dr Goodykuntz? I must say you're disappointing me, my dear fellow. Remember that the weather's sure to be far worse in Pocatello and if Dr Goodykuntz has contracted to give an address tonight, he is already at the auditorium, pouring out inspiration and healing multitudes of sufferers.'

Splendor sat up and groped on the floor for his turban.

'You've shamed me, Carlo. Disregard the foregoing negativism. It's quite true that I am very ill. I may indeed have cancer. No'—he threw a hand towards Reinhart—'no demonstration. I'm not whining. If this burning pain in my solar plexus gets worse, I may have to go to Pocatello for treatment. You see, the pity is that the physician cannot heal himself; the conjunction of two life forces is called for. But first, my work is cut out for me.'

He rose to his feet, and at the same moment the lights came on—one ceiling bulb behind the partition and several out front.

'There you are!' cried Reinhart. 'The balloon is going up.'

Soon they heard noises of the arriving audience. Now that he had called Splendor back to duty, Reinhart again became reluctant to associate himself with the project. His reluctance turned to terror when, spying around the partition, he saw the Maker's confederates bring in seating facilities and the Maker's chattering girls prepare to use them. The truth was, whores disturbed Reinhart; turning down their solicitations always made him feel like a great swine. In London during the war, he had frequently been almost moved to counter sidewalk propositions with an offer of marriage. Instead of desire, he felt guilt; for the likes of him and a handful of silver, such a woman would recline and accept penetration. This was the female principle reduced to absurdity.

When he turned back to assure his friend that prospects were bright, he saw only an empty turban rolling across the floor from the open window; the bee had fled its hive.

'So what do we do now?' asked the Maker, when that person appeared a moment later from the front of the store.

Nicholas Graves was uproariously pleased at Splendor's flight. He chortled so strenuously that he choked, and one of his whores called from beyond the partition: 'Baby, you dyin'?'

He ordered her not to embarrass him, and said to Reinhart: 'I tole you, I tole you! He never been with it, man, like you and me. He simply run back to noplace.'

'Then I guess that does it,' Reinhart said. 'Tell everybody to go home—and you can keep the money, you earned it. Too bad. I think he's got something, though it's clogged. And you hardly ever run across anybody who believes in anything nowadays. So you can't exactly call him yellow, since a coward wouldn't have had the idea in the first place. I suppose he's just normal, poor guy.'

'There you are!' the Maker shouted. 'Them folks should blow while you shoot me this wisdom in the back room? Man, you got your chance! How often do you find that, nowadays or never?'

Standing before the audience, Reinhart realized that the Maker's adjuration had probably been sinister. He could not really believe that Reinhart was eloquent; therefore he undoubtedly played the sadist, and his furnishing the orator with disguise, bottle of Dutch nerve, and extravagant encouragement was but the instrumentation of his malice. His roomful of thugs and bawds were to be amused by a Caucasian buffoon, One White Crow.

The drying paste had now drawn Reinhart's upper lip into a pronounced snarl. This was the first time he had ever worn a mask other than that issued him by Nature. He stared through the dark-purple sunglasses, on loan from the Maker's aide Winthrop, at an especially menacing criminal, almost as big as himself in the front row of seats. This man wore sideburns which ran down to his mouth, and on the remainder of his face someone had scored a chessboard with a very dull knife. It was doubtful that he had obeyed the doorside sign prohibiting weapons; and impractical to brood about, since he secured his trousers with a garrison belt terminating in a six-inch buckle of solid lead and both sets of his knuckles were ranks of iron rings begemmed with broken glass. He was a terrible, dreadful, evil sight, and returned Reinhart's stare through protuberant eyes like the business ends of blunt instruments.

Reinhart ducked beneath the counter and took another quick shot of gin. While he was there he heard a brute comment from the savage he had temporarily permitted to outface him: 'Come on, shit or git off the pot!'

'You!' said Reinhart, bobbing up. 'You there, that just spoke. Come up here.'

If the man had been frightening before, he was now a perfect horror. He licked his lips and spat between his mastodon feet. In a nonchalant movement of his right hand, he plucked up a small brown neighbor and hurled him at the counter.

'Be of good cheer, brother,' said Reinhart to the victim, who was apparently carried about by the big man for just such demonstrations of contempt. To the brute he said: 'No, I must have you. Denying the power of the Prime Mover is hopeless. That's what Simon Peter did and he was turned into a rock on which was built the Catholic Church. Now I'm going to count to five and say a bit of Latin, which is the tongue of that faith, and if you're not off that box by the time I finish and standing up here like a man—'

'Praise God and not the Devil,' shouted one of the Maker's male shills from the other side of the room.

The criminal lowered his eyes and muttered at his shoes: 'Ah cut anybody who bruise me with Latin, goddammit.'

'Listen to him take the Mighty name in vain, brethren and cistern!' said Reinhart. 'Poor Simon Peter!'

'Now don't you call me that,' warned the thug, fiddling with his leaden buckle. Nevertheless, he was embarrassed, and dug a cigarette from his jacket pocket and broke it into pieces. 'Ah dint come here to be called out of my name.'

'What is your name, brother?'

'Stony Jack,' answered the big man's little victim, who had reseated himself.

'I don't mean you.'

'Neither do I,' said the small man, who had a bad right eye like a cracked marble. 'I mean him.'

'*Stony!*' shouted Reinhart. 'What did I tell you about Peter becoming a rock? Your name is already petrified, brother.'

'All right,' grumbled the monster. 'I'm comin'. Just don't go laying any Latin on me.' Erect, he was larger than Reinhart, and carried his great shoulders as an ox a yoke.

'Just put your back against the counterfront, brother, and face the audience,' Reinhart ordered, smirking drunkenly. 'There's nothing to be afraid of. The Latin I promised was *sic transit gloria mundi* and that can work as well for the good as for the bad.'

From the bloc of prostitutes in the center of the audience, a girl sprang up and announced her name as Gloria Monday. Like her sisters in law, she was dressed exceedingly drab and had a voice to match; Reinhart saw that streetwalking was a pretty dreary business, not in the least exotic or even sexy.

'Very well, Gloria, you come up here too.'

While she was on her way, Stony Jack glowered at Reinhart. 'I got to stand here with a hoor? I never been so insulted in mah life.' He brought his iron-and-glass knuckles to the countertop and gouged a peevish mark through its veneer of filthy oilcloth.

'Gloria Hallelujah!' It was the Maker himself who shouted, immensely pleased that one of his people was making out.

'Now,' said Reinhart. 'Here on my left is Stony Jack, about 250-odd pounds of force, and on my right is Gloria Monday, about 120 pounds of desire. In the middle, representing the mind, is me, Dr Lorenz T. Goodykuntz of Pocatello, Idaho. This meeting was called by the most brilliant of my students, Splendor G. Mainwaring of this city, but at the eleventh hour he was called away to save a life, and fortunately I was on hand to substitute.'

Gloria leaned against the counter and watched Reinhart with the open mouth of awe, two front teeth missing. Small wonder that the Maker never had a penny. Very miffed, Stony stared blackly at his little assistant in the front row. Reinhart coughed and got another drink sub rosa, being conscious of his high responsibility, in which Splendor no longer figured.

He was masked and under a false name. He addressed a roomful of pariahs who had been bribed, threatened, or tricked into coming. The very light that shone down from above was neither his nor theirs; the building was condemned, its late proprietor in durance vile, its latest lessee in flight. The whole situation, indeed, was just like life, and at the same time that it didn't matter, it was very serious. Though not sober.

'How many among you wish you hadn't been born?' Reinhart asked. While the audience labored over this, some persons putting up both hands, some one, and one man, way in the back, apparently three, Gloria whispered to Reinhart: 'Sir, you want me to say yiss or no?'

'Just tell the truth, my dear.'

'Then I don't know.' She stuck a finger in her ear.

Stony Jack complained, 'That's the foolest thing I ever heard.'

'Ah,' said Reinhart, a bit topheavy from the turban. 'Now you see why I picked these two astute individuals.' He asked Stony: 'Why is it a fool question?'

Flattered, the big man scratched his chin with the rings, which were unavailing against his thick hide. Reinhart saw he had made a tactical error in ceasing to provoke Stony, who might begin to fancy himself a thinker—which is death to the intelligence. He hastily gave his own answer.

'Exactly, because nobody can do anything about it. But kindly observe, my friends, the differences of response between the female and male of the species. The man, pugnacious, positive, dominant, strikes out at the fate which dooms him—because nobody lives forever, everybody eventually fails. Yet he will not admit it. No, he says, meaning Yes. But the woman, not an instrument but a receptacle, is unable to answer at all, which is as much as to say Yes, meaning "You're not asking the right question." If you have observed, women never answer questions. This is because they are capable of producing new life—a capability which men fiercely resent, so sooner or later they throw the woman down and punish her with the

weapon Nature has given them for the purpose, and the
result of course is that she produces the very new life the
resenting of which caused her to be knocked down and
jabbed in the first place. Therefore love is a battle with each
side winning a Pyrrhic victory.'

Gloria Monday never took her loving eyes from his false
face. On the other hand, Stony had begun to grouse in
Anglo-Saxon expletives. As to the audience, Reinhart had
lost even the Maker, who was edging out the street door.
Normally inarticulate, Reinhart felt he could talk all night
through the mask, just throwing things out and letting
them naturally gravitate into order. But when drunk he
also had a fine sense of the lines of communication between
human beings. Unworried—being neither a Southerner
nor a humanitarian, he cherished the differences among
races—at this point he reached under the shelf and brought
forth his gin bottle, drained it into his throat, and broke it
on the counter with a splendid noise and spray of
fragments.

'So much for that. I'm not here to bury life but to
recognize it. If I learned one thing from the sovereign of
Andorra when I served as his medical advisor, it was:
Above all, do no harm and always uphold the dignity of
human life. That's as easy, and as hard, to do whether
you're a king or a criminal. So all of you have a good chance.
Listen to me tell you about the kingdom of Andorra. The
palace, which sits on a hill above a green plain, is made out
of porphyry, a red stone that gets its color from the blood
that is shed in battles and soaks into the earth. The
particular stones for this palace were mined at Thermo-
pylae, a place in Greece where centuries ago a handful of
Spartans fought to the last man against a horde of Persians
and thereby saved their dear country from the foul
invader. But the towers, which are really minarets and
take after the great temples of Islam, are made of alabaster
so white that the snow looks yellow by comparison.

'But it seldom snows there except at Christmas time and
then the sun comes out hot soon after and dries it up so

that there's no slush to get into your boots or sidewalks to be shoveled. The rest of the year it's warm enough to swim all day, and sufficiently cool at night to sleep under one blanket only. The vineyards, heavy with purple and golden grapes, stretch down the slopes behind the palace and on to the horizon, and are thronged with winsome young women with amber hair, who wear only a thin kind of short toga to the midpoint of their supple thighs.

'Now, the Andorrans were a brave, warlike people centuries ago, as everybody was at one time or another—for example, take your Assyrians, who are now extinct; or your Swedes, who fought in the Thirty Years' War but haven't done much since except lie in the sun and turn brown—there's a bit of irony for you folks who were born with a tan . . . The problem always is how to maintain the spirit while indulging the body. The Andorrans have done this by a shrewd device, having discovered that there are two kinds of people, which we may call the hurters and the hurtees. The first get their satisfaction by working their will on somebody else. The second like to be imposed upon. So every Saturday in Andorra the entire populace comes to the great square before the palace and line up, according to type, on one side or another, and the hurters proceed to kick the piss out of the hurtees. . . . I apologize to the ladies. I was carried away by enthusiasm for the point I was making.'

His sunglass lenses were dirty, and several times he caught himself about to clean them, to do which he would have had to reveal his face. Though he was too drunk to worry for his own sake, and too humble to suppose he would be recognized as other than what he claimed to be, he dared not risk exposure for fear of the deleterious effect it would have on the dear audience, who had absolute faith in Dr Goodykuntz. He saw respect on those brown faces: either that or noncomprehension; anyway, not pain.

'Ah,' he shouted, 'how grand it is to be a Negro! Wonderful, just wonderful. You people have more fun than anybody. And while they are frequently niggardly to

you, there's not a white person alive who doesn't see in you
a symbol of romance and adventure. What is the synonym
for "exciting"? *Colorful!'*

Stony Jack, picking his teeth with a switchblade knife,
asked: 'You being sour-castic?'

'Not necessarily,' Reinhart answered. 'Gloria Monday,
am I right or wrong?'

She thought about it, hunched in her ancient green
coat, her hair like a flight of starlings. 'Well, I always kept
myself clean, not like some of them girls you see who don't
take a baf between now and next Christmas. And while I
drink some muscatel now and again and have smoked a
stick of pot, I never fool with H, and there ain't nobody can
say I do, though they may be them who try—'

'Put a sock in it, baby,' called the Maker from the
doorway. He had doubtless picked up the phrase in
England, when he ran his action at Bridgwater. 'We come
to hear the Reverent Dr Goodykuntz, not you troubles,
which are endless.'

For the first time the audience responded as a unit: they
coughed. Reinhart's skull, very warm under the turban,
was wet with perspiration, and his glasses had fogged. He
saw glimmers of the essential truth here and there, but
couldn't seem to maintain a firm hold on it. So far he had
delivered a series of disconnected notes, all sound enough
as far as they went, but what his listeners needed, not to
mention himself, was synthesis—the kind of thing
Splendor was so good at, and the real Dr Goodykuntz,
neither of whom were present, though the audience and
Reinhart were, neither of whom had come voluntarily.
This situation in itself was enormously significant.

'We all,' Reinhart said, 'are in a world we never made, to
use a cliché—and what cliché isn't necessary?—but as
long as we are in it, we might as well make the best of
what may be a mistake. I don't mean we *have* to love
anything or anybody—I discussed that just after the war
with a fellow in Berlin, Germany; in fact, haha, he was a
German; and decided that necessity and love don't mix. I

just mean that it might be nice if we do . . . if we love something, that is. Otherwise life is inclined to get pretty dreary, the electricity is turned off for non-payment of the bill, the telephone never rings except when it's people who want to swindle you, drugs fall from the medicine cabinet, friends let you down, and you never satisfy your parents, nor they you, and unkind people circulate lies about Gloria Monday. But furthermore, what I mean is, perhaps we should try loving even that dreariness and then it wouldn't be so bad, or at least we can see that, in its own way, life is interesting. After all, there it *is*.'

Stony Jack looked over a dirty Band-Aid on his right cheekbone, then spat upon the floor. 'I was wrong afore. This *here* is the foolest thing I ever heard.'

'But you have to admit,' said Reinhart, 'that if it is the foolest, then it is interesting, because it never happened before. And did you ever think of this: that *each new minute is occurring for the first time.* I'm sorry we don't have a wall clock here, to make the principle more obvious, for it's the most extraordinary phenomenon of a life that is filled with them. For example, I am not the same person who began this sentence, but am several seconds older, all the little molecules of my blood are elsewhere in my veins than they were at the outset, my liver is slightly older, heart, lungs, pancreas, etc., have slightly degenerated. The same is also true of you. You are not the same people who earlier entered this building and took your seats; you are, indeed, some minutes nearer to the grave—if we look on the dreary side of the matter. But take heart! So long as time moves, so do possibilities open up. Keep waiting one minute more!'

Reinhart was excited now, believing he had got to fundamentals and then showed a way out—for who wanted to drive life into a corner and leave it there? Better to dissipate it in the space between here and Neptune, like a meteorite bursting into cosmic dust. That is to say, he was all for expanse instead of contraction, but being at the same time an agoraphobe, he was suddenly struck hard by his essential contradiction and fainted, staying out for approximately thirty-two seconds, during which his turbaned head descended to his folded arms on the counter.

He awoke to hear the Maker shouting: 'O noble holy man, thou fallest into a trance!' and could not be sure whether his confederate was authentically impressed or merely resourceful. He himself was very drunk, but felt more desperately than ever his obligation.

'Let me tell you more about Andorra,' he easily resumed, never having trouble with a place he knew nothing about—whereas he could have said very little about Ohio—'where they have a national lottery whose first prize is half a million dollars. And here's the feature: *everybody is guaranteed to win it once in his life.*'

'I be goddam if I gotta stan' here listen to this,' said Stony, and lumbered to his chair, his jacket-back a great wrinkled sky of tweed lightning.

'Kin I stay?' asked Gloria Monday. 'Them other girls always pesterin' me.'

'Sure,' shouted Reinhart. 'Anybody can do anything he wants.' He punched at the atmosphere, which seemed to disbelieve him, but the Maker's claqueurs, long silent, rallied feebly: some merely with 'Yeah': others demanding: 'Tell it to me, O Doc!'

'You're damned right I'll tell it,' Reinhart roared back, the encouragement for some reason making him belligerent. 'I'll tell it to the Lord.'

'The blessed Lord above?' muttered Gloria Monday, looking shyly at Reinhart as if to ascertain whether that was the one he meant.

So as not to be sacrilegious, in case there actually was a standard God of the type in which he did not believe, Reinhart changed his tune slightly, no point in offending. 'I'll tell it to Zeus.' He really had a modicum of faith in the old Greek gods,who always did something crummy but feasible to human beings and certainly never considered dying for their sake.

This all made a big hit with Reinhart's listeners, a group that used silence, distended eyes, and fish mouths for their important demonstrations. The orator regretted his long-held conviction that Negroes were a noisy bunch. He also noticed that the latter half of the room was now empty, though he had actually seen no departures. That they were a devious crowd was at least confirmed.

As long as there was still some purpose in so doing, he withheld from himself the realization that he had failed, since it surely took a while for his kind of wisdom, expressed with his kind of energy, to claim their kind of attention. Certainly any moment now he could expect the classic Negro response: they would rise as one man, screaming ecstasy, and cavort in the aisles. . . . One of the brush hairs fell off his lip. He was over the hump towards twenty-two, and already conscious of certain losses. Real estate was his game and not evangelism, yet he had told the truth about Andorra, which he had made up on the spot. He wished terribly that everybody would win, that you could look nowhere without being blinded by grandeur. He also wished he had either drunk more or drunk less.

The Maker's white coat and black visage had disappeared from the street doorway. Reinhart got a premonition of doom when he saw the color combination with which they had been replaced: policeman's midnight blue and Slavic-red face, but the paste helped keep his upper lip stiff, and he remarked to Gloria Monday: 'How nice! An officer of the law, of all people, has come to join our devotion.'

But she had vanished, probably using Splendor's route through the back window. As had Stony Jack and his small lackey—and indeed every other human being in excess of Reinhart and the uniformed newcomer. A nimble people; at the outset there had been thirty or forty souls in the room, and though Reinhart had seen nobody actually taking leave, now there were none. For a host of reasons he did not himself follow suit: pride, torpor, intoxication, his disguise, and, most important, he knew the patrolman as yet another schoolfellow from before the war.

So he stood, or swayed, his ground, and when the officer had reached the counter, said: 'Hi, Hasek.'

'Hi, Reinhart,' answered Hasek, an incurious man. Far be it from him to ask after Reinhart's unprecedented getup and environs.

'God, Hasek, it must be all of three-four years.'

'All of it,' said Hasek, his cheekbones a foot apart and his hairline beginning at his eyebrows.

'Still on the force?'

'Yes, sure.' Hasek blinked little round eyes.

Reinhart made an overamiable mouth and, indicating his headdress, said: 'I'm a little drunk, Hasek, but I guess that's not against the law. Hahaha.'

Very solemn in his blue hat, Hasek agreed: 'That is correct.'

'Uh, just what was it you wanted, Hasek? I've been giving a speech.'

'Oh.' Hasek scratched his ass with the nightstick. His belt was like a big charm bracelet, with pistol, bullets, handcuffs, flashlight, notepad, holster for twin pencils, two kinds of whistle, leather billy, first aid packet, and a book of green summonses whose white strings were intertwined into a sort of rag-doll head. 'I reckonized you right off in your Mason outfit.'

'Hell,' said Reinhart, 'they make you carry a hardware store.

Something was laboring under Hasek's low forehead, and at last produced issue. He suffered a slow spasm of mirth and said: 'It's a living.'

'*It's a living!*' Reinhart repeated, as if it were a riot. 'That's pretty funny, Hasek.' Laughing, he deftly covered his lip with one hand, went underneath it with the other, and plucked off most of his mustache. He removed the turban, cradling it in his elbow like a football, which left only the purple glasses between him and austere naturalism.

'Now what was it you wanted, Hasek?'

'Why.' Seen directly, the patrolman was not nearly so rubicund as he had appeared through the sun lenses; not for a moment, that is; then the blood rose in his cheeks and he averted his juju-bean eyes. 'Why, we booked this Nigerro. Why, and you know who he is? Old Splendor Mainwaring is who. That good old sonbitch who runs every touchdown I ever blocked for. I loved that Niggero like a brother, and I onetime busted the mouth of the left guard from Cheeseman High for hollering "coon" in the scrimmage. So now the dumb shine turns out to be a user. And it is very embarrassing to me on the force when the chief brings him in and cuffs him to the radiator with me on the desk having to book him. All the while he rides me like he used to on the field: "Keep your butt down. Hit 'em low. Sixty-three, forty-two, *hike!*" '

'Hasek, Hasek! Explain yourself!' shouted Reinhart. 'Splendor Mainwaring was right here in this room not two hours ago. How could he have committed a serious crime within such a short period? Besides, he was sick.'

'You don't need no time nor anything but your own person to take dope,' Hasek explained. 'It's a peculiar crime in that respect. The only thing that's more peculiar is suicide, which is a crime, but the punishment for it is unenforceable, if you get my drift.'

'That I understand, Hasek,' said Reinhart, who felt he was dreaming all this. 'But I tell you there must be some mistake. Splendor taking dope! It's ridiculous. He is a nonchemical physician, among other things.'

Hasek removed his cap and rubbed his elbow against the isinglass liner, to match which there was a round bald spot in the center of his crown. 'I ain't supposed to remark on charges against accused, whose rights include counsel of his own choice, in lieu of which court will appoint same. Due process, habeas corpus on posting of specified bail, prisoner remanded in custody of, etc., etc., a jury of his pears, hear ye, hear ye. Very interesting stuff, Reinhart. How long you been a counselor at law? I remember you was always very bright in reading English, was you not? Miss Beeler used to give us them poems by Woolworth and others. Well, if you want we can go down to the jail to see your client.'

'He sent you here for me?'

'Precisely.'

'One minute, Hasek,' Reinhart demanded belligerently. 'Your name's *not* Hasek! It's Capek, Michael Capek.'

'Correct.'

'Then why did you let me go on saying Hasek?'

'Rules of the force,' said Capek. 'No harassment of nor rudeness to the taxpayer unless apprehended in an act where a violation of law is evident. If you want to file a complaint against me, my number is Three.'

Reinhart found his coat back of the partition; turned out the lights (no use being profligate with the cleaner's current); hung onto the turban and glasses, which should have to go back to their owners; considered closing the windows and doors but decided the hell with it, why did he have to take responsibility for everything in the world?; and started with Patrolman Capek for the stationhouse.

Nobody Knows The Trouble

BASIL BOOTHROYD

PEOPLE ARE TALKING to themselves more.

No.

More people are talking to themselves. And different people. A better class. I find this disturbing as I go about London, and so may you, going about wherever you go about. Harrogate, perhaps. Bude.

They used to be gutter-shufflers, men in other men's overcoats belted with coarse string, hunting for dog-ends. Kicking a failed drinking fountain. Delving in litter baskets for a decent newspaper, sitting on a low wall at rumoured points of call for the charity soup van. All running the aggrieved private commentary.

The language was basic. Some bastard had upset them. Several. Sods and bastards, they would say, and look right through you, so at least it was someone else they had it in for. Everyone else. Even finding a dog-end, they stowed it away with a curse. The world owed them a longer one than that.

Standing in an alcove on Blackfriars Bridge the other

week, watching a cardboard box sink, a man half turned with two very basic w**ds just as I passed contentedly by. The morning being sunny, and my reflexes pleasurably limp, I at first took this for a greeting, and slowed to respond in kind. He was gripping some property in a knotted duster and wearing an incongruously new tweed hat. He completed the turn and looked right through me.

'I'll show bloody Arthur.'

Moving on, I speculated. What was his history? Why was life so harsh? Where had he got the hat? Should I have given him 50p?

We better-adjusted and more buoyant souls have a sixth sense about when to give 50p and when not. Not, I thought, was right this time. He could have got proud, resentful. Violent. But I wondered during the day.

Going home in the afternoon I was more or less addressed by a small man with a huge beard in the Embankment Gardens, his back to that plinth that used to have a statue on it until somebody snapped it off and just left the feet. 'Bitch,' he said, looking up at the River Room of the Savoy. 'Just the gate was worth that.'

My 50p in his palm gave no offence, but touched off a fresh thought. 'Call yourself a Prime Minister?' After counting the coin's sides he dropped it into a carrier bag, printed in red, CARLSBERG.

They would often talk to themselves about the bloody Government.

I don't know why I use the past tense. They're still around. But these new people are joining them. Even women, and of a superior kind. One of these, boarding a cab I was paying off at Charing Cross, shook a good little umbrella at the back of the driver's neck. Of course, anyone could be ridiculous, she said, but nineteen square yards was—. Then the gears drowned her. She wore a quality raincoat, orange. Couldn't have been more than thirty.

Same day, a much older woman, in what I took to be genuine ocelot, joined me at Victoria in an otherwise empty compartment, and said quite loudly as we pulled out:

'It's not ducks.'

'Pardon?' I said.

She said, 'What?'

The conversation lapsed. Just after Redhill there was a threat of revival. She made it over nine hundred dollars, she said, looking on the floor for something. I didn't take it up.

There are differences between the new soliloquisers and the old. Their circumstances are more comfortable. I'm thinking of the men, preponderant in the new wave, though you never did get women, comfortably placed or not, with eyes down for cigarette butts, or seeking a good read in the trash cans. But would you expect a plump, well-tailored lawyer, still in his white bands and waiting to cross the Strand to the Wig and Pen, to make quite a long speech about a little cow called Enid? I was waiting on the same kerb, so I assure you. Why the other house, he demanded, for God's sake? She knew they were pewter.

Possibly neuter. None of my business. Still, you can get caught up. But when I edged closer to the moving lips they were speaking of others matters, intermittently blotted out by heavier items of traffic. 'Out of the question, cranberries . . . some sort of testimonial, you're crazy . . .'

He gave a sharp bark, perhaps a laugh, threw an arm out wide, hitting his knuckles on a lamp post, before diving across between two buses.

That's another difference, the use of gesture. Very rare with the string belt and knotted duster lot. They have an immobility, more of a slumping. Even an accepting palm comes up slowly, as if under water. But the new men, smart and brisk, tend to reinforce the points they make to themselves. As they walk and talk they chop things off with the edge of the hand, just in front of their expensive ties, dismiss them, put an end to that whole nuisance. 'Not from Formosa,' a man was saying outside Harrods the other week, passing at a fast pace in the direction of the Royal Geographical Society—'not ball bearings.' He chopped them right off. A man coming the other way, in trousers so dazzlingly golf that they should have had a single glove

hanging from the hip pocket, had to step off the pavement
to give play for his Nazi salute, or one-armed 'Drop dead'
motion. He wasn't going to have it at any price. It was
ludicrous. Whatever it was. I didn't quite hear. It could have
been lemons. Lemmings.

He caught himself at it, perhaps glimpsing from an eye-
corner the ball bearings chopper, and firmly shut his
mouth to a tight line. It may have checked utterance, but I
noticed, as he rejoined the pedestrians, that he was pushing
his troubles behind him with a double-handed scooping,
and I expect he was again telling himself his plans for
dealing with them.

It's disturbing, as I say, to see these expressions of stress.
Particularly creeping up the social scale, as they
undoubtedly are. Most of these citizens are solid. Two-car
households, is my guess. Freezers. At the other end,
polished executive desks, heavy stationery. A failed
drinking fountain doesn't touch them. You'd want a hell of a
big duster to knot their property up in. Their wallets
sprout credit cards like tambourine ribbons. Crocodile
briefcases instead of sharp-handled lager adverts.

Is that the problem? Do they miss the small delights?
The unexpectedly long dog-end? The unhurried sinking of
a cardboard box?

Nobody knows. Myself, I can only pass on my
observations. With a touch of irrepressible complacency.
There but for the grace of God, I thought, not for the first
time, as a man came towards me on the St James's Park
footbridge, trim, purposeful, one arm outflung as if
forbidding the swimming mallards below to take wing. He
was talking to himself under his narrow-brimmed
Whitehall bowler. It was nothing to do with him, he said,
nothing. How many more times? Take it back to bloody
External Relations.

There but for the grace of God, indeed.

'Pardon?' he said, slowing as we drew abreast.

I said, 'What?'

'There but for what?' he said.

So it's still spreading. I find that disturbing.

My Painful Jaw

J. P. DONLEAVY

I WALKED THROUGH where people and women with legs crossed and furs sat on sofas and a man with white gloves pointed me into an elevator with gleaming brass doors. When it was nearly full they closed and green lights were buzzing and binging and I said five please. The doors opened. Before me a grill, a cage, a man in there. I took off a watch and with my wallet and some change put them into an envelope, pinched it up with a machine and handed it through a hole to the man. I walked down the rows of dark green lockers in near silence and darkness. Turning up a row and pulling on a light, I opened a little green door and took off my clothes.

When I went down some back stairs in my athletic garments I bounced on my rubber soled boots. I went into a room and put a pair of leather gloves on my fists and beat a bag like mad. I skipped rope watching my calves in the mirror. I went over to a window and looked out across the street into living rooms and kitchens or just on the sills at plants.

You could smell the sweat coming from me. I could. And I sat down. Stretch out in these soft warm towels and rest my hairy legs. People come in. Where of course some fear to tread because of fists. Around the walls are pictures of fighters with muscles others with smiles but all standing ready to punch. Most said hi, sat down and whenever they looked at me said boy you're in good shape. I said o no not really, my midriff is fatty and all the while I'd slowly expand out my chest. Then a bouncy man came in throwing blows in all directions looked at me and said how about a few rounds. I tried to look away, I didn't know where to hide my fists. But the eyes would be on me looking for any fear so I said certainly.

We got in the ring. Bong, the gong. Out in the center ring I threw what was a feeler or to see if perhaps he might stand well away from me in anxiety but biff right on my nose and bang on my jaw this man started beating me around the place. I didn't want to turn and run outright because they might think I wasn't taking my beating like a man. So I hid under my gloves to try to give the impression that I was only playing. He knocked me right through the ropes and in spite of everything I made an effort to giggle with o it's nothing I like a good fight but a tooth dropping out of my mouth just produced a splutter. I think my adversary said sorry old man and something in me made me smile through the blood as if I were only resting that round.

He put it to me, have you had enough old man. I said I like a good workout, gets up a sweat. I almost mentioned blood too. I rested in my corner waiting for the bell. When it rang I came out with my customary feeler to size up his style for my special zip punch which I am reluctant to use. We circled around. I must admit I stayed my distance only of course because my zip punch can be fatal at close quarters. The fight had aroused interest in the room, people pushing to see. I had firmly made my decision to use the zip. I think he knew what was coming because he kept his guard high, the only nearly adequate defense against this punch. I waited for the corner of my eye to see a few more people gather, and then I moved in. I brought it from the hip, my right knee slightly flexed, weight well forward on the balls of the feet. The last thing I heard was the little audience catching a collective breath.

They told me later when I was dressed and showered that for awhile they didn't think I'd come around and someone even suggested giving me artificial respiration as well as the salts. But it was generally agreed that in the final analysis it was better that this had happened because the zip punch, especially with the stance I was employing, would have been deadly. My opponent now wearing a bow tie clapped me on the back and said I was a hard man to hit and are you sure you're all right old man. I was horrified when my mouth said I'd very much like to have another workout with you sometime.

An Historic Night at the Old Vic

CARYL BRAHMS & S. J. SIMON

NIGHT. ALL OVER England, from tallow candles, from paraffin containers, from gas mantles, lights beckon enticingly. But nowhere do they burn more brightly than in our gay metropolis.

The season has been a triumph. Jenny Lind has said farewell and Caruso has not yet arrived. Sarah Bernhardt has brought tears to the eyes of J. T. Greim, but George Bernard Shaw seems to be preferring Duse. Mrs Charles Kean, very firm of purpose, has seized Mr Charles Kean's dagger. Dame Marie Tempest has had her first audition, and the Jersey Lily has gone to the South of France. So, with all these artistic events out of the way the great British Public feels free to enjoy itself in any manner it pleases.

Quite a lot of it is congregated at the old Aquarium Music Hall at Westminster, where three men have elected to fire a cannon. They have dragged the cannon into the centre of the stage, they have aimed it to land its projectile into a net, and now they are loading it. At this precise

moment the ammunition is easing itself into the barrel.[1]
It is Zazel, the lady cannon ball.

It is a comfort to know that on this same evening Her Royal
Highness the Princess Victoria is being taken to a
pantomime—*Old Mother Hubbard or Harlequin and Tales of the
Nursery.*
An historic night at the Old Vic.
As usual the place is crowded.
Grimaldi, the lovable familiar clown, is making his
farewell appearance.[2] Joey, who sat between a codfish and
a huge oyster that opened and closed its shell in time to the
music, and who is said to have moved half the audience to
tears with his melancholy ditty, 'An Oyster crossed in
love.' Joey, who having crippled himself with leaps and
tumbles so dangerous that he always has to have an
understudy in the wings, waiting to take on when he
knocks himself out. Joey, who has made them laugh so
often with his pilfering and his sausages and his red-hot
poker. Joey, who, eight years later, is to die in penury, but
unsupplanted.
The audience are strung up to the occasion. Never have
they laughed so loudly at the quips of the comics. Never
have so many strong men been moved to so many tears at
the warbled lament of the Bird in the Gilded Cage.
But at the moment it is the interval.
Relaxing after its efforts, the audience sits at small tables
on the floor, quaffing, chaffing, coaxing. Bloods, blades and
dandies vie with one another in attracting the feminine
eye. And the feminine eye is well in evidence, determined to
be attracted.
In a corner, alone at a table, a little man, slightly thin on
top and slightly dusty all over, is trying to keep his eye on

---

[1] 'It's wonderful fun to be shot from a gun.'
[2] Our Uncle insisted on being present at Grimaldi's farewell performance. Our
Villain insisted on taking our Uncle to the Old Vic. Our publisher insisted on
both. What could our authors do?

every part of the floor at once. He is the Observation Scout from the Society for the Stimulation of Morality and the Encouragement of Good Taste. He is here to-night to collect statistics upon the Easy Acquaintanceship of the Unintroduced. The blades and the belles are keeping him busy.

Now comes a drawing away of skirts. The Clutterwicks and the Shuttleforths have arrived. They are, of course, cutting each other dead.

Naturally the ladies are still doing this safe at home in their back drawing-rooms. But the wretched Benjamin, surrounded by dependable henchmen, has taken a night off from the feud.

So has Pelham Clutterwick, with Archie and Algy in support.

It is a pity therefore that they find they have booked adjoining tables.

Waiters, balancing large trays, make their way among the lounging audience. Cigars, cheroots and even cigarettes are being smoked shamelessly, until the vast dome is as hung with smoke as your own back drawing-room when someone has carelessly turned the wick too high.

Why then does our villain look so dismayed? Is not our Uncle Clarence at his table laughing hugely at the quips, weeping copiously at the gilded Birds, and refreshing himself with gusto from the tall beaker at his side?

Well, that is just the point.

Since our villain's last visit Emma Cons has taken over the old Vic.

The beaker contains barley water.

Uncle Clarence is sober.

Already he has stopped weeping twice to mention that confounded thirty thou'. Heavy weather for our villain. He eyebrows our Uncle.

'Let us go to the Aquarium,' he suggests, 'the gin is good there.'

But Uncle Clarence has caught sight of Number 18 on

the song sheet. He dotes on Grimaldi.
'Later, my dear fellow, later,' he says.
Our villain scowls. It is indeed difficult to fuddle an Uncle
on barley water—neat or diluted.

Behind the scenes four famous ballerinas are cutting each
other dead.
Taglioni, Cerito, Grisi and Grahn have been prevailed
upon to dance simultaneously in a *pas de quatre*. Their silence
is icy, but their looks are eloquent.
The overwrought impresario who has prevailed upon
them is pacing up and down outside the stage door at Her
Majesty's Theatre, where they are due to appear.
Another wilful horse!
The interval is nearly over. In a box the lovely Lady
Caroline Lamb is watching her friends arriving in time for
the cream of the performance. There come Mr and Mrs
Disraeli—the poppets. There's funny old Mr Gladstone
who does so disapprove of her, and here is that amusing
creature Mr Boz. And—good gracious—there's her
husband! She wonders if she ought to wave.
Lady Caroline sights our villain. Heavens—what fine
moustachios! And what a flashing smile. Fascinated Lady
Caroline flashes back at Spencer Faggot.
'You are animated to-night, my dear,' remarks the
Princess Lieven.
Lady Caroline blushes. Oh, dear! She has been caught
flirting in public. To cover it up she changes the subject.
'Is your cousin Armand still in Paris?' she enquires.
The Princess Lieven sighs. 'Poor Armand, he has fallen in
love with a complete invalid.'
'How tragic,' says Lady Caroline.
'Every day,' says the Princess Lieven, 'he takes his fiancée
white camellias.'
Lady Caroline Lamb makes a mental note. A charming
touch. She must tell Mr Sardou. . . .
In a pino boudoir at the Paris Opera Armand's invalid is

dying. Her aria brings tears to the conductor's eyes.

. . . and, thinks Lady Caroline Lamb, she must also tell Signor Verdi. . . .

Now that the fashionable crowd has arrived all the tables are occupied. The Observation Scout from the Society for the Stimulation of Morality and the Encouragement of Good Taste is having a busy time. At a centre table Mr Disraeli toasts his wife with all the courtesy of a Mr Pitt at Balmoral. Mrs Disraeli glows, dimples and blows him a kiss. Our Observation Scout eyes them doubtfully. Have they met before? . . .

The wretched Benjamin is thirsty. He beckons a waiter. But Archie Clutterwick shouts 'Garçon,' and the waiter, pleased by this mode of address, hurries over to him.

The wretched Benjamin is confronted with a problem. Should he glare at the bounder or ignore him utterly? He tries both.

The loyal Algy turns to his best friend.

'Archie,' he says, 'it is a pity that we did not go to the Great Exhibition.'

'Tomorrow,' says Archie vaguely. 'Or perhaps next week.'

A pair of practised eyes have been directing a hopeful gaze at him. But Archie loves his Belinda. Bored, he turns his back on them.

The Observation Scout subtracts one from his total.

Uncle Clarence is quite put out. He has lost his gold repeater again. It must have dropped out of his pocket. He turns to our villain.

'How is the Enemy?' he asks.

Spencer pulls out a gold repeater. 'Just time,' he announces, 'to pop over and see the irresistible, irreplaceable, irremovable Archie Harradine singing "Pretty Little Polly Perkins" at the Late Joys.'

'No,' says Uncle Clarence firmly. One gathers that he does not approve of these new-fangled entertainments.

'You can sing the chorus,' tempts our villain.

Nothing like singing choruses to make an Uncle thirsty.

But our Uncle is not listening. His eyes are riveted on Spencer's gold repeater—dash it, it's exactly like his own! 'I had a repeater like that, once,' he says wistfully.

'I noticed that,' says Spencer tucking it quickly away.

Our Uncle broods. The barley water has tempered the toddy. Now he will have to buy himself a new gold repeater. More expense, demmit! And that reminds him. Thirty thousand pounds! But how to approach it tactfully?

'By the way,' he hazards, 'can you call to mind anything you may have forgotten?'

'Not a thing,' says Spencer Faggot airily. 'Not a mortgage, not a bastard, not a loaded dice.'

'An admirable man,' thinks the upright Uncle Clarence. Such difficult things to remember, too! And he forgets nothing. He sips contentedly at his barley water. Then a shade crosses his face. 'Except of course that thirty thousand pounds! Perhaps a broader hint. . . .'

'How is your luck at cards?' he enquires boldly.

Like magic a pack of cards appears on the table.

'Cut,' says Spencer, 'and we'll see.'

But Uncle Clarence is already shuffling.

A pretty pass. Our villain thinks quickly. He knocks the cards out of our Uncle's hands.

'My mistake,' he says. 'I thought you were a fortune-teller.'

'A curious mistake,' thinks Uncle Clarence. But the word fortune reminds him of something. Our villain owes him one. A very small fortune—Uncle Clarence plays whist for pleasure—but it is the principle of the thing. . . .

Striving to create a diversion our villain suggests leaving for the Tivoli, the Mogul, Vauxhall Gardens, Drury Lane or even the Great Exhibition. But our Uncle is not listening. He is brooding himself into an ugly mood. If the fellow refuses to take a hint there is nothing else for it. Uncle Clarence will come down to brass tacks.

'Young man,' he begins. 'Let me remind you . . .'

'Cut the cackle and get to the 'osses.'

Uncle Clarence starts. But the little man with the loud voice at the back of the pit is not bawling at him. He is telling the chairman to pipe down and bring on the equestrian turn.

The chairman, Lord George Sanger, looked pained. Was it for this that he had left his circus? But he brightened as he reminded himself that it was less than a hundred years before Nikita Balieff would be drawing an enormous salary for doing the same thing in broken English.

'Mademoiselle Lala,' he announced, 'and her waltzing Horses.'

The orchestra leapt into a waltz. It was the 'Blue Danube'.

Be-ribboned and be-belled, with a rose wreath round its neck, sleek, shiny and white, and rearing on its hind-legs, appeared a performer. It was certainly a horse and it was definitely rotating.

Top-hatted, top-booted, be-curled, tight-laced and dressed mainly in a French flag, Mademoiselle Lala, whip in hand, advances to take up her pose with a jaunty air.

'French,' explains Pelham Clutterwick. He claps vigorously.

On the point of clapping also, the wretched Benjamin stops himself. No Shuttleforth is allowed to like the same turn as any Clutterwick.[1]

Mademoiselle Lala cracks her whip. Nothing happens. She cracks it again. The solitary performer looks up. It is still a white horse. It is still rotating. But it is beginning to feel rather lonely.

There is a fusillade of cracks. Mademoiselle Lala, smile obliterated by a scowl, picks up her skirts and with a little whisk disappears daintily into the wings.

Conscientiously the white horse continues its rotating.

There is a rumpus in the wings. A black horse, its bells missing, its ribbons awry, its ears pricked, comes unwillingly, from the wings. It is on all fours. It is trying to

---

[1] Queensbury rules.

eat its wreath. Behind, pushing it, is Mademoiselle Lala.
'Waltz, you bastard!' she snarls.
Lord George Sanger drops his cigar.
'Nelly,' he entreats. 'In heaven's name remember your French!'

Our Uncle Clarence is getting restless. All through the dancing horses, all through the Beautiful Picture in the Beautiful Golden Frame,[1] and all through the still-surviving lady surrounded by knives, he has been trying to get down to brass tacks. But somehow he can never hold Spencer's attention. He is glad the dear fellow is enjoying the performance, but they really must get this matter settled so that he can enjoy it too.

'Young man,' he begins again, 'let me remind you of a certain night, three months ago, when at my brother's house we played whist together. Now I play the game for pleasure. . . .'

But just as our Uncle is about to get right down to the rockbottom of the brass tacks, Lord George Sanger bangs with his hammer on the table. Eloquently he announces a new turn.

Our villain applauds loudly.

Clutterwicks and Shuttleforths eye each other. Which of them is to applaud this one?

A mournful little man, with black eyebrows, red nose and the wide malleable mouth that has been God's gift to the Comedian, from the first Widow Twankey to Bert Lahr, comes on to the stage and tries to hang his open-lidded top-hat on the painted lamp-post of the street scene. It falls down. There is a bang on the drum.

With those thick black eyebrows the comedian signals his reproach to the conductor.

The House is in convulsions.

Barely on a minute, and Dan Leno has got them right between the ribs.

But Uncle Clarence is a little deaf. He goes on talking to Spencer Faggot.

[1] ('It was only A.')

'. . . you made a debt of thirty thousand pounds,' he is pointing out vividly. 'You had not brought your cheque book with you. You asked me for loan. . . .' He breaks off, and looks irritably at the twirling moustachios. 'Spencer— are you listening?'

'No,' says our villain frankly. 'I don't think Dan Leno is funny.'

At the Aquarium Music Hall the battle music that heralds the firing of the human cannon ball has worked itself up to its most dramatic moments. A fanfaronade of trumpets, a martial roll of the drums, and the chief gunner, busbied and bewhiskered, goes through the motions of lighting a torch and applying it to the powder.

The roll of drums loudens to a roar.

Eyes focus. Necks crane. The audience leans forward.

But where is Zazel?

The flustered gunners gather round the barrel. They heave. They tug. They consult together.

The human cannon ball is wedged immovably inside the barrel.

At the Old Vic, young Mr Compton Mackenzie has arrived in the middle of the *pas de quatre*. He has not been drinking barley water.

On the stage the four ballerinas gravely dance. Taglioni, Cerito, Grisi and Grahn, trailing long ballet skirts like precise clockwork clouds. To see their air of young Goddesses doing the world a favour, you would never suppose that they were keeping a sharp eye open for one another's technical weaknesses.

The audience is reduced to silence. Not so young Mr Compton Mackenzie. To him the Goddesses are standing still and the Old Vic is revolving around them.

Something must be done about this!

Tearing off his opera cloak, he flings it at the revolving

walls. A poor missile, but the best he can find.

It falls on Uncle Clarence.

On the stage the *pas de quatre*, in a closing cadenza, drifts into its final group. The rose-crowned ballerinas sustain their famous pose like an old print coming to life.

'Dainty,' says Uncle Clarence, emerging from Mr Compton Mackenzie's cloak.[1]

The curtain falls. The rapt house breaks into wave after wave of applause. The unwrapt Uncle Clarence disengages himself from wave after wave of Mr Mackenzie's cloak. Our villain pounces on it and slings it round his own shoulders. He can always use an opera cloak.

'How well he looks in his borrowed plumage,' thinks Uncle Clarence. Every inch a villain. If he had not met Spencer Faggot in his own brother's house he would no doubt have thought him an unscrupulous, dishonest, ill-bred wastrel who borrowed thirty thousand pounds with no intention of ever paying it back. But no—his manners were perfect. Still—that reminded him.

This time he would be brutally frank.

'About this thirty thousand pounds,' he began laboriously.

But Spencer Faggot had caught Lord George Sanger's eye.

'Later,' he says. 'Later. I'm on next.'

Surprised Uncle Clarence consults his song sheet.

No. 16. A Musical Trio. The Marx Brothers.

'Why bless my buttons,' he says. 'So you are.'

Our villain twirls his moustachios. He looks more like Groucho Marx than ever.

'We may have been a flop on the halls,' he says, 'but we top the bill in Hollywood.'

---

[1] When Mr Compton Mackenzie recounted this story in a broadcast in 1940, he unaccountably stated that the theatre was the Alhambra and that the ballerina around whom the walls appeared to be rotating was Madame Adeline Genée. But was he in any fit state to remember clearly? We fear not, for in his broadcast he made no mention of our Uncle Clarence.

At the Lyceum Don Pedro is measuring wits with Beatrice.

'To be merry best becomes you,' he tells her. 'For, out of question you were born in a merry hour.'

'No, sure, my Lord, my mother cried,' says Beatrice. 'But then a star danced, and under that was I born.'

She is Ellen Terry.

A stir runs through the Old Vic.

No. 23. Grimaldi.

The boxes pick up their opera glasses. The pit lays aside its oranges. Blades lose interest in their belles, Mr and Mrs Disraeli hold hands. Lady Caroline Lamb stops chattering. A painted hussy sits down beside the Observation Scout. He does not notice her. Tier upon tier, emotion spreads and rises until lumps come to throats in every part of the house even before the clown begins to say good-bye.

Silence falls. The curtain goes up.

Joey is on.

The whole house cooes at him.

Here is their dear Joey with his face painted in the familiar way, with the red and white triangles and tufts of every clown.

The applause subsides. A shiver runs through the house. Grimaldi, being totally unable to stand, is playing his scene seated in a chair. His body is broken from forgotten tumbles in past Harlequinades.

Yet as the scene goes on the audience is almost shocked to find itself roaring with laughter again at the old trouper's drollery.

There are tears in the eyes of Lady Caroline Lamb. The Clutterwicks and the Shuttleforths are blowing their noses. To hell with the feud! . . .

Grimaldi's turn is over. The applause dies away. As soon as silence can be obtained and he can summon up sufficient courage to speak, Joey advances to the footlights and delivers, as well as his emotions permit, the following address:

'Ladies and gentlemen,

'In putting off the clown's garment, allow me to drop also the clown's taciturnity, and address you in a few parting sentences. I entered early on this course of life, and leave it prematurely. Forty-eight years only have passed over my head—but I am going as fast down the hill of life as that older Joe—John Anderson. Like vaulting ambition, I have over-leaped myself, and pay the penalty in advanced old age. If I have now any aptitude for tumbling, it is through bodily infirmity, for I am worse on my feet than I used to be on my head. It is four years since I jumped my last jump—filched my last oyster—boiled my last sausage—and set in for retirement. Not so well provided for, I must acknowledge, as in the days of my clownship, for then, I dare say some of you remember, I used to have a fowl in one pocket and sauce for it in another . . .'

It is with no trifling difficulty that Grimaldi reaches the conclusion of this little speech, although the audience cheers loudly and gives him every possible expression of encouragement and sympathy.

But though he has finished he stands, still in the same place, bewildered and motionless, so moved that the little power his illness has left him wholly deserts him.

Unashamedly Uncle Clarence is wiping his eyes.

'Makes me forget everything,' he admits. Our villain, back at his side, brightens.

But something is worrying Uncle Clarence. He had got down to brass tacks, he had been brutally frank, and then he had let himself get distracted. It was high time that he stood no nonsense.

'You owe me thirty thousand pounds,' he says. 'A cheque will oblige.'

'A trifle,' says our villain airily. From his pocket he produces some loaded dice. 'Roll you for it?'

But Uncle Clarence is adamant.

'Sir,' he says. 'Your cheque first. Then we roll.'

Spencer Faggot thinks quickly. 'Play you at snooker?'

'Not even at Battledore and Shuttlecock,' says Uncle Clarence, although he is a dab at this sport.

Spencer thinks quickly again. These brass tacks are deuced awkward. To give our Uncle confidence he pulls out his cheque book and allows him to catch a glimpse of a counterfoil.

'. . . Fifty thou' to Tattersalls. . . .'

But this only hardens our upright Uncle. A man of substance evidently, he reasons. Then why does he not pay him his thirty thousand pounds?

Our villain is cornered. Desperately he plays for time.

'The date?' he asks.

Uncle Clarence tells him.

'The amount?'

Uncle Clarence obliges again.

'I'll be forgetting my own name next,' says Spencer Faggot prophetically.

At his table in the corner the Observation Scout is continuing his count of too easily acquainted couples.

'Eighty-two . . . eighty-four . . . eighty-six . . .'

'Might I borrow your song sheet?' asks the painted hussy who has seated herself at his table.

Absently he passes it across.

'Ninety-two . . . ninety-four . . . ninety-six . . .'

The chairman bangs with his hammer on the table.

'And now,' he announces, 'I have the honour to present the irresistible, irrepressible, irresponsible—LOLA MONTEZ.'

A swirl of skirts, a clatter of castanets, a tap of defiant heels, a whisking hip and la Montez is on.

To see those flashing eyes, that dark smouldering promise, and the tilt of the head crowned with its high comb and framing laces, you would never suppose that there stood Betty James of Limerick.

'Caramba,' curses Uncle Clarence with pride. He thinks he is saying 'brava'.

La Montez possesses twenty-six of the twenty-seven points essential to the Spanish dancer. This is the considered opinion of a sober critic writing in Warsaw.

Those points enumerated are: Three white—the skin, the teeth, the hands; three black—the eyes, eyelashes, the eyebrows; three red—the lip, the cheek, the nails; three long—the body, the hair, the hands; three short—the ears, the teeth, the legs; three broad—the bosom, the forehead, the space between the eyebrows; three full—the hips, the arms, the calves; three small—the waist, the hands, the feet; three thin—the fingers, the hair, the lips.

'All these perfections are Lola's, except as regards the colour of her eyes, which I, for one,' states the eminent critic, 'would not wish to change. Lola's silky hair, rivalling the gloss of the raven's wing, falls in luxuriant folds down her back. On the slender delicate neck, whose whiteness shames the swan's down, rests the beautiful head. How, too, shall I describe Lola's bosom? Words fail me to describe the dazzling whiteness of her teeth. . . .'

On and on he raved but so engrossed was he in the drawing up of the inventory of her charms that he never noticed that she could not dance.

Fortunately Lola herself has noticed this long ago and has devised a technique of her own for distracting attention from it. Picking up a missile she would throw (and hit) the most important member of the audience. Her beauty did the rest.

The orchestra embarks on a *jota*. They are almost as breathless as la Montez. Already it is high time to look round for something to throw. At our villain's table a waiter is depositing quill, ink and wafers.

'Now sir,' says Uncle Clarence grimly. 'Your cheque.'

Lola has found her missile. It is a portrait of Ludwig of Bavaria of the school of Herkomer. The *jota* grows quicker and quicker. Capering wildly Lola looks round for a target.

She sights Mr Disraeli, but he is beating time with evident delight. She looks at Mr Gladstone—out. She catches Prince Albert's eye—'*Pas de plaisanterie, Madame!*'

Pelham Clutterwick's finger is resting on his third waistcoat button. The wretched Benjamin has been revolving his ear ceaselessly. Sucks to the Clutterwicks if a Shuttleforth should get socked.

The orchestra is playing relentlessly. La Montez, like the lady in the song, is doing the fandango all over the place 'Mr Thackeray—rash! Salmon or Gluckstein—short-sighted! Mr Hall Caine—a Manxman! Sir William Parry—a mistake.'

The tempo quickens. She will have to hit somebody soon.

But lo, there comes into her twirling horizon a pair of melting orbs, admirable eyebrows and agitated moustachios. The very man!

Taking careful aim at Spencer Faggot our dancer throws, and hits our Uncle Clarence.

Sucks to the Clutterwicks.

Our villain thinks quickly. While our Uncle is enveloped and indeed almost extinguished by King Ludwig of Bavaria, he seizes the quill and writes furiously.

'Pay Uncle Clarence. . . .'

But, reader, do not be misled. This order to pay, scrawled hurriedly while our Uncle's eagle eye is obscured by a canvas of the school of Herkomer, is unlikely to survive the close scrutiny of the Baring Brothers.

At the Aquarium things have arrived at a pretty pass. They have changed the powder. They have played the battle music three times. They have rung the curtain up and down, and they have pushed an unwilling sword-swallower out in front of it to distract the audience. He is so demoralized he can hardly swallow a dagger.

And still Mademoiselle Zazel has failed to emerge from the barrel of the gun.

But now they are ready for one last try.

The sword-swallower, dagger but half-way down, is twitched away like a toy from a child before its birthday, and once again the weary orchestra churns out the battle music. The roll of the drum is two beats behind. The drummer's wrists are tired.

And here is Zazel being helped into her barrel. But this time they are cutting out the bows, the kissed fingers, the coquetry.

The turn has become a job of work.

Grimly the head assistant prepares to fire the gun. Without much hope his satellites stuff their fingers in their ears.

Bang!

A dainty form is flying through the air. It lands on the edge of the net and rolls itself into the centre. There it sits up, sighs with relief and smiles.

'*Me voici*,' says the human cannon ball.

The audience are taken by surprise. They had not been expecting this for a moment.

It is four o'clock in the morning.

In a stucco love nest in St John's Wood the Observation Scout from the Society for the Stimulation of Morality and the Encouragement of Good Taste awakes with a start. He looks at the painted hussy sleeping peacefully beside him. An awful thought occurs to him.

Ought he to include himself in his report on Couples too easily acquainted?

Focusing Session

KINGSLEY AMIS

'WHAT DOES IT mean?' asked Brenda.

'Well, sensate ought to mean endowed with sense or senses, as dentate if it occurs must mean endowed with teeth, but I don't see how any sort of focusing can be endowed with any sort of sense. I think they wanted an adjective from sense and noticed or someone told them sensuous and sensual were used up and they noticed or someone told them a lot of words ended in -ate. Makes it sound scientific too. Like nitrate. And focusing, well. Homing in on? No? Concentrating? Something like that.'

'I see. But what does it mean?'

'Christ, love, I don't know. Getting you, getting one interested in the other person physically, something like that I should think. Anyway, we know what we're supposed to do.'

'Yes. Darling, you're not to be cross but I must ring Elspeth before we start. She said she'd ring me today or tomorrow and I *know* it'll be while we're doing our focusing if I don't get in first. You know.'

'Check.' As just disclosed, Elspeth was of the Alcistis-Mrs Sharp sorority though, living as she did on the far side of London at Roehampton, less to be feared. 'You take as long as you have to. I'll be in the study.'

Jake finished putting the lunch plates in the rack on the metal draining-board and went where he had said. The study had been made out of what had been not much more than a spacious box-room and the kneehole desk, the celebrated red-leather armchair and a pair of Queen Anne bookcases left little space for anything else, but even he could see that the turquoise carpet was a pretty shade and went well with the wallpaper and Madras cotton curtains.

With the intention not so much of getting in the mood as of keeping up the good work he glanced at a couple of papers that lay on the desk, had been lying there in perfect security since the previous Thursday, even though it was now Monday and Mrs Sharp had by standing arrangement attended the house on the Friday and that very morning. For both times Brenda had been at home and, as in many a (or many another) case of hypernormal powers, Mrs Sharp's were severely curtailed or even curbed altogether by the presence of a third party. Jake picked up one of the papers.

M27 (he read) I find the thought of sexual intercourse with a willing female somewhat under the age of consent, say 14-15 yrs

    1 very pleasant
    2 fairly pleasant
    3 a little unpleasant
    4 very unpleasant

In so far as he could make himself address his mind to the problem, he found he thought all four. The age thing didn't come into it: the attractiveness of any willing female past puberty depended for him on her attractiveness, though as far as he knew he had in practice confined himself to those of 16 yrs and over. What counted was the immediacy or lack of it. Some time or other in Hawaii or somewhere, very pleasant; on this next trip to Italy, fairly pleasant; by the end of next month in Orris Park, a little unpleasant; here and now, very unpleasant. Even that wasn't quite right because of the difference between the thought of sexual intercourse and the thought of the thought of it. If he could snap his fingers and boof, there he was in mid-job, very pleasant; if she were really actually in fact standing a yard away on the precise point of starting to show how willing she was, very unpleasant. Not unpleasant, either, just as much as his old man needed to set it trying to haul itself up into his abdomen. But he couldn't write all this down, especially since the question was obviously nothing to do with any of it. Like the good examinee he had always been (best classical scholarship of his year at Charterhouse, First in Mods, best First of his year in Greats) he asked himself what was expected here, what was being looked for. A means of sorting out the child-molesters from the gerontophiles, why yes, and no doubt of making the finer distinction between the inhibited who welcomed any accepted restriction and the robust sturdy husky hardy hearty etc. He ticked 2 and picked up the other paper.

A fantastically beautiful girl with an unbelievable figure wearing a skin-tight dress cut as low as it possibly could be is looking at me with eyes blazing with uncontrollable passion (he read). With lazy languorous movements she peels off the dress and reveals herself as completely stark naked and utterly nude. Her breasts are so enormous that there is hardly room for them on her thorax. They are rising and falling with irresistible desire as with her shapely hips swaying lazily she glides over and stands insolently before me with her hands on her curving hips and her colossal breasts jutting 100 words out at me. I tear off all my clothes and she gives a tremendous gasp of astonishment and admiration and awe. She lies down on a bed which is there.

There was more, but he was still 73 words short of the 600 minimum set by Rosenberg and had already been compelled to introduce two additional girls, the first with immense breasts, the second with gigantic ones, for the sake of variety. He felt that this must violate some important canon of the genre but could find no other alternative to direct repetition. It was not that he had been idle; this was the fourth draft. The first, which had said all he really wanted to say on the matter, had consisted only of nouns, verbs, prepositions, pronouns and articles and been 113 words long; gamma minus at best. Well, he had to find those 73 somewhere before setting off for Harley Street the next morning. What about a black girl? With Brobdingnagian breasts? No no, with gleaming ebony skin. Mm. . . . The trouble was that being white himself he tended to think about white girls when he thought about girls at all.

Brenda tapped softly at the open door. 'All right?'

'Right.'

He followed her across the small landing, where a Bengal rug lay, and into their bedroom. Here, in a drill they had been through many times together, they lifted off, folded and laid down on an ottoman the patchwork quilt she had expertly made. Again by tradition, lapsed in this case, she slipped off to the bathroom and he quickly undressed and got into bed. He felt calm and yet uneasy, quite resolved to carry out orders but unable not to wish that something harmless in itself would prevent what was in prospect. After a minute he turned over so that he would have his back to Brenda when she reappeared. She had treated with exemplary seriousness Rosenberg's letter about her need to lose weight, had joined the local group of Guzzlers Anonymous at the first opportunity and had already taken off six ounces, but that wasn't going to be enough to make her feel all right about being seen naked, which she had avoided for the past year or more, he supposed.

There was a patter of arrival behind him (she moved lightly for so large a woman) and she got in and snuggled up to him with wincing and puffing noises.

'Ooh! It's freezing. It's supposed to be the middle of April and it's like January.'

'Would you like to turn the other way?'

'No, this is fine for me. Had you heard of comfort eating before?'

'What?'

'Comfort eating. What Dr Thing said I'd been going in for because of feeling sexually inadequate. Had you heard of it?'

'I think so, anyway it's clear enough what it's supposed to mean, which is all balls. If there's anybody who feels sexually inadequate it's me and I haven't started eating my head off. Just another example of thinking that if you name something you've explained it. Like . . . like permissive society.'

'I don't think you're always meant to go in for comfort eating when you feel sexually inadequate. And in any case what makes you think you're the one who feels it so terrifically you leave everybody else standing, how adequate do you think I feel when I think about things and look back, that's what I'd like to. . . .'

Brenda, who had started talking at some speed, stopped altogether because a jet was passing and even at this range she would have to shout rather and she was bad at shouting. A part of the window-frame buzzed for a short time as it always did on these occasions. Eventually Jake said, 'My fault. I just got fed up and guilty and ashamed. Of course you must feel inadequate if we have to use the word, but I can tell you there's no need for you to, it's all me, we went into that.'

'I know we went into it, but we decided it must be me as well as you.'

'You may have thought so, but it wasn't what we decided.'

'Well I think it was. And of course it is, it's obvious. Anyway I'm warm enough now. Hadn't we better get on with it?'

'All right.' Grunting, Jake turned over so as to face his wife. They intertwined their legs in a friendly way.

'Tell me again what we're meant to do.'

'We take it in turns to stroke and massage each other anywhere but what you used to call down below.'

'Did I? Anyway I bags you start.'

'Okay. Lift up . . . Put your arm . . . That's right.'

He started stroking the back of her neck and her left shoulder and upper arm. She sighed and settled herself more comfortably, moving her head about on the pillow. A minute or so went by.

'Is that nice?' he asked.

'Yes. Are we meant to talk?'

'He didn't say we weren't to, the doctor, so I suppose it's all right.'

'Good.'

But neither did any more talking for the moment. With his glasses off, Brenda's face was a bit of a blur to Jake but he could see her eyes were shut. By his reckoning, the second minute was just about up when she said,

'Did the doctor say we weren't to have a kiss?'

'No.'

'Let's have one then.'

He couldn't have said how long it had been since they had kissed each other on the mouth, probably less than twenty-four hours, but it was longer since he had noticed them doing that. Their mouths stayed together for a time, again showing friendliness, this time roughly of the sort that, on his side, he would have shown an amiable acquaintance in public at a New Year's party. He thought Brenda was putting about the same into it. The kiss ended by common agreement.

'Well, that was all right . . . ' he said.

'. . . as far as it went. We'll get better, darling. Lots of ground to be made up.'

'Yes—your turn now.'

'To what?'

'Stroke me the way I was stroking you.'

'Oh yes. Will the same sort of place suit you? Round here?'

'Fine.'

'I'm sorry I'm so fat,' said Brenda after a moment.

'That's all right, I mean you couldn't help it and you've started doing something about it.'

'Yes. Do you think I ought to do something about my hair?'

'What's the matter with it?'

'Matter with it? It's all grey, or hadn't you noticed?'

'Of course I'd noticed. It's a very nice grey. A, an interesting sort of grey.'

'Wow, you make it sound terrific. I could have it dyed back to something like what it used to be. They do jolly good dyes these days.'

'Oh but you can always tell.'

'Not if it's done properly. And supposing you can tell, what about it, what's wrong with that?'

'Well, it looks a bit . . .'

'A bit what? A bit off? A bit bad taste? A bit not quite the thing? A bit mutton dressed up as lamb?'

'Of course not. Well yes, a bit, but that's not really what I . . . I just think it looks ugly. Because it's unnatural.'

'So's make-up unnatural. So's shaving armpits. So's you shaving.'

'All right, just ugly then.'

'I wasn't going to have it bright red or bright yellow or bright purple, just something like what it used to be like, which was brownish mouse if you remember. No I think you think it's sort of out of place.'

'I doubt if we're supposed to talk as much as this.'

'Not that you care.'

Jake looked mildly startled. 'What do you mean?'

'You're not enjoying this are you, me stroking you? Your face went all resigned when I started. Are you?'

'I'm not disenjoying it.'

'Thanks a *lot*,' said Brenda, stopping stroking.

'No don't. What else could I have said? You knew

anyway. And it isn't you. With this it really isn't you. You
said we'd got a lot of ground to make up. We've only just
started.'

'All right, but I reckon it's your turn again now.'

'Fair enough.'

'Did the doctor say you weren't to stroke my tits?'

'No.'

'Well, you can stroke them then, can't you?'

'I suppose so.'

'Only suppose so? They aren't down below are they?'

'No, but they're sort of on the way there. Put it like this,
if down below's red and your arm's green, that makes your
tits amber.'

'Yes, I see. Perhaps we'd better be on the safe side and
not.'

'On the other hand of course, it'd be a natural mistake to
make, so if it is, if it would be a mistake you'd think he'd
have made sure of saying so, you know, oh and by the way
non-genital includes tits, excludes them rather, I should say
breasts. No, mammary areas.'

'You mean we can?'

'I don't see what harm it could do, do you?'

'Fire away.'

He fired away for a full two minutes. She stayed quite
passive, eyes again shut, breathing slowly and steadily,
giving an occasional contented groan. No doubt what he
was doing, or how he was doing it, bore a close resemblance
to its counterpart of a couple of years before, but there was
no means of comparison because he had felt so different
then, in particular felt more. What he felt now was an
increasing but still never more than mild desire to stop
doing what he was doing. In itself each motion he made was
unequivocally if only by a little on the pleasant side of the
pleasant/unpleasant borderline; the snag was there were
so many of them. Patting a favourite child on the head or
indeed stroking a beloved animal (to single out two
activities he had never felt much drawn to) became
unnatural if continued beyond a certain short time, however

willing child or animal might be to let things go on. My
God, another twenty-five minutes of this?—it was a good
job he was such a faithful doer of what doctors told him to
do. Hadn't Rosenberg told him to carry on with this
bleeding sensate-focusing carry-on for *up to* half an hour?
Twenty minutes was that, wasn't it? So was ten. And five.
But to argue so was to use advertiser's mathematics.
Amazing reductions at Poofter's, up to twenty per cent on
all furnishings. Daily brushing with Bullshitter's fluor-
idated toothpaste reduces cavities by up to thirty per cent,
in the case you happen to be looking at by only point-
nought-one of one per cent but what of it, and also of
course helps fight (not helps *to* fight) tooth decay, alongside
drinking things and not eating toffee all day long. Daily
brushing with candlewax or boot-polish would also reduce
cavities by up to something or other and help fight tooth
decay. There were enough laws already but surely there
ought to be one about up to, restricting it to, oh, between
the figure given and half of it. Helping fight things would
be rather more of a—

'Isn't it about time for my turn?' asked Brenda.

'Oh, er . . . yes I suppose it is. I sort of lost count of time.'

'Carried away. No I don't mean that darling, forget I said
it, I was just being frightfully silly. Now on this round I
think we might . . .'

'Hey!'

'What's the matter?'

'Supposed to be non-genital.'

'That's non isn't it, there?'

'Well yes, but only—'

'Genital's genital and non's non.'

'But the spirit of the—'

'Sod the spirit. And even the spirit doesn't say you're not
supposed to enjoy it.'

'I don't think we ought to—'

'Shut up.'

After a little while, Jake began to breathe more deeply,
then to flex and unflex his muscles. Forgotten feelings,

located in some mysterious region that seemed neither body nor mind, likewise began to possess him. Brenda sighed shakily. He pressed himself against her and at once, try as he would, the more irresistibly for his trying, which was like the efforts of a man with no arms to pick up a pound note off the pavement, the flow reversed itself. In a few more seconds he relaxed.

'Oh well, that's that,' he said.

'No it isn't. Only for now. It shows there's something. What do you expect at this stage?'

'What I expect at *this* stage, and what I shall no doubt get, is about twenty more minutes of an experience I wasn't looking forward to and which has turned out to justify such . . . mild forebodings. It isn't you, it's me.'

'Don't think you're the only one, mate. It isn't you, it's me cuts both ways, you know. You're not blaming me, that's how you mean it, but you're not taking me into consideration either. What about that?'

'Yes. Yes, you're right.'

'If you had—been considering me, you might have wondered what I was doing telephoning Elspeth when all I needed to do to make sure we weren't interrupted was take the receiver off. That's right. Putting off the evil hour. Giving way to mild whatnames. It wasn't you, it was me. Now you'd better start stroking again, uncongenial as it may be. The doctor said you were to.'

'It's not un*congenial*, it's just—'

'No, not there. Do my back.'

He started doing her back. 'You said it was nice before, when I was on your shoulder and arm. Was it? Is this?'

'Oh yes. Not tremendous, but nice.'

'Sexy?'

'No,' she said as if he had asked her whether she had said yes or no. 'Nice all the same. I like all that sort of thing, massages and sauna baths and whatnot. You don't, do you?'

'Never been able to see the point of it.'

'I suppose it's just how you're made. I suggest what we do

now is go on for however long it is and not mind too much how we get there, talk or recite or sing as long as we put in the time.'

'Yes. The idea must be to get us used to touching each other again.'

'Start to get us used.'

Gun Law

BRUCE JAY FRIEDMAN

TRUE TO HIS compassionate style, Chief Guster took LePeters's years of fringe homicide work into account and after blinking at the age requirements, slipped him into the detective training course, a one-month programme that included classroom skull sessions, heavy work on the firing ranges, on-the-job field trips with seasoned homiciders, and sessions at the morgue learning to relax around stiffs. In among high-sideburned, heavy-necked young pups, LePeters at forty had a few things going for him. Like an ageing hoop star in his last great year, he was slow to get down court and had little elastic in his legs. None the less, he wasted few motions, looked carefully for openings, and when he saw one, took his shots with great deliberation and rarely missed, breaking open many a ball game. Another valuable playing card for LePeters was his faithless wife, off on location with a film-making stud. In a strange way, this deceived state gave him enormous powers of concentration, a rigidly tunnelled vision that served him well at such critical times as the first fifteen minutes of viewing a fresh homicide victim. After all, if he let his thoughts wander, inevitably they would collide with his wife and he didn't need that. Better to keep his thinking bull's-eye straight. This power of pinpoint thinking was enormously useful on the firing range, a place where breathing, control of the stomach muscles, and an almost Zen-like ability to close out the entire world except for the centre of the target were much more important than aim, good vision, and young, colt-like muscles. Young dicks in training, their minds no doubt on pussy, had a tendency to trigger-jerk their .38s, to more or less jump the gun. LePeters, his thoughts for the moment as sanitized as those of a Ganges holy man, squeezed evenly, building up a record for accuracy that had old-time range men buzzing. On the difficult pop-up targets or 'Hebes in the Weeds', a form of shooting that tested judgement, a fledgling dick more often than not would fire brilliantly but recklessly, gunning down a silhouette he was later told was only 'some poor innocent guy taking a leak in the bushes'. A split-second slower to fire, LePeters made sure to slaughter only kill-crazy pop-ups who were unmistakably bent on homicide.

Thus, LePeters's comparatively advanced years and his faithless wife combined to form a cement-like mixture that firmed up his spine and pulled his character together. Slowly he developed a clenched and measured new style, hesitating before he spoke, looking at the world with dead eyes—the ideal point of view for a new dick. Early in the programme, as a test of nerves, trainee dicks were exposed not to an autopsy, which was small potatoes by comparison, but to a mummification case, considered, in LePeters's bureau, to be the worst of homicides. Such victims, who were either hung, or hung themselves, in the fierce wind and moistureless open air, often wound up thirty feet long and had to be carried in by a team of four instructors and displayed not in the morgue, which was too confined, but in the basement-level detectives' bowling alley. A single glance at the poor endless beanpole of a

victim was enough to make three out of four young dicks
hit the dirt in a swoon. Viewing his first mummification
case, LePeters chewed hard on a strip of Dentyne yet kept
his feet. Using his new, streamlined thinking style, he
allowed himself only a single speculation: that the fellow
had probably been a short guy who'd finally, in death, been
able to reap a kind of vengeance on the big boys who had
always towered over him.

In the many-tentacled world of homicide, fledgling dicks
soon moved towards specialities. Some were obviously
going to become 'hardware freaks', experts in locks,
windows, murder weapons, an ability to determine how
killers gained entry, what road they had used to clear out.
Others moved towards 'clockwork', zeroing in on time
questions of all kinds, terribly useful in the solutions of
crimes. When did the dicks arrive? At precisely what time
had the homicide occurred? When did 'rigger' set in?
LePeters saw quickly that his strength as a homicider was
going to lie in this ability to 'read a body'. Quite early in his
training he subscribed to the golden rule of homicide: 'A
dead body is your best friend.' That is, stiffs, instead of
being justifiably furious at having been knocked off and
clamming up, were more than co-operative during
investigations, and in a sense, had plenty of life left in
them. Most inexperienced dicks first checked a dead man's
face, falling for the old saw that somewhere in a victim's
expression was a mirror reflecting the one who'd laid him
out. Early on, LePeters saw that faces were invariably
neutral and somewhat benign, as though the victim were
in great shape and didn't have a worry in the world.
Contrarily, hands were a thousand times more expressive,
sometimes defiant, often still terror-struck, on rare
occasions gently bemused. It was more difficult than most
murderers knew to slip a weapon into a dead man's hand in
the interest of steering investigators around to suicide as a
motive. On no occasion would a stiff grab a gun firmly;
more often than not it would let the weapon dribble free as
if to say, 'Not on your life, buddy.' Very often, hands told

the entire story. On one occasion, late in the training, LePeters accompanied a seasoned old pro to the scene of a homicide and noticed that the victim's hands seemed to be formed in globular shapes, as though describing a girl with great bazooms. LePeters pointed this out to his instructor and indeed it eventually turned out that a gorgeous, heavy-chested wench had been an accomplice to the crime. Grateful to LePeters, the old-timer rewarded LePeters with a beautifully decorated rubber sheet, standard equipment for every homicide squad car and used to cover bodies in the streets so that irate store-owners could never complain that their business was being chased away. LePeters was amazed not at how easy it was to snuff out a human life, but what a major problem it turned out to be. It took a keen marksman to kill himself with a bullet in the heart, shots often caroming around the rib cage like runaway pinballs and landing with relatively little damage on the other side. A detective who'd had a bullet whistle through his ticker had been known to walk a mile to his squad, tell a few jokes to his sidekick, go out dancing that night, and expire hours later after enjoying a terrific night's sleep. Was there a better example than Detective Teener, LePeters's sidekick? Rarely had a dick been so pared down by gunfire, yet there he was, cavorting about with a hot little second wife and getting along just fine. Once dead, the body was far from finished, too, and LePeters wondered at the way nature had conspired to help a stiff fight back and put homiciders on the trail of the sonofabitch who did him in. Dragging along massive concrete blocks, a slender drowning victim would eventually come bobbing to the surface, brimming over with evidence. A lime-pit case would be discovered months after death, in relatively great shape, having used the lime as a preservative. Most remarkable of all was man's prostate gland. In an effort to eliminate all traces of sex and age, racket men would toss their victim into a shack and burn it to the ground. Yet the prostate never burned. Though all about it lay in cinders, the stalwart little gland would inevitably be found vigorous, unvanquished, in mint condition, ready to sing to the high heavens about the victim's age, sex, and other evidential goodies.

LePeters kept a loose-leaf scrapbook of homicidal nuggets that might some day be useful in turning the tide of a difficult investigation. He noted such apparent trivia as the fact that it was easy to misjudge the weight of the drowning victim. Puffed up to Macy's Thanksgiving Day float size by long exposure to the water, a victim might actually tip the scales at a svelte 110 pounds. Then, too, it was wise not to stand around and leisurely smoke a cigarette while a man was drowning, confident that he'd show his face three times before going down for keeps. Many victims went down once and stayed down, particularly if they were of Italian descent. Though it was certainly tempting, a detective must resist taking mugging Coney Island-type pictures with homicide victims, since hammy poses such as these often showed up in the tabloids and were bound to throw a dick's integrity open to question. It was important to keep all notes in a loose-leaf scrapbook so that the pages pertaining to a particular homicide could be dragged into court, and the rest of the book left behind. Many a dick, who'd taken his entire notebook along, had been embarrassed on the stand when a sheaf of wild Havana orgy shots had tumbled to the floor, thereby throwing his testimony 'down the toilet', to use the courtroom phase.

As LePeters got deeper into the course, he became even deadlier with his gun, keeping it in what appeared to be an over-sized, stiff-leathered, frontier-type holster. Though younger dicks sunk fortunes into velvety baby-leathered rigs and appeared to be 'well-hung', LePeters knew that in a tight situation a .38 might stick in a soft holder and result in one dead homicider. Creakily stiff, polished leather, for all of its old-fashioned appearance, meant a smooth, reliable draw. On the range, LePeters employed a relaxed style, casually slipping his free left hand into his side pocket and being hooted down for shooting like a dude. Yet LePeters had learned, by instinct, that a pocket hand provided the steadiest anchor for dead-eye firing. Before long, one by one, the youngest dicks, envious of LePeters's astonishing scores begrudgingly took up the deceptively dandified style.

LePeters took his gun everywhere, never comfortable unless he felt the friendly unbalanced weight of it against his chest; he was delighted when holster friction began to wear out the lining of his best suit jacket, a trademark of the experienced homicider. Finally, he understood the typical dick who felt like half a man without his weapon and even went to the lengths of wrapping it in cellophane in the morning so it could be worn in the shower. LePeters, along with the other dicks, was scornful of 'grease jobs' or foreign made guns, treasuring his all-American Smith and Wesson .38. As a younger man, freshly bar-mitzvahed, LePeters had kicked off each morning by solemnly winding the sacred phylacteries or 'tifiln' around his arm until he finally grew bored and stored them away. Now, each morning, he leaped out of bed and put in twenty minutes of 'dry-shooting' in his bedroom, propping up two or three radical quarterly magazines as targets, in the prescribed manner. What a distance he had travelled.

As the end of the month drew near, LePeters, though a loner through the programme, joined the younger dicks in speculation about the nature of the final exam, different for each group of graduates. One morning, LePeters sat in class, idly jiggling a few cartridges, while an instructor lectured about statements from dying victims. 'A deathbed statement is admissible as evidence,' said the experienced old homicider, 'but the well-trained dick takes all precautions to make sure that the victim goes ahead and dies. Otherwise, he'd be laughed out of court.' As he added a few notes to his bulging loose-leaf, LePeters saw a little old lady walk into the classroom, dust around a bit, and then slip out. 'How many of you noticed that poor little old lady?' the instructor asked. Before any of the dicks could raise their hands, he was passing out papers and saying, 'If you didn't see her, you are out of luck. She was your final examination.' Designed to test the dick's power of observation, the test consisted of twenty-five multiple choice questions, and one essay, all involving the little old lady's appearance, her rights if she were a homicide suspect, how to conduct an investigation if she were a victim. Momentarily panicked, LePeters saw the entire month of hard work going down the drain. He thought back to his senior year at college when he had literally fainted over an economics final in which the entire exam hinged on a knowledge of grange organization. He actually knew the answer cold, but the possibility that he might not have was too much for him and had knocked him out of the box. But this was a different LePeters. Loosening his collar, sucking in his breath, LePeters waded in and startled himself by how much he remembered about the little old lady, her swarthy complexion, her sarcastic expression, the distinctive little old lady smell of her. Quickly gathering confidence, he flashed through the multiple choices, rapped out an essay and was the first to finish: with enormous cockiness, he sauntered up to the front desk, tossed his paper at the instructor and asked, 'What else you got?'

The Agony of Captain Grimes

EVELYN WAUGH

TWO DAYS LATER Beste-Chetwynde and Paul were in the organ loft of the Llanabba Parish Church
'I don't think I played that terribly well, do you, sir?'
'No.'
'Shall I stop for a bit?'
'I wish you would.'
'Tangent's foot has swollen up and turned black,' said Beste-Chetwynde with relish.
'Poor little brute!' said Paul.
'I had a letter from my mamma this morning,' Beste-Chetwynde went on. 'There's a message for you in it. Shall I read you what she says?'
He took out a letter written on the thickest possible paper. 'The first part is all about racing and a row she's had with Chokey. Apparently he doesn't like the way she's rebuilt our house in the country. I think it was time she dropped that man, don't you?'
'What does she say about me?' asked Paul.
'She says:

' "By the way, dear boy, I must tell you that the spelling in your last letters has been *just too shattering* for words. You know how terribly anxious I am for you to get on and go to Oxford, and everything, and I have been thinking, don't you think it might be a good thing if we were to have a tutor next holidays? Would you think it *too* boring? Some one young who would fit in. I thought, would that good-looking young master you said you liked care to come? How much ought I to pay him? I never know these things. I don't mean the drunk one, tho' he was sweet too".'

'I think that must be you, don't you?' said Beste-Chetwynde; 'it can hardly be Captain Grimes.'

'Well, I must think that over,' said Paul. 'It sounds rather a good idea.'

'Well, yes,' said Beste-Chetwynde doubtfully, 'it might be all right, only there mustn't be too much of the school master about it. That man Prendergast beat me the other evening.'

'And there'll be no organ lessons, either,' said Paul.

Grimes did not receive the news as enthusiastically as Paul had hoped; he was sitting over the Common Room fire despondently biting his nails.

'Good, old boy! That's splendid,' he said abstractedly. 'I'm glad; I am really.'

'Well, you don't sound exactly gay.'

'No, I'm not. Fact is, I'm in the soup again.'

'Badly?'

'Up to the neck.'

'My dear chap, I *am* sorry. What are you going to do about it?'

'I've done the only thing: I've announced my engagement.'

'That'll please Flossie.'

'Oh, yes, she's as pleased as hell about it all, damn her nasty little eyes.'

'What did the old man say?'

'Baffled him a bit, old boy. He's just thinking things out at the moment. Well, I expect everything'll be all right.'

'I don't see why it shouldn't be.'

'Well, there is a reason. I don't think I told you before, but fact is, I'm married already.'

That evening Paul received a summons from the Doctor. He wore a double-breasted dinner jacket, which he smoothed uneasily over his hips at Paul's approach. He looked worried and old.

'Pennyfeather,' he said, 'I have this morning received a severe shock, two shocks in fact. The first was disagreeable, but not wholly unexpected. Your colleague, Captain Grimes, has been convicted before me, on evidence that leaves no possibility of his innocence, of a crime—I might almost call it a course of action—which I can neither understand nor excuse. I daresay I need not particularize. However, that is all a minor question. I have quite frequently met with similar cases during a long experience in our profession. But what has disturbed and grieved me more than I can moderately express is the information that he is engaged to be married to my elder daughter. That Pennyfeather, I had not expected. In the circumstances it seemed a humiliation I might reasonably have been spared. I tell you all this, Pennyfeather, because in our brief acquaintance I have learned to trust and respect you.'

The Doctor sighed, drew from his pocket a handkerchief of *crêpe de chine*, blew his nose with every accent of emotion, and resumed:

'He is *not* the son-in-law I should readily have chosen. I could have forgiven him his wooden leg, his slavish poverty, his moral turpitude, and his abominable features; I could even have forgiven him his incredible vocabulary, if only he had been a *gentleman*. I hope you do not think me a snob. You may have discerned in me a certain prejudice against the lower orders. It is quite true. I *do* feel deeply on the subject. You see, I married one of them. But that, fortunately, is neither here nor there. What I really wished to say to you was this: I have spoken to the unhappy young woman my daughter, and find that she has no particular inclination towards Grimes. Indeed, I do not think that any daughter of mine could fall as low as that. But she is, for some reason, uncontrollably eager to be married to somebody fairly soon. Now, I should be quite prepared to offer a partnership in Llanabba to a son-in-law of whom I approved. The income of the school is normally not less than three thousand a year—that is with the help of dear Diana's housekeeping—and my junior partner would start at an income of a thousand and of course succeed to a larger share upon my death. It is a prospect that many young men would find inviting. And I was wondering, Pennyfeather, whether by any chance, looking at the matter from a businesslike point of view, without prejudice, you understand, fair and square, taking things as they are for what they are worth, facing facts, whether possibly *you* . . . I wonder if I make myself plain?'

'No,' said Paul.'No, sir, I'm afraid it would be impossible. I hope I don't appear rude, but—no, really, I'm afraid . . .'

'That's all right, my dear boy. Not another word! I quite understand. I was afraid that would be your answer. Well, it must be Grimes, then. I don't think it would be any use approaching Mr Prendergast.'

'It was very kind of you to suggest it, sir.'

'Not at all, not at all. The wedding shall take place a week to-day. You might tell Grimes that if you see him. I don't want to have more to do with him than I can help. I wonder whether it would be a good thing to give a small party?' For a moment a light sprang up in Dr Fagan's eyes and then died out. 'No, no, there will be no party. The sports were not encouraging. Poor little Lord Tangent is still laid up, I hear.'

Paul returned to the Common Room with the Doctor's message.

'Hell!' said Grimes, 'I still hoped it might fall through.'

'What d'you want for a wedding present?' Paul asked.

Grimes brightened. 'What about that binge you promised me and Prendy?'

'All right!' said Paul. 'We'll have it to-morrow.'

The Hotel Metropole, Cwmpryddyg, is by far the grandest hotel in the north of Wales. It is situated on a high and healthy eminence overlooking the strip of water that railway companies have gallantly compared to the Bay of Naples. It was built in the ample days preceding the war, with a lavish expenditure on looking glass and marble. To-day it shows signs of wear, for it has never been quite as popular as its pioneers hoped. There are cracks in the cement on the main terrace, the winter garden is draughty, and one comes disconcertingly upon derelict bath chairs in the Moorish Court. Besides this, none of the fountains ever plays, the string band that used to perform nightly in the ballroom has given place to a very expensive wireless set which one of the waiters knows how to operate, there is never any note paper in the writing room, and the sheets are not long enough for the beds. Philbrick pointed out these defects to Paul as he sat with Grimes and Mr Prendergast drinking cocktails in the Palm Court before dinner.

'And it isn't as though it was really cheap,' he said. Philbrick had become quite genial during the last few days. 'Still, one can't expect much in Wales, and it is something. I can't live without some kind of luxury for long. I'm not staying this evening, or I'd ask you fellows to dine with me.'

'Philbrick, old boy,' said Grimes, 'me and my pals here have been wanting a word with you for some time. How about those yarns you spun about your being a shipowner and a novelist and a burglar?'

'Since you mention it,' said Philbrick with dignity, 'they were untrue. One day you shall know my full story. It is stranger than any fiction. Meanwhile I have to be back at the Castle. Good-night.'

'He certainly seems quite a swell here,' said Grimes as they watched him disappear into the night escorted with every obsequy by the manager and the head waiter. 'I daresay he *could* tell a story if he wanted to.'

'I believe it's their keys,' said Mr Prendergast suddenly. It was the first time he had spoken. For twenty minutes he had been sitting very upright in his gilt chair and very alert, his eyes unusually bright, darting this way and that in his eagerness to miss nothing of the gay scene about him.

'What's their keys, Prendy?'

'Why, the things they get given at the counter. I thought for a long time it was money.'

'Is that what's been worrying you? Bless your heart, I thought it was the young lady in the office you were after.'

'Oh, Grimes!' said Mr Prendergast, and he blushed warmly and gave a little giggle.

Paul led his guests into the dining room.

'I haven't taught French for nothing all these years,' said Grimes, studying the menu. 'I'll start with some jolly old huîtres.'

Mr Prendergast ate a grapefruit with some difficulty. 'What a big orange!' he said when he had finished it. 'They do things on a large scale here.'

The soup came in little aluminium bowls. 'What price the ancestral silver?' said Grimes. The Manchester merchants on the spree who sat all round them began to look a little askance at Paul's table.

'Someone's doing himself well on bubbly,' said Grimes as a waiter advanced staggering under the weight of an ice pail from which emerged a Jeroboam of champagne. 'Good egg! It's coming to us.'

'With Sir Solomon Philbrick's compliments to Captain Grimes and congratulations on his approaching marriage, sir.'

Grimes took the waiter by the sleeve. 'See here, old boy, this Sir Solomon Philbrick—know him well?'

'He's here quite frequently, sir.'

'Spends a lot of money, eh?'

'He doesn't entertain at all, but he always has the best of everything himself, sir.'

'Does he pay his bill?'

'I really couldn't say, I'm afraid, sir. Would you be requiring anything else?'

'All right, old boy! Don't get sniffy. Only he's a pal of mine, see?'

'Really, Grimes,' said Mr Prendergast, 'I am afraid you made him quite annoyed with your questions, and that stout man over there is staring at us in the most marked way.'

'I've got a toast to propose. Prendy fill up your glass. Here's to Trumpington, whoever he is, who gave us the money for this binge!'

'And here's to Philbrick,' said Paul, 'whoever *he* is!'

'And here's to Miss Fagan,' said Mr Prendergast, 'with our warmest hopes for her future happiness!'

'Amen,' said Grimes.

After the soup, the worst sort of sole. Mr Prendergast made a little joke about soles and souls. Clearly the dinner party was being a great success.

'You know,' said Grimes, 'look at it how you will, marriage is rather a grim thought.'

'The three reasons for it given in the Prayer book have always seemed to me quite inadequate,' agreed Mr Prendergast. 'I have never had the smallest difficulty about the avoidance of fornication, and the other two advantages seem to me nothing short of disastrous.'

'My first marriage,' said Grimes, 'didn't make much odds either way. It was in Ireland. I was tight at the time, and so was every one else. God knows what became of Mrs Grimes. It seems to me, though, that with Flossie I'm in for a pretty solemn solemnization. It's not what I should have chosen for myself, not by a long chalk. Still, as things are, I suppose it's the best thing that could have happened. I think I've about run through the shoolmastering profession. I don't mind telling you I might have found it pretty hard to get another job. There are limits. Now I'm set up for life, and no more worry about testimonials. That's something. In fact, that's all there is to be said. But there have been moments in the last twenty-four hours, I don't mind telling you, when I've gone cold all over at the thought of what I was in for.'

'I don't want to say anything discouraging,' said Mr Prendergast, 'but I've known Flossie for nearly ten years now, and—'

'There isn't anything you can tell me about Flossie that I
don't know already. I almost wish it was Dingy. I suppose
it's too late now to change. Oh, dear!' said Grimes
despondently, gazing into his glass. 'Oh, Lord! oh, Lord!
That I should come to this!'

'Cheer up Grimes. It isn't like you to be as depressed as
this,' said Paul.

'Old friends,' said Grimes—and his voice was charged
with emotion—'you see a man standing face to face with
retribution. Respect him even if you cannot understand.
Those that live by the flesh shall perish by the flesh. I am a
very sinful man, and I am past my first youth. Who shall
pity me in that dark declivity to which my steps inevitably
seem to tend? I have boasted in my youth and held my head
high and gone on my way careless of consequence, but ever
behind me, unseen, stood stark Justice with his two-edged
sword.'

More food was brought them. Mr Prendergast ate with a
hearty appetite.

'Oh, why did nobody warn me?' cried Grimes in his
agony. 'I should have been told. They should have told me
in so many words. They should have warned me about
Flossie, not about the fires of hell. I've risked them, and I
don't mind risking them again, but they should have told
me about marriage. They should have told me that at the
end of the gay journey and flower-strewn path were the
hideous lights of home and the voices of children. I should
have been warned of the great lavender-scented bed that
was laid out for me, of the wistaria at the windows, of all
intimacy and confidence of family life. But I daresay I
shouldn't have listened. Our life is lived between two
homes. We emerge for a little into the light, and then the
front door closes. The chintz curtains shut out the sun, and
the hearth glows with the fire of home, while upstairs,
above our heads, are enacted again the awful accidents of
adolescence. There's a home and family waiting for every
one of us. We can't escape, try how we may. It's the seed of
life we carry about with us like our skeletons, each one of

us unconsciously pregnant with desirable villa residences. There's no escape. As individuals we simply do not exist. We are just potential home builders, beavers and ants. How do we come into being? What is birth?'

'I've often wondered,' said Mr Prendergast.

'What is this impulse of two people to build their beastly home? It's you and me, unborn, asserting our presence. All we are is a manifestation of the impulse of family life, and if by chance we have escaped the itch ourselves, Nature forces it upon us another way. Flossie's got that itch enough for two. I just haven't. I'm one of the blind alleys off the main road of procreation, but it doesn't matter. Nature always wins. Oh, Lord! oh, Lord! Why didn't I die in that first awful home? Why did I ever hope I could escape?'

Captain Grimes continued his lament for some time in deep bitterness of heart. Presently he became silent and stared at his glass.

'I wonder,' said Mr Prendergast, 'I wonder whether I could have just a little more of this very excellent pheasant?'

'Anyway,' said Grimes, 'there shan't be any children; I'll see to that.'

'It has always been a mystery to me why people marry,' said Mr Prendergast. 'I can't see the smallest reason for it. Quite happy, normal people. Now I can understand it in Grimes's case. He has everything to gain by the arrangement, but what does Flossie expect to gain? And yet she seems more enthusiastic about it than Grimes. It has been the tragedy of my life that whenever I start thinking about any quite simple subject I invariably feel myself confronted by some flat contradiction of this sort. Have you ever thought about marriage—in the abstract, I mean, of course?'

'Not very much, I'm afraid.'

'I don't believe,' said Mr Prendergast, 'that people would ever fall in love or want to be married if they hadn't been told about it. It's like abroad: no one would want to go there if they hadn't been told it existed. Don't you agree?'

'I don't think you can be quite right,' said Paul; 'you see, animals fall in love quite a lot, don't they?'

'Do they?' said Mr Prendergast. 'I didn't know that. What an extraordinary thing! But then I had an aunt whose cat used to put its paw up to its mouth when it yawned. It's wonderful what animals can be taught. There is a sea lion at the circus, I saw in the paper, who juggles with an umbrella and two oranges.'

'I know what I'll do,' said Grimes. 'I'll get a motor bicycle.'

This seemed to cheer him up a little. He took another glass of wine and smiled wanly. 'I'm afraid I've not been following all you chaps have said. I was thinking. What were we talking about?'

'Prendy was telling me about a sea lion who juggled with an umbrella and two oranges.'

'Why, that's nothing. I can juggle with a whacking great bottle and a lump of ice and two knives. Look!'

'Grimes, don't! Every one is looking at you.'

The head waiter came over to remonstrate. 'Please remember where you are, sir,' he said.

'I know where I am well enough,' said Grimes. 'I'm in the hotel my pal Sir Solomon Philbrick is talking of buying, and I tell you this, old boy: if he does, the first person to lose his job will be you. See?'

Nevertheless he stopped juggling and Mr Prendergast ate two *pêches Melba* undisturbed.

'The black cloud has passed,' said Grimes. 'Grimes is now going to enjoy his evening.'

The Archaeology Institute

MYLES na GOPALEEN

WE LIVE IN strange times. It can now be revealed that there has been in existence for the past year (notwithstanding anything that may be contained in the Offences against the State Act) a body known as the Royal Myles na gCopaleen Institute of Archaeology (and you can bet your life that the latter term embraces Palaeontology, Eolithic, Palaeolithic and Neolithic Anthropology). Some months ago this body sent an expedition to *Corca Dorcha* (or Corkadorky), the most remote Gaeltacht area in Ireland or anywhere else. Violent excavations have been in progress since, and preliminary reports which are reaching Dublin from the explorers indicate that discoveries are being made which may mean the end of civilisation as we know it; and the end, too, of all our conventional concepts of human, social, artistic, geological and vegetable evolution. If these messages are to be believed, the Corkadorky researches will throw again into the melting pot the whole sad mess of Tertiary Man, Sir Joseph Prestwich's theory of the essentially pleistocene palaeolithic character of the Kent plateau-gravels', Stonehenge, the glacier theories, the 'proofs' of European neolithic eskimo stratigraphs, and even show that the gigantic mammalian skeletons which are honourably housed in our museums are fakes of the first order perpetrated by 'Irish' Iberian flint-snouted morons (c. 6,000 B.C.) who practised the queer inverted craft of devising posterity's antiquities.

Local observers are hourly awaiting the emergence of the Corkadorky Man, who is expected to prove himself the daddy of every other Man ever pupped by scholarly dirt-shovellers. Unlicensed short-wave radio transmitters are standing by to flash the news to the learned societies of the world. Herr Hoernes, the famous author of *Der diluviale Mensch in Europe*, is maintaining a 24-hour watch at the earphones in Stockholm with M. Mortillet, whose *Le Préhistorique* is still read.

A word about this Royal Myles na gCopaleen Institute of Archaeology. There is some mystery about the 'Royal', many commentators holding that the term has reference to the bar of a certain theatre where it is alleged the first meeting was held and the learned objects of the Institute defined. Be that as it may, it would be rash to suppose that the Institute is just a gatherum of clay-minded prodnoses. Every branch of research has a sub-institute of its own and the heavily documented reports of each sub-institute are appraised, co-ordinated, catalogued, sifted, indexed, cross-referenced, revised, checked and digested by the 'Royal Institute', which is essentially an assessive, deductive and archivistic body. Within the 'Royal Institute' you have, for instance, the Institute of Comparative Bronzes. This body is concerned only with time-bronze progressions (mostly based on millennial variations in the obliquity of the earth's orbit) and has already disproved practically every thing that has appeared in *L'Anthropologie: Materiaux pour l'histoire primitive de l'homme*, the somewhat inexact French publication. Then again you have the Association of Superior Muck. This body is composed of chemists who spend their time surveying the testing samples of alluvial

muck and all manner of water-borne ordure. All this goes
to show that the researches now in progress have no
relation to scare journalism, 'all that is best in Irish life',
'progress', or any other shibboleth. It is an exercise in
scientific discovery and deduction. There is no margin for
emotion, conjecture or error. That is why Herr Hoernes
stays up all night in Stockholm.

I have no intention of entering into the contents of the
perturbing preliminary reports I have mentioned, or
describing the larger objects stated to have been dug up. I
illustrate here, however, a few of the smaller and less
disturbing relics which were unearthed. The figures
shown over are carved in stone. As a layman I do not know
what to make of them. The lower stone seems to be a
representation of primitive greyhound racing, with every
chance that our friend in front will clock 30.15. The upper
stone may mean that we once had a national sport of fish-
racing.

An observer on the spot, and who assisted in some of the
excavations, has given me a somewhat far-fetched story
which I pass on for what it is worth (and not, mark you, for
what it is not worth). According to him the primeval
human remains unearthed were fossilized, and bore on the
legs certain serrated markings that suggested corduroy.
Various other aspects of hair remains, neckwear remains
and whatnot provided an impressive accumulation of
evidence that the Corkadorky Man was an Ice Age fly-boy
and the progenitor of the present indefeasible Irish nation.
It will be a nice cup of tea for the GAA if this is proved to be
the case.

I will have more to say on this subject.

A SPECIAL despatch from the explorers sent to
Corkadorky by the Royal Myles na gCopaleen Institute of
Archaeology states that large masses of diorite rock have
been unearthed. The rocks look like adamellite and contain
orthoclase, plagioclase felspar, micropegmanite starch,
igneous hornblende, baking soda, gangrene-pale pyroxene,
not to mention andesine strata tinged with accessory

deposits such as zircan and apatite

The Plain People of Ireland: Begob appetite is right, you'd need a square meal and a pint of stout after that mouthful of chat. What book did you cog all them jawbreakers out of?

Myself: The Encyclopaedia Britannica.

The Plain People of Ireland: And a fine man he is when he's at home, God bless him.

IN CORKADORKY

The savants sent to Corkadorky by the Royal Myles na gCopaleen Institute of Archaeology continue to send back curious despatches. The latest says that the Corkadorky Man is at last a reality. It appears that he is streets ahead of the famous Monmouthshire Man, nor has he anything to fear from Iceland's renowned Stelvik Man. He is one of the most interesting men ever discovered, and while an account of his more singular characteristics must be postponed to a future article, I may say here that one remarkable feature about him is the right index finger. Beyond yea or nay, it is the longest finger ever encountered by anthropologists. The Long Finger of the Corkadorky Man has, in fact, fascinated the explorers, and keeps continually cropping up in their somewhat incoherent messages. There is a long indentation or sign of wear on the top of it and the archaeologists argue that this must be proof of the Man's practice of putting things on the Finger and keeping them there for lengthy periods. 'Lengthy periods' in this context would, of course, mean centuries. This corroboration of the well-known folk idiom about putting things on the long finger is curious and may mean that the Corkadorky Man may explain for us at last why our record in the world as men of affairs has always been so miserable.

From inquiries I have made I am glad to say that no traces of old fossilized meal have been found in the Man's mouth and that the hands bear no traces of cheese or of the despised cheese-paring tool. That is something to be thankful for and something to be going on with.

A roving party from the Myles na gCopaleen Institute of Archaeology have arrived in Killarney and have chosen to start excavating at the bottom of the lakes. It is a safe bet that nobody else in the world would have thought of doing that or anything like it. As usual, the operations have resulted in a flood of wild rumours. Preliminary messages arriving in Dublin say that the explorers have found that the bottom of the lake consists, not of the usual mess of muck and weeds one might expect, but first-grade waterproof concrete. The Institute contends that this (with other proofs they have) goes to show that Killarney is not a divine accident of nature or 'heaven's reflex', but the personal handiwork of our crafty ancestors. If the Institute is correct, the whole hash of lake and mountain with its wealth of sublimely inconsequent *nuance* was carried out with hod, trowel, plumb-line and muck-bucket. It seems also that the whole place is a network of hot pipes and that it is thus that the sub-tropical vegetation effects were got. The pipes are buried at varying depths and are said to be connected with hot subterranean spas in Clare and places even more distant. Apparently what the Institute is getting at is that the whole of Ireland is a vast construction job and that we have nobody but ourselves to thank for our peerless scenery. Sea shells have been found on top of the Devil's Mountain, proving that sea-level soil was heaped up by human agency to make the mountain. It is thought that the Firbolgs (or 'Bagmen') were the slave-artisans who did the carrying work in primitive times. The large hollow left by the excavation necessary to construct even a small mountain was always carefully concreted and filled with water.

The savants who are in Kerry hope to produce a Killarney Man in due course. What they intend to do with him we can only guess.

The Treatment

LEW LANGLEY WAS a very short, immensely broad man with a thunderous, slow-moving voice that rested on the very rockbottom of the lower register. He swung into prominence just twice. Once, dressed in a jerkin, he appeared as a prototypical Welsh bowman in a film about Agincourt, emphasizing the bowed quality of his legs and taking the public's mind off the action by being brought abruptly before the cameras by the director, who was fanatical about the need to uncover the truth about Welsh bowmen. The other time was his appointment to some musical post in Salt Lake City which ended when it was found that his style of singing was doing something to the salt.

But for me Lew Langley's apogee took place in the high summer of 1929.

During his early manhood Lew worked hard at his singing without getting very far. His aim was simply to become the most profound bass who had ever lived, hitting notes so low they would banish performers like Kipnis and

Jetsam to a place among the castrati. For Lew this worked well, but for no one else. Below a certain note he would keep opening his mouth and smiling, showing that the notes he was hitting were making a big impact on Lew, but for people outside Lew nothing came across at all. This meant that whole sections of the songs he sang became fogged and the drift of the ballads he favoured was always elusive. This did not bother anyone, for the songs that Lew favoured added up to a curriculum of every disaster that had ever hit this century and the last. If ever a character in one of Lew's songs set foot on a desert, he would be fighting off delirium and vultures by the end of the first verse; if anyone went down a mine, methane could be seen thickening around every note.

His teacher, Mathew Seewell the Sotto, who loved a light tone of voice and a jovial type of lyric, said that he would never have been able to stand Lew if it had not been for his way of vanishing from vocal view every whip-stitch. Lew helped pucker the brow of a whole decade by standing in front of eisteddfod audiences, opening his mouth wide and gesturing broadly while failing for two thirds of the time to communicate anything but a sense of unease. Many a sub-committee was set up to decide into what eisteddfod category Lew was supposed to fit.

In the operettas that swept across Meadow Prospect like hail, Lew had little better luck. His parts were kept deliberately small. If anyone came in to announce himself as the sole survivor of a plague, a flood, an explosion, this would be Lew, spreading a thickness of doom over the entire hall with one of the great lowing notes of which he was capable when not climbing down into the cellarage.

But even here his wings were wetted. The jealousy endemic in the musical life of Meadow Prospect caused all operatic choruses to cluster in a tight swarm around anyone who had the vocal ball at his feet. They did this with particular ferocity in the case of Lew, not only muffling his tone but, short as he was, blotting him from sight. It was usual in the middle of Lew's announcement of the latest earthquake or bush-fire to see Lew's head bursting like a furious bomb from between the packed thighs of the besieging choristers.

Lew's occupation at this period was that of a modest insurance agent, vending nothing more spectacular than the most meagre kind of funeral benefit. His manner as he approached the door of his clients, was so grave and portentous, his voice, as he requested the penny or twopence contribution, so deep and hollow that many regarded him as bringing too monotonous a note of mortality into a transaction which, from the start, was short on laughs.

In 1926, people decided that they could not stand a long coal strike and Lew. So they persuaded him to go touring in the United States with a male voice party. He had some success. In one of the South Western States some farmers found that one of Lew's middle notes had the power of riveting steers, causing them to turn around, fall still, listen and become fatly placid. He was awarded a florid honorary doctorate in a University so obscure that to this day the FBI maintains that Lew made the whole thing up. He was awarded a professorship in vocal control, which in his case meant how to bring a song to a dead stop with no sense of shyness or anomaly.

In the blazing July of 1929 he returned to Meadow Prospect to attend a large eisteddfod to be held the following month. He wore a heavy fur-collared coat down to the top of his boots, meant to fool the most savage type of Arkansan winter, a hat so stupendously rimmed it would have made Lew, stripped of his coat, look like a hatter's shop window fitting.

He expected to be fêted. He was ignored. Ignored by the eisteddfod committee who regarded Lew as a fakir and a loon. Ignored by the recently widowed woman whom Lew wished to woo.

Lew exhibited his rage. He stalked up and down the fierce central hill of Meadow Prospect, his hat and coat firmly in position. The heat was ruthless. Lew's face grew redder and more apoplectic as the group who sat around in Tasso's Coffee Tavern pleaded with him to use sense and slip out of his stetson and fur before he had a stroke.

The group in Tasso's got to work. They scraped up every fact from the private lives of the eisteddfod committee and the widow. The harvest, it seemed, was dark and astonishing. The committee men were persuaded to let Lew adjudicate the bass solo competition which he did with an impercipience that still inhibits a fair belt of singers in the deeper range. When he delivered his adjudication he kept on his fur-collared coat and it managed to strike a note of sardonic mastery. When he went to offer the widow his compliments we persuaded him to take off his coat so that she could see what she was having in the way of a groom.

If we hadn't he would never have made that trip to Salt Lake City. One more trip up Meadow Prospect hill in that rig would have floored him.

A Matter for the Courts

N.F. SIMPSON

The Court is assembled. The JUDGE, COUNSEL, USHER *and* CLERK *are in their places. The* POLICEMAN *is down* R. *The spotlight down* L *fades.*

KIRBY *exits down* L.

MABEL *appears at the door* R. (*The* PROSECUTOR *rises*)

MABEL. What's going on, Arthur?

USHER. Silence!

PROSECUTOR. The accused is Kirby Groomkirby.

MABEL. Oh, he'll need his suit, then. (*She crosses to the mantelpiece, picks up the coat-hanger with the suit on it, and crosses back*) Come along up, Arthur.

(MABEL *and* ARTHUR *exit* R. *The* POLICEMAN *closes the door*)

PROSECUTOR. M'lord, the facts, as your Lordship is aware, are not in dispute in this case. The accused, Kirby Groomkirby, has admitted in the Magistrate's Court that between the first of August last year and the ninth of April he has been fairly regularly taking life, and since the case was heard there three weeks ago has asked for nine other offences in addition to the thirty-four in the original indictment to be taken into account making a total altogether of forty-three. On the last occasion on which he took a life he was warned by Detective Sergeant Barnes that complaints had been lodged and that action would be taken against him if he failed to conform to the law. It was after this, while he was preparing to repeat the offence, that Detective Sergeant Barnes arrested him.

JUDGE. This would have been his forty-fourth offence?

PROSECUTOR. Yes, m'lord, but it was never carried out.

JUDGE. Because he was arrested.

PROSECUTOR. Yes, m'lord.

JUDGE (*with heavy sarcasm*) It would be a pity to credit him with the wrong number of offences.

PROSECUTOR. He went before the Magistrate's Court on the third of this month where he pleaded guilty and was remanded for sentence. Since then he has asked for the nine other offences to be taken into account.

JUDGE. Are these nine offences exactly similar?

PROSECUTOR. They are exactly the same, m'lord, except that the victims are different.

JUDGE. Naturally the victims wouldn't be the same. What method has he been using?

PROSECUTOR. He seems to have been using the same technique fairly consistently, m'lord. He tells his victim a joke, waits for him to laugh, and then strikes him with an iron bar.

JUDGE (*after pondering for a second*) Is there any previous record?

PROSECUTOR. No, m'lord.

JUDGE. He's been in no other kind of trouble at all?

PROSECUTOR. None at all, m'lord.

JUDGE. I see. (*He writes*)

(*The* PROSECUTOR *sits*)

(*To the Defence*) Yes?

DEFENCE (*rising*) M'lord, I should like to begin by calling Detective Sergeant Barnes to the witness-box.

(*The* USHER *rises and signs to the* POLICEMAN *who opens the door* R.

BARNES *enters* R *and is shown into the witness-box by the* USHER, *who hands him the Bible and swearing card. The* POLICE-MAN *closes the door)*

BARNES. I swear by Almighty God that the evidence I shall give shall be the truth, the whole truth, and nothing but the truth. Detective Sergeant Barnes, Gamma Division.

(*The* USHER *takes the Bible and card and resumes his seat)*

DEFENCE. Sergeant Barnes, you I believe spoke to the accused, and to his parents, shortly before he was arrested?

BARNES. That is so, yes, sir.

DEFENCE. Would it be true to say that you found him very communicative and helpful?

BARNES. He was as communicative as I understand he usually is, yes, sir.

DEFENCE. And helpful?

BARNES. He was quite helpful, yes, sir.

DEFENCE. Whom did you see first, Sergeant Barnes—the accused or his parents?

BARNES. I saw his parents to begin with, sir.

DEFENCE. What did you say to them?

BARNES. I put the position to them, sir, and told them that complaints had been received about their son's conduct . . .

DEFENCE. Yes—I'm sorry to interrupt you, Sergeant Barnes, but perhaps you can tell the Court what in so many words you said on this first occasion?

BARNES. Yes, I think I can remember what I said, sir. When I went in, the first person I saw was Mr Groomkirby, so I addressed what I had to say to him. I said to the best of my recollection, something to the effect that 'It's beginning to add up down at the mortuary, Mr Groomkirby'.

JUDGE (*intervening*) Meaning that you were keeping a check of this man's victims?

BARNES. We were rather pressed for space, m'lord.

JUDGE. I know that, Sergeant. What I'm asking you now is whether your remark 'It's beginning to add up down at the mortuary' referred to this man's victims only, or to those of other people as well?

BARNES. It was a kind of joke, m'lord. I was trying to keep on friendly terms at that stage and I made the remark in a somewhat humorous manner. I went on to say, 'We haven't got the *Albert Hall*, Mr Groomkirby'.

JUDGE. So you weren't giving information?

BARNES. Not what you might call information, no, m'lord.

(*The* JUDGE *returns the ball to the Defence*)

DEFENCE. What did Mr Groomkirby say to you, as far as you can remember, Sergeant Barnes, in reply to that remark of yours?

BARNES. It was Mrs Groomkirby, sir. She said, 'We shall have to have another word with him, Arthur.'

JUDGE (*intervening*) Who is Arthur?

DEFENCE. The father, m'lord.

JUDGE. Arthur Groomkirby?

DEFENCE. Yes, m'lord. (*To Barnes*) Did you get the impression from the conversation you had with the mother and father of the accused, Sergeant Barnes, that they were doing all they could to help their son and take his mind off law-breaking?

BARNES. I got the impression that they were very concerned at the turn things seemed to have been taking, sir.

DEFENCE. And genuinely determined to do what they could for their son, to get him to mend his ways?

BARNES. Yes, sir.

DEFENCE. And the accused—it would be true to say, wouldn't it, Sergeant Barnes, that he rather confided in you?

BARNES. He told me certain things about himself, yes, sir.

DEFENCE. Can you tell his Lordship what you were able to gather from this conversation with the accused—and his parents—about his character in general, and what you think may have caused him to act as he did?

BARNES. He seemed to have a strong desire, m'lord, to wear black clothes. He told me he'd had it for as long as he could remember, and his mother, m'lord, told me the same. For the last year or two he's been studying what he calls 'logical analysis', and this has gradually taken the form of looking for a logical pretext for wearing his black clothes. Prior to that I understand he just wore them without concerning himself about finding a pretext, m'lord.

JUDGE. There's nothing reprehensible in his wanting to be rational about it.

BARNES. No, m'lord. But with the accused it seems to have combined rather adversely with this urge to wear black, m'lord.

JUDGE. In what way?

BARNES. He said he had to have rational grounds for wearing it, m'lord.

JUDGE. Yes?

BARNES. And he hit upon this idea of going into mourning.

JUDGE. For his own victims, I suppose.

BARNES. For his own victims, m'lord.

JUDGE (after pondering for a second) Surely there must have been plenty of people dying from natural causes.

BARNES. He wouldn't wear mourning for anyone he didn't know, m'lord. I put that specifically to him. He said he felt it would be a mockery, m'lord.

JUDGE. Was he sincere about this?

BARNES. I think he was, m'lord, yes.

   (The JUDGE nods imperceptibly to the Defence)

DEFENCE. Could we bring in exhibit nine, m'lord?

   (The POLICEMAN exits down R and, in turn, pulls on NUMBER
   TWO and NUMBER THREE weighing machines.
   The USHER, at the same time, exits down L and pulls GORMLESS on.
   The POLICEMAN then closes the door R and the USHER resumes
   his seat)

I want you to look now, Sergeant, at the weighing machines there in front of the witness-box. Have you seen these machines or machines like them, Sergeant, before?

BARNES. Yes, sir, I have.

DEFENCE. Where did you see them?

BARNES. They were upstairs with a good many more, sir, at the house where I interviewed the accused, sir.

DEFENCE. Are these the ordinary kind of weighing machines such as anyone going into an amusement arcade or into a chemist's shop might expect to find?

BARNES. They are a fairly common type, yes, sir.

DEFENCE. They are in fact, what are sometimes known as 'Speak-your-weight' machines?

BARNES. Yes, sir.

DEFENCE. How many of these machines did you find when you went to the house at which the accused was living?

BARNES. A good many, sir. I didn't count them, but I should say running into several hundred.

DEFENCE. Would the number you saw be consistent with there being five hundred of these machines?

BARNES. It would be consistent with that, yes sir.

DEFENCE. Were you able to discover in your conversation with the accused, Sergeant Barnes, any motive he might possibly have for building up this exceptionally large collection of Speak-your-weight machines?

BARNES. He did refer to them, sir. I didn't set much store by what he said because I thought it sounded a bit far-fetched, but I gathered it was more the volume of sound he was concerned about. He wanted them to be heard over a long distance.

DEFENCE. By anyone in particular?

BARNES. By as many people as possible, sir.

DEFENCE. He was teaching them to sing, wasn't he, Sergeant?

BARNES. That was his intention, sir.

JUDGE. To do *what*?

DEFENCE. To sing, m'lord.

JUDGE. I thought we were talking about weighing machines?

DEFENCE. These are a special type, m'lord, which speak

when subjected to weight and can also be trained to sing. I have had these three brought into the court for this reason, m'lord. There would be no difficulty in arranging for them to sing a short song, or part of a song, if your Lordship would allow.

JUDGE. How long is this going to take?

DEFENCE. It would take a matter of minutes, m'lord.

JUDGE (*unenthusiastically*) Yes I suppose so.

DEFENCE. I am very much obliged to your Lordship. (*He nods to the usher and sits*)

(*The* USHER *rises, takes out a pitch pipe and gives a middle C. After a brief pause,* NUMBERS TWO *and* THREE *launch into the 'Lizzie Borden' song as a duet.* GORMLESS *is silent. The* JUDGE, *in so far as he takes notice of the song at all, remains unimpressed by it. The song ends. There is a pause*)

(*He rises*) Thank you, m'lord.

(*The* USHER *crosses to Gormless*)

One final question, Sergeant Barnes . . .

(*The* USHER *removes the weight from Gormless*)

GORMLESS. 'Fifteen stone ten pounds.'

(*There is a pause for one puzzled moment. The* USHER *returns to his seat*)

DEFENCE (*resuming*) Was anything said to you, Sergeant Barnes, either by the accused or by his parents, that might lead you to believe he was intending eventually to have these weighing machines shipped to the North Pole?

BARNES. Yes, sir. Arrangements were actually in hand for this, sir.

DEFENCE. Did he volunteer any information that might explain this action?

BARNES. Only to say that he wanted them to act as sirens, sir.

JUDGE (*intervening*) Sirens?

BARNES (*in an explanatory manner*) To lure people to the North Pole, m'lord.

DEFENCE. There was a scientific reason for this, Sergeant Barnes, wasn't there?

BARNES. Yes, sir.

DEFENCE. Will you try and enlarge on this for his Lordship, Sergeant Barnes?

BARNES (*to the Judge*) I fancy he had some notion, m'lord, that once these people were at the North Pole, if he could get enough of them together in the one place, he would have very little difficulty in persuading them all to jump at the same moment.

JUDGE. And what inscrutable purpose was this manoeuvre calculated to serve?

BARNES. I think he was more concerned with what would happen when they landed again, m'lord. He was hoping it might have the effect of tilting the earth's axis a little more to one side, m'lord.

JUDGE (*after a pause*) I see.

DEFENCE. This would very likely bring about quite far-reaching climatic changes, would it not, Sergeant?

BARNES. I think something of that kind was what he had in mind, sir.

DEFENCE. A shifting of the Ice Cap, for instance?

BARNES. Yes, sir.

DEFENCE. This might well give rise to a new Ice Age so far as these islands are concerned?

BARNES. In all probability, yes, sir.

DEFENCE. Would it be true to say, Sergeant Barnes, that he was hoping in this way to provide himself with a self-perpetuating pretext for wearing black?

BARNES. Yes, sir.

DEFENCE. By ensuring that for an indefinite period deaths from various causes connected with the excessive cold would be many and frequent?

BARNES. That was at the back of it, yes, sir.

DEFENCE. Thank you, Sergeant Barnes.

(BARNES *stands down and exits* R)

I would like to call Mrs Groomkirby now to the witness-box. (*To the Usher*) Mrs Groomkirby. (*He sits*)

USHER (*rising and calling*) Mrs Groomkirby.

(*The* POLICEMAN *opens the door* R)

POLICEMAN (*calling*) Mrs Groomkirby.

MABEL (*off*) All right, give me time to get downstairs.
(MABEL *enters* R. *The* POLICEMAN *closes the door*)
USHER. His Lordship is waiting, Mrs Groomkirby.
MABEL. Where do I go?
(*The* USHER *shows* MABEL *into the witness-box*)
You feel so public. (*In the witness-box, she becomes somewhat overawed by her surrounding*)
(*The* USHER *hands the Bible and swearing card to* MABEL)
I swear by Almighty God that the evidence I shall give shall be the truth, the whole truth, and nothing but the truth.
(*The* USHER *takes the Bible and card and resumes his seat*)
DEFENCE (*rising*) You are Mabel Laurentina Groomkirby?
MABEL. Yes, sir.
DEFENCE. You are the mother of the accused, Mrs Groomkirby, are you not?
MABEL. Oh, well, yes. I suppose if it's Kirby on trial, I must be. I hadn't realized.
DEFENCE. It would be true to say, wouldn't it, Mrs Groomkirby, that your son likes wearing black?
MABEL. He's worn it all his life.
DEFENCE. He likes wearing black but he doesn't feel justified in wearing it except at the funeral of someone he knows?
MABEL. Well, it's only in the last few years he's come to think like that, really. He always used to just wear it.
DEFENCE. His attitude has changed?
MABEL. It's been very noticeable over the last year or two.
DEFENCE. Can you account for this change in any way, Mrs Groomkirby?
MABEL. Not really—unless his studies have had anything to do with it. He's always been of a very logical turn of mind ever since he was born, but what with all this studying lately he seems to have got a different attitude altogether these last few years.
DEFENCE. Your son is a rather ingenious young man, is he not, Mrs Groomkirby?
MABEL. A lot of people say he is, yes, sir.

DEFENCE. He has a cash register, I believe.

MABEL. That's right.

DEFENCE. What exactly is the function of this cash register, Mrs Groomkirby? What does your son use it for?

MABEL. It was an egg-timer to begin with, and then he gradually came to rely on it more and more for other things.

DEFENCE. When it was an egg-timer—can you tell his Lordship how it worked?

MABEL. Well, sir, it was rigged up in the kitchen with the telephone on one side of it and the gas stove on the other. He likes to have his eggs done the exact time—just the four minutes ten seconds—or he won't eat them. He just goes right inside himself. So he rigged up the cash register.

DEFENCE. How did it work, Mrs Groomkirby?

MABEL. He'd got a stop-watch but he wouldn't trust that. He'd trust it for the minutes but he wouldn't trust it for the seconds.

DEFENCE. And so he used the cash register instead?

MABEL. That and the telephone. He had them side by side.

DEFENCE. What was the actual procedure he adopted, Mrs Groomkirby?

MABEL. Well, he'd put his egg on to boil, then he'd stand there with his stop-watch.

DEFENCE. Go on, Mrs Groomkirby.

MABEL. Well, then the moment it said four minutes exactly on his stop-watch, he'd simply dial TIM, wait for the pips, ring up No Sale on the cash register and take out his egg.

DEFENCE. And this was, in fact, the only sequence of actions that took precisely the ten seconds?

MABEL. That's right, sir. He wouldn't eat them otherwise.

DEFENCE. And he worked this out for himself without any assistance whatever from anyone else?

MABEL. Oh, yes. It was entirely his own. And then he started getting dependent on the bell for other things as

well. Eating first; and now practically everything he does
he has to have a bell rung.

DEFENCE. To come back to this question of the black
clothes, Mrs Groomkirby.

MABEL. They've as good as told him that if ever he were
to part with his cash register it would mean total paralysis
for him.

DEFENCE. Yes. You say your son, Mrs Groomkirby, has
always liked wearing black. Will you tell his Lordship in
your own words about this attachment to black clothes?

MABEL. Well, sir, all his baby things were black. He had a
black shawl and rompers and even down to his bib were all
black, and his sheets and pillow-cases. We had everything
in black for him as soon as he was born. People used to stop
in the street and remark about him. He's never worn
anything white. Sometimes when he was in his pram
people used to say he looked like a wee undertaker lying
there. We got it all planned before he was born that if we
had a white baby we were going to dress him in black—or
her in black if it had been a girl—and if either of them were
black we'd have everything white, so as to make a contrast.
But when he came he was white so we had the black.

JUDGE (intervening) Is your husband a coloured man, Mrs
Groomkirby?

MABEL. He's an insurance agent, sir.

JUDGE. Yes, but is he coloured?

MABEL. Well, no, sir. Not so far as I know.

JUDGE. What I'm trying to get from you, Mrs
Groomkirby, is the simple fact of your husband's racial
characteristics. Does he, for instance, have any negro
blood?

MABEL. Well—he *has* got one or two bottles up in his
room, but he doesn't tell me what's in them.

(The JUDGE *looks blankly at Mabel for a moment and then relin-
quishes the matter*)

DEFENCE. There's one more thing I should like to ask you,
Mrs Groomkirby. Each of your son's forty-three victims
was struck with an iron bar after having been told a joke.

Would it be true to say that your son, Mrs Groomkirby, went to considerable trouble over these jokes?

MABEL. He went to very great trouble indeed, sir. He sat up to all hours thinking out jokes for them.

DEFENCE. Can you tell his Lordship why your son went to all this trouble with every one of his forty-three victims, when there were a number of far simpler methods he could have used?

MABEL. I think for one thing he rather took to the humorous side of it. And for another thing he always wanted to do everything he could for these people. He felt very sorry for them.

DEFENCE. He wanted to make things as pleasant as possible for them even at some considerable trouble and inconvenience to himself?

MABEL. He didn't mind how much trouble he went to, as long as they ended on a gay note.

DEFENCE. Thank you, Mrs Groomkirby.

> (*The* USHER *signs to Mabel to stand down.*
> MABEL *comes from the witness-box and exits* R)

(*He begins his final speech to the Judge*) M'lord, in asking you to take a lenient view of this case, I am not underestimating the seriousness of the offences this young man has committed. They are very grave breaches of the law, and no-one realizes this now more than he does himself. He has made very considerable efforts to find other ways of satisfying this—in itself quite harmless, indeed laudable—desire for a logical pretext, but so far, unfortunately, he has met with little success. He has had this scheme involving the weighing machines. We may think this to have been a somewhat grandiose scheme and that there could be very little hope of its succeeding, or even indeed of its being universally acceptable were it possible to adopt it. The important thing is that it has been worked out by this astonishingly resourceful and gifted young man as the result of a determination to avoid by every means in his power any further breach of the law in satisfying this craving he has for black clothes. He has gone to very great trouble and expense in training these weighing machines, m'lord, with the intention not of sitting idly down beside them to listen to and enjoy the fruits of his labour himself, but of keeping himself indirectly from coming into conflict with the law. In my respectful submission, m'lord, this very complex personality with whom we are dealing is not in any ordinary sense of the word a killer; he is, on the contrary, a kindly, rather gentle young man, not given to violence—except in this one respect—and showing himself to be quite exceptionally considerate of others even to the extent of arranging, at considerable personal sacrifice of time and energy, for them to die laughing. I would therefore ask your Lordship to pass as light a sentence as, in your Lordship's judgement, is warranted in this very exceptional case. (*He sits*)

(KIRBY *enters R, crosses to Gormless and replaces the weight. He then crosses to C and raises his arms as though to conduct. The* JUDGE *addresses* KIRBY, *who, startled, falls to his knees facing the Bench*)

JUDGE. There have been too many crimes of this nature: people killing a number of victims—forty-three in your case—from what appear to be, and indeed often are in themselves, laudable motives. Your counsel has made an eloquent plea for you, and two people have been willing to come into the witness-box—one of them the detective who arrested you—and give a favourable account of you. But from your forty-three victims—not a word. Not one of those forty-three has felt under any obligation to come forward and speak for you, notwithstanding the great trouble we are told you went to in furnishing them with laughing matter. And what about the iron bar you used? Was this also chosen and wielded with the well-being of your victims in mind? I think not. Your mother has said that you wear black. This is not surprising. Such a taste seems to me to be in perfect conformity with the career you have chosen to embark upon. I am not greatly influenced by the reasons that have been put forward for your having this apparently irresistible craving—they seem to me to have very little bearing on the matter. It is becoming more and more an accepted feature of cases of this kind that in the course of them the Court is subjected to a farrago of psychological poppycock in which every imaginable ailment in the nursery is prayed in aid. As for your desire to find a logical pretext, this is the one redeeming feature I have been able to find in this case. But you could have come by a pretext in any one of a number of quite legitimate ways. I have no doubt at all that at least a score of undertakers could have been found whose advice and assistance you could have had for the asking. Instead you chose another way, a way which has led you straight to this Court. You began a few months ago by telling your first joke to your first victim and then striking him with an iron bar. What did you get out of it? The excuse to wear black for a day or two. Was it really worth breaking the law in order to be able to wear black for forty-eight hours? And then a little later on came your second murder, and the opportunity to wear black again for a short time. And so it has gone on: victim after victim, until even you could not have expected the authorities to overlook it any longer. Indeed, Detective Sergeant Barnes warned you quite explicitly what would happen if you broke the law for the forty-fourth time. There seems to me to be not the smallest shred of excuse for these repeated offences. As for this diabolical scheme to send weighing machines to the North Pole, which we have been told is so ingenious, the less said about it the better. If the song we have just had to listen to in this court is in any way typical of the kind of thing we were to have been regaled by from the North Pole, it would be hard to imagine what sort of person would have been enticed there by it—or having got there would want to remain for long within earshot, still less be in any fit state to jump up and down. In deciding upon the sentence I shall impose in this case, I have been influenced by one consideration, and it is this: that in sentencing a man for one crime, we may well be putting him beyond the reach of the law in respect of those crimes which he has not yet had an opportunity to commit. The law, however, is not to be cheated in this way. I shall therefore discharge you.

Walter Slurrie Goes to Washington

RICHARD CONDON

WALTER GOT IN touch with me again the year after he ran for Congress from Dallas and won the election. He was married, he said. They had a little boy. They were living in the 3500 block on Potomac in Highland Park, Dallas.

A Dallas Citizens' Committee had chosen him as their candidate and had backed him to get the nomination and, despite the fact that Walter ran as a Republican and that Texas was a traditional Democratic state, he had been elected by a large plurality. We had watched him run from the 66th floor at Felsenburshe City in New York. Probably one of the dirtiest campaigns ever staged in American politics. Also, Walter's Dallas Citizens' Committee would not stand up to any close examination. But candidates have to find money somewhere and we are told that a lot of hoodlums are hat-over-the-heart patriots. The real question was: Where did the Citizens' Committee find Walter? Another good question might have been: Why did they find him?

The Dallas Citizens' Committee had advertised for a

candidate who was 'a married man with a good war record
and experience as a lawyer who wished to dedicate himself
to public service'. Any applicant had to be Texas-born and
under thirty-five. Two hundred and eleven people applied
for the job. The committee chose Walter.

The year Walter ran there were a half-dozen crucial
contests going on around the country. Walter's was mildly
interesting because he was a Republican running against a
Democratic incumbent in a Democratic situation. What I
couldn't put together with all the years I had known Walter
was the filthiness of the campaign he ran. He just wasn't
that sort of fellow. I considered that, of the two of us,
Walter was the more purposeful about how he wanted
politics to be run. I was a mercenary. I was the turncoat
Democrat who was now hustling the Republicans for a
buck. My job was to hustle both parties but make it look as if
the Felsenburshes were committed Republicans. To hustle
both parties I used elected politicians, of which Walter was
now one.

Walter's Dallas campaign was so low and so degrading to
the electoral system that I wanted to hear him tell me about
what made him do it. He couldn't have needed to be elected
that badly. But there were too many other campaigns
spinning around the country.

Then he called me two months after he had been
installed in the House. We made a date to meet in Dallas,
but before I go onto what occurred at that meeting just let
me lay out what Walter's campaign had been like.

His incumbent opponent was Fred Carl Haskins.
Haskins flew his own plane, was on the board at the Dallas
Country Club, and was personally as well as politically
popular. He had a good record in Congress after three
terms in office. He was a solid citizen, old-family, who
may have taken one or two drinks too many, around whom
Walter built a fantasy.

Walter smeared him with an almost untested issue in
American politics. Churchill had made his Iron Curtain
speech at Fulton. Harry Truman had gotten the country's

toes wet in it by setting up his Loyalty Boards, but the thing had never been presented as a direct threat/choice at the voter level.

The issue was threateningly foreign, something the voters had heard of vaguely before but found it hard to evaluate in terms of their own lives, because it was such a remote and improbable phenomenon. But Walter brought the smell of it and the fear of it very close to them. He rubbed their faces in its foreignness, its distinct probability.

It was also vaguely familiar because in the 20s Hearst had shrieked against the Wobblies and Palmer had thundered that America must be saved from them. But there had been Babe Ruth, C.C. Pyle, Dempsey, and flag-pole sitters available too, and so much more on the side that celebrated life. Anyway, Americans hadn't shown any interest in politics yet beyond the courthouse. They turned to politics with a bang when the Bomb was dropped and Walter had the great good luck to drag his malevolent issue in almost immediately after that.

Walter's 'Save America from Communist Infiltration' issue was redhot and unexploited. Russians were as foreign as any foreigners could get. They had a sick alphabet, morbid writers, and a very low regard for human life. They had been shaky, undefined allies during the war but everybody knew that Uncle Joe was pretty tricky, except that Walter didn't let it lie there just like that.

He used a pendulum response. He nourished fears: fears that the peace wouldn't last. He filled the vacuum created by the disappearance of the Nazis.

I was given the privilege of a preview of how Walter's axe would fall, splitting the country in half, while he was still in the Navy, at some desk job at Newport News. We met by chance in the lobby of the Carlton, always glad to see each other as two surviving pseudo-lawyers. Walter went to great lengths to thank me for having had something to do with getting him a job early in the war with the OPA, something which I couldn't remember at all at the time.

Walter actually invited me to dinner that night, a famous first for Walter, something that is nearly certain to happen in anybody's lifetime. He was in full uniform, which most grandly would have outranked my discarded Marine corporal's stripes. We went to an Italian restaurant called the Villa d'Este, where he astonished me by introducing the proprietor, a thug named Dom G. Everyone is an insider somewhere. Walter was not given a check for the dinner, but on the other hand neither was I. The food was on the ouch side for anyone who had ever eaten with Marie; a red sauce joint.

Walter hadn't changed. He was the same, plodding, intent grind who preferred to punish one idea at a time until it lay bleeding. He was always willing to settle for less.

He said he wanted some professional advice. 'I have the chance to go into active politics, Charley,' he said. 'I've been talking it over with a priest in the Navy and with some other people.'

'A priest?'

'Yes. He was my—chaplain. He isn't a professional politician, of course. I'd like to confirm a few points with you.'

'Why not?'

'I am a lawyer. I have a good war record. I am wearing the leadership stripes of a lieutenant-commander—I was promoted yesterday, by the way. I am devoutly interested in doing a job for constituents and I think I have discovered a new and vital issue for the American people as they face the unknown of a post-war world.'

'Is that so? Where will you run?'

'Texas.'

'Salopado?'

'No. One of the cities.'

'Congress?'

'Well, that's the idea.'

'What's the new issue?'

'In strictest confidence?'

'Why not?'

'You can talk it after I start to use it,' he said gravely. He leaned forward. 'Charley, this isn't off the top of my head. I've read a lot of books—and you know how I go about studying a book—about political ideologies and economics and propaganda and I have proven the whole thing to my satisfaction—in theory anyway.'

'Proven what?'

'Proven that there is a demonstrable, incipient danger of Communism taking over the government of this country.'

'Whaaaat?'

'Right at this moment it might not seem so. But I have solid information that the Russians are pressing us for an exchange of intelligence teams, for example, which would be deadly if it is allowed to happen. They are going to try to infiltrate our government at every level. If they can penetrate our intelligence organizations, and Colonel Donovan has already endorsed the idea, then they can infect other American institutions to which access is so much easier.'

'Like where, Walter?'

'Well, name it. Our communications industries. Our churches. The new visual radio medium which may grow into something important. It would be easy to worm into our educational system and our political organizations, including Mr Truman's United Nations. Bribe and conscript. They will come to us pretending to be friends until they can fill their Trojan horses to capacity. Then they will strike in the dead of the night to overthrow our government to replace it with Communism.'

'Jesus, Walter, I thought the war had bankrupted the Russians.'

He took a deep breath, then expelled it carefully as he spoke. 'Charley, through channels that represent one of the strongest, most cohesed organizations in the world, a unitary force with access to hidden plans and facts inside Europe, Asia and sources deep within this country, I have been privileged to study this thing from every direction. What I have been told, what I have read and remembered,

has convinced me that this country is now facing a
terrifying Communist peril.'

I didn't doubt that Walter believed he had fallen upon a
treasure of truth, what I doubted was his judgment in
unraveling it. Walter wasn't an intelligent fellow. He was
shrewd, he could imitate and simulate all the attitudes of
cogent wisdom, but he had no judgment and no selectivity.

'Still—no offense Walter—but it is an election gimmick,
isn't it?'

'Well, yes. In the confining sense it is the lever that will
put me into Congress where I will be able to fight and
protect the American people from what then goes far
beyond the gimmick stage and becomes a national peril.
What I propose to take over will become the core of our
national security.'

'But are you going to use this in Texas of all places? Do
you have any reason to believe that they know what
Communism is or give a damn if they do?'

'If they don't know right now, they will,' he answered
calmly. 'And, by God, the entire country will know within
the next two years. When I campaign on this issue, it is just
possible that people who are soft on Communism might
get hurt, but I'll even do that gladly because it has to be
done.'

I tried to see Walter from the new perspective he was
offering me, but I couldn't. He was the same faltering
Walter who was sure to botch up another shot at the
dignified eminence that meant so much to him. He was
telling me that he was going to get himself elected against
an incumbent Democrat in Texas on an issue that would have
him warning a country which had just won a world war. He
was going to try to tell those people that he would be
protecting them from total infiltration and possession by a
foreign power that had just lost 35,000,000 people in the
same war and was lying gasping on its back from need,
perhaps ten thousand miles from Texas.

I tried to talk around his nonsense, hoping it would go
away. 'Walter, can you remember how upset you were

when you discovered that we were going to pay a few dozen drunks two dollars apiece to vote the straight ticket for us, using the names of other people who had died before they wouldn't have bothered to vote on Election Day?'

'Yes. And I remember the gangsters you hired to intimidate the voters who did turn out. And the police you paid to look the other way. That will never happen in my kind of politics.' His voice had found its natural self-righteousness. He held my forearm. He was waxing eloquent, which was Walter's single talent beyond his pale innocence. 'It was because of politics like that, and the Eastern bankers, and the Eastern establishment press that we were dragged into war. Hitler had right on his side. Ask any military man. He would have whipped the Russians for us. So the rest of us, my people in Texas, had to fight that Easterners' war in order to keep America for Americans by standing off foreign ideologies and loathsome alien conceptions. Yes, Charley, I remember that Election Day in 1935.Why do you ask?'

'Did you vote in 1935, Walter? Or in '36? Or in '40?'

'What about the gangsters?'

'I was the one who told you that. Did you ever *see* anybody being intimidated by a hired gangster at the polls? We had outgrown that even in 1935. Forty years ago they used hoodlums in ghettos to force people out to vote when they didn't even understand what voting was. They were disenfranchised people who had fled their governments, who feared and hated governments, who couldn't speak, read, or write English. So the Organization had people they could recognize, slum hoodlums who spoke their languages, herd them out to the polls so that they could turn their kids into doctors and police chiefs. How do you think this country works, Walter? It is an ongoing struggle to persuade the people to reason out a government that can make better lives for them.'

'B-movie stuff,' he sneered. Walter even sneers when he is praying if he thinks God doesn't agree with him. Anyone

can imagine how easy it is to want to punch him right in his
mush when he sneers.

'And Americans can not only speak, read, and write now
—because of strong laws—but maybe they can even think.
By voting more they have less to complain about.'

'We have gotten off the subject, Charley.'

'Right. Now—you want my professional opinion on
whether you have a good election gimmick. I say—sure. It
is a great election gimmick. But what I was starting to say
is, this time it really is buying drunks' votes and hiring
those gangsters you object to so much.'

'I don't understand that.'

'You will be lying to them, won't you? You are going to
tell them that some cockeyed theory is absolute gospel fact,
as if you held documents in your hand which proved how
many Communists had infiltrated the government, which
you do not have. You will be saying in effect that you are a
liar, therefore they should buy protection from you with
their votes to save them from being burned in their beds.'

'Do you really see it that way, Charley? Will voters see it
that way? I knew you were just testing my thesis with
hypothetical questions but you've brought up something I
had not anticipated.'

'Don't worry about it.'

'Why shouldn't I?

'What do Texans know about elections in New York
forty years ago?'

'That's right. Thank you, Charley. Now—tell me
straight out—what do you think of my plan?'

'Will it get you elected, you mean?'

'Yes. That's where I want your opinion.'

'I think it will all the way, Walter. It may even be the
coming thing in politics. It's so simple.'

'That's wonderful.'

'Mind if I throw in a little lecture? Sort of singing for my
supper?'

'Please. Go right ahead.'

'Walter, politicians may seem to continue on without

much reference to the people, but whatever they do is the will of the people.'

'But—where does that affect my plan?'

'I just wanted to talk about how one idea can proliferate in politics. Let's say you run on a platform of warnings about a Communist takeover. Maybe in California a candidate is running on an issue of pensions for teenagers and in Ohio a man seeks office by offering free admission to race tracks. Well, people like me, the professional survivors in politics, would watch the people react to each issue, then measure the issue's usefulness against the plurality it produced for the candidate against other pluralities. The issues that get the best results are then moved along by people like me, to other candidates in following elections and, if these issues produce bigger and bigger pluralities all because of the accident of one man trying it out absolutely blind in Texas, a great national issue is produced.'

'That is absolutely wonderful,' he said exultantly. 'I knew I could count on you to tell me the truth.'

That was the moment when Walter foretold his own future. That was the isolated second when Walter and I, unconsciously, exchanged hats and styles. Suddenly it was as though I were marching along toward some kind of a demonstration in civics and Walter were sprinting straight toward corruption. Not that I knew it then. But we were both beginning the long journey along each other's divergent railway tracks, both of us lost.

Walter Slurrie, the 1947 anomaly, a Texas Republican, won his election. His plurality was the greatest in his state and all other states where contests on new issues were run. I was on the phone talking to other political managers about it for almost a week. The professional consensus favoring Walter's issue was overwhelming, because it seemed to work so well and produce such golden results. With anti-Communism, Walter had built the boys a vote-getter, and they were all busy gearing up for the next election, in hundreds of local, state, and federal elections where Walter, with his flashing Red Crusade, was still the national star. 'This little son-of-bitch may just have laid out the issue of the 50s for us,' Pop said. 'Are you sure this is the same long, blond drink-of-water with those busy eyes, the one who stayed with us and run out on Margaret?'

'The same one, Pop.'

'The shitty lip-licker you went to law school with?'

'That's him. Walter Slurrie.'

'I can't believe it. A shifty night court lawyer coming up with a great stunt like that. That priest musta thought of the whole thing. The boys are gonna make a lot of deals with this one, Charley, even if the Republicans are going to be carrying the ball this time.'

Walter campaigned to establish in the prepackaged prejudices of Dallas voters that his opponent was subversively and dangerously Communistic, already acting as an advance agent of the Soviet government in the Congress. Further, twenty-six workers were paid to conduct a telephone canvass of individuals listed in the Dallas telephone directory to spread the word that Walter's opponent's twenty-year-old daughter was spreading gonorrhea throughout the city.

It is hard to imagine how anyone could be free enough from self-doubt to be able to run a campaign like that. Back-to-back the two charges ruined Walter's opponent's family. The AP carried a sidebar out of Heppner, Oregon, three years later that the daughter had killed herself. By that time Walter's opponent had already become a stumbling drunk and an outcast. But the campaign sent Walter to Washington as a crusader and gave all American constituencies the greatest fake issue to rally round since William Jennings Bryan and the Cross of Gold.

London's Villages

MILES KINGTON

Has the little grocer's shop near you closed down recently? Does your local sub-postmistress now wear a sari? Got a choice of wine bars but no pub you like? Chances are you're in one of London's new villages!

The Village Bookshop This is not for selling new books. Nor, curiously, second-hand books. It markets review copies and remainders, that is, books which the publishers could not sell and which the reviewer did not wish to keep. Who would want to buy books like that? Villagers, of course.

Ye New Village Pubbe People often imagine that pubs receive only interior revamping. Not so. The most important changes take place outdoors. It is no use installing varnished wood, inglenooks and Space Invaders, if the outside of the pub is not repainted in brown-purple with scrolly writing proclaiming that the brewers are really 'Purveyors of gins, whiskies and other fine liquors', that here can be found 'real London ales' and that behind the pub is a small square of concrete known as 'a family beer garden'.

London village pubs have a star system, as follows:

* Dart board
** American pool
*** Separate room marked Billiards
**** Live rock or jazz most evenings
***** A theatre upstairs

The Blind Shop Not for the benefit of the blind, any more than the Third World shop is for the Third World. Here the villagers buy blinds depicting rural scenes to hang in their basement windows, and to remind them of their country cottages which they cannot get to this weekend.

The Asian Shop Not just any old Asian shop, of course, because they are everywhere, just as are Chinese take-aways, Indian restaurants and next-day cleaners *or* photo developers. To be a *real* village Asian shop, it must have the courage to feature at least ten things not available at the ordinary post office: eg persimmons, lychees, mangoes, yams, plantains, coriander, kumquats, pomegranates, yaws, beri-beri and continental tomatoes as big as an elephant's navel.

The Little Restaurant with gaily painted red chairs and a vase of fresh flowers on each table. Whether it sells pizzas or local hamburgers or doner kebabs does not matter. The important thing is to have gaily painted red chairs and a vase of fresh flowers on each table. Oh, and waiters in something stripey. That way you can get the true village feeling of a French café. Breton crêpes followed by Calvados are best. Or was that 1979? Well, it's probably come back by now.

The Village Wine Bar An antique shop which also sells wine by the glass, at antique prices.

The Print 'N' Repro Shop Here, in their traditional studio, the print workers pursue their ancient craft of putting a piece of paper in a Xerox machine and pressing a knob. You may also buy gaily coloured German felt-tip pens, and packets of envelopes which work out at only 6p each.

Heliogabalus Or Nostradamus. Or Jabberwocky. Any polysyllabic name will do to describe the village shop which sells traditional posters of James Dean, postcards of the less daring Impressionists and greeting cards with a deflating message on page 3.

Mr Scoff's Delicatessen The village food shop. Here you can buy authentic French bread made each day in London, pâtés made in pottery bowls, and bags of smoked salmon odds and ends to make your own smoked salmon mousse out of. The proprietor of the shop *must* (a) have a paperback out under his own name, (b) be delightfully camp without actually being gay, (c) appear in the shop in person at least once a year.

The Village Cinema Not, of course, an Odeon or ABC (except perhaps if it has recently had a preservation order) but one with a folk name such as Screen on the Green, Flicks in the Sticks or the Bionic, Golders Green. Here, during the afternoon and evening, villagers can see all the German, Japanese and Woody Allen films they ought to see, often on the very day they are reviewed in the *Guardian* (the village newspaper). At 11.15 begins the late night session of films they *want* to see, like *Casablanca, Singing in the Rain* and *Jules et Jim*, or any film that has a preservation order on it.

The Flour Shop And nothing is browner than real flour, or more lumpy, or more full of bits of stone (hence the label 'stone ground'). The traditional village maidens in their gay village Martini aprons will sell you buckwheat, sesame seeds, basmati rice or Canadian cracked rye, or indeed anything for which there is no recipe in your cookery books, at traditional village prices. No wonder they all look bonny and plump-cheeked, while the customers look pale and underfed. You can also buy here organic vegetables and fruit. Organic means, generally, twice the price; specifically it means wizened (apples), gnarled (carrots), or brown (white cabbage).

Ye Antique Shoppe There are two quite distinct kinds of antique shop, both tremendously valid.

(1) The antique shop which is never open. It displays huge pseudo-Chinese pieces of furniture or monumental Victorian parlour objects in a dark dusty interior never besmirched by customers. That is, junk.

(2) The antique shop which is always open, manned by a dealer reading a paperback. It sells functional antiques. That is, pieces from a bygone era which could still be used. That is, battered household articles. That is, junk.

(3) Sorry, there's a third as well. The Bourneville Tin Shop. That is, the shop which sells anything with a trade name on it. Like ashtrays marked Bovril. In other words, junk.

The Tile Shop Every village must have a tile shop, preferably where the butcher's used to be, for meat is an unnecessary and probably harmful luxury but tiles are a necessity. There are two kinds of tile shop. One sells shiny tiles made in Italy and featured in *Vogue*. The other sells rough brown earthy tiles, either made in Morocco by unshaven, underpaid natives or crafted in Wiltshire studios by unshaven, underpaid arts graduates. Tile shops always open with a special opening sale; after two years, when all the villagers have tiled their bathrooms, they have a special closing sale.

The Street Market In some villages in London there still survive street stalls that sell fruit and veg, flowers and whelks. Their occupants are not genuine London villagers, merely jumped up tradesmen from the East End. Their coarse cries, clumsy stalls and messy habits are not authentically representative of true London village life and can safely be ignored.

The Local Craft Shop Villagers like to support local crafts. Especially they like to support the local crafts of Portugal (painted pottery), the Philippines (dangly rope objects), Peru (ponchos) and Penzance (brown coffee mugs).

The Stripped Pine Shop The most ancient London village craft, dating back to the primeval mists of the 1960s, is the art of stripping pine. Nobody knows for sure how it is done; no one has the faintest idea what happens to all that flaked black grot which is stripped off pine, and must amount to a hundred tons a year; nobody can begin to imagine from where come all those dressers and kitchen tables and desks. Nobody would dare ask. It is simply a mystery for which we must all be thankful. Prices of stripped pine are expressed in an ancient village language, by the way; eg £AF/AO.

Ye Olde Rocke 'N' Rolle Shoppe Villagers do not buy records; they rent them for taping and sell the lease back at a slight loss. The racks are full of every LP ever made by Genesis and Billy Joel; the walls are festooned with boxes of total Verdi operas and the entire Haydn symphony range, for Haydn was the Sanderson of the orchestra. Do villagers line *their* walls with boxes? The only music not found here is English folk music, which has no place in a London village.

The Architect's Workshop Under the spreading indoor palm the village architect works, conscious that passers-by are staring through his open-plan window over his open-plan shoulder and wondering what he is designing. He is designing one-room extensions and back additions for other villagers, of course; or the smallest lavatories in the world for restaurants; or wine bar decors; or simply workshops for other architects. If asked to build a house, he would not know what to do.

The Fishmonger A very lucky village will have a fish shop, complete with marble slabs, chips of ice, a wall chart of fish in six languages and a few fish mentioned in Elizabeth David. Peak time of the year is September, when the villagers have just come back from their village holidays in the Dordogne and remember that monkfish is really called 'lotte' or are still keen enough to do their own *moules marinières*.

The Village Natural Shoe Shop All natural things are brown (rice, sugar, eggs, coffee mugs, Academy Cinema posters, trees) and leather is no exception. Do not buy white shoes; they have been over-refined till there is no nutrition in them. Get shapeless brown moccasins from your village shoe shop. They are the real thing.

The Children's Opera Group As a sort of cultural crèche, larger London villages keep their children out of mischief on winter evenings by allowing them to make an opera. Well, they don't actually allow *them* to make an opera of course; that can be safely left to Ben Britten. If it's a really go-ahead village, they will actually commission Stephen or Nicholas or Darryl (whom someone in the village knows awfully well) to write a new opera, and get his friends to play in the band. Everyone agrees that the opera is too good not to be heard again, but it never is. The opera is performed in the village progressive church which for two months is jam-packed with the local village musicians. They are not seen there during the other ten months of the year.

Mr K*a*p*l*a*n

LEONARD Q. ROSS

FOR TWO WEEKS Mr Parkhill had been delaying the inescapable: Mr Kaplan, like the other students in the beginners' grade of the American Night Preparatory School for Adults, would have to present a composition for class analysis. All the students had had their turn writing the assignment on the board, a composition of 100 words, entitled 'My Job'. Now only Mr Kaplan's rendition remained.

It would be more accurate to say Mr K*A*P*L*A*N's rendition of the assignment remained, for even in thinking of that distinguished student, Mr Parkhill saw the image of his unmistakable signature, in all its red-blue-green glory. The multicolored characters were more than a trade mark; they were an assertion of individuality, a symbol of singularity, a proud expression of Mr Kaplan's Inner Self. To Mr Parkhill, the signature took on added meaning because it was associated with the man who had said his youthful ambition had been to become 'a physician and sergeant', the Titan who had declined the verb 'to fail': 'fail, failed, bankropt'.

One night, after the two weeks' procrastination, Mr
Parkhill decided to face the worst. 'Mr Kaplan, I think it's
your turn to—er—write your composition on the board.'
Mr Kaplan's great buoyant smile grew more great and
more buoyant. 'My!' he exclaimed. He rose, looked around
at the class proudly as if surveying the blessed who were to
witness a linguistic *tour de force*, stumbled over Mrs
Moskowitz's feet with a polite 'Vould you be so kindly?' and
took his place at the blackboard. There he rejected several
pieces of chalk critically, nodded to Mr Parkhill—it was a
nod of distinct reassurance—and then printed in firm
letters:

My Job A Cotter In Dress Faktory
Comp. by
H*Y*

'You need not write your name on the board,'
interrupted Mr Parkhill quickly. 'Er—to save time . . .'

Mr Kaplan's face expressed astonishment. 'Podden me,
Mr Pockheel. But de name is by me *pot* of mine
composition.'

'Your name is *part* of the composition?' asked Mr Parkhill
in an anxious tone.

'Ya*ssir!*' said Mr Kaplan with dignity. He printed the rest
of H*Y*M*A*N K*A*P*L*A*N for all to see and admire.
You could tell it was a disappointment for him not to have
colored chalk for this performance. In pale white the
elegance of his work was dissipated. The name, indeed,
seemed unreal, the letters stark, anemic, almost denuded.

His brow wrinkled and perspiring, Mr Kaplan wrote the
saga of A Cotter in Dress Faktory on the board, with much
scratching of the chalk and an undertone of sound. Mr
Kaplan repeated each word to himself softly, as if trying to
give to its spelling some of the flavor and originality of his
pronunciation. The smile on the face of Mr Kaplan had
taken on something beatific and imperishable: it was his
first experience at the blackboard; it was the moment of
glory. He seemed to be writing more slowly than necessary

as if to prolong the ecstasy of his Hour. When he had finished he said 'Haü Kay' with distinct regret in his voice, and sat down. Mr Parkhill observed the composition in all its strange beauty:

My Job A Cotter In Dress Faktory
Comp. by
H*Y*M*A*N K*A*P*L*A*N

Shakspere is saying what fulls man is and I am feeling just the same way when I am thinking about mine job a cotter in Dress Faktory on 38 st. by 7 av. For why should we slafing in dark place by laktric lights and all kinds hot, for Boss who is fat and driving fency automobile? I ask! Because we are the deprassed workers of world. And are being exployted. By Bosses. In mine shop is no difference. Oh how bad is laktric light, oh how is all kinds hot. And when I am telling Foreman should be better conditions he hollers, Kaplin you redical!!

At this point a glazed look came into Mr Parkhill's eyes, but he read on.

So I keep still and work by bad light and always hot. But somday will the workers making Bosses to work! And then Kaplan will give to them bad laktric and positively no windows for the air should come in! So they can know what it means to slafe! Kaplan will make Foreman a cotter like he is. And give the most bad dezigns to cot out. Justice.
Mine job is cotting Dress dezigns.
T-H-E E-N-D

Mr Parkhill read the amazing document over again. His eyes, glazed but for a moment before, were haunted now. It was true; spelling, diction, sentence structure, punctuation, capitalization, the use of the present perfect for the present—all true.

'Is planty mistakes, I s'pose,' suggested Mr Kaplan modestly.

'Y-yes . . . yes, there are many mistakes.'

'Dat's because I'm tryink to give *dip ideas*,' said Mr Kaplan with the sigh of those who storm heaven.

Mr Parkhill girded his mental loins. 'Mr Kaplan—er— your composition doesn't really meet the assignment. You haven't described your *job*, what you *do*, what your work *is*.'

'Vell, it's not soch a interestink jop,' said Mr Kaplan.

'Your composition is not a simple exposition. It's more of a—well, an *essay* on your *attitude*.'

'Oh, fine!' cried Mr Kaplan with enthusiasm.

'No, no,' said Mr Parkhill hastily. 'The assigment was *meant* to be a composition. You see, we must begin with simple exercises before we try—er—more philosophical essays.'

Mr Kaplan nodded with resignation. 'So naxt time should be no ideas, like abot Shaksbeer? Should be only *fects?*'

'Y-yes. No ideas, only—er—facts.'

You could see by Mr Kaplan's martyred smile that his wings, like those of an eagle's, were being clipped.

'And Mr Kaplan—er—why do you use "Kaplan" in the body of your composition? Why don't you say "I will make the foreman a cutter" instead of "Kaplan will make the foreman a cutter?" '

Mr Kaplan's response was instantaneous. 'I'm so glad you eskink me dis! Ha! I'm usink "Keplen" in de composition for plain and tsimple rizzon: becawss I didn't vant de reader should tink I am *prajudiced* aganst de foreman, so I said it more like abot a strenger: "*Keplan* will make de foreman a cotter!" '

In the face of this subtle passion for objectivity, Mr Parkhill was silent. He called for corrections. A forest of hands went up. Miss Mitnick pointed out errors in spelling, the use of capital letters, punctuation: Mr Norman Bloom corrected several more words, rearranged sentences, and said, 'Woikers is exployted with an "i", not "y", as Kaplan makes'; Miss Caravello changed 'fulls' to 'fools', and declared herself uncertain as to the validity of the word 'Justice' standing by itself in 'da smalla da sentence'; Mr Sam Pinsky said he was sure Mr Kaplan meant *'opprassed voikers of de voild*, not *deprassed*, aldough day are deprassed *too*,' to which Mr Kaplan replied, 'So ve bote got right, no? Don' *chenge* "deprassed", only *add* "opprassed".'

Then Mr Parkhill went ahead with his own corrections, changing tenses, substituting prepositions, adding the definite article. Though the whole barrage Mr Kaplan kept shaking his head, murmuring 'Mine goolness!' each time a correction was made. But he smiled all the while. He seemed to be proud of the very number of errors he had made; of the labor to which the class was being forced in his service; of the fact that his *ideas*, his creation, could survive so concerted an onslaught. And as the composition took more respectable form, Mr Kaplan's smile grew more expansive.

'Now, class,' said Mr Parkhill, 'I want to spend a few minutes explaining something about adjectives. Mr Kaplan uses the phrase—er—"most bad". That's wrong. There is a word for 'most bad". It is what we call the superlative form of "bad".' Mr Parkhill explained the use of the positive, comparative and superlative forms of the adjective.' "Tall, taller, tallest." "Rich, richer, richest." Is that clear? Well, then let us try a few others.'

The class took up the game with enthusiasm. Miss Mitnick submitted 'dark, darker darkest'; Mr Scymzak, 'fat, fatter, fattest'.

'But there are certain exceptions to this general form,' Mr Parkhill went on. The class, which had long ago learned to respect that gamin, The Exception to the Rule, nodded solemnly. 'For instance, we don't say "good, gooder, goodest", do we?'

'No, sir!' cried Mr Kaplan impetuously.' "Good, gooder, good*est*"? Ha! It's to leff!'

'We say that X, for example is good. Y, however, is—?' Mr Parkhill arched an eyebrow interrogatively.

'Batter!' said Mr Kaplan.

'Right! And Z is—?'

'High-cless!'

Mr Parkhill's eyebrows dropped. 'No,' he said sadly.

'*Not* high-cless?' asked Mr Kaplan incredulously. For him there was no word more superlative.

'No, Mr Kaplan, the word is "best"! And the word "bad", of which you tried to use the superlative form . . . it isn't "bad, badder, baddest". It's "bad" . . . and what's the comparative? Anyone?'

'Worse,' volunteered Mr Bloom.

'Correct! And the superlative? Z is the—?'

' "Worse" also?' asked Mr Bloom hesitantly. It was evident he had never distinguished the fine difference in sound between the comparative and superlative forms of 'bad'.

'No, Mr Bloom. It's not the *same* word, although it—er—sounds a good deal like it. Anyone? Come, come. It isn't hard. X is *bad*, Y is *worse*, and Z is the—?'

An embarrassed silence fell upon the class, which, apparently, had been using 'worse' for both the comparative and superlative all along. Miss Mitnick blushed and played with her pencil. Mr Bloom shrugged, conscious that he had given his all. Mr Kaplan stared at the board, his mouth open, a desperate concentration in his eye.

'*Bad—worse*. What is the word you use when you mean "most bad"?'

'Aha!' cried Mr Kaplan suddenly. When Mr Kaplan cried 'Aha!' it signified that a great light had fallen on him. 'I know! De exect void! So easy! *Ach!* I should know dat ven I was wridink! *Bad—voise—*'

'Yes, Mr Kaplan!' Mr Parkhill was definitely excited.

'Rotten!'

Mr Parkhill's eyes gazed once more, unmistakably. He shook his head dolorously, as if he had suffered a personal hurt. And as he wrote 'w-o-r-s-t' on the blackboard there ran through his head, like a sad refrain, this latest manifestation of Mr Kaplan's peculiar genius: 'bad—worse —rotten; bad—worse . . .'

France and the French

ROBERT MORLEY

DURING THE FIRST World War, the punishment for homosexuality in the French army was execution. However, if you were an officer you were allowed a final charge against the enemy, on the understanding that you got yourself shot. In one rather exceptional case the accused, who was the heir to enormous wealth and a proud title, was granted special leave from the battlefields until he had managed to consummate his marriage and procreate an heir. Eight months after he was killed in action, a child was born—a girl. That's the French for you—they take every trick but the last.

But for an Englishman there is always the fear that the French will win in the end. Every now and then one of my friends will put it to the test and retire with his ill-gotten gains to perch on one of those green-brown hills at the back of Cannes. But I am always struck by the sense of suspended animation which envelops him when he has acquired the sun blinds and the swimming pool. Once he has collected the sunshine and the gin, and of course the

English papers, he is constantly obsessed with the price of butter.

My attitude to France was, I suppose,inherited from my father, who always felt perfectly at home there because he never attempted to talk or make friends with the natives. He admitted that there were certain things they did better than we did—sex and gambling, for instance—neither of which is true today. When I was sixteen and had left my last school, he decided that I should go into the Diplomatic Corps. He used to play bridge at his club with the Greek Ambassador, and usually won his money. 'They are a very decent class of fellow,' he told me. 'You'll enjoy being an Ambassador. Come on,' and having prized some money from his trustees, spirited me across the Channel to Tours, where he had been told the best French was spoken. Twenty-four hours in Tours shook him. He found himself encircled by the French. Hitherto he had always had his back to the sea, and a good hall porter at his elbow. In Tours there wasn't even a good hotel.

'You don't care for this, surely?' he asked me. 'You wouldn't be happy here? There's nothing to do.'

'Learn French?' I asked him.

'Yes, but not here.' He was already fingering the money entrusted to him for my further education. We left for Monte Carlo that afternoon. 'This will be better for you,' my father assured me. 'You get all nationalities here. In the Diplomatic Service you'll find you have to mix.' My parent was anxious not to leave me alone with the wrong *ambiance*. *Ambiance* was one of his four French words. His other three were *Le Bon Dieu*.

'I believe,' he would reiterate, 'in *Le Bon Dieu*, which is why I find the Church of England service so frustrating.'

'You never go,' my mother told him.

'That is why,' he told her. '*Le Bon Dieu* is everywhere except in an English church.' There was no arguing with Father, while the money lasted, at any rate. In Monte Carlo it didn't last very long, about ten days, and we were posting breathlessly home before the cheques bounced. In France it was an offence for cheques to bounce, and Father dreaded not arrest, but banishment from the casinos.

I myself was arrested in France when I was eight years old. I had swung a fishing line off the jetty and caught the hook in my thumb. I was led away by a gendarme, with blood streaming from my hand. As he marched me through the streets I sobbed, not with pain, but with terror. True, he took me to a doctor, and not the police station, but why didn't the fool tell me what he was doing? An English Bobby would have given me a toffee and told me I was a brave little chap. The French are a logical people, which is one reason the English dislike them so intensely. The other is that they own France, a country which we have always judged to be much too good for them. France has for centuries blocked our way to Europe. Before the invention of the aeroplane, we had to step over them to get anywhere. I was particularly conscious of this geographical fact as a child, because I lived at Folkestone, where the Channel is at its narrowest, and the packet sailed daily for Boulogne. When the gales blew, my nurse used to take me down to the Harbour to watch the homecoming passengers staggering down the gangplank, and crawling across the cobblestones to the Pavilion Hotel for a steadyer. 'Serve them right,' she would tell me. 'That's what you get for going abroad, Master Robert.' Intolerance was one of the subjects she taught me in the nursery, and I was a willing pupil.

For me intolerance is still the adrenalin in the vein of society. Without it we should perish, with it we get into trouble. The intolerance of white to black, Gentile to Jew, rich to poor, and vice versa makes for battle, murder and sudden death. It also keeps everyone who stays alive fighting fit for a short time. In the intolerance league, the British are still top—an unaccustomed position for this old country these days. Over the years we have hung labels round the necks of foreigners. Americans are brash, Spaniards lazy, Germans gross, Turks treacherous, Russians dangerous and the Italians pathetic. We suffer them to live in their own lands only because they have to be there to be ready to fetch and carry for us when we have our holidays.

It is this concept of the British as the absentee landlords of the world that has served us so splendidly in the past, but it is one that the French have never accepted. They persist in believing that France belongs to them. The argument has been going on for some centuries. At various times in our history we have had to resort to fisticuffs, and one day no doubt we shall have to do so again. But it would be foolish not to recognise that the present is a period of stalemate, and there is little we can do just at the moment but pay up and look pleasant. We don't like paying bills any more than the French do, but at least we struggle to do so. When De Gaulle died, his epitaph was spoken by the landlord of my local inn. 'I'm sorry the old chap's gone, but he never paid the bill for Dunkirk, did he?'

Another fact I learned in my nursery was that the Frogs were a violent lot. In those days every revue, and most musical comedies, contained an Apache Number, in which a French Cad in sidewhiskers and a tight fitting black suit assaulted a girl in slow tempo around the stage. The girl wore, as we believed all Frenchwomen did, a slit skirt, and had her hair pulled a good deal before being finally knocked down, rolled over and abandoned. She would lie unconscious on the floor until resuscitated by her partner for the curtain call.

Years later I had my earlier impression of the French confirmed, while staying in the Rue de Rivoli. The Rue de Rivoli, as most readers probably know already, is an absurdly long colonnaded street, running from the Place de la Concorde to the Louvre, and a good way beyond. For a time when I was making a picture in Paris, I lived at the Hotel Brighton, and had a bedroom overlooking the Tuileries Gardens. In the evening, after a day's shooting, I would repair to the bar and sit watching the television before dinner. If it was raining, and it usually seemed to be,

I would then walk under cover to a restaurant in the Place Vendôme.

One evening, as I stepped into the Arcade, I saw at a distance of two hundred yards, a man carrying a body emerge from a lighted doorway and crossing the pavement, attack the colonnade with his victim's head. Half a dozen times he swung his human battering ram, and then casually abandoning it, let what was left of it fall into the gutter, and returned to the bistro. I suppose I could have arrived on the scene quicker, but when I did, the horror and fright I felt had been replaced by righteous indignation. With scarcely a glance at the crumpled corpse, I tore into the café and into the half a dozen silent, sulky Frenchmen who sat there. A torrent of pidgin French, stage argot and half-remembered phrases from the Folies Bergères poured from my lips.

'*Bêtes sauvages! Canaille! Méchants hommes! Quelle bêtise, quelle exposition formidable! Que va dire Le General? Appellez les gendarmes!*' I looked round for the man who had committed the crime, but could not identify him, yet they had all been there. They had watched, they had done nothing, and now a man lay dead in the gutter, and still no one moved.

'*Ambulance!*' I shouted, '*Appelez un ambulance, vite, vite!* Very well, if you won't do it, I shall.' I seized the telephone, and realized I hadn't the slightest idea how to proceed. I pushed the receiver into the hands of the one I took to be the proprietor. '*Appellez,*' I ordered. '*Appelez, vite! Pas de nonsense! Attendez!*'

I really had them mesmerized. I think in that brief instant I realized why it is Englishmen are so good in a crisis. Slow to anger, perhaps, but when we are roused our fury is really magnificent. '*Venez!*' I reiterated, '*venez, vite!*' and for the first time employing physical force, drove my finger deep into the patron's chest. There was a hint of menace now in the way in which he replaced the receiver on its stand. His eyes were fixed on something at the back of me. I spun round, ready for a surprise attack, to find the corpse had now got to his feet and was dusting himself off. Then he started to laugh. I can never forgive him that laugh. I like to think he was concussed, but I can never be sure. All I know is I had to pay for the telephone call before I could leave the bistro.

But at least on that occasion I didn't have a Frenchman on my side. The French are never on anyone's side for very long. When they capitulated in 1941, the general feeling in my country was that at last we could get on and win the war. 'Now we know where we are,' we told each other. I was making another picture at the time and the mood in the studio when we heard that Paris had fallen was one of quiet optimism. Only the director was silent and apprehensive.

'Come,' I said to him at luncheon, 'surely the rushes can't have been all that terrible. No worse than yesterday's, at least.'

'It's not the rushes for once,' he told me. 'It's Paris. You wouldn't understand what Paris means to me. It's the last place left in Europe where one can purchase genuine chamois leather gloves, buttoning to the armpits.'

I imagine if chamois leather gloves are being stitched these days, the British have the monopoly. It is curious how the pole of sexual permissiveness has shifted. Now it is the French who are the Puritans and we the libertines. A friend of mine, who recently had a few hours to kill in Nice, decided to spend them in a brothel. Being a writer, the word bordello came eventually to his lips and his need manifested itself to the hall porter of the hotel in which he was lodged. He was directed to an appartment on the Front, and in the parlour explained to the proprietress that what he enjoyed most was a sound whipping. A moment later and he was back on the Promenade des Anglais, Madame's rebuke still ringing in his ears: '*Pardon, monsieur, c'est une maison serieuse.*'

'Of course,' he told me when he recounted the incident, 'I may not have made myself understood.'

It's always a mistake trying to speak French to the Frogs. As Noel Coward once remarked when he was sustaining a role at the Comédie Française, 'They simply don't understand their own language.' How true. 'Place de la Concorde,' you say to the taxi driver, and he sits uncomprehending while you repeat your instructions a dozen times before he consents to shrug his shoulders and get going. Once he has secured you as his passenger, he will take his time before deciding on the destination. 'Place de la Concorde,' he will suddenly announce, braking abruptly, and turning the cab round come scuttling back from the Bois de Boulogne where he has been enjoying a skelter at your expense. In England a taxi driver doesn't make the foreigner pronounce Waterloo twenty-seven times before conveying him to the railway station. He doesn't have to. He knows he's going to miss the boat train anyway, because of the traffic jam.

The French and Ourselves these days both keep boarding-houses. Our windows face each other, but whereas there is usually a sign hanging up in our front parlour advertising vacancies, the French always seem to be *Complet*. When an American rings the bell over the road, the door is opened immediately. There is little fuss, hardly any formality, no questions asked. He just signs the book and pays up. Naturally, we on this side expect him to pay up, but before doing so there are a whole lot of questions to be answered. Is he respectable? How long will he be staying? Whom are we to notify if he dies? What is his purpose in coming? Was his mother an Armenian? We don't mind if she was, but we like to know.

Every year, little pieces of the white cliffs of Dover crumble away and fall into the Channel, which you might think would have the effect of increasing the distance between our coast lines yet today the French stand nearer to us than ever, and with the Hovercraft service, a projected Channel Tunnel and the Common Market, we seem to be in danger of actually touching. It will not be an easy embrace, if I have my way.

The other day, deciding to find out for myself how real is the danger of a final clinch, I bought a ticket on a

Hovercraft, a vehicle of which I have always been slightly ashamed, believing it to be another British invention which failed to jell, and imagining the South Coast of my beautiful land littered with these rusting giants, and set sail for Boulogne. True, when I came upon it in Dover, it was stranded, apparently helpless on the sand, but a spirit of optimism prevailed among its attendants. Concrete ramps had been constructed leading to the doors of the monster and soon passengers were being invited to climb on board. I found the loading procedure unnerving. Care has to be taken lest the thing should tip sideways, and when I stepped on to the port side, two other passengers were hastily urged forward on the starboard deck. Hovercrafts apparently cannot decide whether they are boats or planes. Lifebelts are circular, but on the other hand there are air hostesses, young ladies with bossy manners in identical uniforms, barking instructions and soliciting orders for duty-free demon alcohol and Customs-exempt cancer sticks. For those of us who have never worked on the roads, Hovercraft travel is perhaps the nearest they will get to operating a pneumatic compressor. Once aloft, they are not, of course, grasping it by the handle, but actually bouncing up and down in the saddle. Sucking up a gin and tonic through a straw—conveying a glass to my lips nearly knocked my teeth out—I learnt that the fellow in the next jump seat was paying his first visit to France. He was planning to return that evening, reckoning he would be able to see all he wanted to of 'abroad' in six hours, provided he wasn't poisoned by the grub.

My own plans called for a rather longer visit. I didn't propose to return for twenty-four hours, just in time to scuttle through my stage door on Monday night in time to receive the customers. Visiting France while one is acting in the London theatre always adds excitement to the trip. I have never yet been posted as a defaulter, but there's always a first time. The nearest I ever came to it was when David Tomlinson flew me to Le Touquet, and on the way home his engine started to cough. On that occasion I wasn't worried so much about missing a single performance, but the rest of the run.

Boulogne served in the war as a bomb dump for returning allied missions who had failed to locate their intended target further inland. It has been rebuilt with both eyes on the car ferry. I was reminded of a Christmas toy for eight-year-olds. The nursery floor is covered with sections of motorway, some of it not yet assembled. Stepping out, except along the promenade, is unattractive and dangerous.

The French cannot bear to look out through a restaurant window without being able to read the price of the crustacea and coq au vin they are consuming, in reverse. They insist on being constantly reminded of the cost of living expressed in rump steak and chips. The only thing that makes us British suspicious lest the French have more of the stuff than we have, is they never think of anything else. A nation always ready to put its hand in anyone's pocket except its own. I chose a bistro where I could glimpse the sea between the lines of graffiti, and after lunch joined the proprietor and his friends for a discussion on the Common Market. Everyone agreed that it was in our interest to join. Meanwhile it was in their interest to pop over on the Hovercraft and shop in Dover.

After luncheon I took a taxi and drove over to Le Touquet. In the Casino, in the vast hotels, on the deserted plage, nothing stirred. For most of the year Le Touquet is a ghost town, only coming to life for a few short weeks in the high summer. Out of season its mood is set by the shells of the great hotels standing derelict in the forest, like the ruins of Ankhor Vat. Legend has it that Le Touquet died just as the war was ending, the result of a drunken escapade by four American airmen who wanted a little action. If you want action these days, Le Touquet is the last place in which to find it. Perhaps the French never intended to rebuild it. Perhaps they didn't want to be reminded of the English milords who patronized the place between the wars, accepting that in any case they wouldn't come back

even if they could afford to. Those stuffed shirts who cried
'*Garcon!*' and '*Banco!*', and competed on the golf links and
polo grounds for perpetual challenge cups given by English
clubs and British regiments, and presented personally to
the victors by the Prince of Wales or Gladys Cooper. In
those days we actors used to queue up at the barrier at
Victoria Station on Sunday mornings to catch the boat
train with our share of the week's booty, anxious to join
our betters on the green turf or across the green baize. We
were bound for a continent to which we British have never
really belonged, but which in those days we really believed
belonged to us.

It was dark when I returned to Boulogne. The ferry had
stopped running, the waterfront was deserted. I had
dinner in the empty hotel dining-room, and went to bed. In
the morning when I got into the bath there was no soap.
When I stepped out of it, there was no towel. I rang the bell,
and no one came. Eventually, to stop myself shivering I
dried myself on a sheet, calculating how much the French
must have saved themselves over the years by not
providing their customers with soap or bath towels.

Nowadays they don't even come when the customer
calls. They surely can't imagine that it's our turn to answer
the bell?

Mrs Robbins

RANDALL JARRELL

PEOPLE DID NOT like Mrs Robbins. Mrs Robbins did not like people; and neither was sorry. She was a South African—not a native, not a Boer, a colonial. She had been a scholar once, and talked somewhat ostentatiously of *her work*, which she tried *to keep up*. To judge from her speech, she was compiling a Dictionary of Un-American English: if lifts and trams ever invade the North American continent, Pamela Robbins is the woman to lead them. Often, when you have met a true Englishwoman—the false ones are sometimes delightful—you feel that God himself could go no further, that way. Mrs Robbins existed to show what he could do if he tried.

For Mrs Robbins understanding anybody, having a fellow-feeling for anybody, admitting anybody else exists, were incomprehensible vices of Americans, Negroes, continentals, cats, dogs, carrots. She was 'half British phlegm and half perfidious Albion', according to Gertrude Johnson, who loved to refer to Pamela as the Black Man's Burden; any future work on Mrs Robbins will have to be based on Gertrude's. This *half . . . half* formula was Gertrude's favourite. She had said that the President was 'half *jeune fille*, half *faux bonhomme*.' I hadn't liked her formula for Pamela, so I accepted her description of the President with bored matter-of-factness, as if she'd told me that he was half H_2 and half SO_4; but then I thought, 'It's so, it's so.' Sometimes Gertrude was witty without even lying.

For Mrs Robbins life was the war of one against all; in this she was another Gertrude, a commonplace, conventional jointed-hardwood Gertrude. (Yet her conception of this war was that of a Hessian prince of the eighteenth century, while Gertrude's was that of the director of some War of the Future, a war in which the inhabitants of the enemy country wake up one morning to find that they have all been dead a week.) Mrs Robbins asked: 'If I am not for myself, who then is for me?'—and she was for herself so passionately that the other people in the world decided that they were not going to let Pamela Robbins beat them at her own game, and stopped playing.

Once Mrs Robbins had a long and, in its later stages, surprisingly acrimonious argument with several of her guests (to Americans English manners are far more frightening than none at all) about a book of Evelyn Waugh's called *Brideshead Revisited*. She believed it to be a satire on the Roman Catholic Church, since she was sure that its author was 'too intelligent a man' to believe in 'all that'. Her guests had a few good arguments, and she had many bad ones: yet, say what she might, the guests stayed unconvinced. Finally she exclaimed, drawing herself up: 'I have lived among the English aristocracy, and I know.' I had always loved Cleopatra's 'The man hath seen some majesty, and should know,' but·before this I had never really *heard* it.

Mrs Robbins fought to acquire as much—not merit; what did she know about merit?—as much prestige or position or face as possible. Since, as everybody knows, the English never boast, there was nothing she didn't feel free, feel obligated, to tell you about herself: she was her own tombstone. For her mankind existed to be put in its place. She felt that the pilgrim's earthly progress is from drawer to drawer, and that when we are all dead the Great Game will be over. Mrs Robbins poured tea as industrial chemists pour hydrofluoric acid from carboys.

To hear her was to be beginning to despair. Constance Morgan's beloved Dr Rosenbaum once murmured, like the Spartan boy: 'I do nodt like de tune she says zings to.' Gottfried Rosenbaum, that kindly—or as some people said, that crazy—composer, could as easily have pronounced the Hottentot click sounds Mrs Robbins had grown up among (though to hear her, she seemed to have been born in an airliner over the Cape of Good Hope, and to have arrived in Sussex on the second day) as he could have pronounced *th*. He said *d* a third of the time, *t* a third of the time, and *z* a third of the time, and explained, smiling, that after a few years, ass zhure ass Fadt, these would merge into the correct sound. It is true that his *d* and *t* and *z* were changing, but not in the direction of any already existing sound: his speech was a pilgrimage towards some *lingua franca* of the far future—'vot ve all speak ven de Shtate hass videredt avay,' as he would put it.

It never was the individual sounds of a language, but the melodies behind them, that Dr Rosenbaum imitated. For these his ear was Mozartian. To hear him speak French, if you didn't try to understand what he was saying, was as good as attending *Phèdre*: he seemed a cloud that had divorced a textbook of geometry to marry Guillaume Apollinaire—when you replied, weakly, *Yes*, it was in the accents of Matthew Arnold appreciating Rachel. Without realizing it, Dr Rosenbaum imitated for a few minutes the characteristic tune of whatever person he had been talking to—you could tell immediately whether he had been having a conversation with one of the professors educated at the City College of New York or with one begun at Indiana and finished at the Harvard Graduate School.

But even his Unconscious knew enough to refuse to imitate Mrs Robbins. Her every sentence sang itself to a melody so thin-lipped, so emptily affected, so bloodless, so heartless, so senselessly and conclusively complacent, that it was not merely inhuman but inanimate, not merely lifeless but the negation of life—as you listened plants withered, the landscape grew lunar, the existence of *Paramecium*, of molds and spores, of the tobacco mosaic virus came to seem the fantasy of some Utopian planner; her voice said that there is nothing.

To understand what Pamela Robbins was one didn't need to listen to what she said, to understand English, to understand human speech; the Afghans, who had never learned to make the slightest sense out of, discrimination between, *Here* and *Get down!* and *Bad dog!*—they knew what Mrs Robbins was, and as she fed them wagged their tails distrustingly. They ate like horses—no, that isn't fair, they ate horses; anything but horsemeat, in those quantities, would have been beyond the Robbins' means.

If I tell you that Mrs Robbins had bad teeth and looked like a horse, you will laugh at me as a cliché-monger; yet it is the truth. I can do nothing with the teeth, but let me tell you that she looked like a *French* horse, a dark, Mediterranean, market-type horse that has all its life begrudged to the poor the adhesive-tape on a torn five-franc note—that has tiptoed (to save its shoes) for centuries along that razor-edge where Greed and Caution meet. This dark French look was, I suppose, Mrs Robbins' 'Norman blood' coming out; for surely the Normans must have taken along with them on the Conquest some ordinary Frenchmen.

The Three Henries

SELLAR & YEATMAN

Chapter XXVI
Henry IV. A Split King

WHEN HENRY IV Part I came to the throne the Barons immediately flung their gloves on the floor in order to prove
1. That Richard II was not yet dead
2. That Henry had murdered him.
Henry very gallantly replied to this challenge by exhibiting Richard II's head in St Paul's Cathedral, thus proving that he was innocent. Finding, however, that he was not memorable, he very patriotically abdicated in favour of Henry IV, Part II.

Renewed Educational Ferment
Even Henry IV, Part II, however, is only memorable for having passed some interesting laws against his *Old Retainers*, ie butlers and sutlers, who had irritated him by demanding *Liveries*, requiring to much *Maintenance*, etc. He also captured the Scottish Prince James and, while keeping

him as a sausage, had him carefully educated for nineteen years; finding, however, that James was still Scotch, Henry IV Part II lost interest in education and died.

Chapter XXVII
Henry V. An Ideal King

ON THE DEATH of Henry IV Part II, his son, Prince Hal, who had won all English hearts by his youthful pranks—(such as trying on the crown while his father lay dying, and hitting a very old man called Judge Gascoigne)—determined to justify public expectation by becoming the *Ideal English King*. He therefore decided on an immediate appearance in the Hundred Years War, making a declaration that all the treaties with France were to be regarded as dull and void.

Conditions in France were favourable to Henry since the French King, being mad, had entrusted the government of the country to a dolphin and the command of the army to an elderly constable. After capturing some breeches at Harfleur (more than once) by the original expedients of disguising his friends as imitation tigers, stiffening their sinews, etc. Henry was held up on the road to Calais by the constable, whom he defeated at the utterably memorable battle of AGINCOURT (French POICTIERS). He then displaced the dolphin as ruler of Anjou, Menjou, Poilou, Maine, Touraine, Againe and Againe, and realizing that he was now too famous to live long expired at the ideal moment.

Chapter XXVIII
Henry VI. A Very Small King

THE NEXT KING, Henry VI, was only one year old and was thus rather a Weak King; indeed the Barons declared that he was quite numb and vague. When he grew up, however, he was such a Good Man that he was considered a Saint, or alternatively (especially by the Barons) an imbecile.

Joan of Ark

During this reign the Hundred Years War was brought to an end by *Joan of Ark*, a French descendant of Noah who after hearing Angel voices singing *Do Ré Mi* became inspired, thus unfairly defeating the English in several battles. Indeed, she might even have made France top nation if the Church had not decided that she would make an exceptionally memorable martyr. Thus Joan of Ark was a Good Thing in the end and is now the only memorable French saint.

The Wars of the Roses

Noticing suddenly that the Middle Ages were coming to an end, the Barons now made a stupendous effort to revive the old Feudal amenities of Sackage, Carnage and Wreckage and so stave off the Tudors for a time. They achieved this by a very clever plan, known as the *Wars of the Roses* (because the Barons all picked different coloured roses in order to see which side they were on).

Warwick the Kingmaker

One of the rules in the Wars of the Roses was that nobody was ever really King but that Edmund Mortimer really ought to be: any Baron who wished to be considered King was allowed to apply at Warwick the Kingmaker's, where he was made to fill up a form, answering the following questions:

1. Are you a good plain crook?
2. Are you Edmund Mortimer? If not, have you got him?
3. Have you ever been King before? If so, state how many times; also whether deposed, beheaded, or died of surfeit.
4. Are you insane? If so, state whether permanently or only temporarily.
5. Are you prepared to marry Margaret of Angoulême? If Isabella of Hainault preferred, give

reasons. (Candidates are advised not to attempt
both ladies.)
6. Have you had the Black Death?
7. What have you done with your mother? (If *Nun*,
    write *None*.)
8. Do you intend to be I (*a*) a Good King.
                       (*b*) a Bad King.
                       (*c*) a Weak King.
                    II (*a*) a Good Man.
                       (*b*) a Bad Man.
    (Candidates must not attempt more than one in
    each section.)
9. How do you propose to die? (Write your answer in
    BLOCK CAPITALS.)

Sweet Sixteen

JEFFREY BERNARD

ALL WEEK MY my thoughts have continually returned to the business of Mr Ike Ward. Doubtless you'll remember he was the man born a slave and who has just died aged 119. Well, it's not so much the longevity that astounds me, more the fact that he was married 16 times. Was he, I wonder, trying to tell us something? What was tremendously bucking was to read that he'd outlived all 16 of them too. To defuse and render harmless 16 wives is no mean feat; there may be hope for me yet. Assuming he got married for the first time when he was 19—as I did—then this gives him a batting average, so to speak, of just over 6 years, which isn't bad compared to my pathetic 4. Of course, in the unlikely event of a woodcutter with one acre of land being able to afford an attorney, he could conceivably have been married 16 times in as many years. This means he could have been pining or laughing for the past 84 years depending on his attitude towards women. I should have thought it a fairly slaphappy one myself. But why do the deed so many times? It was reported that he never wore glasses so it's possible that he never saw them coming. Perhaps he regarded them as mere chattels, 16 consecutive housemaids in fact, and I believe a team of journalists from the *Guardian* are flying out to Florida to investigate such a possibility.

The other thing is why did *they* marry *him*? (I know why they married me and that was because they thought I was someone who never actually existed.) Now you wouldn't, under normal circumstances, be exactly enraptured or captivated if, on looking up from your embroidery or latest Cartland novel, you saw that you were being approached by a 19- or 90-year-old, black, non-spectacle-wearing woodcutter bearing a diamond engagement ring in the calloused palm of an extended hand. No. You'd probably say to yourself, 'Who dis crazy man?' before throwing the remains of your water melon at him.

The fact remains that 16 succumbed to a line of chat that has sadly gone unrecorded for posterity and me this evening. D'you think that, in the afternoon of his life, he ever reflected on them? Mustn't he have got confused, especially if he was having affairs on the side? I'm exactly 70 years younger than him and already I've forgotten whether it was Jacki or Jill who caused the scar on my left knee cap. But that's beside the point and an aside from a mere meddler in a marriage. Incidentally, Mr Ward was always in perfect health and he died just one day after he entered a nursing home for the first time in his life. It doesn't say a lot for the American medical profession, does it?

Yes, what could that line of chat of his have been? Could it have been a simple 'Hallo, honey chile' accompanied by a smile so sweet and sincere that they swooned at his sawdust-covered boots, or did he simply soft-talk them into it with the latest news such as the result of the Jack Johnson/Tommy Burns fight or the gunfight at the OK Corral? I've a hunch that he was one of those boring men who make a pass at every single female they meet. Or perhaps he had odd talents like being able to do card tricks, make a good mint julep, balance six wine glasses on his head or hop a hundred yards on one leg in 30 seconds. (I myself, at the age of 14, quite hypnotized our charwoman with my ability to roll cigarettes at great speed.)

But they say it's pure chemistry, don't they? He may have exuded a strange body odour such as musk, orange blossom, or Southern Comfort. Perhaps when you held his hand, looked deep into his eyes and listened to him humming 'Old Man River' you just knew he was Mister Ike Right. Anyway, a little late in the day I know, I shall drink to his health. Sixteen times.

The Pukey

NIGEL DENNIS

MR TROY'S REFUSAL to have a pukey in the house had
caused enormous trouble in the family. 'Pukeys are nasty,
degenerate things,' he said: 'they make filthy messes all
over the floor, they corrupt the young, they interrupt
homework and sap the nation, and we have nowhere to put
one.' His wife would answer: 'Well, well, we are getting
distinguished, aren't we? It seems we're the Duke of
Devonshire. Let me tell you that Blanche and Mabel both
have pukeys in their drawing-rooms, and far from being
corrupted, they are happier.' Young Miss Troy appealed to
her father's sense of status, saying: 'Everywhere I go,
Father, it's always: "What did your pukey do last night?" I
have to admit we haven't got one.' 'Oh, all right,' said Mr
Troy, after a couple of years, 'I'll let the pukey-man come
and give a demonstration.'

A few days later, the man arrived with the pukey and put
its box against the wall opposite the fireplace. When Mrs
Troy asked: 'Won't it catch the draught there?' the pukey-
man only laughed and said: 'The point about a pukey,

madam, is that it's bred to be insensible.' 'But it is *alive*, isn't
it?' asked Mrs Troy quickly, 'because we'd never pay for
something dead. And if it's alive, won't the dog resent it?'
'Both dog and budgie will be unconscious of it, madam,' said
the pukey-man, 'a pukey speaks only to a human brain.'
'Well, cut the brainy cackle and open the box,' said Mr Troy
roughly.

Let us admit at once that the first impression the pukey
made on Mr Troy was a good one. Even lying stupefied on
the carpet, its eyes had a wondering gaze that fell hardly
short of sweetness. 'It's not just going to flop down like
that all the time, is it?' asked Mr Troy, to hide the fact that
he liked it so far. 'Give it a minute, my dear sir!' begged the
pukey-man, 'it's hardly got its bearings.' 'Pay him no
attention!' exclaimed Mrs Troy, 'he's been picking on
pukeys for years.' 'Oh, what shall we *call* it?' cried Miss
Troy.

She had hardly spoken when the pukey shuddered from
snout to stern and let its muzzle fall right open, showing
six rows of vivid pink gums and bubbles of sparkling saliva:
'No teeth; that's curious!' muttered Mr Troy. Then, with
no warning, it vomited all over the carpet—a perfectly-
filthy, greenish-yellow mess—causing Mrs Troy to cry
spontaneously: 'Oh, the filthy little beast!' and Miss Troy
to say: 'Oh, Mum, don't *fuss!*' and Mr Troy to say: 'I told you
it would foul everything up. Take the little brute away!' 'An
ounce of patience, if you please,' asked the pukey-man, 'or
how can it grow on you?' 'I'm sure that's true   and I don't
mean I don't like it,' said Mrs Troy, rallying. 'Isn't it actually
good for the carpet?' Miss Troy asked the pukey-man, 'I
know the Vicar said, reasonably used, it was.' 'That is
perfectly correct, Miss Troy,' said the pukey-man, 'it's not
the vomit but the abuse of it.' 'Now, there's a remark I
always like to hear,' said Mr Troy.

At that moment the pukey, which had been staring at its
own emission in a rather vague, contented way, changed its

expression entirely. A sort of pathetic anguish came over its whole face: it held its snout sideways and looked at Miss Troy in a pleading, tender way. 'Oh, *look!*' cried Mrs Troy, 'it's trying to say it didn't mean bad.' They were all wrenched by the pukey's fawning expression, and when it slobbered and grovelled and brownish tears dripped from the corners of its eyes, Mrs Troy could have hugged it. 'Damned sentimental, hypocrital brute!' said Mr Troy, 'I still reserve my judgement.' But he was the first to jump in his seat when the pukey, suddenly throwing-up on to the carpet a clot of gritty mucus, followed this up with a string of shrieks and groans. Everyone was deafened except Miss Troy, who sensed at once that the pukey was illustrating the dilemma of girls of her own age in search of happiness. 'Why, bless my soul!' said Mrs Troy soon, 'it's trying to have *sex*, that's what it is'—and sure enough, the pukey was now twisting its hind-parts in the most indecent way, and rubbing its flanks on its own vomit. 'I'll not have that in *my* house,' said Mrs Troy, pursing her lips, 'it's just plain filth, and showing-off.' 'My dear madam, it never actually *gets* there,' said the pukey-man: 'nothing ever really *happens.*' 'Oh, Mother, you and Father make everything seem obscene!' said Miss Troy, 'even love.' 'Well, as long as it only suggests but can't actually do it, I don't mind,' said Mrs Troy, watching the pukey with a new curiosity. 'My mind is still unmade up,' said Mr Troy.

Worn out, it seemed, by sexual frustation, the pukey lay still for a moment. Then, suddenly fixing its eye on Mrs Troy, it gave her such a glare of horrible malignancy that she reached for her husband's arm. Next minute, there was a dreadful spectacle: throwing itself into a spasm of rage, the pukey began tearing and biting at its own body, like a thing bent on suicide. 'Stop it! Stop it! Put the lid on!' screamed Mrs Troy, 'it's cruel, and drawing blood.' 'Frankly, you'll have to adjust to that madam,' said the pukey-man, 'because it fights more than anything else.' 'Oh then, that's decisive for me,' said Mr Troy, 'because I love to see a good scrap.' 'It *is* the men who like that best,' agreed the pukey-man, as the pukey went through the motions of winding its entrails round the throat of an enemy and jumping on his face. 'I don't *mind* its fighting,' Mrs Troy said grudgingly, 'but I'll put its lid on if it overdoes it. I like *beautiful* things best.' The words, alas, were hardly out of her mouth when the pukey, sighting backwards over its spine like a mounted cowboy firing at his pursuers, shot her full in the face with an outrageous report. 'Now, no grumbling Mother!' screamed poor Miss Troy, knowing her mother's readiness to take affront. 'But it's *not* nice!' protested Mrs Troy, fanning herself with an evening paper. 'Oh, Mother, can't you see it *means* nothing?' cried Miss Troy, 'it's not like *us*, with our standards.' 'Standards or no,' said Mrs Troy, 'I never saw Mabel's pukey do that to *her*.' 'Ah, but this is an improved model, madam,' said the pukey man.

'Am I correct in supposing,' asked Mr Troy, 'that nothing substantial ever comes out of its rear end anyway?' 'That is correct, sir,' answered the pukey-man, 'all secretion and excretion are purely visual and oral. The vent is hot air at most: hence, no sand-box.' 'Yet it has a belly on it,' said Mr Troy, 'I know because I can see one.' 'You can see a belly, sir,' answered the pukey-man, 'but you can't see any guts, can you?' They all laughed at this, because it was so true.

After throwing-up another couple of times ('Mercy, what a messy little perisher it is!' said kind Mrs Troy), the pukey became inordinately grave and a whole rash of wettish pimples spread over its face. 'Well, you are in luck!' said the pukey-man, jumping up as if genuinely interested, 'it never does this more than once a week at most. Can you guess what it is?' They all racked their brains, guessing everything from sewage farming to guitar-playing, and still couldn't imagine; until Miss Troy, who was the quickest of the family, screamed: '*I* know! It's *thinking*!' '*Mes compliments*, young lady,' said the pukey-man, bowing.

They all watched the pukey thinking because it was so

unexpected; but none of them really liked it. 'When it vomits, it only makes me laugh,' said Mr Troy, 'but when it thinks, *I* feel like vomiting.' 'I just feel nervous and embarrassed, like it was something you'd seen and shouldn't,' said Mrs Troy, and even Miss Troy for once agreed with her mother, saying, 'You feel it's only doing it as a change from being sick, but it's the same really.' 'Don't judge it too hardly,' said the pukey-man, 'surely the wonder is that with no brains it can think at all.' 'Has it really no brains?' asked Mr Troy, curious. 'No, sir,' said the pukey-man: 'that's *why* its thinking makes you sick.' 'Funny sort of animal, I must say,' said Mr Troy, 'thinks without brains, bites without teeth, throws up with no guts, and screws without sex.' 'Oh, *please* stop it thinking!' begged Mrs Troy. 'I had an experience once that smelt like that.' At which words, the pukey's pimples disappeared completely and, lying prone with its paws out, it gave Mrs Troy a smug, complacent look, showing all its gums in a pleading whimpering. 'Oh, the little angel! It wants to be congratulated for having thought!' cried Mrs Troy: 'then we *will*—yes! we *will*, you smelly little darling—you little, stinking, clever, mother's thing!' 'I find that touching, too,' said Mr Troy, 'no wonder there's so much nicker in pukeys.' 'It's for love and culture, too, Dad,' Miss Troy reminded. 'Thank you, Miss Troy,' said the pukey-man, 'we breeders tell ourselves that too.'

During the next hour the pukey did all manner of things—such as marching like the Coldstream Guards, dancing and balancing on one paw like Pavlova, folding its arms like a Member of Parliament, singing the national anthem, plucking away at its parts mysteriously, fighting like mad, and making such vulgar explosive noises at both ends that the Troys were all left speechless with wonder. What charmed them as much as anything was feeling that the pukey made no distinction about what it did: whether it was fawning or screeching, or thinking or puking, it made it all like the same, because it loved each thing equally and looked at you always so proudly for it. 'I can only say you breeders must be jolly highly-skilled,' summed-up Mr Troy, 'to root out all the natural organs and still poison the air.' 'It's more a sixth sense than a skill,' said the pukey-man modestly, 'and one which your wife, I may say, seems to have instinctively.' This was the first compliment Mrs Troy had had since she gave birth to Miss Troy, and to cover her natural embarrassment she said sharply, 'Well, put its lid on again now and take it away. We'll come and fill out the Never-never forms tomorrow.'

With the pukey gone, it wasn't like the same home. The walls seemed to have been sprayed with a dribble the colour of maple-syrup and dead flies kept dropping from the ceiling. The state of the carpet was beyond description, although the last thing the pukey had done before the lid closed was puff a sort of scented detergent powder over the stinking mess it had made. But the Troys were much too impressed to worry about the room: they could only think of buying the pukey and doing this every night. 'It baffles me,' said Mr Troy, as they went to bed: 'it's not human, it's not mechanical, it's not like any animal I've ever known.' 'What it leaves on the carpet is human through-and-through,' said Mrs Troy, and they all laughed at this because it was so true.

The Tattooed Lady

PATRICK RYAN

MADAME ISABELLE WAS not only the Most Picturesque Tattooed Lady in the World she was also the largest. Twenty-three lovable stones of her, there were, as Fat Woman in Cadwallader's International Circus before Morry Lishman, Camberwell's Tattoo Artist to Crowned Heads, married her for her canvas.

'When I first set eyes on her lovely pink acres, Gutty,' he told me on his deathbed, '"My Gawd!" I said to myself, "here's my chance to move into CinemaScope. Now I can get free from the frustration of niminy-piminy dragons and pierced hearts and I Love Mum. At last I got elbow-room for the epics."'

He was a pre-Raphaelite genius of the needle and converted his wife into one Stupendous Epidermal Epic. From whichever quarter you came upon Madame Isabelle, melodrama met your eye. Only above the neckline was her frame untouched by pigment. The Valley of Death lay between her shoulder-blades, and the Light Brigade galloped into the jaws of hell, bug-eyed through shot and shell from the Russian artillery ranged about her left armpit. The Battle of Hastings bayeuxed across the small of her back, on one mighty thigh Charles I lost his head to the chopper, while over on the other Marie Antoinette gave up hers to the guillotine. Cowboys and Indians raced up her left arm, Turks massacred Armenians down the right. Lincoln met his death on her diaphragm and, above the decorous hammock of her sequined brassière—Cadwallader's was strictly a family show for readers of a family magazine—lay Morry's masterpiece . . . the Battle of Trafalgar.

Across the vasty deeps of her upper chest, on a rippling blue sea, against a crimson sunset, the British Fleet drove under full sail headlong into the guns of the French and Spanish ships ranked on the sinister side. From the prow of *Victory*, Nelson waved one-armed defiance at Villeneuve, prancing bearded on *Bucentaure*. Guns smoking, flags flying, decks awash with blood and heroes, the wooden walls surged into battle and gave Isabella star-quality down among us freaks.

It was one and six to see her motionless, but, for an extra bob and after the ladies had left the tent, Morry would put on the record of '1812' and Bella would do her 'Storm at Sea'. Genteelly, and eschewing all hula abandon, she would jog up and down like a horseman in a Noh play, and the contending fleets would pitch and toss in the quivering waves, now swinging together so that the opposing admirals could each have spat the other in the eye, then swaying apart again as her muscle-control tempest cleft the blue waters. It was a most artistic performance, and when Bella was really in the joggling groove, she could send petty-officers sea-sick.

If Morry's boundless cupidity had not driven him to take folding money from an Empire Loyalist for needling the Union Jack on his prize bull, Bella would likely have passed the rest of her days happy enough under his decorative thumb.

'Keep an eye on her for me, Gutty,' he said, a couple of days before we laid him away with the hoof-marks immemorial in his buttocks. 'She's right moony and butterscotch romantic under all that adipose. A proper mark for some soft-talking Lothario if she's left to think for herself.'

Though my own secret passion for Bella bade me reject such critical opinion, she soon confirmed from her own lips that there wasn't just a thin woman inside her struggling to get out, but a fifty-three-year-old Madame Bovary thirsting for True Romance and the opportunity to fill her Amorous Vacuum.

'I've never been one to speak ill of the departed, Gutty,' she said, 'but little Morry, rest his soul, was never really Mr Right for me.'

'He loved you, Bella.'

'He loved me the way Mr Gobelin loved his tapestry.'

'He looked after you all right. He always saw you got your grub.'

'Only to keep his needlework inflated. He knew if I lost weight what would happen to this lot.' She tapped the Battle of Trafalgar. 'All them sailors shrunk down to matchsticks and the warships wrinkled up like rubber dinghys.'

'Biggest naval disaster in the history of tattooing.'

'For him it would have been. In looking after me, Morry was just protecting his professional reputation. But now he's gone, poor dear, I've got a feeling Mr Right'll be coming along any day.'

'Maybe he's come along already, Bella. Maybe he's been around here all the time.'

'Who has?'

'I have. I've been in love with you ever since you first came to Cadwallader's as a mere girl of eighteen-stones-four.'

'You, Gutty? All these years?'

'Yes, Bella. But propriety forbade me to speak out to a married woman. I love you for your nature, not just because you're fat. May I, Bella, be your Mr Right?'

'I'm very sorry, old love, but I'm afraid you can't. No

offence meant, of course, but you can't really expect a sensitive woman like me to go a bundle on an India-Rubber Man, can you now?'

And, sadly, a middle-aged India-Rubber Man at that. What had I, Gutta-Percha Godfrey, to offer any woman but a two-way stretch skin, extensible ear-lobes, and the facility to rub out lead-pencil with my nose?

Despite Bella's premonitions of romance, she didn't strike much luck during the next season. The only likely beau who came back-stage bearing flowers and ostensibly bent on her autograph, was a man in Pontefract, who finished up sticking a pin in her bow-front to settle a bet as to whether she was all McCoy or just inflated. I was cultivating high hopes that as time went round she would fall my way, when, on the last day at Llandudno, fate put the bellows to her flickering flame of Bovary. A handsome little gent, a keen-eyed Mr Magoo sporting a Cuttle-beard and a monocle, bounced into the tent after close-down.

'Madame Isabella,' he bowed. 'Otto Sodermann, your devout admirer and humblest servant.'

He presented a bunch of roses that looked big even on Bella.

'I've seen you,' she said, blushing, 'down there every night this week looking at me through horse-racing binoculars.'

'A feast of beauty for my eyes, dear madame. Such form, such fleshly profusion!' He kissed ecstatic fingertips. 'If only Rubens could have lived to paint you!'

'How come, Mr Sodermann,' I asked suspiciously, 'you like the ladies so fat?'

'I have Egyptian blood in my veins. In the Land of the Pharaohs they like a lot of woman at a time. Renoir, Madame Isabella, would have wept at the splendour of your shoulders.'

'Really, Mr Sodermann,' she simpered. 'You never ought to say such things.'

He knelt suddenly in her vast shadow and kissed her

hand just where the tail-end cowboy took off from the wristbone.

'Call me Otto and make me eternally happy. Add the gift of friendship to your extravagance of priceless beauty.'

'Well, honestly, you do go on, don't you . . . Otto.'

'Hold on a bit—about all this priceless beauty,' I cut in. 'What about all those tattoos?'

'Insensitive Philistine!' he cried. 'You india-rubber infidel! Have you no soul? Does the inner beauty shining from that peerless face not blind your plebeian eyes to all else? I see no tattoos in the light that shines from that lovely smile.'

'You rotten ox, Gutty,' said Bella. 'Drawing attention at a time like this.'

Otto followed the show around for a month, prancing about Bella like Beau Nash on a hot tin roof, dazzling her with courtly compliments, extolling bulk as the ultimate criterion of pulchritude, and generally giving her the full, gilt-edged old madam. I did my best to compete with his blandishments, but a gutta-percha Romeo whose social forte lies in using his lower lip as a catapult just can't compete with a sawn-off, silver-tongued Casanova.

I could understand Bella going down like two tons of coal before his campaign but I couldn't for the life of me see what Otto, at fifteen years her senior and outweighed by a clear sixteen stones, could possibly be after in chasing her. When he finally popped the question in Barnstaple and was rapidly accepted, I wondered if we hadn't got a well-heeled, sixty-eight-year-old lunatic on our trail.

'I told you, Gutty,' said Bella, almost airborne with rapture like a betrothed dirigible, 'that Mr Right would come along in the end. And, in spite of all the rotten things you keep saying about Otto, I'm inviting you to the wedding Saturday week just for old time's sake.'

Faced with the prospect of spending the autumn of my days in a state of unrequited love. I decided to do a depth-probe on Mr Sodermann. Wriggling over transoms and squirming through fan-lights comes dead easy to an india-rubber man, and I gave his hotel-room a Paul Drake going-over while he was out with his fiancée in two double-seats at the pictures. And I found ammunition which, even at this late hour with the banns called and the wedding-cake in the oven, might still win back my Bella, if fired at the explosive moment. I caught her alone on the night before the wedding.

'Now that you're really getting hitched, my dear,' I said, 'I'm just going to admit that the best man won and do all I can to see that you make a happy marriage.'

'That's nice, Gutty. I don't like you being all upset.'

'As a first gesture, I want to draw your attention to a personal point and trust you won't take offence about it.'

'I won't take on. What is it?'

'The Battle of Trafalgar.'

'My old chest-tattoo?'

'To you, Bella your chest. To Otto . . . the bosom of his bride.'

'But he never notices my tattoos. He told you so.'

'Normally, Bella, everyday, maybe he doesn't. But is a bridal night an everyday occasion?'

She looked down across the cascade of her chins and her happy eyes clouded over.

'I never really thought about it that way,' she said doubtfully. 'And I have bought a real negligent nightdress. But I can't do nothing about it now. You can't get Trafalgar off me overnight.'

'Maybe not,' I said, producing my bottles, 'but they do camouflage battle-ships.'

Bella made a handsome couple of brides next day in her brand-new wedding suit as Rudolph, our eight-foot giant, took her down the aisle to give her away. Otto was dapper as Ascot and hopping anxious for the off. I sat myself anonymously down among the giraffe-necked ladies and the knee-high dwarfs. I waited till the parson got to the piece about 'if any man can show just cause . . .'

'I've got just cause,' I cried. 'He's not wedding that woman for love. He's just after the pictures on her chest.'

'The pictures on her chest?' said the parson.

'You've got it,' I said, running up the aisle to show Bella her bridegroom's photograph in the *Tattoo Collector's Quarterly Gazette*. 'There he is, in black and white . . . Otto Sodermann, Europe's No. 1 Collector of Decorated Skins, standing beside a selection from his gallery of over two hundred mounted Tattoos of All Nations.'

'The man's a latex lunatic,' said Otto. 'Please proceed with the ceremony.'

'You won't want to,' I said, 'without Morry Lishman's latest masterpiece . . . Allow me, my dear.'

I unbuttoned my dumbstruck Bella's jacket to reveal the scoop-necked chiffon blouse beneath.

'The Battle of Trafalgar!' shouted Otto. 'It's gone!' Nelson was no more, Villeneuve had disappeared, and not a single ship sailed the ocean of Bella's chest. Never a spot of colour flecked her skin and a shining baby-pink desert stretched from shoulder to shoulder.

'Bleached out, Mr Sodermann,' I said, 'by a new system of Japanese Instant Electrolysis. Do you want our Bella now without her Battle of Trafalgar?'

'Sacred blue!' he snarled. 'Name of a name of a dirty pig.'

He picked up his coat-tails and ran out of the church, hotly pursued by dwarfs and giraffe-necked women. Bella collapsed in my arms and Rudolph, backed by Waldo the Strong Man, held me up.

'It's all over now, my love,' I comforted her. 'He only wanted your Trafalgar for his collection. A deceased wife's pelt is her husband's legal property and he calculated that, with all the weight you carry, it wouldn't be long before he got legitimate chance to frame it among his souvenirs.'

'Oh, Gutty,' she wept, 'what a fool I've been.'

'Never mind, Bella,' I said. 'I'll just ask the vicar if I can take over where Otto left off and we'll all live happily ever after. We'll soon get that nailpolish off your thorax. And even if it brings the tattoo off with it, we can always get by on my elasticity.'

And the parson, after some ecclesiastical demur which

he overcame when Waldo threatened him with karate, took up from where he had left off and set little rubber wedding-bells a-tinkling in my heart.

Ill Met By Moonlight

STANLEY REYNOLDS

STROLLING INTO MY local newsagents the other morning to
ask about the possible whereabouts of my monthly supplies
of *Household Beautiful* and *Tidy Home*, the little old lady, a most
mumsie-looking apparition with an electric blue rinsed
head of hair and zircon encrusted goggles, was standing
neath the usual line-up of barely clad doxies on the main
magazine display shelf, bemoaning the state of the world. I
don't know what channel this newsagent lady can receive
on her telly but I never seem to see the same shows.
Apparently there had been a sex education film on during
the children's hour the afternoon previous. Feeling a bit
salty, I said, 'Sex education films, aren't there any street
corners any more?'

This brought a laugh from one of the ancients who was
thumbing through a glossy mag full of naked jades. But the
newsagent lady was not amused. 'That's very satirical, I'm
sure, bighead,' she said, 'but just look at this.' She then
thrust a copy of that morning's *Daily Mirror* at me. Under
the headline SEX LESSONS FOR RAPISTS I read the following
intelligence from New York:

'*Rapists are being cured of their criminal urges,*' I read aloud, '*by being taught the art of seduction.*'

'Not so much with the mouth, mush,' the lady newsagent snapped for the venerables who had been casting nostalgic, amorous glances at the girlie mags had turned all ears. Unable to resist an audience I nevertheless continued the public reading.

'*The amazing lessons in love are given at a New York clinic in a test scheme paid for by the American Government.*'

A few of the old fellows interrupted me there and started complaining about how they failed to emigrate to the States back in '28 when they had the chance to get in on the ground floor of civil aviation or talking pictures; America, they said, was truly the land of opportunity whereas here they had to queue for a simple hernia operation.

'*Treatment,*' I went on, '*is based on the theory that rapists have never understood how to seduce women and therefore become frustrated and angry. So volunteers are shown how to chat up girls, and woo them.*'

The old boys grumbled about having been born too soon, tossed aside the girlie mags, purchased *Fishing Times, Today's Angler, Field and Stream* and other such outdoors mags, and shuffled out and round the corner to the tea-shop which passes for European sidewalk café life in the grey, pebble-dashed Liverpool suburbs we live in. I picked up *Household Beautiful* and headed home, and the reader has perhaps already grasped that I am the domestic sort; I suppose I am what you could call a grass widower, an unmarried father, the head of a one-parent family, and no longer a lady's man.

Leading a quiet sort of life and not getting out much any more, I had thought that rape in this permissive age was a thing of the past. But just after reading that item in the *Mirror* about the seduction school in New York I was taking a taxi into the heart of downtown Liverpool to see yet another wholesome, Easter Holiday family type picture, when I noticed a large sign painted on the side of a wall. 'Women,' it said, 'Reclaim the Night'. Puzzled, I asked the cab driver what this meant.

'The ladies,' he said, 'don't like gettin' raped when they

are staggerin' home after not bein' able to pick up a guy in one of de drinkin' clubs dat are all around here.' This area we were passing through was the twilight area.

Since then I have been puzzling over the whole business of rape, wooing, seduction and sex education. In the old days, in my boyhood in America, my sex education, like all other boys' sex education, was conducted on street corners. My first afternoon seminars were held outside the Highland Fruit and Soda Fountain at the corner of Hampden and Nonotuck Streets in Holyoke, Mass., and I later did an advanced level course on the street corner outside the Wayland Drug Store at the corner of Wayland Square and Weybossett Street in Providence, Rhode Island. These were given by older boys, some of whom were so mature and worldly wise they were forced to shave twice and sometimes even three times a week.

In their essence the whole of these tutorials could be boiled down to one simple rule of thumb which was 'When they say, "No" what they really mean is "Yes".' Later, of course, one learned that there were more sophisticated girls who had to be wooed. 'Listen, honey,' the would-be seducer would have to whisper, 'you had a hamburger, you saw a show.'

I suppose any warm words are better than a sock on the jaw, and as my own sex life as a sex life is practically null and void, I thought perhaps I should try the gift of golden speech on some young lady rather than simply drag her down to the boozer and ask the barman to fill her up. With this in mind I borrowed a clean shirt, a fiver, and a telephone number from my 18-year-old son and bracing myself with several fingers of Old Vulturine Genuine Japanese Scotch Whisky type drinking fluid, given to me by a seafaring man who obviously harboured some secret grudge against me, I telephoned the bimbo, whom I had met casually a couple of times.

Putting on my best Charles Boyer voice I coo-ed, 'Why, hello, there, Brenda, you remember me, Ambrose's dad?

Yeah, that's right, the one with the cold sore and the little
crinkly eyes with the red rims. Well, the strangest thing
has been happening—in all my dreams I search for you, but
I do not find even the echo of your footsteps, my darling.'
   'You bin smokin' them funny cigarettes?' she said. 'And
since when are you French?'
   'I got a frog in my throat,' I explained. 'But forget the little
details. They are as nothing to what has been going on inside
me. Where have you been hiding, thief of my heart?'
   'I bin to Manchester last week,' she said, 'to see Iggy Pop,
but I haven't been going out too much recently me self.'
   'Well,' I said, 'there is no rest for me, sleep has left my
bed. I blink into the darkness wondering how I can steal the
beauty from your face.'
   As ill fate would have it this Brenda agreed to meet me at
a bistro in town—'Me Mam,' she explained, 'might not
understand me goin' out with a fella old enough to be me
Dad, if we had one, a Dad, I mean.' Luckily the bistro was
badly lighted and the girl, who was 26 and had been playing
the older woman with my eighteen-year-old, sort of
screwed up her eyes and paid me the compliment of saying
I didn't look quite as old as I obviously was and that I did,
indeed, look something like my eldest son in the dusk with
the light behind me, only I was more sort of fallen apart at
the seams.
   Over a few demi-jugs of what such young gents as my
eldest boy call 'leg openers', I attempted to ply her with
honeyed words while the tape recorder in the bistro blared
out a song the entire lyric of which seemed to be six nasal
adolescents screaming, 'We don't want no aggrovation!' I
did not allow this to hinder my research.
   'O my sinner,' I whispered, 'let us spend this night
together.'
   'Ya what?' she asked.
   I filled her glass and went on, 'My mind whispers,
"Come, let us run away," but I am afraid, my Brenda, of
that long journey.'

'Yeah,' she said, 'I went to Newcastle to see the Ded
Byrds play last month and the car broke down on the M62.
Shockin' it was.'

'I look at you, Brenda, and long to live with you for ever.'

At this point the punk rockers on the tape stopped
singing and that last line of mine was bellowed to a silent
room. The waitress sniggered. Brenda kept beating time to
the rock music which, evidently, was still playing inside her
own head.

'But at least, my beautiful sinner,' I said, 'we will spend
tonight together. Stay a night until our enemy the cock
shall crow.' I do not wish to appear immodest but when I
delivered that line I had to hand it to myself. 'Roll over
Charles Boyer,' I said, 'and tell Errol Flynn the news.'

'Hey!' Brenda said, coming to life, 'I don't like that'sort of
talk. I can't stand no smut of any kind.'

She had already whipped through a bit of the red ink
they were selling in this place, and wishing to avoid a
drunken scene with a young harridan I hastily explained
the poetic nature of the farmyard reference. 'Aw!' she
said, 'I hate the country. There's nothin' to do there and the
TV reception is usually somethin' shockin'.' But then her
eyes lighted up. 'Say,' she said, 'the way you talk, it's kind of
queer. I suppose that's why at your age you ain't got a wife.'

'I got three sons.'

'Yeah,' she said scornfully, 'I always heard they were the
worst kind. Not that I got anything against you guys,
except you talk funny. And me Mam says they can be real
good friends with a woman.'

Seeing how the evening had progressed and seeing how I
was down to my last quid and a handful of small change, I
said, 'Speaking as strictly as a pal, Mizz Brenda, you think
you might cough up for the next round?'

'Say,' she said, 'what kind of a fag is a fag like you
anyway, comin' out practising all that dirty queer talk on a
girl and then tryin' to borrow money from her. A real man
never would borrow money from a girl but then we sort of
know what kind of a man a man like you is.'

There were a few more minutes of a fairly hairy time between Mizz Brenda and my goodself and in the end I lent her my last quid for a taxi home. I had just enough for a half pint at the pub next door with a long walk home to the suburbs the only thing standing between a sadder and wiser man's good night's sleep. Inside the pub there were a couple of leering oafs discussing their success with women. They looked like the types who would have to pull a sawn-off shotgun on a girl to get so much as a goodnight kiss, but from what they were saying they had mastered the new art of seduction which they are teaching nowadays in New York.

One thug, who looked incapable of human speech, pointed a dirty thumb at what looked like a respectable enough young lady sitting in a corner. He had picked her up the night before, he told his mate.

'How's it go?' the lout with him asked.

'Do I ever miss?' the punk asked, leering. 'I just walked up to her, right in here it was, and I says, "Hey, babe, you go?" '

'An' what did she say?' the other asked.

'She said, "I do now, you smooth talkin' sonofagun".'

Walking home through Liverpool's twilight zone I was feeling a bit nervous, wishing they'd hurry up and reclaim the night for both men and women alike, but then my friend the taxi driver pulled up and offered me a free ride home. 'What's money?' he asked philosophically. 'Can money buy you happiness? Can money buy you the love of a good woman?'

'Yes,' I said.

'Yeah,' he said, 'I always thought so too.'

A Visit in Bad Taste

ANGUS WILSON

'HE LOOKS VERY much older' said Margaret. 'It's aged him dreadfully and made him servile.'

'I should imagine that prison does tend to kill one's independence' said her husband drily.

'Oh yes that's all very well, Malcolm, you can afford to be rational, to explain away, to account for. But he's my brother and no amount of reasons can make it any better to have him sitting there fingering his tie when he talks, loosening his collar with his fingers, deferring every opinion to you, calling old Colonel Gordon sir, jumping up with every move I make. It's like a rather pathetic minor public schoolboy of nineteen applying for a job, and he's sixty, Malcolm, remember that—sixty.'

'I think you know' said Malcolm Tarrant, as he replaced his glass of port on the little table by his side 'that public school has always meant a lot more to Arthur than we can quite understand. The only time that I visited him in Tamcaster I was struck by the importance that they all attached to it. As a bank manager there and a worthy citizen of the town it was in some kind of way a passport to power, not just the place you'd been at school at. And now, I imagine, it's assumed an importance out of all perspective, a kind of lifebuoy to a drowning sailor. We're inclined to imagine prison as peopled with public schoolboys, each with a toothbrush moustache and an assumed military rank, "ex-public schoolboy gaoled," but they only make so much of it because it's so unusual. God knows what sort of awful snobbery the presence of a "public schoolman" arouses among the old lags, or the warders too for that matter—people speak so often of the horrors of War but they never mention the most awful of them—the mind of the non-commissioned officer. Depend upon it, whatever snobbery there was, Arthur got full benefit from it.'

Margaret's deep, black eyes showed no sign of her distress, only her long upper lip stiffened and the tapir's nose that would have done credit to an Edward Lear drawing showed more white. The firelight shone upon her rich silver brocade evening dress as she rustled and shimmered across the room to place a log on the great open fire. She put the tiny liqueur glass of light emerald—how Malcolm always laughed at her feminine taste for crème de menthe!—upon the mantelpiece between the Chelsea group of Silenus and a country girl and the plain grey bowl filled with coppery and red-gold chrysanthemums.

'If you mean that Arthur is vulgar' she cried 'always has been, yes, yes. At least, not always' and her thin lips,so faintly rouged, relaxed into tenderness 'not when we were children.But increasingly so. My dear, how could I think otherwise, married to that terrible little woman.—"How do you keep the servants from thieving, Margaret?"—"Give that class an inch and they'll take an ell"—dreadful, vulgar little Fascist-minded creature.'

'Dear Margaret' said Malcolm, and he smiled the special smile of admiring condescension that he kept for his wife's political opinions. 'Remember that in Myra's eyes you were a terrible Red.'

'It isn't a question of politics, Malcolm' said his wife and she frowned—to her husband she was once again the serious-minded, simple student he had found so irresistible at Cambridge nearly forty years ago. 'It's a question of taste. No, it was a terrible marriage and a terrible life. It was the one excuse I could make for him at the time. To have lived for so many years against such a background was excuse enough for any crime, yes, even that one. I felt it all through the trial as I sat and watched Myra being the injured wife, with that ghastly family round her.'

'That's where we differ' said Malcolm and for a moment his handsome, high-cheekboned face with its Roman nose showed all his Covenanting ancestry 'I could never excuse his actions. I tried to rid myself of prejudice against them, to see him as a sick man rather than as a criminal' it was not for nothing one felt that the progressive weeklies were so neatly piled on the table beside him 'but when he refused psychiatric treatment the whole thing became impossible.'

Margaret smiled at her husband maternally as she speared a crystallized orange from its wooden box with the little two pronged fork. 'It must be wonderful to have everything all cut and dried like you, darling' she said 'only people don't fit into pigeon holes according to the demands of reason. Arthur would never go to a psychoanalyst, you old goose; in the first place he thinks it isn't respectable, and then deep down, of course, he would be frightened of it, he would think it was witchcraft.'

'No doubt you're right. No doubt Arthur does still live in the Middle Ages' he moved his cigar dexterously so that the long grey ash fell into the ashtray rather than on to his suit, he narrowed his eyes 'I still find his actions disgusting, inexcusable.'

'Offences against children' said Margaret and she spoke the phrase in inverted commas, contemptuously 'I suppose there is no woman whose blood does not get heated when she reads that in the newspaper. But somehow it all seemed so different when I saw it at the trial. Arthur seemed so shrunken and small, so curiously remote for the principal actor, as though he'd done it all inadvertently. He probably had, too,' she added fiercely, striking the arm of her chair with her hand 'in order to forget that dreadful, bright woman—that awful, chromium-plated, cocktail-cabinet, old-oak-lounge home. And then those ghastly people—the parents—there are some kinds of working class people I just cannot take—servile and defiant, obstinate and shifty. I believe every word Arthur said when he told of their menaces, their sudden visits, their demands for money. Oh! they'd had their pound of flesh all right' she said bitterly 'in unhappiness and fear. Even the children, Malcolm, it sounds so moving in the abstract, poor little creatures not comprehending, their whole lives distorted by a single incident. When Rupert and Jane were little, I used to think that if anyone harmed them I would put his eyes out with hot irons. But these children weren't like that—that cretinous boy with the sudden look of cunning in his eyes and that awful, painted, oversexed girl.'

'It's a pity you ever went to the trial' said Malcolm, but Margaret could not agree. 'I had to suffer it all' she cried 'it was the only way. But that Dostoyevskeyan mood is over. I don't want any more of it, I want it to be finished.' She fitted a cigarette into one of the little cardboard holders that stood in a glass jar on her work-table, then suddenly she turned on her husband fiercely 'Why has he come here? Why? Why?' she cried.

'I imagine because he's lonely' said Malcolm.

'Of course he is. What can be expected? But he'll be just as lonely here. We aren't his sort of people, Malcolm. Oh! Not just because of what's happened, we never have been. This isn't his kind of house.' She thought with pleasure of all they had built up there—the taste, the tolerance, the ease of living, the lack of dogmatism. Her eyes lighted on the Chelsea and the Meissen figures, the John drawings, the Spanish metal-work, the little pale yellow spinet— eclectic but good. Her ears heard once more Ralph Tarrant telling them of his ideas for Hamlet, Mrs Doyle speaking of her life with the great man, Professor Crewe describing his theory of obsolete ideas, Dr Modjka his terrible meeting with Hitler. Arthur had no place there.

'You want me to ask him to go' said Malcolm slowly.
Margaret bent over the fire, crouching on a stool in the
hearth, holding out her hands to the warmth. 'Yes' she said
in a low voice 'I do.' 'Before he's found his feet?' Malcolm
was puzzled. 'He knows I think that he must move
eventually, but for the moment . . .' 'The moment!' broke
in Margaret savagely. 'If he stays now he stays for ever, I'm
as certain of that as that I stand. Don't ask me *how* I know, but
I do.' 'Ah! well. It won't be a very pleasant talk' said her
husband 'but perhaps it will be for the best.'

Only the frou-frou of Margaret's skirt broke the silence
as she moved about the room, rearranging the sprigs of
winter jasmine, drawing the heavy striped satin curtains
across to cover a crack of light. Suddenly she sat down
again on the stool and began to unwrap some sewing from
a little silk bundle.

'I think the last chapter of Walter's book very
pretentious' she said in a voice harder and clearer than
normal. 'He's at his worst when he's doing the great
Panjandrum.'

'Poor Walter' said Malcolm 'You can't go on playing Peter
Pan *and* speak with the voice of authority . . .'

They had not long been talking, when Arthur came in.
His suit looked over-pressed, his tie was too 'club', his hair
had too much brilliantine for a man of his age. All his
actions were carried out overconsciously, with military
precision; as he sat down he jerked up his trousers to
preserve the crease, he removed a white handkerchief
from his shirtcuff, wiped his little toothbrush moustache
and cleared his throat—'Sorry to have been so long' he said
'Nature's call, you know.' Malcolm smiled wryly and
Margaret winced.

'You don't take sugar, do you Arthur?' she said as she
handed him his coffee.

'Will you have a glass of port, old man?' asked Malcolm,
adapting his phraseology to his brother-in-law.

'Oh! thanks very much' said Arthur in quick, nervous

tones, fingering his collar. Then feeling that such diffidence was unsuitable, he added 'Port, eh? Very fruity, very tasty.'

There was a long pause, then Margaret and Malcolm spoke at once.

'I've just been saying that Walter Howard's new book . . .' she began.

'Did you have an opportunity to look at the trees we've planted?' said Malcolm. Then, as Margaret, blushing, turned her head away, he continued 'We ought really to have more trees down, if this fuel shortage is going to materialize. I'll get on to Bowers about it.'

'Oh not this week, darling' said Margaret 'Mrs Bowers is away with her mother who's ill and young Peter's got flu. Poor Bowers is terribly overworked.'

'Next week then' said Malcolm 'I must say I've never known such a set for illness.'

'Give them an inch and they'll take an ell' said Arthur.

The reiteration of her sister-in-law's phrase enraged Margaret. 'What nonsense you do talk, Arthur' she cried. 'I should have thought the last few months would have taught you some sense.' She blushed scarlet as she realized what she had said, then more gently she added 'You don't know the Bowers. Why Mrs Bowers is the best friend I have round here.'

Arthur felt the old order was on its mettle, he was not prepared to be placated. 'I'm afraid my respect for your precious British workmen has not been increased where I come from' he said defiantly.

'I doubt if you saw the British workman at his best in prison' said Malcolm carefully, and as his brother-in-law was about to continue the argument, he added 'No, Arthur, let's leave it at that—Margaret and I have our own ideas on these things and we're too old to change them now.'

Arthur's defiance vanished. He fingered the knot of his tie and mumbled something about 'respecting them for it'. There was a silence for some minutes, then Malcolm said abruptly 'Where do you plan to go from here?' Arthur was understood to say that he hadn't thought about it.

'I think you should' said Malcolm 'Why don't you go abroad?'

'The colonies?' questioned Arthur with a little laugh.

'I know it's conventional, but why not? You can always count on me if you need any money.'

Arthur did not speak for a moment. Then 'You *want* me to go from here?' he asked. Margaret was determined to fight her own battle, so 'Yes, Arthur' she replied 'You must. It won't do here, we don't fit in together.'

'I doubt if *I* fit in anywhere' Arthur's voice was bitter.

Malcolm would have dispelled the mood with a 'nonsense, old man,' but Margaret again took up the task. 'No, Malcolm, perhaps he's right' suddenly her voice became far away, with a dramatic note. 'When Malcolm was at the Ministry in London during the raids and Rupert was flying over Germany, I had to realize that they might both be killed and then, of course *I* wouldn't have fitted in. I took my precautions. I always carried something that would finish me off quickly if I needed it. Remember, Arthur, if anything should happen I shall always understand and respect you.'

Malcolm looked away, embarrassed. These moments of self-dramatization of Margaret's made him feel that he had married beneath him.

Arthur sat, thinking—the colonies or suicide, neither seemed to be what he was needing.

'Well' he said finally 'I'm very tired, I'll be toddling off to bed, I think. A real long night'll do me good.'

Margaret got up and stroked his hair.

'Ee,' he said 'it's a moocky do, lass, as Nurse used to say.'

This direct appeal to sentiment repelled her 'You'll find whisky and a syphon in your room' she said formally.

'Yes, have a good nightcap' said Malcolm to the erect over-military back of his brother-in-law.

'Thank God that's over' he sighed a few minutes later. 'Poor old Arthur. I expect he'll find happiness sometime, somewhere.'

'No, Malcolm' said Margaret fiercely 'it's been an unpleasant business, but if it's not to turn sour on us, we've got to face it. Arthur will *never* be happy, he's rotten, dead. But we aren't, and if we're going to live, we can't afford to let his rottenness infect us.'

Malcolm stared at his wife with admiration—to face reality, that was obviously the way to meet these things, not to try to escape. He thought for a few minutes of what she had said—of Arthur's rottenness—socially and personally—and of all that they stood for—individually alive, socially progressive. But for all the realism of her view, it somehow did not satisfy him. He remained vaguely uneasy the whole evening.

Cricket in the Caucasus

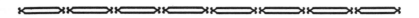

A. P. HERBERT

I

'I TELL YOU what it is, Andrey Andreyevitch,' said Stepan Pepushkin impatiently, 'if the cricket competition does not soon begin it will be dark before it is finished. And then, you know, we shall be hampered by the wolves.'

'What is the hurry?' replied the old man, chewing grass. 'I am too drunk to umpire yet. Natalya Popova cannot find the bats. And, besides, the young men have not yet settled the dispute about the teams.'

'Sometimes,' replied the other passionately, 'I think I see the stars in your old eyes, Andrey Andreyevitch; and sometimes I do not understand you.'

Stepan Pepushkin was a poet. He wore a peaked cap and black knickerbockers. He was eager for the new game, which would bring back poetry to the village, the Commissar had said. 'How can there be a dispute among brothers?' he cried.

'Well, you see, it is perfectly simple,' said the old umpire. 'I think I can stand now. I will get up. What a disgusting creature I am to be drunk on Wednesday! And Olga

Merinin says the harvest will be late. What was I saying, Stepan Stepanovitch?'

'You were raving quietly,' replied the young man. 'There is Natalya, carrying the two bats like torches over her shoulders. How beautiful she is!'

'The young men are quarrelling. Boris Borisovitch has emptied the whitewash pail over Lopakhin; and now we shall have no crease. But all this is highly intelligible when you come to think of it.'

'If I were to kill Maria Andreyevna,' said the poet dreamily, 'would you marry again?'

'Excuse me, the trouble is that our village has been collectivized under the Decree. Everything is in common. We are all in common. We are all brothers. Naturally, therefore, say the young men, we cannot have two teams of brothers playing against each other, for there can be nothing brotherly in trying to get the better of one another. But the Commissar has a paper from Moscow. He says there must be two teams of eleven, each with a captain; but the young men will not have captains. It is all rather unpleasant. I think I shall lie down again.'

'Eleven is a beautiful number,' said the poet. 'Two ones. Two ones—two captains—two bats of forest wood. Some day, Andrey Andreyevitch, I shall go to London where this beautiful game was thought of.'

But the old man was asleep.

Stepan Pepushkin walked over to the debate of the young men. He went straight up to Natalya Popova and kissed her. 'Will you marry me?' he said loudly, because of the noise of the speakers, many of whom were talking in common. She had very brown eyes, like a small cow in springtime. She wore a Tartar skirt and knee-pads for the wicket.

'I think I am engaged to some of the others,' she said. 'Besides, you are a poet, Stepan, and there is no place for poetry now. We should have no food.'

'If I were to write in prose,' said the young man, 'would you love me?'

'Prose is more respectable, to be sure,' said Natalya Popova, 'but, excuse me, every one is active and vigorous now, ploughing and making grain for the State or combating the counter-revolutionaries. You are only a dreamer; Olga Merinin told me she found you feeding nightingales in the wood. What is the use of that when Russia is starving, Stepan Pepushkin? To-day, to take an example, the Committee will not let you take part in the batting. They have appointed you to count the runs. I tell you what is in my mind, Stepan; I am sorry I let you kiss me.'

Stepan smiled dumbly and listened to the speakers.

'Comrades,' shouted Serge Obolensky, the humane slaughterer, 'the solution is evident. We cannot have two hostile teams competing against each other, for this would be to play into the hands of the Capitalist Governments, which seek to divide the workers. But we can all play on the same side.'

'Pravda!' 'Well spoken, Serge!' 'Yashmak!' cried the cricketers.

Big Lubov, the bearded schoolmaster, came to the rostrum carrying a stump. 'I have a proposition.'

'Nitchevo!' 'Chuchuk!' 'A proposition!'

'My proposition is that all runs should be shared in common.'

'Pravda!' 'Yashmak!' 'All runs to be shared in common!'

But Bortsov, the Commissar, stepped forward. 'I have a paper from Moscow. At Moscow they say that you are idle; the grain lies unreaped, the bins are empty.'

'Tchai!' 'Merovestia!' cried the angry villagers.

'Moscow says that the will to compete and act energetically must be born again in you. Therefore they have given you this cricket which the English workers play. Therefore you must have two teams striving for victory, and therefore each worker shall keep his own runs, striving to gain more than his comrade.'

'Kill the Commissar!' cried every one. 'Capitalism!' 'The counter-revolution!'

'I will kill the Commissar!' yelled Big Lubov the

schoolmaster. 'Give me a bat, Natalya Popova,' he said in a softer voice; for Big Lubov loved Natalya.

'There are only two bats,' said the girl, 'and they must be restored to the Government after the game. It would be a pity to break them.'

'*Pravda!*' said Lubov; and he drove the sharp stump which he carried through the Commissar's heart.

'And now let us begin the game,' said the schoolmaster.

II

'Now that we have killed the Commissar,' Serge Obolensky was saying, 'we have no one who can explain the rules of cricket. But Russia is like that.'

'Who wants rules?' said young Nicolai Nicolaievitch. 'Rules were made for the bourgeois.'

'*Pravda.* True. But excuse me, it would be convenient if we could come to some agreement about the method of our proceedings. To take an example, Nicolai Nicolaievitch, we know that there are two sets of stumps, for the Commissar told us so much; but where in the world are we to put them?'

'It is simple enough, Serge Obolensky. We will put one set here and the other over there.'

'Yes, Nicolai,' replied the older man patiently; 'but where?'

'There.'

'I recognize the energy of your mind, Nicolai—but how far away?'

'Give me the Commissar's paper. Twenty-two yards— that is versts. *Cuculin!*' said the young revolutionary in triumph.

'No one in the village can throw a leather ball so far. I tell you what, we will let each man bowl according to his capacity. The strong man shall throw from a great way off and the weak from a little distance. Thus we shall establish equality. Big Lubov, to take an example, must throw at the batsmen from the next field, and I shall throw from here.'

'But,' said the young cynical clerk of the bank, 'suppose

that the strong man pretends to be weak, then he will have an advantage.'

'Then,' said Serge Obolensky simply, 'we shall kill him.'

III

Big Lubov and Natalya Popova were still batting. All the village had bowled the round ball at them, some from this place and some from that. None of the peasants had hit them. Big Lubov defended his body nimbly with his great bat. But the young men did not like to throw the ball at pretty Natalya. They threw it away from her, so that she could not strike it with her bat. So it came about that Lobov had gained seven runs, but pretty Natalya had made none.

Old Volodja's best cow lay in the shade watching the game. Dreamily, sitting on the cow, Stepan Pepushkin wrote the runs in his book. He thought that Natalya was like a tulip.

'Ho, Stepan!' Big Lubov cries, 'how goes the count?'

'Lubov—9 runs,' answers the poet; 'Natalya Popova—7 runs.'

'*Nitchevo!* How is this? Not once has Natalya struck the ball.'

'From time to time I give her a run,' said the poet, 'because she is so beautiful.'

'*Yashmak!*' At first Big Lubov was angry. But he loved Natalya and he shrugged with good temper. When Big Lubov shrugged it was like a storm on the hills. Trees fell down.

'Besides,' said Serge Obolensky cunningly, 'since all the runs are to be shared in common, Lubov Lubovinsky, the question has no significance. Strictly speaking, the count is Lubov—8; Natalya—8.'

'*Botsch!*' shouted the schoolmaster angrily. 'No man or woman shall take *my* runs!' For Lubov had begun to enjoy the cricket, and the will to win was in his great heart, which was shaped like a pear.

'You are a *molak*, Lubov!' cried Nicolai Nicolaievitch. 'Run-hog! *Menshevik!*'

'Bowl, thou,' replied the big man with a threatening motion, 'or I will bat thee.'

Presently Lubov had made 13. Stepan gave Natalya two more runs because of the pretty curve of her waist, which was like a prow of a small ship. Natalya Popova was 9.

Then Alexis the blacksmith took the ball.

Lubov cries out: 'Ho! Blacksmith, you come too close! Stand yonder by Obolensky in the farther field!'

But Alexis throws the ball strong and low and strikes the schoolmaster in the stomach.

'Yashmak!' 'Hit!' 'Lubov is out!' cry the peasants.

'The blow was irregular,' cries the batsman angrily. 'He came too near. What is the verdict, Andrey Andreyevitch?'

All eyes turned to the aged umpire. But the umpire was still asleep.

'He is drunk,' said Serge Obolensky.

'I tell you what,' said Lubov, 'is it not a very extraordinary thing that all the time, while we have been playing this game, the umpire was lying drunk at the place called square-leg, and none of us perceived it?'

'Russia is like that,' said Serge Obolensky. 'My father's sister kept beetles in her bedroom and fed them on sunflower seeds. Nobody knew.'

'Practically speaking,' the schoolmaster remarked logically, 'the game, so far, has not been happening, for the official, in a manner of speaking, was not present. It follows therefore that I am still batting.'

'In that case,' said the cunning Nicolai, 'you have not made 13 runs, but no runs.'

'Pravda!'

Lubov weakened. He thought that none of the peasants would make so many as 13 runs.

'Besides, as you will be the first to appreciate, Lubov Lubovinsky, this umpire is only a mouthpiece for the voice of the people. Indubitably he is incapable; but what of that? The voice of the people has said that you are out.'

'Out!' 'Out!' 'Slava!'

Lubov with a bad grace gave up the bat, saying, 'As for

you, Andrey Andreyevitch, to-night I will give you to the wolves.'

The old man woke. 'The queer thing is, brother,' he said, 'that I have forgotten your name.'

'Russia is like that,' said Serge Obolensky.

'I have just remembered,' said Big Lubov unpleasantly, 'that I have a pistol in my breeches pocket. If any brother or comrade makes more than 13 I will shoot him through the head.'

IV

All the peasants batted in turn and were thrown out. Boris Polunin was stunned. Michael Andrid ran away. Only Natalya Popova remained always at the stumps, Natalya had 11 runs; but Stepan would not give her any more now for fear of Big Lubov's pistol. Alexis the blacksmith had made 7. The others had made nothing. Meanwhile Big Lubov had become exceedingly dogmatic and unpopular. When the last man was out he said, 'Well, it must be evident to all of you that Lubov Lubovinsky has gained the victory.'

The angry shouts of the villagers drowned his speech; and Alexis the blacksmith said, 'Excuse me, the affair is not concluded. Stepan Pepushkin has not yet tried his skill.'

'*Pravda!*' 'Stepan!' 'Pepushkin the poet will put the schoolmaster down.'

They summoned Stepan to the stumps, and gave the ball to Nicolai Nicolaievitch. The young poet was overjoyed to be batting with Natalya. On his way to the stumps he took her in his arms and kissed her.

'Your hair is like the wild jasmine which grows in the Caucasus,' he said. 'Now, Natalya, if I am not mistaken, you are going to see that I am not a dreamer only.'

Nicolai prepared to throw, but the poet stepped forward, lifting his hand. 'Excuse me, Nicolai Nicolaievitch,' he said, 'but, do you know, this is a highly significant moment? Here am I, a young man who never in his whole life has played with bat and ball before. I have never been clever with my hands. At carpentry and needlework I was the duffer of my school. I never could knit or tie up parcels. Truly, I don't know anyone so clumsy with his fingers. I am always dropping my tea-cup, upsetting things, pushing things over. As you see, Nicolai, I am quite unable to tie my cravat in a presentable bow. The only tool I was ever able to use was a lead pencil. And yet—'

'Pardon my abruptness, Stepan Pepushkin,' said Nicolai, 'but if you are going to relate to us the history of your life it seems to me that the fieldsmen had better sit down.'

'That is as you please, Nicolai Nicolaievitch.' And all the peasants sat down on the grass.

'As I was saying,' the batsman continued, 'the extraordinary thing is that here I am with this really most unfamiliar instrument in my hands, and, do you know, I am superbly confident? I am absolutely convinced that I am going to succeed in the game, and gain more runs than this blustering schoolmaster. Is it not remarkable?'

'*Pravda*,' said the bowler, yawning slightly.

'The reason for all this is, I think, perfectly evident. It is Natalya—Natalya Popova, standing there with her Government bat like a torch of a new truth. Now that the Union of Soviet Republics has inscribed cricket upon its advancing banners I think you will agree that we shall conquer the world. Cricket was the one thing that Holy Russia lacked. Cricket will save Russia. Cricket——'

'Excuse me,' Serge Obolensky, rising to his feet at mid-off; 'night is falling, Stepan Pepushkin; the grass is wet with dew, and I perceive that wolves are gathering at the borders of the field. It would be convenient to most of us if we could continue the game.'

'By all means,' answered the poet. 'But do you know, in spite of my confidence it has now occurred to me that men are but mortal and the future is uncertain? It is just possible that Nicolai Nicolaievitch will kill me with the ball. Permit me therefore to embrace Natalya Popova before we begin.'

'Naturally, Stepan Pepushkin.'

This ceremony concluded, the poet prepared to defend himself. Nicolaievitch threw the ball very hard at his head. Stepan put his bat before his face, and the ball, touching it, flew into the forest, scattering the wolves.

'Run, Natalya Popova!' cried the poet, and they ran.

Old Volodja, the long-stop, was fat and slow. They ran nine runs.

The ball was carried back at length, and Stepan, panting, faced Nicolaievitch again.

Big Lubov stepped forward. 'I tell you what,' he bellowed, 'I have just realized that all this business is simply a waste of time. When you come to think of it, there are crops to be garnered, cattle to be tended, cows to be milked. The moon is rising, and here we all are throwing a leather ball at Stepan Pepushkin. Is it not preposterous? What in the world does it matter, I ask myself, whether Stepan gains more runs than Lubov or not? Naturally it is most unlikely that he will overcome me; but will the State be any the better for it if he does? Andrey Andreyevitch is asleep again. Let us all go to the village and drink *tchai*.'

'What you say is extremely reasonable,' said Serge Obolensky, 'but, excuse me, you should have said it before. It is evident that Stepan Pepushkin has a talent for the game, and it would not surprise me if he were to overcome you.'

'*Pravda!*' '*Yashmak!*' cried the peasants, who hated the schoolmaster.

Nicolaievitch threw the ball at Pepushkin's face a second time. The poet struck the ball towards the wood.

'Run, Natalya!'

'I run, Stepan. So thou run also!'

A big wolf runs out of the wood and takes the ball in its mouth.

'Run, Volodja! The wolf has the ball. Follow and help him, Boris Borisovitch!'

The wolf runs into the wood. Volodja runs after the wolf. Boris Borisovitch runs after Volodja. Serge Obolensky runs after Borisovitch. Alexis the blacksmith runs after Obolensky. Olga Merinin runs after Alexis. Nicolai Nicolaievitch runs after Olga Merinin. The other peasants follow; and last of all, Andrey Andreyevitch, waking up, totters into the wood, where the wolves devour him with the others.

Only Big Lubov remains in the field, watching with a sour smile Stepan and Natalya run up and down, hand-in-hand, between the stumps. Stepan has made two-hundred-and-ninety-four. Out of breath, he pauses; Natalya folds her strong arms about him.

'You are a true man, Stepan Pepushkin,' she whispers. 'We will go to Moscow together and make flypapers for the Government.'

But Big Lubov has picked up the Commissar's paper.

'It is all very well,' he says spitefully, 'but, do you know, Pepushkin, we were playing without the bails? Moscow says that without the bails the game does not exist.'

Natalya wept.

'After all, then, Stepan, I find that I do not love you.'

'Russia is like that,' said Stepan Pepushkin.

A Year in Miniature

RUSSELL DAVIES

AS 1980 DREW to a close, bringing with it the end of Second World Olive Oil Year (and conceivably the beginning of Third World Third World Year, or World), I felt that nothing could ever be the same again, or different, or anything. How wrong I was! The events of 1981 have unrolled beneath us like some giant gaudy carpet in eezi-care Strolon, and I for one have frequently felt grateful to be a denizen of a reliably foam-backed society with two-year warranty. Why, was it only last Ascot Week that the Toyota Pipe and Drum Band was formed up in Bonnie Scotland, sending the inaugural strains of 'I Belong to Honshu' winging over the Campsie Fells at little or no cost to the average motorist? Was it just a few short months ago that Demis Roussos, the Warbling Wigwam, went on a diet and lost 7½ stone? It is said that Demis was able to recurtain his entire water-skiing lodge with his old pyjamas; and such was the improvement in his singing that the record company seriously considered putting the hole back in the middle of his LPs, instead of two tactful millimetres off to the side as heretofore. Slimming has been one of the year's success stories. University rector Alfonso Cardau of Valladolid was in the middle of a lecture about his own method this summer, when his trousers fell down. His point was proved.

It has of course been a terrific year for royalty. Every plumber worth his solder must have burst with pride when he learnt that the Prince and Princess of Wales would be honouring, with their wedding, the very onset of International Water Supply and Sanitation Decade. And there was something in it for glaziers, too—for no sooner was the warmer weather with us than King Juan Carlos of Spain fell through a glass door by his swimming pool. POUM! it went. Then the Duchess of Kent appeared at Wimbledon in a 'jewelled neck brace'. ('I suppose you haven't got anything for a jewelled neck?' 'Well I dunno, yer Worship, I got this ole brace, that'll prop it up pro tem, wot you reely want is an Austriopath . . .') But there will no longer be any Beauty Queens in Illinois. Thanks to the Illinois Women's Will Bill, or some such legislation, competitors of this type will now be known as Royal Persons. But there is a widespread feeling that this is one of those innovations that just may not catch on, like the experimental plastic football turf at Royal Person's Park Rangers.

Of the several sensations in the dental world, not the least shattering to the family concerned occurred in Carlisle, where Frank Little was playing pool when he fluked his false teeth into the bottom pocket. There is something unwelcoming about the idea of thrusting your arm down a dark hole in the expectation of finding teeth; so it was some time before a Leisure Appliances Engineer arrived to restore Frank to custodianship of his incisors. Better a long wait, however, than an unseemly grappling for possession, such as occurred this summer in Idabel, Oklahoma, where dentist Curtis Brookover, enraged at the alleged non-payment of false-teeth fees by housewife Mrs Lee Stoval, called on the lady, pinned her to the carpet and actually hauled his property out of her face. When last heard of, she had sued him for assault, he had counter-sued for a bite on the finger, and the whole thing was set for a good few years in court. The law here probably has no teeth either.

Lawsuits were generally worn on the head this year. A man in Bournemouth was mugged and his wig stolen—was it, indeed, a mugging or a wigging?—and Mr Paul Gregory of Burslem went before an industrial tribunal to claim compensation from Arthur Badger Ltd, who had sacked him for turning up to work in a trilby hat trimmed with plastic effigies of Kermit the Frog. Found to be 50% to blame for this career setback, Mr Gregory was awarded the curious sum of £797 which, a friend surmised, he would probably put to appropriate use by honouring the behavioural traditions of the newt family. In Harwich, meanwhile, a Dutch lady was prevented from entering the country on the grounds that she had a rat concealed in her headscarf. How this was discovered was never made clear, unless the rumour is true that her companion was carrying a stool-pigeon up his trouser-leg. The rat and the lady were friends; she had rescued it from an experimental laboratory. HM Customs, however, are no respecters of rodents, and would have destroyed the tragic creature on the spot if it had not cheated the exterminator: with a tiny cry, it leapt upon a VAT form, devoured about half of it, and died in terrible agony.

On the whole, America did poorly out of the last twelve months. The nation lost its hold on our own Lynsey de Paul, who returned to Heathrow insisting that the break-up with James Coburn was not her fault; she had 'leaned over backwards to make sure the relationship was for pure mutual pleasure'. There was a certain technical interest in this for physiologists, who had been wondering what steps had been taken—step-*ladders* even—to compensate for the eighteen inches difference in heights. Ex-President Nixon gave up his Manhattan apartment. A gorgeous place, but costing a fortune to whitewash. Little difficulty in raising the purchase price was experienced by the buyer, Syria. American business failure of the year was the compassionate hot-line phone-in service set up by computer salesman Paul White. 'Curse-aholics Anonymous' was intended to help succour those unfortunates who just can't stop swearing. In his first six weeks of operation, Mr White got 2000 calls, every one of them abusive. When finally even the Tell-the-time machine began to inform him that it was ten o'goddam clock exactly, he gave up. California, in its turn, has had to admit that its water and weather are unsuitable for making seaside rock. That is why Los Angeles has placed an order for one million sticks of 1984 Olympic Rock with the Fylde Coast Confectionery Company of Blackpool. The sticks will have 'Los Angeles 1984' written all through them and profit written all over them and have already been denounced by hard-line Republican dentists as a pinko attack on America's teeth (see above).

Brighton's nude beach celebrated its first anniversary. Mr Tillard, assistant director of Brighton council's resort services department, said, 'The beach has been very well used,' and 'We've had letters from all over the world asking for details.' So if you'd like to know more about how to use a beach well, just get in touch with Mr Tillard. It's just as well to be sure. Some girls went nude bathing in Minorca this summer and were arrested. They pointed out the signs reading 'Nudists Only', and the police pointed out the nearby wartime defence observation post from which the naughty old anthropologists who had put up the signs were watching the whole proceedings through powerful binoculars and a cloud of steam. Yet worse was the experience of Mr Thomas Brady, a company director from Harrow on holiday with four convent-educated daughters (his own). Their first-choice hotel being full, and the second within coughing distance of a cement factory, they finally moved on to a third place, arriving at dead of night. When they awoke to survey the scene from the balcony, they found whole tribes of nudists dangling at them in

accusing fashion. 'When we looked below to the drive,'
reported Mr Brady, 'there were people with nothing on
cleaning their cars.' One must agree that the sight of squeaky
flesh wobbling over a Volvo was probably for fetishists
only. It is to be hoped the Bradys did not get back to
Heathrow in time to witness the incident where an Arab
traveller, overcome by heat, took off his trousers and
underpants in the concourse. You've never seen a terminal
like it—pandemonium everywhere. It took police some
minutes to convince the fellow that, privileged though the
British public was to receive such a rare insight into the
Gulf States, discretion was the better part of Allah.

   Of the year's many mysteries, the most outstanding was
the case of the medical records found dumped in vast
quantities on almost every vast-quantity dump in the land.
Confidential information from these sources must surely
now be in the hands of unscrupulous dustmen. Already it is
rumoured   that   Reginald   Bosanquet   wears   a   Hair
Credibility Augmentation; that Magnus Pyke's insurance
policy incorporates an Arms Limitation Treaty; and that
Her Majesty the Queen Mother's ostrich-feather hats are
actually her hair. But otherwise the medical news is fair.
Mr Roger Thatcher, the Registrar-General (funny the
lines of work the Thatchers have gone into, now we've all
had the sense to get proper roofs) tells us that there are
now 1800 people in this country who are 100 years old or
more. This is not staggering when you consider that
Socrates is still playing football for Brazil, but it's not bad. If
only doctors would get it consistently right. They told poor
Mrs Rosa Sutterby of Wisbech that she had ten years to
live, and this year she died. Mind you, they told her in 1907.
She was 107 when she finally accepted medical advice.

   One thing about the coming year. I think the weather
will improve. God is getting the message, and precipita-
tions are going to be more nourishing again. Some months
ago, a Swedish pastor started bombarding his congregation
with bananas to wake them up, and I think a similar effect
was wrought upon the Almighty: hence the very helpful

showers of Co-op sausages reported this year in the Devonport area. It wouldn't have pleased the Israelites, but it's made Jack Scott and a lot of housewives very happy.

As for 1981, one thing is certain. It will go down in history as one of the years.

Here We Are

DOROTHY PARKER

THE YOUNG MAN in the new blue suit finished arranging
the glistening luggage in tight corners of the Pullman
compartment. The train had leaped at curves and bounced
along straightaways, rendering balance a praiseworthy
achievement and a sporadic one; and the young man had
pushed and hoisted and tucked and shifted the bags with
concentrated care.

Nevertheless, eight minutes for the settling of two
suitcases and a hat-box is a long time.

He sat down, leaning back against bristled green plush,
in the seat opposite the girl in beige. She looked as new as a
peeled egg. Her hat, her fur, her frock, her gloves were
glossy and stiff with novelty. On the arc of the thin,
slippery sole of one beige shoe was gummed a tiny oblong
of white paper, printed with the price set and paid for that
slipper and its fellow, and the name of the shop that had
dispensed them.

She had been staring raptly out of the window, drinking
in the big weathered signboards that extolled the

phenomena of codfish without bones and screens no rust could corrupt. As the young man sat down, she turned politely from the pane, met his eyes, started a smile and got it about half done, and rested her gaze just above his right shoulder.

'Well!' the young man said.

'Well!' she said.

'Well, here we are,' he said.

'Here we are,' she said. 'Aren't we?'

'I should say we were,' he said. 'Eeyop. Here we are.'

'Well!' she said

'Well!' he said. 'Well. How does it feel to be an old married lady?'

'Oh, it's too soon to ask me that,' she said. 'At least—I mean. Well, I mean, goodness, we've only been married about three hours, haven't we?'

The young man studied his wrist-watch as if he were just acquiring the knack of reading time.

'We have been married,' he said, 'exactly two hours and twenty-six minutes.'

'My,' she said. 'It seems like longer.'

'No,' he said. 'It isn't hardly half-past six yet.'

'It seems like later,' she said. 'I guess it's because it starts getting dark so early.'

'It does, at that,' he said. 'The nights are going to be pretty long from now on. I mean. I mean— well, it starts getting dark early.'

'I didn't have any idea what time it was,' she said. 'Everything was so mixed up, I sort of don't know where I am, or what it's all about. Getting back from the church, and then all those people, and then changing all my clothes, and then everybody throwing things, and all. Goodness, I don't see how people do it every day.'

'Do what?' he said.

'Get married,' she said. 'When you think of all the people, all over the world, getting married just as if it was nothing, Chinese people and everybody. Just as if it wasn't anything.'

'Well, let's not worry about people all over the world,'he said. 'Let's don't think about a lot of Chinese. We've got something better to think about. I mean—well, what do we care about them?'

'I know,' she said. 'But I just sort of got to thinking of them, all of them, all over everywhere, doing it all the time. At least, I mean—getting married, you know. And it's—well, it's sort of such a big thing to do, it makes you feel queer. You think of them, all of them, all doing it just like it wasn't anything. And how does anybody know what's going to happen next?'

'Let them worry,' he said. 'We don't have to. We know darn well what's going to happen next. I mean. I mean—well, we know it's going to be great. Well, we know we're going to be happy. Don't we?'

'Oh, of course,' she said. 'Only you think of all the people, and you have to sort of keep thinking. It makes you feel funny. An awful lot of people that get married, it doesn't turn out so well. And I guess they all must have thought it was going to be great.'

'Come on, now,' he said. 'This is no way to start a honeymoon, with all this thinking going on. Look at us—all married and everything done. I mean. The wedding all done and all.'

'Ah, it was nice, wasn't it?' she said. 'Did you really like my veil?'

'You looked great,' he said. 'Just great.'

'Oh, I'm terribly glad,' she said. 'Ellie and Louise looked lovely, didn't they? I'm terribly glad they did finally decide on pink. They looked perfectly lovely.'

'Listen,' he said. 'I want to tell you something. When I was standing up there in that old church waiting for you to come up, and I saw those two bridesmaids, I thought to myself, I thought, "Well, I never knew Louise could look like that!" Why, she'd have knocked anybody's eye out.'

'Oh, really?' she said. 'Funny. Of course, everybody thought her dress and hat were lovely, but a lot of people seemed to think she looked sort of tired. People have been saying that a lot, lately. I tell them I think it's awfully mean of them to go around saying that about her. I tell them they've got to remember that Louise isn't so terribly young any more, and they've got to expect her to look like that. Louise can say she's twenty-three all she wants to, but she's a good deal nearer twenty-seven.'

'Well, she was certainly a knock-out at the wedding,' he said. 'Boy!'

'I'm terribly glad you thought so,' she said. 'I'm glad someone did. How did you think Ellie looked?'

'Why, I honestly didn't get a look at her,' he said.

'Oh, really?' she said. 'Well, I certainly think that's too bad. I don't suppose I ought to say it about my own sister, but I never saw anybody look as beautiful as Ellie looked today. And always so sweet and unselfish, too. And you didn't even notice her. But you never pay attention to Ellie, anyway. Don't think I haven't noticed it. It makes me feel just terrible. It makes me feel just awful, that you don't like my own sister.'

'I do so like her!' he said. 'I'm crazy for Ellie. I think she's a great kid.'

'Don't think it makes any difference to Ellie!' she said. 'Ellie's got enough people crazy about her. It isn't anything to her whether you like her or not. Don't flatter yourself she cares! Only, the only thing is, it makes it awfully hard for me you don't like her, that's the only thing. I keep thinking, when we come back and get in the apartment and everything, it's going to be awfully hard for me that you won't want my own sister to come and see me. It's going to make it awfully hard for me that you won't ever want my family around. I know how you feel about my family. Don't think I haven't seen it. Only, if you don't ever want to see them, that's your loss. Not theirs. Don't flatter yourself!'

'Oh, now, come on!' he said. 'What's all this talk about not wanting your family around? Why, you know how I feel about your family. I think your old lady—I think your mother's swell. And Ellie. And your father. What's all this talk?'

'Well, I've seen it,' she said. 'Don't think I haven't. Lots of people they get married, and they think it's going to be great and everything, and then it all goes to pieces because people don't like people's families, or something like that. Don't tell me! I've seen it happen.'

'Honey,' he said, 'what is all this? What are you getting all angry about? Hey, look, this is our honeymoon. What are you trying to start a fight for? Ah, I guess you're just feeling sort of nervous.'

'Me?' she said. 'What have I got to be nervous about? I mean. I mean, goodness, I'm not nervous.'

'You know, lots of times,' he said, 'they say that girls get kind of nervous and yippy on account of thinking about—I mean. I mean—well, it's like you said, things are all so sort of mixed up and everything, right now. But afterwards, it'll be all right. I mean. I mean—well, look, honey, you don't look any too comfortable. Don't you want to take your hat off? And let's don't ever fight, ever. Will we?'

'Ah, I'm sorry I was cross,' she said. 'I guess I did feel a little bit funny. All mixed up, and then thinking of all those people all over everywhere, and then being sort of 'way off here, all alone with you. It's so sort of different. It's sort of such a big thing. You can't blame a person for thinking, can you? Yes, don't let's ever, ever fight. We won't be like a whole lot of them. We won't fight or be nasty or anything. Will we?'

'You bet your life we won't,' he said.

'I guess I will take this darned old hat off,' she said. 'It kind of presses. Just put it up on the rack, will you, dear? Do you like it, sweetheart?'

'Looks good on you,' he said.

'No, but I mean,' she said, 'do you really like it?'

'Well, I'll tell you,' he said. 'I know this is the new style and everything like that, and it's probably great. I don't know anything about things like that. Only I like the kind of a hat like that blue hat you had. Gee, I liked that hat.'

'Oh, really?' she said. 'Well, that's nice. That's lovely. The first thing you say to me, as soon as you get me off on a train away from my family and everything, is that you don't like my hat. The first thing you say to your wife is you think she has terrible taste in hats. That's nice, isn't it?'

'Now, honey,' he said, 'I never said anything like that. I only said—'

'What you don't seem to realize,' she said, 'is this hat cost twenty-two dollars. Twenty-two dollars. And that horrible old blue thing you think you're so crazy about, that cost three ninety-five.'

'I don't give a darn what they cost,' he said. 'I only said—I said I liked that blue hat. I don't know anything about hats. I'll be crazy about this one as soon as I get used to it. Only it's kind of not like your other hats. I don't know about the new styles. What do I know about women's hats?'

'It's too bad,' she said, 'you didn't marry somebody that would get the kind of hats you'd like. Hats that cost three ninety-five. Why didn't you marry Louise? You always think she looks so beautiful. You'd love her taste in hats. Why didn't you marry her?'

'Ah, now, honey,' he said. 'For heaven's sakes!'

'Why didn't you marry her?' she said. 'All you've done, ever since we got on this train, is talk about her. Here I've sat and sat, and just listened to you saying how wonderful Louise is. I suppose that's nice, getting me all off here alone with you, and then raving about Louise right in front of my face. Why didn't you ask her to marry you? I'm sure she would have jumped at the chance. There aren't so many people asking her to marry them. It's too bad you didn't marry her. I'm sure you'd have been much happier.'

'Listen, baby,' he said, 'while you're talking about things like that, why didn't you marry Joe Brooks? I suppose he could have given you all the twenty-two dollar hats you wanted, I suppose!'

'Well, I'm not so sure I'm not sorry I didn't,' she said. 'There! Joe Brooks wouldn't have waited until he got me all off alone and then sneered at my taste in clothes. Joe Brooks wouldn't ever hurt my feelings. Joe Brooks has always been fond of me. There!'

'Yeah,' he said. 'He's fond of you. He was so fond of you he didn't even send a wedding present. That's how fond of you he was.'

'I happen to know for a fact,' she said, 'that he was away on business, and as soon as he comes back he's going to give me anything I want, for the apartment.'

'Listen,' he said. 'I don't want anything he gives you in our apartment. Anything he gives you, I'll throw right out the window. That's what I think of your friend Joe Brooks. And how do you know where he is and what he's going to do, anyway? Has he been writing to you?'

'I suppose my friends can correspond with me,' she said. 'I didn't hear there was any law against that.'

'Well, I suppose they can't!' he said. 'And what do you think of that? I'm not going to have my wife getting a lot of letters from cheap traveling salesmen!'

'Joe Brooks is not a cheap traveling salesman!' she said. 'He is not! He gets a wonderful salary.'

'Oh yeah?' he said. 'Where did you hear that?'

'He told me so himself,' she said.

'Oh, he told you so himself,' he said. 'I see. He told you so himself.'

'You've got a lot of right to talk about Joe Brooks,' she said. 'You and your friend Louise. All you ever talk about is Louise.'

'Oh, for heaven's sakes!' he said. 'What do I care about Louise? I just thought she was a friend of yours, that's all. That's why I ever even noticed her.'

'Well, you certainly took an awful lot of notice of her today,' she said. 'On our wedding day! You said yourself when you were standing there in the church you just kept thinking of her. Right up at the altar. Oh, right in the presence of God! And all you thought about was Louise.'

'Listen honey,' he said, 'I never should have said that. How does anybody know what kind of crazy things come into their heads when they're standing there waiting to get married? I was just telling you that because it was so kind of crazy. I thought it would make you laugh.'

'I know,' she said. 'I've been all sort of mixed up today, too. I told you that. Everything so strange and everything. And me all the time thinking about all those people all over the world, and now us here all alone, and everything. I know you get all mixed up. Only I did think, when you kept talking about how beautiful Louise looked, you did it with malice and forethought.'

'I never did anything with malice and forethought!' he said. 'I just told you that about Louise because I thought it would make you laugh.'

'Well, it didn't,' she said.

'No, I know it didn't,' he said. 'It certainly did not. Ah, baby, and we ought to be laughing, too. Hell, honey lamb, this is our honeymoon. What's the matter?'

'I don't know,' she said. 'We used to squabble a lot when we were going together and then engaged and everything, but I thought everything would be so different as soon as you were married. And now I feel so sort of strange and everything. I feel so sort of alone.'

'Well, you see, sweetheart,' he said, 'we're not really married yet. I mean. I mean—well, things will be different afterwards. Oh, hell. I mean, we haven't been married very long.'

'No,' she said.

'Well, we haven't got much longer to wait now,' he said. 'I mean—well, we'll be in New York in about twenty minutes. Then we can have dinner, and sort of see what we feel like doing. Or I mean. Is there anything special you want to do tonight?'

'What?' she said.

'What I mean to say,' he said, 'would you like to go to a show or something?'

'Why, whatever you like,' she said. 'I sort of didn't think people went to theaters and things on their—I mean, I've got a couple of letters I simply must write. Don't let me forget.'

'Oh,' he said. 'You're going to write letters tonight?'

'Well, you see,' she said. 'I've been perfectly terrible.

What with all the excitement and everything. I never did thank poor old Mrs Sprague for her berry spoon, and I never did a thing about those book ends the McMasters sent. It's just too awful of me. I've got to write them this very night.'

'And when you've finished writing your letters,' he said, 'maybe I could get you a magazine or a bag of peanuts.'

'What?' she said.

'I mean,' he said, 'I wouldn't want you to be bored.'

'As if I could be bored with you!' she said. 'Silly! Aren't we married? Bored!'

'What I thought,' he said, 'I thought when we got in, we could go right up to the Biltmore and anyway leave our bags, and maybe have a little dinner in the room, kind of quiet, and then do whatever we wanted. I mean. I mean—well, let's go right up there from the station.'

'O, yes, let's,' she said. 'I'm so glad we're going to the Biltmore. I just love it. The twice I've stayed in New York we've always stayed there, Papa and Mamma and Ellie and I, and I was crazy about it. I always sleep so well there. I go right off to sleep the minute I put my head on the pillow.'

'Oh, you do?' he said.

'At least, I mean,' she said. ' 'Way up high it's so quiet.'

'We might go to some show or other tomorrow night instead of tonight,' he said. 'Don't you think that would be better?'

'Yes, I think it might,' he said.

He rose, balanced a moment, crossed over and sat down beside her.

'Do you really have to write those letters tonight?' he said.

'Well,' she said, 'I don't suppose they'd get there any quicker than if I wrote them tomorrow.'

There was a silence with things going on in it.

'And we won't ever fight any more, will we?' he said.

'Oh, no,' she said. 'Not ever! I don't know what made me do like that. It all got so sort of funny, sort of like a nightmare, the way I got thinking of all those people getting married all the time; and so many of them, everything spoils on account of fighting and everything. I got all mixed up thinking about them. Oh, I don't want to be like them. But we won't be, will we?'

'Sure we won't,' he said.

'We won't go all to pieces,' she said. 'We won't fight. It'll all be different, now we're married. It'll all be lovely. Reach me down my hat, will you, sweetheart? It's time I was putting it on. Thanks. Ah, I'm so sorry you don't like it.'

'I do so like it!' he said.

'You said you didn't,' she said. 'You said you thought it was perfectly terrible.'

'I never said any such thing,' he said. 'You're crazy.'

'All right, I may be crazy,' she said. 'Thank you very much. But that's what you said. Not that it matters—it's just a little thing. But it makes you feel pretty funny to think you've gone and married somebody that says you have perfectly terrible taste in hats. And then goes and says you're crazy, beside.'

'Now, listen here,' he said. 'Nobody said any such thing. Why, I love that hat. The more I look at it the better I like it. I think it's great.'

'That isn't what you said before,' she said.

'Honey,' he said. 'Stop it, will you? What do you want to start all this for? I love the damned hat. I mean, I love your hat. I love anything you wear. What more do you want me to say?'

'Well, I don't want you to say it like that,' she said.

'I said I think it's great,' he said. 'That's all I said.'

'Do you really?' she said. 'Do you honestly? Ah, I'm so glad. I'd hate you not to like my hat. It would be—I don't know, it would be sort of such a bad start.'

'Well, I'm crazy for it,' he said. 'Now we've got that settled, for heaven's sakes. Ah, baby. Baby lamb. We're not going to have any bad starts. Look at us—we're on our honeymoon. Pretty soon we'll be regular old married

people. I mean. I mean, in a few minutes we'll be getting in
to New York, and then we'll be going to the hotel, and then
everything will be all right. I mean—well, look at us! Here
we are married! Here we are!'

   'Yes, here we are,' she said. 'Aren't we?'

The Wild Life of Suburbia

RICHARD GORDON

SUBURBIA IS BEAUTIFUL. You can tell from the advertisements.

The houses are beautified with satin-finished craftsmen-fitted double-glazed picture windows. They contain beautiful things, like reproduction oak-stained old country plant stands, and a set of Currier and Ives porcelain Christmas bells.

The cars are beautiful, buffed every Sunday with the savagery of a dentist scaling teeth. So are the people, scoured in the sauna, swaddled in Thermolactyl, wearing beautiful quartz watches with 50 functions including alarm facility and lap timer, tippling beautifully tinted drinks from personalized Edwardian goblets, and holidaying in beautiful places with their beautiful 5-piece saddle-stitched light tan wipe-clean vinyl luggage collection.

Even the books are beautiful, designed to be part of the furniture of life with an introduction by Dr A. L. Rowse.

The suburban countryside in which I live is superb—pH tested, cleansed with paraquat dichloride and diquat dibromide, nourished like a sickly child on glyphosate, benomyl, dinocap, formothion, buprimate and chealated manganese. By comparison, that shrinking open space between the end of one city's suburbs and the start of the next, slashed by motorways, ravaged by chain-saw and bulldozer, lethal with pesticides, is as inhospitable to animal fur and feather as the polar icecap to human skin and bone.

Wildlife is flocking after mankind to the comfort and convenience of the suburbs. Only in such soft security can it survive. Darwin rules, OK?

My South London suburb already supports an endogenous fauna of gerbils, goldfish, cats, dogs and children.

The gerbil, ever-whirring on its little metal treadmill, symbolizes suburban man's scuttle through life, reaching nowhere until one morning he too is found cold in his cage. The goldfish swim lazily in their ponds beside the crazy paving, under the ineffective fishing rods of the gnomes, indicating his frustration at ever hooking life's glittering prizes, even those from the football pools.

Suburban man fondles the cat to enjoy the purring sensuousness he no longer receives from suburban woman, except after ladies' night at the Rotary. All suburban dogs suffer Freudian anal eroticism, from enforced constipation under the council by-laws concerning footpaths.

Children are the best trained suburban pets. Suburban mothers distrust natural instincts like natural fibres, and rear their young according to a book by a millionaire doctor living in America. The parents later insist, on pain of fierce punishment, their offspring be honest, truthful and sexually continent, because they so despairingly wish they were themselves.

Upon this ecology have crept hedgehogs, weasels, stoats, grass snakes, squirrels, moles, badgers, and brown-shelled Roman snails (taking some time from their habitat in the Cotswolds—they can be baked stuffed with garlic butter, though less to suburban taste than tinned gazpacho).

From the colour aerials, the moping owl complains to the moon. The collar-dove mimics the cuckoo, causing frenzied writing to the local newspapers in early spring. The repetitive song-thrush maddens anyone foolish enough to install the GPO's new style bird-call telephone. We suburbanites are the world's conservationists, without needing to create all the self-righteous fuss of Greenpeace.

The scent which invigorated Mr Jorrocks and inflames the Anti-Blood Sports League blows through bedroom windows opened upon a new suburban day. The fox is our most interesting and subtle invader. I see one vixen regularly, curled asleep on the recliner left overnight on the patio. She expects a petit beurre from the Teasmade, before loping languidly through the laurels to stare hungrily towards the neighbours' breakfast bar, in hope of a tossed bacon rind or handful of Special K.

So wily an animal sees no need to seek its usual menu of pheasant and fowl, rabbit and rat, when prepacked convenience food is so abundant. A crash between carport and oil-tank proclaims the view of a fox as stridently as John Peel's horn in the morning. Reynard has broken from his herbaceous covert to tip over the rubbish bin and rummage for a balanced diet.

My memoirs of a suburban fox-hunting man include the discovery after a dinner party of scattered avocado skin and prawn shells, clean-picked, crunched bones from the frozen duck, a chewed carton of bright pink strawberry mousse among scraps of silver paper from the dolcelatte. Our Beaujolais Villages drained of its dregs, the panatella ends from the ashtray, the disappearance of an After Eight squashed under the heel of an unsteady guest, indicated the completed enjoyment of a meal of civilized delicacy.

The earths of *canis vulpes suburbanensis* are securer than those of its country cousins, which are always likely to be trodden by keepers or ramblers. Ours inhabit cuttings where man dare not venture without fear of prosecution by British Rail. Dog, vixen and cubs are often displayed in the morning sunshine, comfortable among the scraggy bushes and disposed prams, fridges and pieces of cars, enjoying the ludicrous sight of humans packed into trains like battery hens. Suburban foxes are not simply tame towards man. They are also damn supercilious.

One pads amongst the azaleas and rhodos in our floodlit garden at night, staring through the lounge windows to watch the *News at Ten*. I would not boast that it takes an intelligent interest in the affairs of the human world. More likely, it just wants to see the weather forecast. An American Express card lost from the garden furniture is probably pledging my credit at Harrods' game counter. When my Nino Cerruti aftershave crashed from the bathroom windowsill, a fox appeared and rolled in it. The animals are becoming as beautiful as the people. Last autumn, our open sports car rolled from the garage and decimated the topiary opposite. From the rank stink, a fox had jumped in and released the handbrake. They will soon learn to drive, which could be useful in getting the children to school.

In the suburbs of New York they have raccoons as we have foxes.

Foxhunting in suburbia is performed by the council, on the Hitlerian principle of gassing anything assessed as distasteful or unnecessary. The men in white suits with their little van are clearly ineffective, because the suburban fox population is increasing with the confident fecundity of the human one.

The Masters of Foxhounds Association is as right as honest in its belief of hunting as a vulpine contraceptive. We have the ingredients for a meet. Our local livery stable offers a string of serviceable horses upon which suburban children in hard hats dream of Princess Anne. We could conscript a pack of hounds—lively and disciplined, if varied. A visit to Moss Bros is the remaining necessity. A stirrup cup at the local and away through the morning rush-hour, with a new set of hunting calls to cover such eventualities as *Gone To Earth Wrong Way Up One-Way Street.*

The fox has immutable snob value. Ours never molest the semi-dets and split-levels. They roam only the backyards of desirable residences, with heated garages for frosty mornings, deafening stereo equipment, video recording systems incorporating remote control slow-down capacity, four brands of malt whisky, tailored-made kitchens, a Volvo as well as a Mercedes, perpetual motion Black Forest clocks, finely-tooled leather executive cases, detachable suite covers, matching made-to-measure curtains, water softener, personal stationery on luxurious watermarked paper and floral dreamy duvets.

I am gratified that my suburban home has the distinction of emitting a better class of garbage.

The Tooth

ROBERT BENCHLEY

SOME WELL-KNOWN saying (it doesn't make much difference what) is proved by the fact that everyone likes to talk about his experiences at the dentist's. For years and years little articles like this have been written on the subject, little jokes like some that I shall presently make have been made, and people in general have been telling other people just what emotions they experience when they crawl into the old red plush guillotine.

They like to explain to each other how they feel when the dentist puts 'that buzzer thing' against their bicuspids, and, if sufficently pressed, they will describe their sensations on mouthing a rubber dam.

'I'll tell you what I hate,' they will say with great relish, 'when he takes that little nut-pick and begins to scrape. Ugh!'

'Oh, I'll tell you what's worse than that,' says the friend, not to be outdone, 'when he is poking around careless-like, and strikes a nerve. Wow!'

And if there are more than two people at the experience-meeting, everyone will chip in and tell what he or she considers to be the worst phase of the dentist's work, all present enjoying the narration hugely and none so much as the narrator who has suffered so.

This sort of thing has been going on ever since the first mammoth gold tooth was hung out as a bait to folks in search of a good time. (By the way, when *did* the present obnoxious system of dentistry begin? It can't be so very long ago that the electric auger was invented, and where would a dentist be without an electric auger? Yet you never hear of Amalgam Filling Day, or any other anniversary in the dental year. There must be a conspiracy of silence on the part of the trade to keep hidden the names of the men who are responsible for all this.)

However many years it may be that dentists have been plying their trade, in all that time people have never tired of talking about their teeth. This is probably due to the inscrutable workings of Nature who is always supplying new teeth to talk about.

As a matter of fact, the actual time and suffering in the chair is only a fraction of the gross expenditure connected with the affair. The preliminary period, about which nobody talks, is much the worse. This dates from the discovery of the wayward tooth and extends to the moment when the dentist places his foot on the automatic hoist which jacks you up into range. Giving gas for tooth-extraction is all very humane in its way, but the time for anaesthetics is when the patient first decides that he must go to the dentist. From then on, until the first excavation is started, should be shrouded in oblivion.

There is probably no moment more appalling than that in which the tongue, running idly over the teeth in a moment of care-free play, comes suddenly upon the ragged edge of a space from which the old familiar filling has disappeared. The world stops and you look meditatively up to the corner of the ceiling. Then quickly you draw your tongue away, and try to laugh the affair off, saying to yourself:

'Stuff and nonsense, my good fellow! There is nothing the matter with your tooth. Your nerves are upset after a hard day's work, that's all.'

Having decided this to your satisfaction, you slyly, and with a poor attempt at being casual, slide the tongue back along the line of adjacent teeth, hoping against hope that it will reach the end without mishap.

But there it is! There can be no doubt about it this time. The tooth simply has got to be filled by someone, and the only person who can fill it with anything permanent is a dentist. You wonder if you might not be able to patch it up yourself for the time being—a year or so—perhaps with a little spruce-gum and a coating of new-skin. It is fairly far back, and wouldn't have to be a very sightly job.

But this has an impracticable sound, even to you. You might want to eat some peanut-brittle (you never can tell when someone might offer you peanut-brittle these days), and the new-skin, while serviceable enough in the case of cream soups and custards, couldn't be expected to stand up under heavy crunching.

So you admit that, since the thing has got to be filled, it might as well be a dentist who does the job.

This much decided, all that is necessary is to call him up and make an appointment.

Let us say this resolve is made on Tuesday. That afternoon you start to look up the dentist's number in the telephone book. A great wave of relief sweeps over you when you discover that it isn't there. How can you be expected to make an appointment with a man who hasn't got a telephone? And how can you have a tooth filled without making an appointment? The whole thing is impossible, and that's all there is to it. God knows you did your best.

On Wednesday there is a slightly more insistent twinge, owing to bad management of a sip of ice water. You decide that you simply must get in touch with that dentist when you get back from lunch. But you know how those things are. First one thing and then another came up, and a man came in from Providence who had to be shown around the office, and by the time you had a minute to yourself it was five o'clock. And, anyway, the tooth didn't bother you again. You wouldn't be surprised if, by being careful, you could get along with it as it is until the end of the week when you will have more time. A man has to think of his business, after all, and what is a little personal discomfort in the shape of an unfilled tooth to the satisfaction of work well done in the office?

By Saturday morning you are fairly reconciled to going ahead, but it is only a half day and probably he has no appointments left, anyway. Monday is really the time. You can begin the week afresh. After all, Monday is really the logical day to start in going to the dentist.

Bright and early Monday morning you make another try at the telephone book, and find, to your horror, that some time between now and last Tuesday the dentist's name and number have been inserted into the directory. There it is. There is no getting around it: 'Burgess, Jas. Kendal, DDS. . . . Courtland—2654.' There is really nothing left to do but to call him up. Fortunately the line is busy, which gives you a perfectly good excuse for putting it over until Tuesday. But on Tuesday luck is against you and you get a clear connection with the doctor himself. An appointment is arranged for Thursday afternoon at 3.30.

Thursday afternoon, and here it is only Tuesday morning! Almost anything may happen between now and then. We might declare war on Mexico, and off you'd have to go, dentist appointment or no dentist appointment. Surely a man couldn't let a date to have a tooth filled stand in the way of his doing his duty to his country. Or the social revolution might start on Wednesday, and by Thursday the whole town might be in ashes. You can picture yourself standing, Thursday afternoon at 3.30, on the ruins of the City Hall, fighting off marauding bands of reds, and saying to yourself, with a sigh of relief: 'Only to think! At this time I was to have been climbing into the dentist's chair!' You never can tell when your luck will turn in a thing like that.

But Wednesday goes by and nothing happens. And Thursday morning dawns without even a word from the dentist saying that he has been called suddenly out of town to lecture before the Incisor Club. Apparently, everything is working against you.

By this time, your tongue has taken up a permanent resting place in the vacant tooth, and is causing you to talk indistinctly and incoherently. Somehow you feel that if the dentist opens your mouth and finds the tip of your tongue in the tooth, he will be deceived and go away without doing anything.

The only thing left is for you to call him up and say that you have just killed a man and are being arrested and can't possibly keep your appointment. But any dentist would see through that. He would laugh right into his transmitter at you. There is probably no excuse which it would be possible to invent which a dentist has not already heard eighty or ninety times. No, you might as well see the thing through now.

Luncheon is a ghastly rite. The whole left side of your jaw has suddenly developed an acute sensitiveness and the disaffection has spread to the four teeth on either side of the original one. You doubt if it will be possible for him to touch it at all. Perhaps all he intends to do this time is to look at it anyway. You might even suggest that to him. You could very easily come in again soon and have him do the actual work.

Three-thirty draws near. A horrible time of day at best. Just when a man's vitality is lowest. Before stepping in out of the sunlight into the building in which the dental parlour is, you take one look about you at the happy people scurrying by in the street. Carefree children that they are! What do they know of Life? Probably that man in the silly-looking hat never had trouble with so much as his baby teeth. There they go, pushing and jostling each other, just as if within ten feet of them there was not a man who stands on the brink of the Great Misadventure. Ah well! Life is like that!

Into the elevator. The last hope is gone. the door clangs and you look hopelessly about you at the stupid faces of your fellow passengers. How can people be so clownish? Of course, there is always the chance that the elevator will fall and that you will all be terribly hurt. But that is too much to expect. You dismiss it from your thoughts as too impractical, too visionary. Things don't work out as happily as that in real life.

You feel a certain glow of heroic pride when you tell the operator the right floor number. You might just as easily have told him a floor too high or too low, and that would, at least, have caused delay. But after all, a man must prove himself a man and the least you can do is to meet Fate with an unflinching eye and give the right floor number.

Too often has the scene in the dentist's waiting room been described for me to try to do it again here. They are all alike. The antiseptic smell, the ominous hum from the operating rooms, the ancient *Digests*, and the silent, sullen group of waiting patients, each trying to look unconcerned and cordially disliking everyone else in the room—all these have been sung by poets of far greater lyric powers than mine. (Not that I really think that they *are* greater than mine, but that's the customary form of excuse for not writing something you haven't got time or space to do. As a matter of fact, I think I could do it much better than it has ever been done before.)

I can only say that, as you sit looking, with unseeing eyes, through a large book entitled *The War in Pictures*, you would gladly change places with the most lowly of God's creatures. It is inconceivable that there should be anyone worse off than you, unless perhaps it is some of the poor wretches who are waiting with you.

That one over in the arm-chair, nervously tearing to shreds a copy of *The Dental Review and Practical Inlay Worker*. She may have something frightful the trouble with her. She couldn't possibly look more worried. Perhaps it is very, very painful. This thought cheers you up considerably. What cowards women are in times like these!

And then there comes the sound of voices from the next room.

'All right, Doctor, and if it gives me any more pain shall I call you up? . . . Do you think that it will bleed much more? . . . Saturday morning, then, at eleven . . . Goodbye, Doctor.'

And a middle-aged woman emerges (all women are middle-aged when emerging from the dentist's office) looking as if she were playing the big emotional scene in *John Ferguson*. A wisp of hair waves dissolutely across her forehead between her eyes. Her face is pale, except for a slight inflammation at the corners of her mouth, and in her eyes is that far-away look of one who has been face to face with Life. But she is through. She should care how she looks.

The nurse appears, and looks inquiringly at each one in the room. Each one in the room evades the nurse's glance in one last, futile attempt to fool someone and get away without seeing the dentist. But she spots you and nods pleasantly. God, how pleasantly she nods! There ought to be a law against people being as pleasant as that.

'The doctor will see you now,' she says.

The English language may hold a more disagreeable combination of words than 'The doctor will see you now.' I am willing to concede something to the phrase 'Have you anything to say before the current is turned on.' That may be worse for the moment, but it doesn't last so long. For continued, unmitigating depression, I know nothing to equal 'The doctor will see you now.' But I'm not narrow-minded about it. I'm willing to consider other possibilities.

Smiling feebly, you trip over the extended feet of the man next to you, and stagger into the delivery room, where amid a ghastly array of death masks of teeth, blue flames waving eerily from Bunsen burners, and the drowning sound of perpetually running water which chokes and gurgles at intervals, you sink into the chair and close your eyes.

But now let us consider the spiritual exaltation that comes when you are at last let down and turned loose. It is all over, and what did it amount to? Why, nothing at all. A-ha-ha-ha-ha-ha! Nothing at all.

You suddenly develop a particular friendship for the dentist. A splendid fellow, really. You ask him questions about his instruments. What does he use this thing for, for instance? Well, well, to think of a little thing like that making all that trouble. A-ha-ha-ha-ha-ha! . . . And the dentist's family, how are they? Isn't that fine!

Gaily you shake hands with him and straighten your tie. Forgotten is the fact that you have another appointment with him for Monday. There is no such thing as Monday. You are through for to-day, and all's right with the world.

As you pass out through the waiting room, you leer at the others unpleasantly. The poor fishes! Why can't they take their medicine like grown people and not sit there moping as if they were going to be shot?

Heigh-ho! Here's the elevator man! A charming fellow! You wonder if he knows that you have just had a tooth filled. You feel tempted to tell him and slap him on the back. You feel tempted to tell everyone out in the bright, cheery street. And what a wonderful street it is too! All full of nice, black snow and water. After all, Life is sweet!

And then you go and find the first person whom you can accost without being arrested and explain to him just what it was that the dentist did to you, and how you felt, and what you have got to have done next time.

Which brings us right back to where we were in the beginning, and perhaps accounts for everyone's liking to divulge their dental secrets to others. It may be a sort of hysterical relief that, for the time being, it is all over with.

Grand Tour 2000

E. S. TURNER

THE RICKSHAWMAN who took me from Boulogne to Le Touquet, some ten miles distant, was an idle old rascal, for ever grumbling about the head wind and making excuses to stop and light up a Gauloise. His curiosity about the purpose of my travels was intense; and when I told him that I was bound for the People's Republic of Italy he let go of the shafts and crossed himself, pitching me headlong on to the *chausée deformée*.

The torpor of the Age of Leisure lay heavy on the countryside. Although it is the custom to lie abed until noon, as in England, the people look utterly drained. All the eating-places bore notices saying *Fermé: Jour de Repos*; but French eating-places always did.

In Le Touquet I booked in at the once-palatial Westminster Hotel. Here, until the world's oil ran out, Rolls-Royces and Lagondas used to be parked six deep. It is now a 'religious house'; that is to say, it is run by a colony of sebaceous young Californians practising their cult of universal massage. After one or two misunderstandings I slept in a field.

The luxury shops in the forest, formerly filled with *objets de grande luxe*, were stuffed with the ubiquitous electronic trash with which people now beguile their idleness. An avalanche victim detector bore a label *'Pour l'enfant'*.

Horse-drawn stage-coaches are few and hideously expensive. I travelled to Tours by one of the 'auto-drive' rail-cars, paying a hairy member of the Lost Generation to operate the other end of the rocker-arm. He told a pathetic story of how he had left his four children to look for some institution to subvert, but could not face the fact that everything had been subverted already. For hours we sweated through a dismal landscape to tumbledown fun centres, sacked theme parks, recreation areas like wildernesses, wilderness camps like nothing on earth, abandoned safarilands, dude concentration camps—the residue of a bold experiment designed to occupy the waking energies of the workers made redundant by technology. But the population had rapidly wearied of these 'facilities'. Most had sunk into sloth, the rest into the black economy.

The peasants, of course, continue to till their fields, fatuously chatting to each other by walkie-talkie when they could just as easily communicate direct. Nothing is more ridiculous than an old woman beeping and bleeping away as she piles up the beetroots.

What extraordinary riffraff one meets on the Grand Tour: knaves peddling locks of Margaret Thatcher's hair; jolly Senegalese with huge back packs full of old Barclaycards, which they are convinced are of untold value; quacks with pills to cure the craving for employment; itinerant spoon-benders from Israel; Arab mendicants who once flew their own Learjets; dreadful old hags left over from the sexist wars; fugitives from psychodrama workshops; sock-sniffers, lost in a world of their own; youths of twenty with their brains already addled by music; embittered thesis-writers thrown on the streets when sorely-tired nations rose up against the universities . . .

In the old airport at Lyons, which like all airports now serves as a general caravanserai, I met the legendary Wild Boy of the Camargue, today's nearest approach to a Noble Savage. Abandoned by his parents, he had been brought up from infancy by a roving herd of sociologists and was thus unable to communicate intelligibly or to distinguish right from wrong. The Wild Boy took my hand with a smile of unearthly innocence and then bit my fingers to the bone.

Near Vittel in the Vosges I had my first good meal in an institution I had never hoped to see: a Michelin 4-star restaurant. It is kept going by factory executives from La Vallée des Usines, where privileged workers turn out electronic baubles round the clock. The sight of the workshops ablaze with lights all night is like something from the mid-twentieth century.

The executives have their own spa where their livers are serviced. Most of the other spas in these parts are over-run by religious cultists. Some of them have seized the demilitarised citadels on the Meuse and the Rhine, from which they descend to raid the trout pools and the frog farms, even attempting to levy tithes on the peasants' crops. Others rise up from old Maginot forts to seize women for brain-washing and worse.

Switzerland at last! As I feared, the country is like a shabby adventure playground, with a Tellorama wherever one turns. The authorities have even revived an ancient practice, once condemned by Ruskin, of inviting travellers to fire off howitzers in order to set echoes rolling among the peaks. Does not this start off avalanches? I enquired. So much the better, was the unfeeling reply; then families can try out their electronic avalanche victim detectors, which are such fun to use. I shuddered. Now that the Toll of the Road is no more, there is a deadly craving everywhere for accidents.

The British Consul in Geneva said I was the first British traveller to call on him for five years. His grandfather, he said, had once met Guy Burgess and wished he hadn't. He then affixed a note to the door reading *Fermé: Jour de Repos* and closed it in my face.

On the Italian border, above Domodossola, was all the disagreeable apparatus of a People's Republic: watch towers, barbed wire, minefields, road blocks. But it was at once obvious that the Italians, those children of Nature, lacked the surliness to operate this nonsense effectively; and fortunately the Soviet Union, now the Sick Man of Europe, lacks the will to put pressure on its satellites. I had expected my books to be denounced as pornographic; instead, the smiling Carabinieri tried to sell me Swedish magazines. I had expected to be issued with coupons for meals and to be directed to a bugged bedroom. But I was courteously told that, if I had been fool enough to come this far, they would not dissuade me from the folly of continuing, and that I could do as I wished.

From the frontier I descended the Alps by Basket Trail. It is an idea borrowed from Funchal, Madeira and one simply slides down the foothills in a succession of wicker sledges, through avenues of beggars, stoned by *bambini*, pillaged by snatch-thieves and yapped at by dogs. At one point I slithered under a motorway viaduct on which a linear town had been built and the townsfolk cheerfully pelted me with refuse.

As in the Soviet Union, the grand hotels, especially in the thermal establishments, are occupied by the common people. The menfolk, however, instead of recovering from the supposed fulfilment of norms, are treated for the stresses of unemployment. It is something we shall yet see in England.

I had hoped to view many Old Masters in Italy, but they

have long since been smuggled out to the rapacious auction-houses. To its shame, the Uffizi Gallery in Florence could muster only a few old Pirelli calendars. But Florence still attracts English aesthetes, to judge from the lissom high tenors thronging the Ponte Vecchio.

How superb is Rome without its motor traffic, even if the quarrelling rickshawmen are the scum of Europe. I followed faded signs reading 'To The Atheist Museum' and soon found myself at the Vatican. The Pope had long since returned, in defiance of the Kremlin, and I was privileged to see him on the balcony, flanked by very old pictures of Lenin and Marx to which I fancied he made a somewhat unpapal gesture when blessing the crowd. At all events a solemn titter ran through the throng. The Pontiff took the opportunity to rebuke those of his audience who still wore jeans, despite proven evidence down the generations that these constricting garments are destructive of human fertility.

That night the city celebrated its Festival of Pandemonium. The combined tumult of electronic music-makers, massed carillons, rickshawmen's klaxons, burglar alarms, anti-rape screechers and howling briefcases was fully worthy of the Infernal City in its motorised prime. I was glad I had made my way there and I could not wait to leave.

Don Carlo

ANTHONY BURGESS

THE LIBRETTO, as far as I could tell with my small Italian, was wordy but sound. There are very few plots available to the librettist—or to the novelist for that matter—and Ricciardelli's was the one that found its best expression in *Romeo and Juliet*. The title was Pirandello-like: *I Poveri Ricchi*. The Corvi are rich and the Gufi are poor. Gianni Gufo loves Rosalba Corvo. The Corvi forbid marriage. Old Man Corvo loses his money, and Old Man Gufo is left a fortune by a forgotten uncle in America. Now the Gufi forbid marriage. Old Man Corvo nevertheless gets drunk with Old Man Gufo and the two become friendly. Corvo offers to invest Gufo's fortune for him, and Gufo says yes. Corvo's scheme fails, and both families are now poor. The boy and girl may marry with everybody's halfhearted blessing. But Gianni and Rosalba are now so accustomed to clandestine trysts that they lose interest in each other when they are free to kiss in the open. So the two families (and this was stolen from Rostand) pretend a great enmity which they no longer feel and the lovers love each other again. Telegrams arrive speaking of restored fortunes for both families. Embraces, bells, wine, curtain. This story had to be put across in seventy minutes, with the terrace of the Corvo house overlooking a piazza full of choral market stallholders. Ricciardelli's lyrics and recitative were far too wordy and overbrimmed with poetic colour: leave colour to the music. Domenico needed a greater variety of forms—trios, quartets, quintets as well as duets—and he needed the pithiness which an admirer of D'Annunzio could not easily provide. Indeed, he needed what I was not—a new da Ponte.

I worked not in Nice but in Monaco, in the Condamine on the rue Grimaldi. I had a bare and airy topfloor apartment rented, on a six-months lease, from a M. Guizot who was visiting Valparaiso. When I had finished the first draft I telegraphed Domenico in, or just outside, Taormina. He came. I hired a piano, a tinny Gaveau. He stayed. We ended with two versions of the libretto, one in Tuscan, the other in a kind of American with the title *The Richer the Poorer*. I learned a lot of Italian. He learned something about English prosody. He began to dream of doing something popular for the New York stage. He had no strongly individual musical style but could imitate anybody. This opera was mainly in the style of late Puccini, with acerbities stolen from Stravinsky. It had a ragtime sequence and a drunken duet. A drunken quartet would not fit into the narrative pattern, but the finale was loud and vinous.

While Domenico warbled and struck chords on the wretched Gaveau in the long bare salon, I worked on my novel two rooms away. This was *The Wounded*, about the legless man coming back from the war (poor Rodney) and nobly trying to make his betrothed marry another, a whole man. But his betrothed is blinded in a car accident and the whole man who has fancied her no longer does so. So the two maimed marry and live happily and beget limbed and sighted children. This sounds worse than it really is, though, *pace* Don Carlo Campanati, it is still pretty stupid. What I was trying to do at that time was, in a sense,

Shakespearian. I was taking a story that could not fail to be popular, especially when adapted to the screen, as *The Wounded* was in 1925, and attempting to elevate it through wit, allusion and irony to something like art.

And all during this time I lived a loveless life. Domenico, without my telling him, divined quickly what and how I was and regretted that he could not help. He took the train to Ventimiglia once a week, sometimes twice, and came back looking rested. I for my part bitterly masturbated, sometimes seeing, as I approached climax, the figure of Don Carlo spooning in soup and shaking his head sadly. I tried to purge some of the rage of my loneliness in housework and cooking, though Domenico was a better cook than I and an old woman came in to clean three times a week. Friends, we were friends, he said, as well as brothers in art, but—ah, that kind of love seemed to him, if I would forgive him saying so, an abomination.

When Don Carlo came from Paris to stay with us for two days, I looked guiltily at him, as though his image had been a real presence. He had come, he said, when he had done panting from the long climb to the top storey, to play roulette.

'Is that,' I asked, getting him a whisky with a little water, 'permitted? To a priest, that is?'

'The first shareholders of the Casino,' he said, 'were the Bishop of Monaco and Cardinal Pecci. And you know what Cardinal Pecci became.'

'Pope Leo the Thirteenth,' Domenico said.

'We must exorcize the puritan in you,' Don Carlo said, roguishly wagging his whisky at me without spilling a drop. 'You think there is something irreligious about gambling. But it is only the opposing of one free will to another—'

'Talking of exorcism,' I said. 'Domenico promised that you would tell me the whole story. About this boy in Sardinia possessed by devils or what ever they were—'

'Domenico has no right to promise anything on my behalf. It's of no interest to you, who would not believe it anyway.'

'What right have you to say what I believe and what I do not?' I asked, and that made him grunt as at a light blow struck at an ailing liver. He said:

'It is a thing I do. Indeed, any priest. But some do it better than others. Some take a chance.'

'What do you mean—a chance?'

'You bring me back to what I was trying to say. One free will against another—that of the player, that of the little white ball on the big wheel—'

'You mean that figuratively? You mean an inanimate object can really have free will? What *do* you mean?'

'I am rebuked. You must soften the rebuke with more whisky.' I took his empty glass. 'I mean,' he said, while I poured, 'that what cannot be predicted looks very much like free will. I meant no more than that. I need,' he said to his brother, 'a necktie. I must go in as one of the laity. I must not scandalize the faithful. It is bad enough,' chuckling, 'to scandalize the faithless.'

'Me? You mean me?' I said, giving him his fresh whisky.

'Why not you? You are not of the Church. You are not one of the faithful. Ergo you are one of the faithless. Does that annoy you?'

'I would,' I said sadly, 'be one of the faithful if I could. If the faith itself were more reasonable. I was in the faith, I know all about it.'

'Nobody knows all about it,' Don Carlo said.

'It's easy for you,' I said, somewhat loudly. 'You've put off the needs of the flesh. You've been gelded for the love of God.'

'Gelded? A rare word, I think.'

'Castrated, deballocked, deprived of the use of your *coglioni*.'

'Not deprived,' he said in no gelding's voice. 'No, not deprived. We choose what we wish, but nobody may choose deprivation. I will take a bath now.'

He took a very loud splashing bath, singing what sounded like highly secular songs in a coarse dialect. He shouted, in the same dialect, what sounded like a complaint

about the lack of a bath towel. 'I'll take it,' I said to
Domenico, who was scoring what looked like a semiquaver
run for the strings at the round centre table. I got a towel
from the corridor cupboard and took it to Don Carlo. He
stood in the swimming bathroom, squeezing a blackhead
on his chin. His eyes flashed from the mirror at my
entrance. He was naked, of course, bigbellied but also
bigballocked, with roadworker's arms and shoulders, very
hairy everywhere. He took the towel without thanks,
began to dry himself, balls and belly first, and said:

'If all goes well, it will be dinner at the Hôtel de Paris. But
some light nourishment is called for before we go. Bread.
Salami. Cheese. Wine.'

'Certainly, Father.'

'What is your father?' he asked sternly.

'A dentist.'

'In England?'

'In the town of Battle in East Sussex. The name
celebrates the disaster of Senlac, when the Anglosaxons
lost to the invading Normans.'

He dried his shoulders, exposing his balls and what the
Romans called *dumpennente* without shame. 'And when are
you going home?'

'I have no intention of going home. Not yet.'

'It is not now the invading Normans,' he said. 'It is what
some call the intangible visitation. You have read the
newspapers?'

'You mean influenza?'

'The Anglosaxons are being invaded worse than most. It
is a cold country. February is a cold month there. A long
war ends and a long winter follows. Paris suffers too, I lost
three students this week. I hope you do not have to go
home.'

I shivered, as though the influenza were being conjured
here in mild safe Monaco by this naked priest. 'Why did you
mention my father?' I said. 'Have you some occult vision of
his succumbing to the—?'

'*Occult*,' he bawled. 'Do not use that word to me.' And he

pushed me out of the bathroom.

'Occult,' I bawled back through the shut door. 'It only means hidden. It only means concealed.' But he was singing again.

I was sulky and vaguely fearful as we walked together up the road which separated the Condamine from the Casino. But I was maliciously glad too that Don Carlo was puffing and wheezing from the steep climb. Also the February sea wind was stiff, and he had to hold on hard, grumbling, to his black trilby, while Domenico and I wore sporty caps that could not be buffeted off. We were in country daywear, though of course with stiff collars, while Don Carlo was in wrinkled alpaca and an overtight shirt of his brother's, the tie rich but not modest. He looked like a cynical undertaker. He was panting hard when we reached the Casino, while Domenico and I, with breath to spare for the crescendo, were singing a chorus from our opera:

> Money isn't everything–
> It's only board and bed,
> The only thing distinguishing
> Being living, being dead
> (So I've heard said).

Domenico liked those ings and had stressed them in the orchestration with triangle and glockenspiel.

But there was no grumbling when Don Carlo began to play. Domenico and I staked our few francs at roulette and promptly lost them, but Don Carlo was rapt in the miracle of winning. We were, of course, in the 'kitchen', not one of the salles privées for the rich and distinguished. It was the depressed postwar time and there were not many playing. We had heard that the Société des Bains de Mer was being saved from bankruptcy only by the pumping in by Sir Basil Zaharoff of thousands out of his armament millions. We had seen him and his Spanish mistress, the Duquesa de Marquena y Villafranca, getting out of a huge polished car outside the Hôtel de Paris. He wanted to take over the principality and instal himself as its ruler; his fat mistress longed to be elevated to princess. He never came into the gaming rooms; he did not believe in gambling.

'*Messieurs, faites vos jeux.*'

And there was Don Carlo playing consistently *à cheval*, greedily wanting a return of seventeen times his stake. He got it too, twice. The plaques were piling up. Then he went into an anthology of other possible stakings: *en plein*, which should have brought him thirty-five times his money but didn't; *transversale*—I think it was 25, 26, 27—and there he won, eleven times his stake. *Carré? Quatre premiers?* He shrugged at losing: you only got an eightfold return. He went back to horseback, his stake on the line between 19 and 22. By God, it came up. Then he put three hundred francs on 16, *en plein.* He lost. Muttering something to himself, he tried a *sixain*, putting his plaque on the line dividing 7, 8, 9 and 10, 11, 12. It came up—five times the stake. He shrugged. He returned to that damned intractable *en plein*—16. He approached it cautiously, with a fifty-franc stake. He lost. '*Basta, Carlo*', his brother said. Don Carlo frowned, grunted, then seemed *sotto voce* to curse. He reverted to putting three hundred francs, the 'kitchen' upper limit, on 16 once more: the curse was on his timidity. The croupier span the *cylindre.*

'*Les jeux sont faits, rien ne va plus.*'

There were about ten round the table. Domenico and I dared not, of course, breathe. A middleaged man with only three fingers in his left hand and on his right eye a black patch kept his singular gaze on Don Carlo's face, as though his study were gamblers' reactions to their own selfimposed hells. A silverhaired beldam seemed ready, blue at the lips, to suffer cardiac arrest on Don Carlo's behalf. 'Oh my God.' That was myself. Don Carlo looked sternly at me and my vain nametaking. Then he looked at the wheel, where the ball was just rolling to rest.

On 16. He went: 'Ah.'

'The luck,' I said infelicitously, 'of the devil.' He did not seem to hear. He hugged his chips to his bosom, then threw

one, in the incense-splashing swipe of the Asperges at high
mass, at the croupier. The croupier, who had never, to my
knowledge, seen him in his life before, said: *'Merci, mon père.'*
Don Carlo sketched an unabashed blessing and moved
away from the table.

'That's wise,' I said.

'Trente-et-quarante,' he said.

'No, Carlo, no. *Basta.'*

'Roulette,' Don Carlo said, 'is really for children. Trente-
et-quarante is for men. Tonight I feel myself to have,' and
he frowned at me humorously, 'the devil's luck.'

So we watched him while he sat at the trente-et-
quarante table with untrustworthy looking Milanese and
Genoese who had come over the border for the weekend.
He quipped with them in various dialects while the seals of
the six new packs were broken. Trente-et-quarante is
simpler than roulette, since it deals not in specific numbers
but in *pair, impair, couleur* and *inverse,* but the stakes are
double those of roulette: it is the serious gambler's game.
Don Carlo staked *à cheval* most of the time. He seemed to
know more about it than anybody there, including the *chef
de partie,* and, stacking his winner's plaques in two high piles,
he delivered a little lecture or sermon on the mathematical
probabilities of recurrences—card rows to the value of 40
coming up only four times, as compared with thirteen
times for a row of 31 and so on. He aspersed gratuities at
the croupiers, then got up sighing with content as from a
heavy meal. But the heavy meal was to come: he had
promised us that.

Before cashing his chips he hesitated, looking back at the
gaming salon with; in his eyes, the signs of a lust not sure
yet whether it was satisfied. 'Two things I have not done,'
he said. 'The *finales sept* and the *tiers du cylindre sud-est.* In both.
cases *par cent,* I think. I think I shall do them now.'

'*Basta, Carlo.'*

'What in the name of God—'

'You are too ready,' he told me, 'with your casual use of
the holy name of the Lord God. The *finales sept par cent* is one

hundred francs on 7 and 17 and 27. The other one is one hundred francs *à cheval* on the numbers on the southeast segment of the wheel—'

'Where did you learn all these things?' I asked. 'Is it a regular part of theological instruction in Italy?'

'Have you read,' he counterasked, 'but I know you have not so there is no point in asking, the books of Blaise Pascal?'

'I know the *Pensées·* I glanced at the *Provincial Letters.* You have no right to assume to assume—'

'The holy and learned Pascal was first to use the word *roulette.* He was much concerned with the mysteries of chance. He also invented the calculating machine and the public omnibus and the watch on the wrist. The mystery of numbers and of the starry heavens. Who are you to sneer and scoff and rebuke?'

'I'm not sneering and scoffing and. I merely asked—'

'You would do well to think about the need for harmless solace in a world full of diabolic temptation. I will *not* play the *finales* and the *tierce.*' As though it were all my fault that he was thus deprived of further harmless solace, he sulkily cashed his plaques. He was given a lot of big notes, some of which he dropped and Domenico picked up. Then he began to waddle out. Domenico shrugged at me. We followed.

Despite postwar shortages, the ornate but airy restaurant of the Hôtel de Paris was able to offer us the following:

Saumon Fumé de Hollande
Velouté de Homard au Paprika
Tourte de Ris-de-Veau Brillat-Savarin
Selle d'Agneau de Lait Polignac
Pommes Dauphin   Petits Pois Fine-Fleur
Sorbet au Clicquot
Poularde Soufflée Impériale
Salade Aida
Crêpes Flambées au Grand Marnier
Coffret de Friandises
Corbeille de Fruits   Café   Liqueurs

I had expected little more than a choice of ornate renderings
of the flesh of the pigeons that, wounded by palsied trigger-
fingers in the famous Monte Carlo pigeon shoot, wandering
trustingly pecking round the outdoor tables of the Café de
Paris opposite, were picked up as easily as kittens. But this
was God's plenty and I said so. Don Carlo, after two seconds
of consideration, accepted the term. It cost a lot, but Don
Carlo had the money. For drink we began with champagne
cocktails, went on to a good Chablis and a fine Chambertin,
took a refreshing Blanquette de Limoux with the dessert,
and ended with an acceptable Armagnac in flutes not
balloons. Don Carlo ate with sweating concentration but,
when we arrived at the sorbet, spared time to take in the
charming *belle époque* décor. I said to him:

'This décor of the *belle époque*. You find it charming?'

He said, as I'd expected: 'There is a vagueness about
these expressions. Who says that epoch was beautiful?
Beauty is one of the attributes of the divinity. And
charming, I do not know what is meant by charming.'

'Alluring. Pretty. Pleasing. Ocularly seductive. Unpro-
found but sensuously satisfying. Tasteful and delicate.
Like that lady behind you.'

He grunted, turning, munching the bread that was still
on his breadplate and which he had forbidden the waiter to
clear, to look at an animated woman in a chainstitched-
embroidered dress of very fine black pure silk chiffon.
Ocularly unseduced, he turned round again. 'A frivolous
people,' he said.

'The French?' I said, joyously. 'All the French? The
French in myself? My mother? And what do you mean by
frivolous?'

He wagged his bit of bread at me. 'Remember,' he said,
'that language is one of our trials and sorrows. We are
forced, by the very nature of language, to generalize. If we
did not generalize we would have nothing to say except
such as,' wagging it still, 'this bread is a piece of bread.'

'*Tautologia*,' Domenico said.

'Is language, then,' I said, 'of diabolic provenance?'

'No,' he said, and this time he munched. 'Read Genesis, and you will see that God made Adam call things by name, and that was the birth of language. When Adam and Eve fell, then language became corrupted. Out of that corruption I say that the French are a frivolous people.' And he swallowed his bread. There was nothing more to eat on the table. Don Carlo called for the bill. It was a big one. The table swarmed with paper money.

'This décor of the *belle époque*,' I said. 'You find it charming?'

His response was unexpected. He bellowed at me, so that heads turned: '*Adiuro ergo te, draco nequissime, in nomine Agni immaculati—*'

'*Basta, Carlo.*'

Don Carlo grinned at me without mirth but with a sketch of menace appropriate to the words of exorcism he had uttered. 'That is excessive,' he said. 'That goes too far. I address a little demon only, and I will call it a demon of frivolity. We will burn him out of you yet. We will have you back before you are finished. We will have you *home*.' For the first time ever on hearing that word my eyes pricked, and the charming décor dissolved momentarily in coloured water. 'Now,' he said, 'ask me again about the décor of the beautiful epoch.' I said nothing, though my lips and tongue formed *We?* There was no bread in my mouth but I swallowed as if there were. Don Carlo was, I was learning, formidable. He drew from a side jacket pocket a big cheap watch that ticked at me across the table. 'Seven o'clock mass at Sainte Dévote,' he said. 'You know Father Rougier?' he asked of his brother.

'*La conosco.*'

'I will say mass in my best Parisian Latin,' he said to me. I had forgotten it was Sunday tomorrow, but the days of the week had long ceased for me to have individual flavours; they all tasted of the same loneliness and frivolity, which I termed work. So then, it was after ten and we must walk downhill from Carlo's mount to Carlo's lodging, that he might go to bed and be well rested for his early mass. In the vestibule of the Hôtel de Paris Don Carlo smiled at the

bronze equestrian statue of Louis XIV and then, with
neither malice nor menace, at me. The effigy had been
there only about twelve years, but the raised knee of the
horse had been so often touched for luck that it shone
golden. Don Carlo rubbed it affectionately. Then he turned
to the greeting of a British voice.

'The Don and the Monte. I knew sometime you two
would meet. How are you, *caro Carlo, Carlo querido?*'

'*Muy bien.*' And Don Carlo shook hands with a
palehaired English smiler with a cricketer's body, got up in
the uniform of an Anglican bishop, complete with gaiters.
Domenico was introduced. I too.

'The writer? The playwright? Well, quite an honour.
Saw one of your things when I was back. A real scream.'
This man was the Bishop of Gibraltar. The pale hair was
parted on the right, which in those days was called the girl's
side, and a lock fell engagingly over the left very blue eye.
Looking back on him now I see a fusion of Messrs Auden
and Isherwood, homosexual writers like myself. Most of
the bishop's strong brown teeth were on show as he shook
hands manlily. The Bishop of Gibraltar's diocese extended to
the Côte d'Azur, and one of the earlier episcopal duties had
been to warn the sunning British of the dangers to their
souls of gambling. As I was almost at once to see, those
days were over. What puzzled and a little shocked me was
the amicality subsisting between an Anglican and a
Catholic prelate. 'I saw your brother in the Windy City,' the
bishop said to Don Carlo. 'We had dinner. We played.'

'Craps?' asked, to my further shock, Don Carlo.

'The Idaho variety.'

'What a good idea. You have, ha, *i dadi?*' He rerubbed the
raised bronze pastern.

'*Los dados? Cierto.*'

'*Basta.*' Domenico was visibly tired from eating. I was
weary too, but did not dare, for fear of exorcism, to protest.
So we all went up to the episcopal suite on the third floor,
and in the drawingroom, full of *belle époque* charm, his
lordship served whisky and brought out the dice in a cup of

Florentine leather. Don Carlo lugged forth his big cheap
watch and placed it on the table, where it beat aggressively.
The bishop said:
'Fasting from midnight, of course. The blessed mutter of
the, as the poet has it. Browning, is it not?' he asked me.
'Chicago,' I said, nodding. 'Why, if I may ask with a
writer's professional cheek, Chicago?'
'Anglican matters,' the bishop said, shaking the dice. 'An
episcopal conference. I say no more. Come on, seven,
eleven.' He threw a total of 12 and then of 9 and then of 7
and lost. Don Carlo burlily cast, muttering a prayer, and
got 11, fifteen to one. It was all between the two clerics:
Domenico and I were hopeless. But, ever the inquiring
novelist, I stayed to drink and listen. The bishop, presiding
over an Anglican enclave at the foot of a fiercely Catholic
peninsula, had a special social if not theological relationship
with, ha ha, the sons of the Scarlet Woman. Big Eight: even
money. Hardways: seven to one. Baby wants a new pair of
shoes. Roll dem bones. This was madness. They talked
about colleagues: men with reversed collars were all in the
same business despite the electrified fence of the
Reformation. The third Campanati brother, Raffaele, was
an importer into the United States of Milanese foodstuffs.
He had trouble, there was a kind of Neapolitan brigandage
in Chicago, different from other American cities where the
Sicilians were the dealers in monopoly and violence, which
they termed protection. Craps: seven to one. The bishop
said:
'The big word came up, as you may suppose.'
'*Ecumenico?*' Big Six: even money.
'Early days,' the bishop said. I didn't understand. The
word was new to me, who had done little Greek. But I
began to understand, from fragmentary allusions, how it
was that Don Carlo and the Bishop of Gibraltar knew each
other, indeed were a sort of friends. Nothing to do with
religion, though to do with Rome. His lordship liked
autumn holidays in Rome. Don Carlo, in Rome for a task of
translation of a very knotty document for the Holy

Father's own benefit (English to Italian that was, about capital and labour or something), got to playing bridge with his lordship, not at the time more than a dean. Auction, of course, contract not yet having come in. The bishop proposed a session of contract, though, for the next day, after he had preached to the British and Don Carlo had eaten a long breakfast after his blessed mutter at Sainte Dévote. Contract was the coming version; it would supplant auction totally; had I read the article in *The Times* by the Rev. Causley DD? Did I, for that matter, play? A little auction. You will soon pick up contract. No, I said, alas: I had some writing to do.

At one minute to midnight Don Carlo was served a stiff whisky. He finished it as, all eyes on synchronized watches, the hour came up. Like going into battle, the bishop said. Over the top into Sunday, and the best of luck. 'It's a battle, yes,' Don Carlo said. 'It's all a battle.' And he looked at me as though I were a whitefeathered malingerer. I nearly made some excuse about my heart.

are very likely to be patched up and turned loose upon the world, to beget their kind. But massaged along the backbone to cure their lues, they quickly pass into the last stages, and so their pathogenic heritage perishes with them. What is too often forgotten is that nature obviously intends the botched to die, and that every interference with that benign process is full of dangers. Moreover, it is, like birth control, profoundly immoral. The chiropractors are innocent in both departments. That their labors tend to propagate epidemics and so menace the lives of all of us, as is alleged by their medical opponents—this I doubt. The fact is that most infectious diseases of any seriousness throw out such alarming symptoms and so quickly that no sane chiropractor is likely to monkey with them. Seeing his patient breaking out in pustules, or choking, or falling into a stupor, he takes to the woods at once, and leaves the business to the nearest medical man. His trade is mainly with ambulent patients; they must come to his studio for treatment. Most of them have lingering diseases; they tour all the neighborhood doctors before they reach him. His treatment, being entirely nonsensical, is in accord with the divine plan. It is seldom, perhaps, that he actually kills a patient, but at all events he keeps many a worthy soul from getting well.

Thus the multiplication of chiropractors in the Republic gives me a great deal of pleasure. It is agreeable to see so many morons getting slaughtered, and it is equally agreeable to see so many other morons getting rich. The art and mystery of scientific medicine, for a decade or more past, has been closed to all save the sons of wealthy men. It takes a small fortune to go through a Class A medical college, and by the time the graduate is able to make a living for himself he is entering upon middle age, and is commonly so disillusioned that he is unfit for practice. Worse, his fees for looking at tongues and feeling pulses tend to be cruelly high. His predecessors charged fifty cents and threw in the pills; his own charges approach those of divorce lawyers, consulting engineers and the

Chiropractic

H. L. MENCKEN

THIS PREPOSTEROUS QUACKERY is now all the rage in the back reaches of the Republic, and even begins to conquer the less civilized of the big cities. As the old-time family doctor dies out in the country towns, with no trained successor willing to take over his dismal business, he is followed by some hearty blacksmith or ice-wagon driver, turned into a chiropractor in six months, often by correspondence. In Los Angeles the damned there are more chiropractors than actual physicians, and they are far more generally esteemed. Proceeding from the Ambassador Hotel to the heart of the town, along Wilshire boulevard, one passes scores of their gaudy signs; there are even many chiropractic 'hospitals'. The morons who pour in from the prairies and deserts, most of them ailing, patronize these 'hospitals' copiously, and give to the chiropractic pathology the same high respect that they accord to the theology of Aimée McPherson and the art of Cecil De Mille. That pathology is grounded upon the doctrine that all human ills are caused by the pressure of misplaced vertebræ upon the nerves which come out of the spinal cord—in other words, that every disease is the result of a pinch. This, plainly enough, is buncombe. The chiropractic therapeutics rest upon the doctrine that the way to get rid of such pinches is to climb upon a table and submit to an heroic pummeling by a retired piano mover. This, obviously, is buncombe doubly damned.

Both doctrines were launched upon the world by an old quack named Andrew T. Still, the father of osteopathy. For years his followers merchanted them, and made a lot of money at the trade. But as they grew opulent they grew ambitious, *ie*, they began to study anatomy and physiology. The result was a gradual abandonment of Papa Still's ideas. The high-toned osteopath of to-day is a sort of eclectic. He tries anything that promises to work, from tonsillectomy to the vibrations of the late Dr Abrams. With four years' training behind him, he probably knows more anatomy than the average graduate of the Johns Hopkins Medical School, or, at all events, more osteology. Thus enlightened, he seldom has much to say about pinched nerves in the back. But as he abandoned the Still revelation it was seized by the chiropractors, led by another quack, one Palmer. This Palmer grabbed the pinched nerve nonsense and began teaching it to ambitious farm-hands and out-at-elbow Baptist preachers in a few easy lessons. To-day the backwoods swarm with chiropractors, and in most States they have been able to exert enough pressure on the rural politicians to get themselves licensed. Any lout with strong hands and arms is perfectly equipped to become a chiropractor. No education beyond the elements is necessary. The whole art and mystery may be imparted in a few months, and the graduate is then free to practise upon God's images. The takings are often high, and so the profession has attracted thousands of recruits—retired baseball players, plumbers, truck-drivers, longshoremen, bogus dentists, dubious preachers, village school superintendents. Now and then a quack doctor of some other school—say homeopathy—plunges into it. Hundreds of

promising students come from the intellectual ranks of hospital orderlies.

In certain States efforts have been made, sometimes by the medical fraternity, to make the practice of chiropractic unlawful. I am glad to be able to report that practically all of them have failed. Why should it be prohibited? I believe that every free-born man has a clear right, when he is ill, to seek any sort of treatment that he yearns for. If his mental processes are of such a character that the theory of chiropractic seems plausible to him, then he should be permitted to try chiropractic. And if it be granted that he has a right to do so, then it follows clearly that any stevedore privy to the technique of chiropractic has a right to treat him. To preach any contrary doctrine is to advocate despotism and slavery. The arguments for such despotism are all full of holes, and especially those that come from medical men who have been bitten by the public hygiene madness, *ie*, by the messianic delusion. Such fanatics infest every health department in the land. They assume glibly that the whole aim of civilization is to cut down the deathrate, and to attain that end they are willing to make a sacrifice of everything else imaginable, including their own sense of humor. There is, as a matter of fact, not the slightest reason to believe that cutting down the deathrate, in itself, is of much benefit to the human race. A people with an annual rate of 40 a thousand might still produce many Huxleys and Darwins, and one with a rate of but 8 or 9 might produce nothing but Coolidges and Billy Sundays. The former probability, in truth, is greater than the latter, for a low rate does not necessarily mean that more superior individuals are surviving; it may mean only that more of the inferior are surviving, and that the next generation will be burdened by their get.

Such quackeries as Christian Science, osteopathy and chiropractic work against the false humanitarianism of the hygienists and to excellent effect. They suck in the botched, and help them on to bliss eternal. When these botched fall into the hands of competent medical men they higher hetæræ. Even general practice, in our great Babylons, has become a sort of specialty, with corresponding emolument. But the chiropractor, having no such investment in his training, can afford to work for more humane wages, and so he is getting more and more of the trade. Six weeks after he leaves his job at the filling-station or abandons the steering-wheel of his motor-truck he knows all the anatomy and physiology that he will ever learn in this world. Six weeks more, and he is an adept at all the half-Nelsons and left hooks that constitute the essence of chiropractic therapy. Soon afterward, having taken post-graduate courses in advertising, salesmanship and mental mastery, he is ready for practice. A sufficiency of patients, it appears, is always ready, too. I hear of no complaint from chiropractors of bad business. New ones are being turned out at a dizzy rate, but they all seem to find the pickings easy. Some time ago I heard of a chiropractor who, having once been a cornet-player, had abandoned chiropractic in despair, and gone back to cornet-playing. But investigation showed that he was really not a chiropractor at all, but an osteopath.

The osteopaths, I fear, are finding this new competition serious and unpleasant. As I have said, it was their Hippocrates, the late Dr Still, who invented all of the thrusts, lunges, yanks, hooks and bounces that the lowly chiropractors now employ with such vast effect, and for years the osteopaths had a monopoly of them. But when they began to grow scientific and ambitious their course of training was lengthened until it took in all sorts of tricks and dodges borrowed from the regular doctors, or resurrection men, including the plucking of tonsils, adenoids and appendices, the use of the stomach-pump, and even some of the legerdemain of psychiatry. They now harry their students furiously, and turn them out ready for anything from growing hair on a bald head to frying a patient with the x-rays. All this new striving, of course, quickly brought its inevitable penalties. The osteopathic graduate, having sweated so long, was no longer willing to take a case of sarcoma for $2, and in consequence he lost patients. Worse, very few aspirants could make the long grade. The essence of osteopathy itself could be grasped by any lively farm-hand or night watchman in a few weeks, but the borrowed magic baffled him. Confronted by the phenomenon of gastrulation, or by the curious behavior of heart muscle, or by any of the current theories of immunity, he commonly took refuge, like his brother of the orthodox faculty, in a gulp of laboratory alcohol, or fled the premises altogether. Thus he was lost to osteopathic science, and the chiropractors took him in; nay, they welcomed him. He was their meat. Borrowing that primitive part of osteopathy which was comprehensible to the meanest understanding, they threw the rest overboard, at the same time denouncing it as a sorcery invented by the Medical Trust. Thus they gathered in the garage mechanics, ash-men and decayed welter-weights, and the land began to fill with their graduates. Now there is a chiropractor at every cross-roads, and in such sinks of imbecility as Los Angeles they are as thick as bootleggers.

I repeat that it eases and soothes me to see them so prosperous, for they counteract the evil work of the so-called science of public hygiene, which now seeks to make morons immortal. If a man, being ill of a pus appendix, resorts to a shaved and fumigated longshoreman to have it disposed of, and submits willingly to a treatment that involves balancing him on McBurney's spot and playing on his vertebræ as on a concertina, then I am willing, for one, to believe that he is badly wanted in Heaven. And if that same man, having achieved lawfully a lovely babe, hires a blacksmith to cure its diphtheria by pulling its neck, then I do not resist the divine will that there shall be one less radio fan in 1967. In such matters, I am convinced, the laws of nature are far better guides than the fiats and machinations of the medical busybodies who now try to run us. If the latter gentlemen had their way, death, save at the hands of hangmen, Prohibition agents and other such legalized assassins, would be abolished altogether, and so

Chiropractic

H. L. MENCKEN

THIS PREPOSTEROUS QUACKERY is now all the rage in the back reaches of the Republic, and even begins to conquer the less civilized of the big cities. As the old-time family doctor dies out in the country towns, with no trained successor willing to take over his dismal business, he is followed by some hearty blacksmith or ice-wagon driver, turned into a chiropractor in six months, often by correspondence. In Los Angeles the damned there are more chiropractors than actual physicians, and they are far more generally esteemed. Proceeding from the Ambassador Hotel to the heart of the town, along Wilshire boulevard, one passes scores of their gaudy signs; there are even many chiropractic 'hospitals'. The morons who pour in from the prairies and deserts, most of them ailing, patronize these 'hospitals' copiously, and give to the chiropractic pathology the same high respect that they accord to the theology of Aimée McPherson and the art of Cecil De Mille. That pathology is grounded upon the doctrine that all human ills are caused by the pressure of

misplaced vertebræ upon the nerves which come out of the
spinal cord—in other words, that every disease is the result
of a pinch. This, plainly enough, is buncombe. The
chiropractic therapeutics rest upon the doctrine that the
way to get rid of such pinches is to climb upon a table and
submit to an heroic pummeling by a retired piano mover.
This, obviously, is buncombe doubly damned.

Both doctrines were launched upon the world by an old
quack named Andrew T. Still, the father of osteopathy. For
years his followers merchanted them, and made a lot of
money at the trade. But as they grew opulent they grew
ambitious, ie, they began to study anatomy and physiology.
The result was a gradual abandonment of Papa Still's ideas.
The high-toned osteopath of to-day is a sort of eclectic. He
tries anything that promises to work, from tonsillectomy
to the vibrations of the late Dr Abrams. With four years'
training behind him, he probably knows more anatomy
than the average graduate of the Johns Hopkins Medical
School, or, at all events, more osteology. Thus
enlightened, he seldom has much to say about pinched
nerves in the back. But as he abandoned the Still revelation
it was seized by the chiropractors, led by another quack,
one Palmer. This Palmer grabbed the pinched nerve
nonsense and began teaching it to ambitious farm-hands
and out-at-elbow Baptist preachers in a few easy lessons.
To-day the backwoods swarm with chiropractors, and in
most States they have been able to exert enough pressure
on the rural politicians to get themselves licensed. Any lout
with strong hands and arms is perfectly equipped to
become a chiropractor. No education beyond the elements
is necessary. The whole art and mystery may be imparted in
a few months, and the graduate is then free to practise
upon God's images. The takings are often high, and so the
profession has attracted thousands of recruits—retired
baseball players, plumbers, truck-drivers, longshoremen,
bogus dentists, dubious preachers, village school superintendents. Now and then a quack doctor of some other
school—say homeopathy—plunges into it. Hundreds of

promising students come from the intellectual ranks of hospital orderlies.

In certain States efforts have been made, sometimes by the medical fraternity, to make the practice of chiropractic unlawful. I am glad to be able to report that practically all of them have failed. Why should it be prohibited? I believe that every free-born man has a clear right, when he is ill, to seek any sort of treatment that he yearns for. If his mental processes are of such a character that the theory of chiropractic seems plausible to him, then he should be permitted to try chiropractic. And if it be granted that he has a right to do so, then it follows clearly that any stevedore privy to the technique of chiropractic has a right to treat him. To preach any contrary doctrine is to advocate despotism and slavery. The arguments for such despotism are all full of holes, and especially those that come from medical men who have been bitten by the public hygiene madness, *ie*, by the messianic delusion. Such fanatics infest every health department in the land. They assume glibly that the whole aim of civilization is to cut down the deathrate, and to attain that end they are willing to make a sacrifice of everything else imaginable, including their own sense of humor. There is, as a matter of fact, not the slightest reason to believe that cutting down the death-rate, in itself, is of much benefit to the human race. A people with an annual rate of 40 a thousand might still produce many Huxleys and Darwins, and one with a rate of but 8 or 9 might produce nothing but Coolidges and Billy Sundays. The former probability, in truth, is greater than the latter, for a low rate does not necessarily mean that more superior individuals are surviving; it may mean only that more of the inferior are surviving, and that the next generation will be burdened by their get

Such quackeries as Christian Science, osteopathy and chiropractic work against the false humanitarianism of the hygienists and to excellent effect. They suck in the botched, and help them on to bliss eternal. When these botched fall into the hands of competent medical men they

are very likely to be patched up and turned loose upon the
world, to beget their kind. But massaged along the
backbone to cure their lues, they quickly pass into the last
stages, and so their pathogenic heritage perishes with
them. What is too often forgotten is that nature obviously
intends the botched to die, and that every interference with
that benign process is full of dangers. Moreover, it is, like
birth control, profoundly immoral. The chiropractors are
innocent in both departments. That their labors tend to
propagate epidemics and so menace the lives of all of us, as
is alleged by their medical opponents—this I doubt. The
fact is that most infectious diseases of any seriousness
throw out such alarming symptoms and so quickly that no
sane chiropractor is likely to monkey with them. Seeing his
patient breaking out in pustules, or choking, or falling into
a stupor, he takes to the woods at once, and leaves the
business to the nearest medical man. His trade is mainly
with ambulent patients; they must come to his studio for
treatment. Most of them have lingering diseases; they tour
all the neighborhood doctors before they reach him. His
treatment, being entirely nonsensical, is in accord with the
divine plan. It is seldom, perhaps, that he actually kills a
patient, but at all events he keeps many a worthy soul from
getting well.

Thus the multiplication of chiropractors in the Republic
gives me a great deal of pleasure. It is agreeable to see so
many morons getting slaughtered, and it is equally
agreeable to see so many other morons getting rich. The art
and mystery of scientific medicine, for a decade or more
past, has been closed to all save the sons of wealthy men. It
takes a small fortune to go through a Class A medical
college, and by the time the graduate is able to make a living
for himself he is entering upon middle age, and is
commonly so disillusioned that he is unfit for practice.
Worse, his fees for looking at tongues and feeling pulses
tend to be cruelly high. His predecessors charged fifty
cents and threw in the pills; his own charges approach
those of divorce lawyers, consulting engineers and the

I'm Getting Mallied in the Morning

JOHN WELLS

The Japanese yesterday turned their attention towards the traditional English wedding. Twenty-three leaders of the multi-million pound Japanese wedding industry descended on Britain, intent on finding out what makes the girls back East so enthusiastic about an English marriage.—Sunday Telegraph

TO MANY OF our highly prized and respected readers the Englishman is a funny coot.

All too often the cultivated Japanese traveller, however intelligent, sensitive and adventurous he or she may be, will be tempted to dismiss Joe Bull as a mobile-faced big pink hooligan, the traditional butt of so much wartime humour.

But perhaps it is time, with the greatest possible respect, that our readers took a short passionate look at Mr Bull with a view to exploding, as the Englishman himself would say, a few French ducks.

Consider the very ancient English Wedding Ceremony. In England, when a man and woman, or any similar combination, wish to 'have a fack' it is not the simple business it is in Japan.

Oh no.

Leading Japanese anthropologist Wassamata Wichu has written: 'In more virile and dynamic societies sexual coupling is a hurdle we go flying over with the greatest of ease. In England, thanks to long centuries of decay and energy-draining, a great song and dance is necessary to land Percy in the Pudding.'

The Ceremony we were able to study took place in the charming city of Reeds, in the Northern Province of York-shah.

Despite warnings from our delightful English hosts in London that 'you litre baggers'—an affectionate term meaning 'small friend or companion'—would not understand a word they said in Reeds on account of their pronounced Celtic accent, we found the old ritual both illuminating and as easy to comprehend as falling off a house.

Three weeks before we arrived, the 'Buns of Marriage' had been exhibited at the local Materialist shrine.

We were unable to discover the exact nature of this part of the ceremony, but natives we questioned described it as 'a rot of hokey-pokey', suggesting that some form of dance was involved, perhaps to exorcise the 'Boon in Tooven', or unborn child conceived as a result of a previous Wedding.

The day of the main ceremony began dark and wet, provoking much gesticulation at the sky on the part of the assembling natives, together with exaggerated facial contortions and exclamations in a tone of lugubrious fatalism to the effect that a sky-spirit referred to as 'It' was urinating on them.

Despite the inclemency of the weather, grotesque costumes were much in evidence: feathered head-dresses, terrifying face-paint, and many large silver and gold bags, used, we discovered later, as offensive weapons.

The centre of the ceremonial is a mock battle between two teams of champions selected by the couple, and known respectively as 'Blide Sparrans' and 'Glume Sparrans', which is believed capable of exciting them sufficiently to 'have Itway'.

In ancient times this battle was fought to the death, but today, in keeping with the sleepy, easy-going mood of these carefree islanders, the 'poonjub' is very perfunctory, resulting usually in little more than a few broken noses and the loss of a few teeth, and both teams demand liberal supplies of the locally brewed 'Newcassa Blun' before they will go into action.

The drink, which is passed from hand to hand in brown bottles, is believed to possess aphrodisiac qualities, and produced very alarming symptoms as the day progressed, including violent eye-movements, apparent demon-possession, frothing at the mouth, rolling on the floor, loss of memory, incontinence and subsequent nausea.

We requested to taste it, and were at first told that this would not be possible in the small quantities we were asking for, 'not for nips'. Later however we were offered a bottle by an elderly female celebrant, and found it warm, sweet, and tasting a little like oatmeal soup.

The Materialist shrine had been decorated with flowers for the ceremony, martial music was played on a pipe-organ, and a Materialist monk, flanked by flower-maidens and dressed in what appeared to be a Victorian female nurse's costume with a black petticoat and a white plastic punishment collar, greeted the Wedding celebrants with much eye-rolling and clasping and unclasping of his hands.

Materialist teaching is almost incomprehensible to the foreigner, involving as it does repetitive invocation of the sky-spirit in a ritual distraction of the worshippers' attention while the so-called 'sacred element' is gathered in collecting-bags. But its contribution to the Wedding ceremonial is direct and to the point.

The couple being excited to sexual congress are invited by the monk to think about the others' 'Woldy goods', and to prove their credit-worthiness by exchanging golden

rings, worth only a few yen but the equivalent in England
of half a dozen oxen or twenty sheep.

The couple are dressed for this holy moment in
traditional erotic costumes, the female in a 'baby doll' lace
veil and nightdress, suggesting innocence combined with
great wealth, and the male in the outfit of a nineteenth-
century 'toff' or 'Johnny', the feared hero-villain of
melodrama and pornographic film since time immemorial.

On a blast from the pipe-organ, the couple then turn to
face the rival armies, drawn up on either side of the shrine
and facing to the East, home of the sky-spirit. A march is
played, and as the couple pass down through the centre of
the shrine the eyes of the two opposing factions converge.
Their collective 'woldy goods', or so they believe in the
trance-like state induced by the 'Newcassa Blun', are being
taken away from them by the opposition.

Eyes glassy and teeth bared, the participants move
unsteadily off to the formalised mutual abuse, ripping of
clothes and colourful York-shah violence from which the
couple will, it is hoped, emerge to perform the final act,
boots, dead cats and old tin cans tied to their ankles for luck.

The Night the Bed Fell

JAMES THURBER

I SUPPOSE THAT the high-water mark of my youth in Columbus, Ohio, was the night the bed fell on my father. It makes a better recitation (unless, as some friends of mine have said, one has heard it five or six times) than it does a piece of writing, for it is almost necessary to throw furniture around, shake doors, and bark like a dog, to lend the proper atmosphere and verisimilitude to what is admittedly a somewhat incredible tale. Still, it did take place.

It happened, then, that my father had decided to sleep in the attic one night, to be away where he could think. My mother opposed the notion strongly because, she said, the old wooden bed up there was unsafe; it was wobbly and the heavy headboard would crash down on father's head in case the bed fell, and kill him. There was no dissuading him, however, and at a quarter past ten he closed the attic door behind him and went up the narrow twisting stairs. We later heard ominous creakings as he crawled into bed. Grandfather, who usually slept in the attic bed when he was with us, had disappeared some days before. (On these occasions he was usually gone six or eight days and returned growling and out of temper, with the news that the federal Union was run by a passel of blockheads and that the Army of the Potomac didn't have any more chance than a fiddler's bitch.)

We had visiting us at this time a nervous first cousin of mine named Briggs Beall, who believed that he was likely to cease breathing when he was asleep. It was his feeling that if he were not awakened every hour during the night, he might die of suffocation. He had been accustomed to setting an alarm clock to ring at intervals until morning, but I perusaded him to abandon this. He slept in my room and I told him that I was such a light sleeper that if anybody quit breathing in the same room with me, I would wake instantly. He tested me the first night—which I had suspected he would—by holding his breath after my regular breathing had convinced him I was asleep. I was not asleep, however, and called to him. This seemed to allay his fears a little, but he took the precaution of putting a glass of spirits of camphor on a little table at the head of his bed. In case I didn't arouse him until he was almost gone, he said, he would sniff the camphor, a powerful reviver. Briggs was not the only member of his family who had his crotchets. Old Aunt Melissa Beall (who could whistle like a man, with two fingers in her mouth) suffered under the premonition that she was destined to die on South High Street, because she had been born on South High Street and married on South High Street. Then there was Aunt Sarah Shoaf, who never went to bed at night without the fear that a burglar was going to get in and blow chloroform under her door through a tube. To avert this calamity—for she was in greater dread of anaesthetics than of losing her household goods—she always piled her money, silverware, and other valuables in a neat stack just outside her bedroom, with a note reading: 'This is all I have. Please take it and do not use your chloroform, as this is all I have.' Aunt Gracie Shoaf also had a burglar phobia, but she met it with more fortitude. She was confident that burglars had been getting into her house every night for forty years. The fact that she never missed anything was to her no proof to the contrary. She always claimed that she scared them off before they could take anything, by throwing shoes down the hallway. When she went to bed she piled, where she could get at them handily, all the shoes there were about her house. Five minutes after she had turned off the light, she would sit up in bed and say 'Hark!' Her husband, who had learned to ignore the whole situation as long ago as 1903, would either be sound asleep or pretend to be sound asleep. In either case he would not respond to her tugging and pulling, so that presently she would arise, tiptoe to the door, open it slightly and heave the shoe down the hall in one direction, and its mate down the hall in the other direction. Some nights she threw them all, some nights only a couple of pairs.

But I am straying from the remarkable incidents that took place during the night that the bed fell on father. By midnight we were all in bed. The layout of the rooms and the disposition of their occupants is important to an understanding of what later occurred. In the front room upstairs (just under father's attic bedroom) were my mother and my brother Herman, who sometimes sang in his sleep, usually 'Marching Through Georgia' or 'Onward, Christian Soldiers'. Briggs Beall and myself were in a room adjoining this one. My brother Roy was in a room across the hall from ours. Our bull terrier, Rex, slept in the hall.

My bed was an army cot, one of those affairs which are made wide enough to sleep comfortably only by putting up, flat with the middle section, the two sides which ordinarily hang down like the sideboards of a drop-leaf table. When these sides are up, it is perilous to roll too far toward the edge, for then the cot is likely to tip completely over, bringing the whole bed down on top of one, with a tremendous banging crash. This, in fact, is precisely what happened, about two o'clock in the morning. (It was my mother who, in recalling the scene later, first referred to it as 'the night the bed fell on your father.')

Always a deep sleeper, slow to arouse (I had lied to Briggs), I was at first unconscious of what had happened when the iron cot rolled me on to the floor and toppled over on me. It left me still warmly bundled up and unhurt, for the bed rested above me like a canopy. Hence I did not wake up, only reached the edge of consciousness and went back. The racket, however, instantly awakened my mother, in the next room, who came to the immediate conclusion that her worst dread was realized: the big wooden bed upstairs had fallen on father. She therefore screamed, 'Let's go to your poor father!' It was this shout, rather than the noise of my cot falling, that awakened Herman, in the same room with her. He thought that mother had become, for no apparent reason, hysterical. 'You're all right, Mamma!' he shouted, trying to calm her. They exchanged shout for shout for perhaps ten seconds: 'Let's go to your poor father!' and 'You're all right!' That woke up Briggs. By this time I was conscious of what was going on, in a vague way, but did not yet realize that I was under my bed instead of on it. Briggs, awakening in the midst of loud shouts of fear and apprehension, came to the quick conclusion that he was suffocating and that we were all trying to 'bring him out'. With a low moan, he grasped the glass of camphor at the head of his bed and instead of sniffing it poured it over himself. The room reeked of camphor. 'Ugf, ahfg,' choked Briggs, like a drowning man, for he had almost succeeded in stopping his breath under the deluge of pungent spirits. He leaped out of bed and groped toward the open window, but he came up against one that was closed. With his hand, he beat out the glass, and I could hear it crash and tinkle on the alleyway below. It was at this juncture that I, in trying to get up, had the uncanny sensation of feeling my bed above me! Foggy with sleep, I now suspected, in my turn, that the whole uproar was being made in a frantic endeavour to extricate me from what must be an unheard-of and perilous situation. 'Get me out of this!' I bawled. 'Get me out!' I think I had the nightmarish belief that I was entombed in a mine, 'Gugh,' gasped Briggs, floundering in his camphor.

By this time my mother, still shouting, pursued by Herman, still shouting, was trying to open the door to the attic, in order to go up and get my father's body out of the wreckage. The door was stuck, however, and wouldn't yield. Her frantic pulls on it only added to the general banging and confusion. Roy and the dog were now up, the one shouting questions, the other barking.

Father, farthest away and soundest sleeper of all, had by this time been awakened by the battering on the attic door. He decided that the house was on fire. 'I'm coming, I'm coming!' he wailed in a slow, sleepy voice—it took him many minutes to regain full consciousness. My mother, still believing he was caught under the bed, detected in his 'I'm coming!' the mournful, resigned note of one who is preparing to meet his Maker.'He's dying!' she shouted.

'I'm all right!' Briggs yelled to reassure her. 'I'm all right!' He still believed that it was his own closeness to death that was worrying mother. I found at last the light switch in my room, unlocked the door, and Briggs and I joined the others at the attic door. The dog, who never did like Briggs, jumped for him—assuming that he was the culprit in whatever was going on—and Roy had to throw Rex and hold him. We could hear father crawling out of bed upstairs. Roy pulled the attic door open, with a mighty jerk, and father came down the stairs, sleepy and irritable but safe and sound. My mother began to weep when she saw him. Rex began to howl. 'What in the name of God is going on here?' asked father.

The situation was finally put together like a gigantic jig-saw puzzle. Father caught a cold from prowling around in his bare feet, but there were no other bad results. 'I'm glad,' said mother, who always looked on the bright side of things, 'that your grandfather wasn't here.'

484

Acknowledgements

'The Kugelmass Episode' by Woody Allen, originally published in *The New Yorker*, is reprinted with permission of NEL Ltd from *Side Effects* (1981); 'The Quarrel with Ramlogan' is reprinted with permission of the author and André Deutsch Ltd from *The Mystic Masseur* (1957) by V. S. Naipaul; 'Princess Daisy' by Clive James, originally published in the London Review of Books (1980), is reprinted with permission of the author and A. D. Peters & Co Ltd, 'Leonard as a Lover' is reprinted with permission of Pan Books Ltd from *The Serial* (1978) by Cyra McFadden; 'Jeeves in the Springtime' is reprinted with permission of A. P. Watt Ltd from *The World of Jeeves* (1967) by P. G. Wodehouse; 'Strictly from Hunger' by S. J. Perelman, originally published in *The New Yorker* is reprinted with permission of A. D. Peters & Co Ltd; 'Flag of Inconvenience' (1980) by Keith Waterhouse is reprinted with the kind permission of the author and the proprietors of *Punch* magazine; 'The Love Nest' is reprinted with permission of Charles Scribner's Sons from *The Best Short Stories of Ring Lardner* (1929) by Ring Lardner; 'Conference Purposes' is reprinted with permission of the author and Secker and Warburg Ltd from *The History Man* (1975) by Malcolm Bradbury; 'Appetites' is reprinted with permission of The Bodley Head from *Ulysses* (1937) by James Joyce; 'Sense of Humour' is reprinted with permission of Constable Publishers from *Runyon on Broadway* (1950) by Damon Runyon; 'Identity Crisis' is reprinted with permission of Collins Publishers from *The Tin Men* (1965) by Michael Frayn; 'Here We Go Again' by Arthur Marshall, originally published in the *New Statesman* in 1976, is reproduced with the kind permission of the author and Hamish Hamilton Ltd from *I'll Let You Know* (1981); 'Suicide' is reprinted with permission of Jonathan Cape Ltd from *Portnoy's Complaint* (1969) by Philip Roth; 'Earth to Earth' is reprinted with permission of A. P. Watt Ltd from Robert Graves' *Collected Stories* (1965); 'Red-blooded ¾ rose' by Paul Jennings, originally published in *The Observer*, is reprinted with kind permission of the author from *Oodles of Oddlies* (1963); 'The Soldier in White' is reprinted by permission of Jonathan Cape Ltd from *Catch-22* (1962) by Joseph Heller; 'The Luck of the Irish' is reprinted with permission of Jonathan Cape Ltd from *Conducted Tour* (1981) by Bernard Levin; 'Hotel Superbe v. The Filthistan Trio' is reprinted with permission of A. D. Peters & Co Ltd from *Beachcomber* (1974) by Beachcomber (J. B. Morton); 'The Funeral of the Year' is reprinted with permission of the author and Faber and Faber Ltd from *Lord Malquist and Mr Moon* (1966) by Tom Stoppard; 'Bech Enters Heaven' is reprinted with permission of André Deutsch Ltd from *Bech: A Book* (1960) by John Updike; 'The Fall of the House of Hazelstone' is reprinted with permission of Secker and Warburg Ltd from *Riotous Assembly* (1971) by Tom Sharpe; 'The Eyes of Texas are Upon You' (1959) and 'A Woman of a Certain Class' (1975) by Paul Dehn and 'Scoop' (1980) by Alexander Frater are reprinted with the kind permission of the proprietors of *Punch* magazine; 'How to be Topp' is reprinted with kind permission of Michael Willans from *How to be Topp* (1954) by Geoffrey Willans; 'Blacked Up' is reprinted with permission of Abner Stein from *Reinhart in Love* (1963) by Thomas Berger; 'Nobody Knows the Trouble' (1977) by Basil Boothroyd is reprinted with kind permission of the proprietors of *Punch* magazine; 'My Painful Jaw' is reprinted with permission of The Bodley Head from *Meet My Maker the Mad Molecule* (1965) by J. P. Donleavy; 'An Historic Night at the Old Vic' is reprinted with the kind permission of Caryl Brahms from *Don't Mr Disraeli!* (1940) by Caryl Brahms and S. J. Simon; 'Focusing Session' is reprinted by kind permission of the author from *Jake's Thing* (1978) by Kingsley Amis, published by Hutchinson Ltd; 'Gun Law' is reprinted by permission of Jonathan Cape Ltd from *The Dick* (1971) by Bruce Jay Friedman; 'The Agony of Captain Grimes' is reprinted by permission of A. D. Peters & Co Ltd from *Decline and Fall* (1945) by Evelyn Waugh; 'The Archaeology Institute' is reprinted with permission of the publishers, Granada Publishing Limited, from *The Best of Myles* (1968) by Myles na Gopaleen; 'The Treatment' (1963) by Gwyn Thomas is reprinted with the kind permission of the proprietors of *Punch* magazine; 'A Matter for the Courts' is an extract from *One Way Pendulum* (1960) by N. F. Simpson reprinted by permission of Curtis Brown Ltd, London, on behalf of the author; 'Walter Slurrie Goes to Washington' is reprinted by permission of Hutchinson Ltd from *Death of a Politician* (1979) by Richard Condon; 'London's Villages' (1981) by Miles Kington is reprinted with the kind permission of the proprietors of *Punch* magazine; 'Mr K*a*p*l*a*n' is reprinted with permission of Constable Publishers from *The Education of Hyman Kaplan* (1937) by Leonard Q. Ross; 'France and the French' is reprinted with the kind permission of the author, Robert Morley, from *A Musing Morley* (1974); 'Mrs Robbins' is reprinted by permission of Faber and Faber Ltd from *Pictures From an Institution* (1954) by Randall